D1598610

# A John Haught Reader

# A John Haught Reader

Essential Writings on Science and Faith

John F. Haught

WIPF & STOCK · Eugene, Oregon

A JOHN HAUGHT READER
Essential Writings on Science and Faith

Wipf & Stock
An Imprint of Wipf and Stock Publishers
199 W. 8th Ave., Suite 3
Eugene, OR 97401

www.wipfandstock.com

PAPERBACK ISBN: 978-1-5326-6102-0
HARDCOVER ISBN: 978-1-5326-6103-7
EBOOK ISBN: 978-1-5326-6104-4

Manufactured in the U.S.A.

# Contents

# Introduction

*A JOHN HAUGHT READER* challenges Christian theology to respond forthrightly to the thoughtful concerns of believers, agnostics, and atheists alike about the troubling issues posed by cosmic and biological evolution. The *Haught Reader* compiles selected chapters from nine published books by theologian John F. Haught plus two of his previously unpublished essays. They total 36 separately numbered readings grouped under six subjects: religion and science (Part I), Darwinian evolution (Part II), revelation (Part III), cosmic purpose (Part IV), suffering and death (Part V), and the New Atheism (Part VI). Although their ordering is not chronological, these readings generally follow the historical arc of Haught's magisterial contribution to the understanding of religion and its relationship to science. The readings include Haught's innovative theology of evolution, his critique of religiously-based opposition to evolution, and his rebuttal to atheistic materialism predicated on evolution.

Over the last century, religion has undergone sustained foundational challenges with the growth of secularism and science. Following World War I, scientific developments in astrophysics and evolution captured public attention, philosophy retreated from metaphysics into logical positivism and existentialism, and academics embraced a purely physicalist understanding of the universe. In 1925, philosopher Alfred North Whitehead (1861–1947) labeled this interpretation of nature "scientific materialism," according to which the universe consists solely of "senseless, valueless, purposeless" matter reconfigured by mindless physical and natural laws without transcendent meaning.[1] This materialist worldview destabilized traditional religious verities and engendered an often atheistic interpretation of the universe. By mid-century, the secular intellectual establishment had accepted scientific (or evolutionary) materialism as its reigning metaphysics, and by century-end, the New Atheists were proclaiming materialism a scientific truth and the "God hypothesis" an intellectually indefensible and delusional belief. As the twenty-first century arrived, religion confronted a profound crisis of relevancy. Yet surprisingly, few theologians rose to address this crisis. Among these few theologians, none was more effective than Georgetown Professor John F. Haught.

1. Whitehead, *Science and the Modern World*, 17.

1

During his long and distinguished career as a lay Catholic theologian, Dr. Haught has established an international reputation for his scholarship in systematic and evolutionary theology and for his effectiveness in explaining and defending religion. Haught received his Doctorate of Theology Degree from Catholic University of America in 1970. From 1970 to 2005, he served as professor in the Department of Theology at Georgetown University in Washington DC and as Departmental Chair from 1990 to 1995. In 2005, he left classroom teaching to concentrate on writing and lecturing on theology and evolution, becoming a Georgetown Distinguished Research Professor. To date, he is the author of 21 books, 92 peer-reviewed articles and book chapters, 45 encyclopedia and opinion articles, and 4 published lectures. He has also delivered over 300 invited academic lectures and presentations. These writings and lectures reflect Haught's broad, interdisciplinary interests in physics, cosmology, evolution, and ecology, beyond the purview of most theologians. His recognitions include: the "Owen Garrigan Award in Science and Religion" (2002), the "Sophia Award for Theological Excellence" (2004), the "Friend of Darwin Award"[2] from the National Center for Science Education (2008), and Honorary Doctoral degrees from the University of Louvain (2009) and Chestnut Hill College (2016). In fall semester 2008, Haught held the D'Angelo Chair in the Humanities at St. John's University in New York City.

The best entrée into Haught's collected readings is his initial essay: "My Life in Science and Theology." In this essay, Haught identifies the many authors who influenced his thinking, especially the Jesuit paleontologist Pierre Teilhard de Chardin (1881–1955), the inspiration for his lifelong interest in science and religion. Haught gradually found the medieval theological worldview and prescientific Thomistic philosophy still permeating Catholic theology no longer adequate in the age of modern science, especially after Darwin. Teilhard had convinced Haught that evolutionary science was a gift rather than a danger to Christian theology—a theology needing to refocus on the future of creation as inseparable from the pursuit of personal salvation. Haught grounds his evolutionary theology on this fundamental insight. His theology addresses the purpose and future of the whole universe as a work in progress, emerging continually into fuller being; and he considers that this awakening cosmos requires "the flourishing of a scientifically informed religious faith" to sustain its momentum. Inevitably, Haught confronted the controversy between materialists and creationists, dismissing their misguided debates over cosmic design as blind to the unfolding drama

2. Haught was awarded this title for his testimony in *Kitzmiller v. Dover Area School District* (2005) opposing the teaching of Intelligent Design Theory in high school science classes.

of an awakening universe. The world is not static and complete but evolving and unfinished, Haught observes, and humanity is called to participate constructively in this cosmic adventure. An intimately engaged personal God continuously creates this world by beckoning and not forcing it forward, simultaneously assuring humanity that nothing in this ongoing cosmic story will be lost to eternity.

"Part I: God, Science & Religion" introduces Haught's foundational writings on religion, which he defines as a conscious and appreciative response to the transcendent mystery of existence. Religion constitutes abiding faith in the trustworthiness of existence and a passionate concern for the "infinite and inexhaustible dimension of depth" beneath the surface of existence. God is this depth dimension—*mysterium tremendum et fascinans*—the terrifying yet fulfilling ground for humans coping with anxiety over finitude, meaninglessness, and guilt. Haught also describes religion in this setting as a hope and longing for the future; a willing and courageous acceptance of existential anxiety; an aesthetic quest after the transcendental beauty in being, goodness, and reality; and an unflagging desire and quest after metaphysical truth.

Scientific materialists or naturalists challenge such faith as unfounded, demanding scientific proof of God's existence, as if God were a problem susceptible to scientific solution. As a gracious and self-giving mystery, explains Haught, God inevitably exceeds the horizon of human thought, especially the epistemological bounds of ordinary scientific inquiry. Haught's full critique of materialism comes later in this volume. But reading 8 explains that religion and science (as distinct from scientific materialism) are not only compatible but also mutually supportive and nourishing. Religion fortifies science's a priori faith in the inherent rationality of the universe and in the mind's capacity to comprehend it, while science expands religion's understanding of creation and thereby "broaden[s] the horizon of religious faith."

"Part II: God, Evolution & Darwin" opens with Haught's response to evolutionary materialism and closes with his theology of evolution. Darwin's revolutionary theory radically altered the medieval and Newtonian view of the universe as fixed and eternal—the metaphysics of being that has influenced religious thought for centuries to the very present. In Darwinian evolution, now recognized to include Mendelian genetics, random genetic mutations naturally selected for the organism's survival in a process occurring over immense periods of time accounts for the diversity of species, including human life. Materialists, like the zoologist Richard Dawkins and the philosopher Daniel C. Dennett, assert that a contingent, deterministic, and mindless evolutionary process demolishes the intellectual respectability of religion's providential and creator God. In his response, Haught invites atheists, agnostics, and theists to adopt a deeper understanding of God, creation, and humans in relation to evolution. Pointing to the richly diverse and complex living species—including human life, mind, and subjectivity—he asks whether an apparently blind and mindless evolutionary process alone is a sufficient and ultimate explanation for such creativity and "new forms of being." He answers that Darwinism is methodologically necessary but metaphysically insufficient. Such creativity, for Haught, requires the God of evolution "drawing the world from up ahead . . . toward the future." This entails a metaphysics of the future that accounts for, but does not supplant, the cosmic qualities of chance variations, natural law, and immense time needed for the emergence of real novelty.

Haught faults the response to Darwinism propounded in creation science, intelligent design (ID) theory, and traditional hierarchical theologies. Creationists "trivialize religion" by disputing Darwinism, using a literalist interpretation of the Bible and claiming that this ancient sacred text is scientifically accurate. ID theorists advance a theologically "restrictive" and "lifeless" argument when theology requires a more robust vision to discern the deeper meaning in an evolving universe. Finally, traditional theologies rest on a metaphysics of the present—the eternal and timeless hierarchy of being, informed by Greek philosophy—that largely ignores the temporal creation of new being and "the coming of a new future." Instead, Haught proposes an evolutionary theology focused on continuing rather than original creation; on the imperfect, suffering, and unfinished world; and on the human expectations for the future. In this evolutionary theology, divine grace permits the world to emerge on its own, enabling human freedom and emergent novelty; and divine action is not coercive but persuasive, luring the universe to greater beauty and assuring human redemption from absolute perishing in death. Evolutionary theology provides an understanding (theodicy) of innocent suffering and restores the biblical picture of God's humility and self-emptying love. It represents a reasonable and scientifically informed metaphysics of becoming in which the world is drawn "perpetually toward deeper coherence by an ultimate force of attraction, abstractly identified as Omega, and conceived of as an essentially future reality."

"Part III: God, Science & Revelation" includes writings on the history, role, and value of Revelation Theology, especially as it relates to cosmic origin, evolution, emergence, and futurity. Until Vatican II, Revelation Theology largely concerned creedal propositions addressing unorthodoxy and safeguarding faith rather than interpreting God's relationship to the world. Vatican II broadened and deepened the meaning of revelation to include God's self-revelation and self-emptying in Scripture and in the world. Haught's Revelation Theology recognizes the revelatory character of diverse religious paths and the revelatory value of new scientific information in mediating transcendent mystery. Indeed, Haught finds the new cosmic story a primary source of revelation. It reveals a self-humbling, self-limiting, and self-emptying God who lovingly allows for human freedom and cosmic flowering into the future. In addition, the self-effacing and self-giving divine love embodied in the crucified Christ encourages individuals to accept their own and others' suffering, shame, and "shadow side."

God's revelation in cosmic history also provides answers to the "God question" posed by modern secular and scientific skeptics, and Haught admonishes theologians to communicate such answers at the risk of otherwise becoming irrelevant. The cosmic story reveals truths about reality that are inaccessible—and yet essential—to science, for example: the reason why reality is intelligible, why the cosmos produced human intelligence, why our minds can grasp reality, and why truth exists and is worth pursuing. By persisting in its otherworldly indifference to science, traditional theology inadvertently reinforces today's cosmic pessimism and existential homelessness. Haught leads this critical theological undertaking in his Revelation Theology, intended to "provide an enlivening sense of the *meaning* of the universe that science is now setting before us."

"Part IV: God, Science & Purpose" tackles perhaps the most vexing theological problem posed by modern science—reconciling cosmic purpose and divine providence with a self-actualizing universe that supports proliferating and diversifying life forms due to blind chance, deterministic law, and immense time. For many in the scientific and intellectual community, scientific information suggests a pointless and meaningless reality consisting entirely of valueless matter manipulated by physical and biological laws, thereby rendering traditional religious explanations intellectually untenable and illusory. Accepting his theological responsibility to address the cosmic pessimism of reductive and deterministic materialism, Haught methodically points out the limits of science regarding questions of ultimate purpose (or teleology) and then deconstructs metaphysical materialism, showing it to be a belief system and not a scientific truth. In explaining cosmic purpose, Haught resists the anthropic principle—the notion of a universe physically fine-tuned since the Big Bang for inevitable human life and mind—as bordering on outdated design arguments of natural theology and as centering narrowly on human rather than cosmic evolution.

Though still shrouded in divine mystery, cosmic purpose, for Haught, is "the working out or actualizing of something of self-evident value"; and he finds unquestionable value in the "unimaginably wide display of beauty" emerging in the cosmic story—"the bursting forth of sentience, mentality, self-consciousness, language, ethics, art, religion, and now science."

Haught's teleology effectively synthesizes Whitehead's aesthetic cosmological principle of the intensification of beauty with Teilhard's law of emergent complexity-consciousness and the phenomenon of terrestrial intelligence. He locates the drama of an awakening universe within an Abrahamic theology of God's futurity and promise. In Haught's evolutionary theology, the struggle, suffering, and waste of natural selection and the catastrophic accidents in natural history represent the inevitable byproducts of the universe still aborning, risking suffering and evil in its restless cosmic unfolding of ever-new and harmonious syntheses of novelty with order. Divine providence, for Haught, resides in the emergent and anticipatory character of the universe opening to a salvific future where God reveals "the breadth and depth of feeling to take into the divine life the entire cosmic story, including its episodes of tragedy and its final expiration."

"Part V: God, Suffering & Death" takes aim at much current theodicy—that is, the theological understanding of suffering and death—because of its failure after Darwin to account for the length, breadth, and depth of nonhuman pain, struggle, and suffering in sentient life. In 1996, Pope John Paul II endorsed evolutionary biology, and in 2004, the International Theological Commission deemed contingency "not incompatible" with divine providence. Yet both statements failed to reconcile the apparently wasteful, inefficient, and random events and the vast unmerited suffering of sentient beings in evolution with the providential governance of a loving and caring God. Underlying this failure, for Haught, is Catholicism's adherence to traditional prescientific metaphysics, inadequate for a theodicy explaining the pain and misery of biological and human evolution. Instead, Haught argues that "a shift from the metaphor of divine governance toward that of God as goal—in accordance with the metaphysics of the future—is more appropriate to a theology for an unfinished universe." By identifying human suffering as expiation for original and ongoing human sin, theology remains indifferent to Darwinian evolution, resorts to a literalist biblical reading of Genesis, and assumes human descent from a lost mythical perfection, rather than focusing on a creative and promising future. Conversely, by explaining evolution as an epic drama of biblical "grace, promise, and liberation," theology makes thoughtful contact with Darwinian science and appropriately "locates this drama within the very heart of God." A theology of evolution brings coherence and adventure to life's endeavors, views suffering and death as essential to evolutionary adaptation and promise, and provides assurance that "God is the underlying permanence that fully preserves everything that occurs in the entire cosmic process." Citing William James, Whitehead, and Teilhard, Haught sets forth a theology of evolution which recognizes that human action contributes significantly and indelibly to the universe and carries redemptive meaning, and that divine love takes care "so that nothing that ever happens can be *lost absolutely.*"

"Part VI: God, Hope & Atheism" opens with uplifting descriptions of Christianity's hopeful anticipation of the entire world's unfolding future and closes with devastating critiques of the New Atheists' shallow, misinformed, and contradictory jeremiads against Christianity. Informed by the Bible's promissory perspective and science's evolutionary cosmology, Christianity today understands the ancient "coming of God" as "the promise of a radically new world." To evolutionary materialists, science's retrospective analytics reveals lifeless and mindless matter as merely "masquerading" as mind and consciousness, heading toward final entropic oblivion. To Christians, by contrast, the same science understood prospectively discloses "a vein of promise in this ambiguous cosmos" with "a future whose ultimate depth we may call God." Haught celebrates the ecclesiastical community of faith, which provides access to the reality of revelation. The Church, however, must also recognize the importance of revelation to resonate in our everyday lives, to remain open to scientifically historical study, and to look at the past "to find ways of orienting ourselves toward the future."

Finally, Haught addresses the New Atheists—Sam Harris, Richard Dawkins, and Christopher Hitchens—who claim that "belief without evidence" causes unnecessary human misery, represents a dangerous moral evil, and warrants uprooting and eradication by scientific reason. Their absolute intolerance for faith, however, overlooks their own unprovable faith in science as the only source of truth (scientism), in the comprehensibility of the universe, and in their own critical intelligence, which they claim is entirely due to a mindless Darwinian process. Furthermore, their faith in radical secularism and scientific naturalism ignores the barbarism of atheistic dictatorships like Nazism and Communism, which adopted versions of scientific materialism. Moreover, the New Atheists erroneously understand faith as an intellectually flawed search for scientific understanding. To the contrary, theology understands faith as a state of self-surrender to the dimension of reality "much deeper and more real than anything that could be grasped by science and reason." Haught labels their "soft-core" atheism a self-subverting creed because it assumes that "by dint of Darwinism, we can drop God like Santa Claus, without having to witness the complete collapse of Western culture—including our sense of what is rational and moral." By contrast, hardcore atheists like Nietzsche, Camus, and Sartre recognized and attempted to address the disorienting terror, absurdity, nihilism, and even madness that attend the death of God. The New

Atheists, however, are oblivious to this inevitable consequence of overthrowing religiously inspired Western cultural values, while still remaining "as committed unconditionally to traditional values as the rest of us." In their Darwinian scheme, moral values become "blinded contrivances of evolutionary selection" because without God, as Haught observes, there are no absolute values. For the New Atheists, the Bible fails to deliver their imaginary ideal deity and perfect creation, unconscious that their perfectly designed, eternally splendid world would also be a dead end, devoid of "any life, any freedom, any future, any adventure, any grand cosmic story, or any opening to infinite horizons up ahead."

This book takes the reader on an exciting adventure in the theological ideas of John F. Haught. In lucid, accessible, and compelling prose, he addresses the most fundamental issues and concerns of modern human existence: Is the universe merely the product of mindless, deterministic forces? Is science the only reliable means of understanding the nature of reality? Does reality have any intrinsic meaning and purpose in light of neo-Darwinian evolution? If the answer is yes, how does one access such meaning and purpose? Is religion compatible with science? What reasoned response can religion and theology offer to the modern atheistic sense of nature? Haught answers these and numerous related questions in a stimulating new approach to theology thoroughly informed by developments in modern science and specifically designed for our evolving universe. Whitehead states: "The worship of God is not a rule of safety—it is an adventure of the spirit, a flight after the unattainable. The death of religion comes with the repression of the high hope of adventure."[3] Haught's writings constitute just such an adventure in systematic theology, providing an intellectually exciting and religiously stimulating vision of an optimistic future.

Charles A. O'Connor III, JD, DLS
October 2018

---

3. Whitehead, *Science and the Modern World*, 192.

Dr. O'Connor is a retired environmental lawyer, lecturer in the Graduate Liberal Studies Program at Georgetown University, and author of *The Great War and the Death of God: Cultural Breakdown, Retreat from Reason, and Rise of Neo-Darwinian Materialism in the Aftermath of World War I* (Washington DC: New Academia, 2014) and articles in the Journal *Confluence,* addressing the war's impact on Jewish thought and on Western music. He is a graduate of Harvard College, AB *cum laude* in English (1964), and Georgetown University, JD (1967), MALS (1985), and DLS (2012).

# My Life in Science and Theology

## JOHN F HAUGHT

Georgetown University

BACK WHEN I WAS in my early twenties, I began reading the works of the
Jesuit geologist and paleontologist Pierre Teilhard de Chardin (1881–1955),
prompting my earliest interest in science and religion. From 1966 to 1970 I
studied theology at the Catholic University of America and, while working
on my doctoral thesis, I began teaching part time at Georgetown University
across town in Washington, DC. After getting my degree in 1970, I joined the
faculty there. In the early 1970s, I started developing a course for undergraduates in science and religion at Georgetown and I taught it almost every year
until I retired from teaching in 2005. I was not trained as a scientist, so I had
to do a lot of reading in physics, cosmology, biology, and other disciplines
that most theologians generally ignore. In addition to Teilhard, I began to
work ideas into my teaching and publications that I picked up from the philosophical writings of science-friendly and religiously appreciative authors
such as Alfred North Whitehead, Michael Polanyi, and Bernard Lonergan.
My first book, *Religion and Self-Acceptance* (1976) was a philosophical approach to religion based on Lonergan's theory of knowledge; my second and
third books, *Nature and Purpose* (1980) and *The Cosmic Adventure* (1984),
were more deeply influenced by Whitehead and Polanyi.

What Is God? (1986) reflects my growing interest in other thinkers that
I had been studying and teaching at that time, especially Paul Tillich, Jürgen
Moltmann, Karl Rahner, and Wolfhart Pannenberg. *The Revelation of God
in History* (1988), *What Is Religion?* (1990), and *Mystery and Promise* (1993)
do not focus explicitly on the question of science and theology, but they
indirectly reflect my ongoing interest in the topic. Along with my interest
in science and theology, I later became preoccupied with the question of
the relationship of ecology to religion, which led to the publication of *The
Promise of Nature* (1993). In that book, I argued that any truly Christian
environmental theology must be concerned with the future of creation and
not just with conscious survival beyond death. I became convinced that

Christian spirituality and ecological morality must never again separate the question of personal salvation from that of cosmic destiny.

Since 1993, all of my books have, in one way or another, focused on science and its implications for religion and theology. I based *Science and Religion: From Conflict to Conversation* (1995) on an approach I developed over many years of undergraduate teaching at Georgetown. After writing that book, however, I became increasingly interested in topics related to evolutionary biology. Because of the growing importance of the question of God and evolution in the intellectual world—as well as in the American cultural conversations—and about the scientific and religious status of what has been called "Intelligent Design," I wrote *God After Darwin* (2000, 2007), *Responses to 101 Questions on God in Evolution* (2001), *Deeper than Darwin* (2003), *Is Nature Enough?* (2006), *Christianity and Science* (2007), *God and the New Atheism* (2008), and *Making Sense of Evolution* (2010). Because of an increasing number of invitations to lecture and write on theology and evolution, both nationally and internationally, I decided to leave the undergraduate classroom in 2005 and devote my time to lecturing and writing on the relationship of religion and theology to evolutionary biology and cosmology. A new emphasis on cosmology is reflected in my two most recent books *Resting on the Future* (2015) and *The New Cosmic Story* (2017). In these works, I still draw, in some measure, on the hopeful vision of Pierre Teilhard de Chardin (1881–1955) that I first encountered many years ago.

The just-mentioned notion of intelligent design (ID), I should note, is controversial, primarily because its proponents insist that it should become part of science education and, hence, a topic to be taken up in biology classes in our public schools. Since the modern scientific method looks only for the physical causes of phenomena, however, ID is not really science and should not be part of science education. ID still commands a large following among conservative Christians and Muslims, but, in 2005, after a long trial in Harrisburg, Pennsylvania, Judge John E. Jones struck down the initiative taken by the Dover County school board to make ID part of that district's high school biology curriculum. Because I had already become deeply involved in discussions relating to religion and evolution, I was asked to testify at the Harrisburg trial on behalf of the plaintiffs who were opposed to the teaching of ID in public schools. I did so happily. Joining the expert witnesses from various academic fields, including biology and philosophy, I was the sole theologian to provide testimony at the trial (*Kitzmiller et al. vs. Dover District School Board*). I supported the argument that ID is a somewhat impoverished theological idea, rather than a properly scientific one, and therefore has no justifiable place in public school education. As a result of my testimony, I was later awarded a "Friend of Darwin" award by the National Center for Science Education. I was probably one of the few non-atheists on this list of awardees.

My exposure to Teilhard years earlier had already turned me into someone who believes that evolutionary science has been a great gift—rather than a danger—to theology. Had it not been for that early influence, my academic life could have taken many other directions. I first encountered Teilhard's evolutionary vision soon after graduating from college in 1964. I was immediately swept away by the power and freshness of his thought. I did not realize fully at the time that my excitement was due also to the fact that I was becoming dissatisfied intellectually and spiritually with the medieval theological worldview presupposed by my religious education up until that point. Before encountering Teilhard, I had been studying in a Catholic seminary and was thoroughly schooled in Thomistic philosophy (much of which I was required to read and memorize in the original Latin). To this day, I am grateful for having had the opportunity to study Thomistic thought. However, I began to realize long ago that Thomas's prescientific philosophy, ingenious and adventurous as it was in the thirteenth century, cannot adequately contextualize contemporary science—although there are a few Catholic philosophers and theologians still attempting to forge just such an impossible synthesis. I have high regard for the effort and goodwill behind these attempts, but I have come to think of them as both intellectually and spiritually inadequate to what we now know about the universe in the age of science, especially after Darwin. Many of the severest critics of Teilhard are rigorous Thomists who have yet to appropriate evolutionary science in a serious way.

In any case, I left the seminary soon after the Second Vatican Council and immediately began to pursue a lay career in academic theology. My decision to take up theological studies was also a consequence of my exposure to the writings of Karl Rahner and contemporary biblical scholarship, especially that of my teacher, the Johannine scholar Raymond Brown. To this day, I am grateful for the historical-critical understanding of Scripture that I learned from Brown and others. I was thus enabled to see long ago that scientifically modern biblical criticism liberates theology from the anachronistic impulse to seek scientific information in the Bible and the ridiculous attempt to make ancient scriptures compete with modern natural sciences. This is a lesson that countless Christians and most anti-Christian evolutionists have yet to learn.

As I recall, however, it was mostly due to the excitement I had felt in my very limited acquaintance at that time with Teilhard's Christian vision of nature and evolution that I found myself drawn toward a life in systematic theology. Even though I have sought intellectual support for relating theology to science by studying the works of many other religious think-ers, especially Bernard Lonergan, Alfred North Whitehead, and Michael Polanyi, Teilhard has been my main inspiration, both intellectually and religiously. I am not as uncritical of his thought today as I may have been when I was younger, but I still draw upon the audacity of his deeply religious conviction that acquaintance with science is absolutely essential to under-standing the meaning of Christian faith today.

I want to point out here that even before I came across his writings, Teilhard's bold ideas were already helping to shape some of the theological reflection that would make the Second Vatican Council such an important event in the history of the Church as well as in my personal life. *Gaudium et Spes*, the Council's *Pastoral Constitution on the Church in the Modern World* (1965), was revolutionary for many reasons, including its making the fol-lowing two observations: (1) "The human race has passed from a rather static concept of reality to a more dynamic, evolutionary one. In conse-quence there has arisen a new series of problems . . . calling for efforts of analysis and synthesis" (§5). And (2) "A hope related to the end of time does not diminish the importance of intervening duties but rather undergirds the acquittal of them with fresh incentives" (§21).[4] I cannot read *Gaudium et Spes* without noticing the influence of Teilhard in it—in spite of the fact that the Vatican had censored his writings earlier. In the first decades of the twentieth century, the controversial Jesuit evolutionist and creative religious thinker had already expressed some of the same sentiments that eventually made their way into Vatican II.

Teilhard had developed some of his ideas on God and evolution in *The Human Phenomenon* and *The Divine Milieu* while he was living in China, becoming one of the top two or three geologists of the Asian continent. These two books and countless other shorter writings have made him famous post-humously, but he remained largely unpublished and unknown in his own lifetime. Because of church censorship, he was never given the opportunity that most scholars have of exposing their works to the critique of other ex-perts. No doubt, then, there are deficiencies in his writings that could have easily been avoided and corrected had his church allowed for the circulation of his ideas. After his death in 1955, his lay friends fed his manuscripts to hungry publishers who then distributed them widely. Some of these were immediately devoured by theologians who helped shape the documents of the Council, and so Teilhard's hope for the future of humanity and of our need to take responsibility for "building the earth" greatly influenced one of modern Catholicism's main documents. This is most ironic because, in 1962,

4. Paul VI, *"Gaudium et Spes."*

the same year the Council met for its first session, the Holy Office of the Vatican issued an admonition advising seminary professors and heads of Catholic colleges and universities to "protect the minds, particularly of the youth, against the dangers presented by the works of Fr. Teilhard de Chardin and his followers."[5] Fortunately, I was one of those who escaped such efforts to protect the tender minds of young Catholics.

Because of the theological ferment fostered by Vatican II, my own, previously medieval, spirituality began to evolve into something new. Catholic University—at least while I was a student there—was an intellectually and religiously liberating environment. It was there that I began to supplement my interest in Teilhard with the theology of hope articulated by Protestant theologians Jürgen Moltmann and Wolfhart Pannenberg along with that of Catholic theologians Karl Rahner, Edward Schillelbeeckx, Yves Congar, and many others who had helped shape Vatican II. My scholarly interests became increasingly ecumenical and my doctoral dissertation reflects how Protestant theology helped me to address the question of how to translate the ancient eschatological thinking of the Bible into relevant contemporary terms compatible with science. To deal with the ancient biblical language of promise and hope, however, I had to study hermeneutics, the art and science of the interpretation of texts, on which I wrote my doctoral dissertation. As I look back on my life in theology, I observe that my constant concern to include the whole cosmos within a sweeping biblical vision of promise and redemption was already beginning to blossom in my master's thesis and doctoral dissertation.

Developing a hopeful sense of the cosmic future and of a purposeful universe has continued to be the main preoccupation of my theology. I have maintained, with Teilhard and "process thought," that, in light of geology, evolutionary biology, and contemporary post-Einsteinian cosmology, theology henceforth needs to start out with the observation that the cosmos remains a work in progress. If the cosmos is still coming into being, we need to entertain the thought that something of great importance may be aborning up ahead and that human technology and morally chastened engineering will be increasingly essential to the shaping of the cosmic future, perhaps even in ways that we cannot yet imagine. I have long viewed the cosmos as a drama of awakening and I have continued to argue that the flourishing of a scientifically informed religious faith is essential to sustaining its momentum.

Concern for the cosmic future and for what's *really* going on in the universe has not been a major theme of Western theology until after the

5. Holy Office of the Vatican, "Warning."

emergence of evolutionary science and cosmology. Classical Christianity and its theologies first came to expression at a time when people took for granted that the universe is fundamentally fixed and unchanging. Their otherworldly spiritual instincts reflected a static, vertical, and hierarchical understanding of the cosmos. Today, however, especially because of developments in the natural sciences, we understand that the *whole* universe, not just life and human history, is still in the process of becoming. My writings reflect the belief that if we take seriously the fact that the universe is unfinished, we need to think new thoughts about the meaning of all the traditional theological topics, including God, faith, and the moral life. I have previously outlined the theological implications of an unfinished universe, especially in my recent book *Resting on the Future* (2015). There, as well as in my latest book *The New Cosmic Story* (2017), I have argued that the universe is best understood according to the metaphor of drama rather than that of design. This means that the most important question in science and theology today is not whether "intelligent design" points to a deity or even how God acts in nature but rather whether the cosmic drama carries a hidden but imperishable meaning.

I am quite aware, however, that this sense of the universe as a still unfinished drama has yet to settle deeply into Christian theological awareness in particular and most religious thought everywhere. Most of the devotional life of religious people on our planet still presupposes an essentially immobile universe. Some of our schools of theology still pay scarcely any attention to science. Christian thought and instruction even at non-fundamentalist schools still tend to nurture nostalgia for a lost Eden or look skyward toward a final heavenly communion with God, apart from natural history and the cosmic future. Emphasis on the need to restore a putatively idyllic past, together with a longing to escape from Earth into eternity, still leads theologians to ignore the Abrahamic spirit of adventurous hope which, in my opinion, must once again become the foundation of any truthful and honest Christian worldview.

Meanwhile, intellectual life, philosophy of science, and the assumptions of popular culture remain immersed in a deadening materialist pessimism that unnecessarily undermines all hopes that the cosmos can somehow be saved from absolute death. Like traditional otherworldly theology, contemporary intellectual life is badly in need of revision. Many of the readings in this book, therefore, reflect my conviction that contemporary scientific naturalism is not only spiritually but also intellectually problematic. I argue that, since our universe is still on the move, we may find—at least in principle, without any conflict with science—reasons to anticipate the future transformation of the whole universe into something unimaginably beautiful, as Teilhard has done in many of his works and as Pope Francis recently encouraged us to do in his encyclical, *Laudato si.*[6]

Christian religious hope, along with the religious aspirations of other traditions, needs to be channeled into a common human concern for the cosmic future ("a great hope held in common," as Teilhard puts it) and not just as a training ground to prepare our souls for personal immortality.[7] I am convinced, moreover, that a concern for cosmic destiny will simultaneously include, enrich, and expand our understandable hopes for personal salvation. Moreover, the widening of human hope to include the cosmic future should be ecologically invigorating. Were theology to take seriously the evolutionary understanding of life and the new cosmological sense of an unfinished universe, the natural setting of human aspirations and religious hope would be expansive enough to give new significance to discussions of the relationship between science and faith.

The readings in this book all take for granted that our new sense of the universe as a drama of awakening is spiritually much more consequential than most scientists and religious believers have noticed. The freedom, redemption, and healing that people of faith look for has not yet fully come to pass since the cosmic story that gave birth to them is still far from finished. This means, as Teilhard has rightly indicated, that all religions and all theological speculation are unfinished and, like the universe, they have a dark side, but, since "the universe is still aborning," they may also have a fresh future.[8]

Any religious expectation that is aware of nature's leaning toward the future hopes not only for personal conscious survival after death but also for the fulfillment of the whole cosmos, as Pope Francis urges in his recent encyclical. The promising God of Abraham, who arrives from out of the future when it seems that everything has reached a dead end, may now be sought by looking in the direction of a new future—not only for individual souls but also for the whole universe. Abrahamic faith in the age of science anticipates not only human and personal redemption but also indeed a transfiguration of the whole cosmos into a scene of wondrous beauty. Without setting out to do so, the natural sciences depicting an unfinished cosmos allow room for a new and beautiful future, not just for humanity and for the earth but also for the whole universe. Science's fresh picture of the cosmos as a drama rather than a design gives a new zest and scope to the ancient Abrahamic expectations. Both science and

6. Francis, "*Laudato Si.*"
7. Teilhard, *Future of Man*, 75.
8. Teilhard, *Future of Man*, 75.

faith direct us, accordingly, to look for the advent of an Indestructible Rightness and Brightness that is drawing the whole scheme of things into the unity of new being from out of the future. A destiny that comprises anything less than the whole cosmic story—and perhaps a multiverse as well—cannot be fully liberating for any living being.

## My Approach to Issues in Science and Theology

The objective of most of my recent writing has been to acclimatize faith to the newly discovered story of a cosmos that started fourteen billion years ago and is still in process. At the same time, however, my teaching, speaking, and writing during the last half-century have attempted not only to make room for faith in the age of science but also to fortify faith by exposing it continually to new scientific discoveries. A major obstacle to the realizing of this objective has been the persistence of biblical literalism in the minds of both believers and scientific skeptics. I have found that most scientists who profess hostility to theology have little if any familiarity with modern biblical criticism. As a result, they carry the same literalist assumptions in their reading of ancient holy books as do anti-Darwinian biblical creationists. Nowadays, in the age of science, literalism often takes the form of an unconscious expectation that the Bible—if it is to live up to its reputation as something "inspired" by God—must be the source not only of religious inspiration but also of reliable *scientific* information. This expectation is shared by both creationists and contemporary New Atheists. In my book *God and the New Atheist* I pointed out that Sam Harris, for example, insists that "the same evidentiary demands" that science has to live up to must also be the criterion of truth in religious writings and creeds.[9] He remarks that if the Bible is supposed to have been "written by an omniscient being" (which is how he sums up the idea of biblical inspiration), then it should also be "the richest source of mathematical insight humanity has ever known."[10] It should have something to say "about electricity, or about DNA, or about the actual age and size of the universe."[11] The other New Atheists—Daniel Dennett, Christopher Hitchens, and Richard Dawkins—likewise appeal to the scientific criteria of inquiry in their assessment of the truth-status of scripture. If the Bible is "inspired," they insist, then it must be scientifically accurate and not just religiously motivating.

9. Harris, *End of Faith*, 35.

10. Harris, *Letter to a Christian Nation*, 60.

11. Harris, *Letter to a Christian Nation*, 61.

I have responded to this literalist mentality by insisting that searching for scientific truths in *any* ancient, prescientific, or classical text, religious or otherwise, is an anachronism that transcends mere silliness. And yet, such silliness is almost the norm in contemporary scientific skepticism. The problem is that literalism, whether by atheists or creationists, is a way of avoiding a genuine encounter with deeply hidden meanings—not only in religious texts but also in the story of the universe. Literalism, I have argued, protects the religious fundamentalist from hearing the word of God on the one hand and gives the New Atheists a pretext for mocking ancient religious writings because of their failure to satisfy contemporary scientific criteria of meaning and truth on the other.

Much of my writing is an attempt to articulate an alternative to literalist readings of both religious texts and the new cosmic story. In the writings collected here, I take for granted that theology and science are distinct but compatible ways of understanding and knowing. They cannot contradict each other because they both seek understanding and truth from within formally distinct *horizons* of inquiry. These horizons do not overlap, so they cannot meaningfully compete or conflict with each other. This is because the kind of evidence, the quality of understanding, and the type of confirmation operative in one horizon of inquiry is not identical with what passes as evidence, understanding, and confirmation in the other.

I am using the term "horizon" metaphorically. Visually speaking—and here I am following the Jesuit philosopher Bernard Lonergan—a "horizon" is the field of all the things we can see from a specific point of view.[12] By analogy, a "horizon of inquiry" refers to what can be understood and known by way of a determinate method of understanding and knowing. Accordingly, since the horizon of inquiry characteristic of the natural sciences is distinct from that of theology, there can be no genuine conflict between them. This is such an obvious point, it seems to me, and yet countless contemporary scientists and philosophers claim, unreasonably and without the scientific justification they demand elsewhere, that science alone is epistemologically reliable, and hence that science and theology are irreconcilable ways of reading the world.

To arrive at this verdict, of course, they first make the false assumption that theology is supposed to look at the world—or read the cosmic story—from within the same horizon of inquiry as the natural sciences. Stuffing ancient religious literature by force into the modern scientific horizon of inquiry, they conclude that it no longer deserves our attention. Ancient religious ways of understanding, they agree, fail to base themselves on the kind

12. See Lonergan, *Insight*.

of empirical evidence that modern science requires, so they can never again be taken seriously. In *The God Delusion*, for example, Richard Dawkins rejects what he calls the "God hypothesis" because it cannot compete with or survive our scientific ways of understanding the natural world. For Dawkins (who is far from being alone among contemporary skeptics), it is only within the territory proper to scientific investigation that the idea of "God" can rightly be examined. In his belief system, the only reliable way to arrive at the true understanding of essentially anything is to follow scientific inquiry. I say "belief" because his dismissal of other horizons is not something he can back up by way of scientific experimentation. Dawkins is a true *believer* and not a scientist, inasmuch as he decrees that only one legitimate horizon of inquiry exists. Today, scientific skepticism in general is not the result of following the scientific method but rather of gratuitously assuming that the horizon of scientific inquiry is the only epistemologically permissible way to see, understand, and know anything whatsoever.

## Science and a Personal God

The question arises, however, as to how and why an educated religious person in the age of science could still believe in a personal, caring, interested God. I appreciate the question, but my response to it has been consistent throughout my academic life. Science is not equipped to confirm or deny the existence of a personal God, but the idea of a personal God is completely consonant with what we now know from science. In backing up this point, once again I admit my indebtedness to Teilhard.

Evolution is a process of becoming *more*, of giving rise to *fuller being* over the course of time. But at each stage of evolution, the world can become *more* only by organizing itself around successively new and higher *centers*. Teilhard called this recurrent cosmic trend "centration." Centration occurred very early in cosmic history when subatomic elements organized themselves around an atomic nucleus. Centration happened later when large molecules clustered around nuclear DNA in the eukaryotic cell, still later when the "central" nervous system took shape in vertebrate evolution, and yet again when social insects gathered around a fertile queen.

At present, the latest dominant units in evolution are human persons, but they can only be brought together socially into higher organic syntheses if their unifying centers are *at least personal*. We human persons cannot be fully alive or fully moved to "become more" by clustering around anything that lacks subjectivity, freedom, and responsiveness or that fails to acknowledge our own free personhood. As both Teilhard and theologian

Paul Tillich agree, human persons, at the center of their being, cannot be *fully* attracted to or challenged by anything that is less than personal. Consequently, that which is *most real*—God, if you will—must *at least* be personal. To be fully real and deeply attractive to persons, the centering reality must be a "Thou" and not an "It."

Like Teilhard, I cannot make sense of what goes on in the cosmic drama apart from taking, in faith, the reality of an attracting, transcendent, promising, and *personal* Center to which the universe is awakening. And if, as Christian faith affirms, this Center has entered intimately and irreversibly into the struggle and suffering of life, to me it is not merely interesting but worthy of worship. At the same time, however, I believe with both Tillich and Teilhard that our ideas of God must always be presented not just as personal but also as *suprapersonal* (to use Tillich's term). This means, today, at the very least, in order to merit a religious surrender on our part, God must be thought of as infinitely larger than the immense universe of modern science. An anthropomorphic, one-planet deity is no longer enough.

I believe that modern scientific skepticism's disillusionment with the idea of a personal God is partly due to the fact that our theologies have made God seem too small for the minds and souls of scientifically educated people. The God of evolution and contemporary cosmology, therefore, must be thought of as continually creating the world not by pushing things forward from the past, but by drawing the world in all its wonders towards a new future ahead. This means that the entire process of cosmic creativity finds its destiny only in an unimaginably wide and redemptive compassion transcending the world. Because of the infinitely resourceful being and compassion characteristic of what theology calls God, even if the physical world will eventually "die" of energy exhaustion, as astrophysicists predict, nothing in the cosmic *story* needs to be thought of as ever lost or forgotten, as Whitehead also suggests. Today, theology needs to emphasize that the entire cosmic story—and not just the human soul—is saved and redeemed forever in the everlasting life and love of God.

Finally, like Teilhard, I do not want to exempt my own faith tradition from undergoing the disturbing phase transitions that occur in other evolving systems. In 1933, Teilhard wrote: "I believe Christianity to be immortal. But this immortality of our faith does not prevent it from being subject (even as it rises above them) to the general laws of periodicity which govern all life. I recognize, accordingly, that at the present moment Christianity (exactly like the mankind it embraces) is reaching the end of one of the

natural cycles of its existence." This is "an indication that the time for renewal is close at hand."[13]

It is this call for renewal that has energized my own theological life
and work. I realize that, for many Christians (perhaps even the majority),
a prescientific understanding of the cosmos as static and immobile is the
only legitimate framework for theological reflection. At the same time,
scientific skeptics are uncomfortable with Christian theologies that fail to
acknowledge the depth and expansiveness of the new scientific understanding of the cosmos. For them, prescientific versions of religion and religious
thought do not lift up their hearts and give new incentive to their moral
lives. Contrary to the judgment of cosmic pessimists, however, I believe that
scientific discovery of an awakening universe is completely at home in a
broadly construed theological metaphysics.

Finally, I want to thank Bradford McCall for organizing the following excerpts and Dr. Charles A. O'Connor for his gracious introduction.
(To avoid conflating my present work with what I published earlier, I have
decided to make only minor revisions to the material presented here.)

13. Teilhard, *Christianity and Evolution*, 94–95.

# Books by John F. Haught

- *The New Cosmic Story: Inside Our Awakening Universe.* New Haven: Yale University Press, 2017.

- *Resting on the Future: Catholic Theology for an Unfinished Universe.* London: Bloomsbury, 2015.

- *Science and Faith: A New Introduction.* New York: Paulist, 2013. Later translated into Lithuanian and Chinese.

- *Making Sense of Evolution: Darwin, God, and The Drama of Life.* Louisville: Westminster John Knox, 2010.

- *God and the New Atheism: A Critical Response to Dawkins, Harris, and Hitchens.* Louisville: Westminster John Knox, 2008. Later translated into Spanish, Italian, Dutch, and Vietnamese.

- *Christianity and Science.* Maryknoll: Orbis, 2007. Later translated into Japanese, Spanish, and Portuguese.

- *Is Nature Enough: Meaning and Truth in the Age of Science.* Cambridge: Cambridge University Press, 2006.

- *Purpose, Evolution, and the Meaning of Life.* Ontario: Pandora, 2004.

- *Deeper Than Darwin: The Prospect for Religion in the Age of Evolution.* Boulder: Westview, 2003. Later translated into Korean (*Choice Magazine* Outstanding Academic Title, 2003).

- *Responses to 101 Questions on God and Evolution.* New York: Paulist, 2001. Later translated into Polish, Portuguese, and Korean.

- *God After Darwin: A Theology of Evolution.* Boulder: Westview, 2000. Later tanslated into Italian, Portuguese, Indonesian, Korean, Russian, and Slovak.

- *Science and Religion in Search of Cosmic Purpose.* Editor. Washington: Georgetown University Press, 2000.

- *Science and Religion: From Conflict to Conversation.* New York: Paulist, 1995. Later translated into Romanian, Korean, Persian, Urdu, Indonesian, and Chinese.

- *The Promise of Nature: Ecology and Cosmic Purpose.* New York: Paulist, 1993.

- *Mystery and Promise: A Theology of Revelation.* Collegeville, MN: Liturgical, 1993. Later translated into Portuguese as *Misterio e Promessa.*

- *What Is Religion?* New York: Paulist, 1990.

- *The Revelation of God in History.* Wilmington: Michael Glazier, 1988.

- *What Is God?* New York: Paulist, 1986. Later translated into Spanish and Portuguese.

- *The Cosmic Adventure: Science, Religion, and the Quest for Purpose.* New York: Paulist, 1984.

- *Nature and Purpose.* Lanham, MD: University Press of America, 1980.

- *Religion and Self-Acceptance.* New York: Paulist, 1976.

## Lectures by John F. Haught Published as Booklets by The American Teilhard Association

- *Teilhard, Big History, and Religion: A Look Inside* (Woodbridge, CT: American Teilhard Association, 2015)

- *Darwin, Teilhard, and the Drama of Life* (Woodbridge, CT: American Teilhard Association, 2011).

- *In Search of a God for Evolution: Paul Tillich and Pierre Teilhard de Chardin* (Lewisburg, PA: American Teilhard Association, 2002).

- *Chaos, Complexity, and Theology* (Chambersburg, PA: Anima, 1994).

# Part I: God, Science & Religion

# 1: Depth[1]

IN RELATING TO ANOTHER person, whoever it might be, but especially if it is someone I love, I may observe the following: sooner or later, the other person will do something or say something that will surprise me. It may either delight or disappoint me. But if I am to sustain my relationship with the "other," I will have to revise my impressions of him or her. I will have to move to a deeper level of understanding the other. And, after relating to the other person on this level for a while, I will find occasion after occasion to dig still deeper. Of course, I may resist the invitation to look deeper, and perhaps for the most part I do resist it. But it takes very little experience of other persons to see that there is something beneath the surface of my impressions of them. Other people are not what they seem to be. This is, of course, a truism so obvious that it seems almost too trivial even to mention. But perhaps there is more to it than first appears. Let us dig deeper.

Not only are others not what they seem to be, but the same is true of myself. There is always more to me than is contained in my impressions of myself. My "self-image" does not exhaust what I am. I need not be an expert in depth psychology in order to validate this observation. I need only a little experience of living to be able to see its truth. Looking back a few years, or even a few months or days, I remember that I thought I knew who I was. But new experiences have reshaped my life. New questions, new feelings and moods, new dreams and fantasies, and new expectations of myself have intervened. I now know that I am not what I thought I was. I may assume at this moment that I am not exactly what I seem to be to myself or to others. Why is this so? Why are others not what they seem to be? Why am I not transparent to myself? This is a troubling question, so disturbing in fact that I usually suppress it. I cling to impressions as though they were foundational truths. I resist going deeper. Why?

Let us also take note of the fact that the natural and social worlds present superficial impressions of themselves that we must question. They too are not what they seem to be. In the case of nature the point is easily made by looking at science. Not only religion but also science thrives on the conviction that things are not what they seem to be. For example,

---

1. The following text is an excerpt. Previously published in Haught, *What is God?*, 11–24. Reprinted with permission.

beneath the world of common sense impressions there is a submicroscopic universe of "counterintuitive" physical occurrences that we cannot picture or even imagine. And in the galaxies beyond us there are likewise unfathomable riches of physical phenomena that, if we could understand them, would expose our world of immediate appearances and impressions as a veil of superficiality. We recoil from the abyss that lies beneath the surface of present knowledge, however, and live under the illusion that our sense impressions or our ordinary experiences of space and time are absolutely valid. And even scientists tend to cling tenaciously to their pet paradigms and models in an effort to domesticate science's tempestuous inner voice—"things are not what they seem to be"—even after we have gone deeper and yet deeper in our understanding. The question keeps forcing itself upon us, therefore: why are things not what they seem to be? What is reality that in the case of others, myself and nature it continually evades full disclosure. Why is it that what seemed profound yesterday is today exposed as trivial, or that what impressed me as deep before appears now as rather shallow? What sort of universe are we dealing with if it does not exhaust itself in our impressions of it?

And there is also the social world of institutions, politics, economic arrangements, and their history. In this world that we share in common with others we may once again experience the shallowness of our impressions of things. Though peoples and nations can survive for years and even centuries on the assumption that their own social and cultural ideals and experiences are universally normative, sooner or later the events of history will bring about a serious challenge to this prejudice. The resistance to this revision of perspective will prove to be enormous and people will even go to war to defend the alleged finality of their culture, politics, or economics. But eventually they will have to confess: "we are not what we thought we were. Our previous self-understanding has been superficial and misguided. We must rethink what we are as a society." And so, from a new perspective, occasionally at least, they may look back with amazement at their previous lack of sensitivity regarding their social and political life.

Let us return to our question, then: why is it that, in the case of others, myself, nature, and society, things are never quite what they seem to be? According to Paul Tillich, it is because there lies beneath their surface an infinite and inexhaustible dimension of depth. Perhaps many people would be content to call it a dimension of mystery. But this word, like the word "God" itself, has lost its meaning for many people. And so it might be useful in this context to call this dimension of inexhaustibility beneath the surface of our impressions simply the depth of existence, the depth of reality, the depth of the universe.

In his famous meditation, "The Depth of Existence," Tillich notes that the wisdom of all ages and continents tells us about the road to that depth. What gives the great classics of philosophy, literature, and religion their authority, generation after generation, is that they are the expression of a journey toward depth undertaken by sincere and concerned individuals or peoples throughout history. The reason that they still grip us today is that we sense in them the call of a depth dimension that promises to give more substance to our lives than what we can find on the surface. They hold out the possibility to us that our own lives can be enriched and that an unexpected contentment with life can be ours if we follow them through the difficult but rewarding way to depth. Those whose lives and experiences have been imprinted in the great classics have all witnessed the same experience:

> They have found that they were not what they believed them-selves to be, even after a deeper level had appeared to them below the vanishing surface. That deeper level itself became surface, when a still deeper level was discovered, this happening again and again, as long as their very lives, as long as they kept on the road to their depth.[2]

What name, then, can we give to this dimension of depth?

> The name of this infinite and inexhaustible depth . . . is God. That depth is what the word God means. And if that word has not much meaning for you, translate it, and speak of the depths of your life . . . Perhaps, in order to do so, you must forget ev-erything traditional that you have learned about God, perhaps even that word itself. For if you know that God means depth you know much about Him. You cannot then call yourself an atheist or unbeliever. For you cannot think or say: Life has no depth! Life itself is shallow. Being itself is surface only. If you could say this in complete seriousness, you would be an atheist; but other-wise you or not. He who knows about depth knows about God.[3]

This dimension of depth, therefore, will be the first of the five ideas in terms of which I would suggest that we think about the divine.

What is there in the experience of all of us to which the word "God" is pointing? Tillich's answer is that "God" is a name for the dimension of depth that all of us experience to one degree or another, even if only in the mode of flight from it. We truly experience the depth even though we find it impossible to focus on it—as if it were just another object of

---

2. Tillich, *Shaking of the Foundations*, 56.

3. Tillich, *Shaking of the Foundations*, 57.

vision or scientific investigation. Depth appears more as the horizon of our experience than as a direct object thereof. Its apparent elusiveness is quite compatible with its being the very condition of all of our experience. Perhaps, as we shall see in more detail a bit later, this observation can help us to interpret and tolerate the apparent absence of God. As the geographical horizon is unavailable to us since it recedes as we explore further, so God might be understood in part as the ultimate horizon of all of our experience, always receding, encompassing, and illuminating, but never falling within our comprehending grasp. But in thinking of the divine as the ultimate "horizon" rather than as a controllable object of experience, have we diminished our sense of its reality?

There is a fundamental dimension of human experience that has the peculiar characteristic of being too massive and, let us say it, too real, to be trivialized as a specific object capable of being placed under our comprehending gaze. It is more accurate to say that this dimension comprehends us rather than we comprehend it. We experience this dimension as real even though it is unavailable to our verificational control. In our frustration at not being able to comprehend it, we may be tempted to deny that it exists at all, but this is a futile denial. All we have to do is to recall those moments in our personal life, in our relations with others, nature, and society, when we have been rocked from the surface by something that we could not control. We may have called it "fate" or "circumstance" and we may have cursed it or repressed it. But it would be hard to deny that there was something eminently real about the experience. It is as though something much larger than ourselves, our lives, or even our period of history, swept us into its embrace, even though we may have been unwilling participants in this dislocation. We may have been tempted to think of such events as utterly impersonal and in no way as evidence of any sort of providentially divine care governing the course of our lives or of history. Taken in isolation, these experiences may have constituted for us sufficient evidence of the universe's fundamental indifference to us.

However, there may also have been some moments, after experiencing these "earthquakes," when we found ourselves on more solid ground than previously. The experience of "fate" was also one that led to a deeper "grounding" in reality. We may even have reached the point of being grateful that we went through such difficult straits since they turned out to be the occasion of growth and a contentment that transcends mere gratification.[4] They have made us experience a new level of ourselves and reality. Such earthquakes awakened in us a courage that gave us a deeper sense of being

4. Ricoeur, *Conflict of Interpretations*, 464–67.

alive. The dimension of depth, therefore, is ambiguous. It is both terrifying and deeply fulfilling. In the words of Rudolf Otto, it is a *mysterium tremendum et fascinans.*[5]

The experience of depth has two faces.[6] It is both abyss and ground. The dimension of depth which supports the surface of our lives initially presents itself to us as an abyss. Instinctively, we recoil from an abyss, since it seems to be unfathomable and bottomless, a void in which there are seemingly no supports. To fall into it would mean to lose ourselves. This is the first face the depth presents to us. It is an anxiety-inducing "nothingness" which seems to threaten our very being.

We might gain a more concrete sense of what this abyss means if we conjure up the specter of being utterly alone without the support of other people or of status or possessions. There is probably nothing we humans find more terrifying or try more ardently to avoid than the state of aloneness. One of the reasons for our anxiety about death is that it is an occurrence that we shall have to go through utterly alone. And so we tend to avoid the threat of death, along with other such "existential" threats as meaninglessness and guilt, since it signifies an intolerable solitariness. We bury our lives in objects, persons, and pursuits that seem to offer us a refuge from the abyss of aloneness.

What would happen, though, if we allowed ourselves, or were forced by "circumstance," to plunge into the abyss? Again, the wisdom of those seekers of depth whose insights are buried in the classic texts of our great traditions have some encouragement for us that is worth pondering. They tell us over and over, whether in myth or direct philosophical and theological language, that there is yet another side to the depth. The depth will show itself to us not only as an abyss but also as ground. In the final analysis, the depth is ultimate support, absolute security, unrestricted love, and eternal care. Compared to this ultimate grounding of our existence, we are told, our ordinary supports are shallow, or at least inadequate. Hence there is nothing to fear in loosening our grip on these supports after all, allowing ourselves to be swept into the depths of our life. The reason we can have the courage to open ourselves to the depth, to accept our solitude, is that there is an ultimate ground to our existence, there is an ultimate companionship in our aloneness. The abyss is only one side of the experience of depth and we are tempted to think, as are some important philosophers (like Nietzsche, Sartre, and Camus), that this is the only side. Most philosophers, and all of the major religious traditions, however, have

5. See Otto, *Idea of the Holy.*
6. See Tillich, *Systematic Theology.*

insisted that the final word about the depth is "trustworthy."[7] It is, in Tillich's words, the "ground of our being."[8]

It is this ground of courage, testified to even by serious atheistic thinkers, that helps us, in part, to indicate what we mean by God. The reader may
have experienced occasions in his or her own life when, facing a seemingly
impossible challenge, an unanticipated influx of strength made it possible to
go on. In such experiences, one may have felt a surge of vitality that is absent
in less urgent moments. What "God" means may, in part at least, be hinted
at when we ask for the ultimate whence of this courage and vitality.[9]

## Religion

The wisdom of the great traditions teaches us that the experience of depth
often occurs after or within the experience of despair, disgrace, impoverish-
ment, loss, suffering, and especially the threat of death. Tillich summarizes
this wisdom when he says "there can be no depth without the way to depth.
Truth without the way to truth is dead."[10] This "way" involves not only the
experience of pain and loss but also joy and ecstasy. It is only because we sense
somehow that in the depth lies joy that we have the incentive to abandon
ourselves to the abyss. We surmise that beneath the surface there is something
that does not disappoint and that can bring a kind of contentment that runs
deeper and endures longer than the usual forms of consolation we seek. This
sense gives rise to religion. Religion is the passionate search for depth and for
an ultimately solid ground to support our existence.

In simplest terms, then, religion may be understood as the search for
depth. To those who think that religion's only function is to provide answers,
this may seem to be an unusual and even unacceptable way of understanding religion. However, once we acknowledge that the dimension of depth is
inexhaustible, we must also confess that no present state of understanding
can ever adequately represent this dimension. There is always a "more" that
goes infinitely beyond what we have already grasped. Our relationship to
this transcendent depth can never be one of mastery or possession. Indeed,
to attempt such an absorption of the infinite horizon of our existence into
the scope of our knowledge is repudiated by all the explicitly religious traditions as a deviation from authentic life. Instead, the appropriate attitude to
take with respect to the depth is that of waiting and searching.

7. Ogden, *Reality of God*, 34–38.

8. Tillich, *Courage to Be*, 156.

9. Wilde, *De Profundis*, 18.

10. Tillich, *Shaking of the Foundations*, 55.

But religion is more than a search. For religion is also a confident naming of the dimension of depth. It is the jubilant enunciation of a sense that the depth has broken through into our lives in one way or another. Religion is the symbolic (and at times ritualistic) expression of the shared experience of this depth that has made itself transparent to human consciousness. In order for us to undertake the adventurous quest which we have called religion, we already need at least some sense of what we are seeking. Otherwise, we would not be aroused to seek it at all. Somehow or other, the depth has already insinuated itself into our lives at the same time that it has elusively receded into the distance. One way in which it makes itself provisionally known to us is to embody itself in events, persons, or aspects of nature and history. These then function as symbols that inspire us to trust and that motivate us to look deeper. Religion, therefore, is a surrender to those symbols and stories that give us the courage to seek further.

This view of religious existence recognizes that "there can be no depth without the way to depth."[11] The fulfillment of our deepest longings cannot occur in one instantaneous act of consciousness, though perhaps a radical decision to live irreversibly in trustful waiting may be one that takes place in a single moment. The experience of God as depth involves our embarking on a way, a journey, a pilgrimage with the full awareness that the end of it may lie an infinite distance ahead. Radical waiting is, of all possible responses to our life, the most difficult, the most arduous, the most ungratifying. But it is also, as Tillich says, the most realistic and the most fulfilling, the one that takes the depth most seriously. And it is not as though by this waiting and searching we are deprived of strength to endure joyfully in the present.

In summary, if God is the depth of existence, then religion is the confident search for this depth as well as the celebration of those events, persons, or occasions where the depth has broken through the surface of our lives in an exceptional way. The test of whether we are religious or not is simply whether we are concerned with this dimension of depth. And it is the degree of seriousness whereby we ask ultimate questions, and not the degree of doctrinal certitude, that determines whether we are surrendering to the transcendent depth of our lives—that is, to God.

11. See Tillich, *Courage to Be.*

# 2: Future[1]

AGAIN LET US START with the obvious. I would invite the reader to pause now and attend to the transient character of this moment. Notice how impossible it is to hold on to it, how it slips out of your grasp. Where did it go? It was present a few moments ago, but now its presentness has been lost and another present has slipped into its place. When that earlier moment vanished, did it slip into nothingness? Did it undergo an absolute perishing? The very fact that you can recall it, that it still persists in your memory, is evidence that it did not perish utterly. In some fashion or other, it still lives on. What we call the "past" is the repository of all those formerly present moments whose immediacy has now been lost to us and which have the enduring status of "having been."

For now, though, our focus is not the past. We know that the formerly present moment took up a permanent dwelling in the past. But where did it come from in the first place? That edge of freshness that blended into a present experience lived only for a moment and then perished. Where did it come from? The source of that moment's novelty we refer to as the future.

It is impossible for us to define the future. We cannot hold it out before us as an object of tangible grasp. It evades our comprehension. But we cannot avoid experiencing it or being affected by it. We cannot deny that the future, any more than the dimension of depth, is a part of our experience, even though we cannot bring it into focus. We are constantly being "invaded" by it, "overwhelmed" by it, "carried into" it, or we are simply trying to avoid it. The future is clearly an ineluctable aspect of our experience and not an illusion, though it is too elusive to be turned into an object for our examination in the same sense as, for example, a physical object in front of our eyes. There is something very slippery about the future. But even though it cannot be reified, there is still something inevitable about it.

If there is anything in our ordinary experience that lies beyond our control, it is the relentless conquering of the present by the future. Again, this is so obvious as not to need mentioning. But our approach in each chapter of this book is to begin with the obvious. We start with those experiences which are so matter-of-fact, so taken for granted, that we find it

---

1. The following text is an excerpt. Previously published in Haught, *What is God?*, 25–46. Reprinted with permission.

difficult to talk about them. Certainly, futurity is one of the commonplaces that evades our ordinary focal understanding. It is a dimension that our consciousness dwells in without usually focusing on. Indeed, focusing on it, as we are doing now, is likely to distort the understanding and feeling of it that we have in our spontaneous existence. Nonetheless, we must ask an unusual, strange-sounding question about it: what is the future? Perhaps the reader has never been confronted by such an apparently inane question before. After all, this kind of question seems to fall in the same context as other apparently unanswerable puzzles such as what is matter? What is reality? What is nature? What is truth? What is beauty? Similarly, at first glance, the question "what is the future?" generates little apparent hope for a clear or interesting answer.

Our question "what is the future?" cannot be an interesting one unless we have first felt the confinement of the past. But there is a paradox here. For we cannot feel the past as confining unless in some mode of present experience we have already felt the future. To know a limit as a limit is to be beyond that limit. To recognize the past truly as past means that we already have some vague sense of futurity. The future, even when it seems to be absent, has already quietly insinuated itself into our present subjective awareness. By comparison with the silent horizon of this future, our past shows up in awareness precisely as pastness. If the future has already inserted itself into our present, perhaps we may begin to feel a troubling conflict.

As with depth, the future is fundamentally a *mysterium tremendum et fascinans*. It evokes in us ambivalent responses. We may, and often do, shrink back from it as an awesome and overwhelming terror, as a *mysterium tremendum*. We feel, with some reason, that it will loosen us from our moorings to the safety of the past. This severance may be a difficult one, depending on the degree to which we have made the past or present normative for our life. But the future is also a *mysterium fascinans*, compellingly attractive and promising a fulfillment not yet attained. There is something in us that longs for the future to deliver us from the decay of the past and the boredom of the present. We intuit a healing power in the future. We form images of it in our daydreams, in our symbols, myths, utopias, and in our religions. But as with the dimension of depth, our relationship to the future is ambiguous. The future is both the object of our deepest longing and, at the same time, an horizon that we would like to recede into a less threatening distance. We would rather make the past or present the absolute criterion of our lives than allow ourselves to be carried away into the unfamiliar freshness of the future. Our native openness to the future is usually awakened most intensely in those moments of our life and in periods of human history when the past or present seems insufficient to nurture our longings. This is why a sense of the future takes root most firmly among the oppressed. The reaching out for something radically new does not easily occur in the midst of ease and satisfaction with the status quo. Often it is only when the resources of the past and present have been spent that we begin to open ourselves willingly to the future . . . As in the case of depth, the future is not only an abyss from which we understandably recoil; it is also a ground that promises ultimate fulfillment.

However, not just any particular future is capable of satisfying us. Even if it happens that we arrive at an imagined "utopia" in our individual or social life, we inevitably find that it too will be relativized by the horizon of a future beyond itself. It will be exposed as finite and fragile and we will have to continue our quest. Each particular future is relative, so it turns out to be too narrow to appease the deep hunger for the future that constitutes the dynamism of human and social life. It is apparent that we never arrive completely at the future we long for and that if we momentarily think we have arrived, we are soon disappointed. It may be tempting for some of us then to interpret the future as an infinite void with no ultimate ground and to see our lives as futile forays into this infinite emptiness. The ever receding character of the future may seem to make despair the most honest attitude we can take toward it. More than one philosopher has taken this position.

The name of this infinite and inexhaustible future is God. That future is what the word God means. And if that word has not much meaning for you, translate it, and speak of your ultimate future, of what you hope for in the depths of your desire. Perhaps in order to do this, you must forget many things that you have learned about God, perhaps even that word itself. For if you know that God means the absolute future, you know much about the divine. You cannot then call yourself an atheist or unbeliever. For you cannot think or say: Life has no future! Reality lies only in the past! The present is sufficient! For whoever has a concern about the absolute future is concerned about God.[2]

Here I have substituted the word "future" for depth because the metaphor "depth" is only partly able to illuminate what many people mean by God (as Tillich himself was no doubt aware). What is signified by the term "God" is only fragmentarily conceptualized by reference to the dimension of depth . . . And yet the "depth" metaphor is by itself inadequate for pointing to the reality of what many people understand by God. It needs to be complemented by other ideas. Among these is that of futurity. Particularly in biblical religion,

---

2. Haught paraphrases Tillich, substituting the term "future" for depth. The expression "absolute future" comes from Karl Rahner, *Theological Investigations*, 59–68

the idea of God is inseparable from our experience of the future. The Bible may even be said to have opened up our consciousness to a radically new way of experiencing the depth of reality, namely as essentially future.[3] Even today's secular experience of the future has been influenced by the biblical location of God's reality in the dimension of futurity. This "eschatological" sense that the "really real" world lies up ahead, in the future, is shared by Marxists and capitalist consumer cultures alike—even though they may either explicitly or implicitly deny the existence of God. Ironically, the secularistic way of experiencing the future is an indirect descendant of the biblical optimism according to which God heals and addresses people in history out of an ever-receding future. The idea of God may have dropped out of the picture, but this future orientation has remained alive in many non-religious movements, oftentimes even more vigorously than in theistic settings. Today's biblical scholarship has shown clearly that the ancient Hebrew religious experience differed from that of its contemporaries essentially in its loosening the sacred from its bondage to the circularity of nature's seasons and placing it in the realm of the indefinite historical future. The central challenge for the early devotees of the biblical Yahweh was to forsake the safety of a purely nature-oriented religion and surrender themselves to the uncertainty of living in a history whose promise seemed to lie far off in the future.

If our emphasizing the future in this way seems to downgrade the importance of the past and of tradition, then this impression must be corrected. Openness to the future is the very condition of, and not an obstacle to, recovering the meaning of the past and the important traditions of our human history. The horizon of the future liberates significant events and traditions from the heaviness of merely having been and opens up a space in which they can come to life once again . . . Openness to the future should never occur at the expense of forgetting the suffering of forgotten peoples of the past or the wisdom molded by tragedy that has been deposited in the great teachings of our traditions—but these traditions are intended to instruct us, not to enslave us.

Another way to think about God, then, is as the absolute future. God is not an object of our experience so much as a dimension or horizon of our experience. Not all things that are real are potential objects of human experience. The dimension of futurity, as of depth, is certainly real, without thereby being subject to our intellectual or perceptual mastery. Therefore, perhaps God may be understood less as a potential object of experience than as a dimension, condition, and future horizon of all our experience.

3. See Moltmann, *Theology of Hope*.

As the absolute future, "God" means the irrepressible promise of fulfillment that emerges anew out of the infinite (and seemingly empty) horizon of our future each time we experience disappointment. "God" means the ground of hope that animates us to search further whenever we realize that we have not yet arrived at what we really long for.

## The Absence of God

Locating God's presence in the arena of the future can help us to understand the apparent absence of God. Scientifically oriented philosophers usually challenge theists to show some present evidence of God's reality. They seek something in the manner of a positive, scientific demonstration of God's objective contemporary existence. And when theists fail to adduce such verification, they are accused of fostering an illusion, that is, of being unrealistic. The existence of that which is said to be of ultimate importance is not even as obvious as that of a rock. How can the intelligent, scientifically enlightened person seriously believe in God?

Our answer to this question is simply that the scientific, empirical approach is oriented toward a region of reality—the present—that is insufficiently expansive enough to contain the reality of God. We may think of the appropriate region of God's reality as essentially the future (although also embracing the past and present). Understood as the absolute future, the reality of God lies beyond the limits of what can be grasped in the present. The methods we employ in understanding the present are inadequate for orienting us to the future. Science is fixed on the present or past; it is incapable of dealing with the future since there is no way it can bring the dimension of the yet-to-come under any sort of verificational control. Only imagination suffused with hope can bring the future within view. The reality of God, therefore, must be approached in the same general way as we approach any aspect of the future, namely, by hoping and imagining.

Of course the empiricist will object that future-oriented imagination is a mere extrapolation from our present wishes, that our longing for the future and picturing it symbolically may have nothing to do with "reality." However, this objection applies more to wishing than to hoping and we must carefully distinguish between these two postures. Hoping is an openness to the breaking in of what is radically new and unanticipated. Wishing, on the other hand, is the illusory extension into the future of what we want at the present moment.[4] Wishing is not an openness to the future but rather is oriented entirely from the present. In order to hope, on the other hand,

4. See Williams, *True Resurrection*, 178–79.

we need to relativize our wishing and open ourselves to the prospect of being surprised by the radically new. Such an attitude requires a courageous
asceticism of its own, a painful renunciation of our tendency to cling obsessively to the present or past. Hoping is not an escape from reality, nor is it
as easy as its critics insist.[5] Hoping is an attitude capable of living tolerantly
with the absence of God.

## Religion

If the ultimate environment of our lives is not only depth but also the
absolute future, then we must understand "religion" accordingly. We may
say, then, that religion is not only concern for depth or the expression
in symbol and ritual of a shared sense of depth. Without denying any of
this, we must now add that religion, in connection with the horizon of an
absolute future, is essentially hope.[6]

We must be careful to distinguish hope from other forms of desire.
It may be very tempting to follow the suggestion of Freud that religion is
nothing other than a product of the pleasure principle—that religion is
an illusion, created by an intense desire to escape "reality" and merge in
an infantile manner with maternal nature or a paternal God who would
satisfy our hunger for gratification. We need not deny that there might be
something to what Freud has to say here about the nature of human desire,
but if we understand the idea of God as that which challenges us to open
ourselves radically to the future, we must distinguish what we are calling religion from Freud's position. After all, in Freud's critique, religion is always
understood as a regressive tendency, as a hankering for a lost love-object
from one's past psychic experience.[7] This obsession with the idol of the past
is the very temptation that biblical religion itself disowned, especially in the
prophetic strains of that tradition. The Hebrew prophets would themselves
have agreed with Freud that we humans are able to do better than simply
spend our lives attempting to recover a lost parental love. They might even
have concurred with psychoanalysis that many of our portraits of God are
inevitably overlaid with regressive images of frustrated relations to significant others in our psychic history. But they would have also insisted beyond
this that the place of encounter with God is in hope for a radically new
future rather than in nostalgia for past safeties. They would look back to

---

5. See Williams, *True Resurrection*, 178–79.

6. See Moltmann, *Theology of Hope*, 19–36.

7. See Freud, *Future of an Illusion*.

the past not in order to retrieve it as past but rather to find precedents for looking forward to the surprising action of God in their future.

The heart of religion, in this context at least, may be thought of as hope for an "absolute future." Such hope is not a renunciation of the reality principle if it turns out that the substance of reality lies in the future rather than in the present or the past. There is no evidence that the present and the past exhaust the limits of reality. It may be that the "really real" lies up ahead and that our historical existence is only a fragmentary and inadequate anticipation of this future. Our anticipation of the fullness of reality would then take the form of imagining the future in such a way as to allow for its entrance into the present. A certain kind of adventurous dreaming would be the way in which we would follow the Freudian imperative to "face reality." A failure to construct creative visions that motivate us to action and usher in the future would be a refusal to be realistic. And if the fullness of God's being is essentially future, then realistic religion consists in the hopeful and imaginative quest for this future.

# 3: Freedom[1]

VERY FEW WORDS EVOKE as much positive sentiment as "freedom." At the same time, few words are more difficult to define. Politicians, philosophers, psychologists, and theologians have all discussed the term. And yet, after hearing what they have to say about it, we are still left with the question: what exactly is freedom? One is tempted to paraphrase Saint Augustine's famous lament about his inability to spell out the meaning of time: if no one asks me what freedom is, then I know what it is; but if someone asks me, then I do not know. Freedom can be rendered intuitively vivid through symbols, myths, and stories of heroic struggles for "emancipation" or "liberation." And the sense of freedom is concretized in actually living and acting rather than by reading or writing a book. Any conceptual or theoretical attempt to say what freedom is risks becoming shallow and abstract, and there is a good chance it will partially warp our immediate grasp of the meaning of the term. Nonetheless, perhaps some insight can be gained from a theoretical study of the idea of freedom. After all, just as Augustine could not refrain from telling us what time is, so it is forgivable if we also attempt to speak conceptually about freedom. We know the extent to which ideas have contributed to the formation of our history. Certainly, our experience of freedom in the Western world has been shaped significantly by bold ideas that, in turn, motivated people to work for liberation from various forms of oppression. It is not entirely out of place, therefore, to discuss the idea of freedom in a theoretical way.

What, then, is freedom? As with our intuition of time, we all have an immediate or "naive" grasp of the meaning of "freedom." The same is true of our experience of depth and futurity. We feel them, we dwell in them, and we sense their presence or absence in various degrees. But we cannot objectify them. We cannot hold them out before us in a controlling fashion such as science attempts to do with the objects of its study. We know them more in the mode of being grasped by them than by actually grasping them ourselves. Or we know them in the mode of fleeing from them. The same is also true of our understanding of freedom. We know what it is only if we have been grasped by it—or, in a negative sense, if we have fled from it. If

1. The following text is an excerpt. Previously published in Haught, *What is God?*, 47–68. Reprinted with permission.

we try to lay hold of it ourselves, it slips away from us. Our approach to it must therefore be somewhat indirect; we should not ever expect to have a perfectly clear intellectual grasp of what it is.

There are three ways in which philosophers have typically dealt with the notion of freedom. One way is to understand freedom as something we have, another as something we are, and yet another as something that has us. The first approach views freedom as one of our faculties, the one whereby we make "free choices" among various alternatives that are offered to us. The ability to make free choices is certainly an important aspect of freedom, but free choice is not coextensive with freedom as we shall understand it here. The second approach, exemplified in an extreme way by the French philosopher Jean-Paul Sartre, views freedom as the very essence of human existence. In this view, human reality is freedom in the negative sense, as not being determined by anything beyond itself and, in the positive sense of the creative source of our very identities.[2] This position that we are freedom would be acceptable if we understood freedom as finite and not as absolute in the sense given by Sartre. To say that we are finite freedom is one important way to understand our nature. However, even this second meaning does not give us the depth toward which the word freedom points. For that reason, I shall dwell hereafter on a third meaning of the term. Freedom, in the deepest sense, is something that takes hold of us, not something that we can manipulate ourselves. Moreover, we owe our freedom to choose (freedom in the first sense) as well as the freedom of our finite existence (freedom in the second sense) to our participating in the encompassing freedom (in the third sense) of which I shall speak in the present chapter. Freedom in the third and most substantive sense is the "ground" of freedom in the first two instances.

If we reflect on some very obvious aspects of our experience, as we have done in the previous two chapters, we shall observe that freedom is most appropriately understood as the comprehensive horizon of our existence, rather than as something we possess or, as Jean-Paul Sartre has proposed, something that coincides with our individual existence. As in the case of depth and futurity, freedom, in the sense of something that grasps us, is a *mysterium tremendum et fascinans*. We shrink from it in fear that we will be lost in its embrace and, at the same time, we long for it passionately, intuiting that our personal fulfillment consists of our eventually surrendering to it. We long for the freedom that coincides with our absolute future, but, at the same time, we are reluctant to allow it into our present life.

2. Sartre, *Existentialism and the Human Emotions*, 52–59.

In order to illustrate concretely the ambivalence of our relationship to freedom, let us look especially at the experience of coming to grips with our own personal identities. Have there been times when we came up to the point of knowing that we really are not fully definable in terms of our immediate surroundings? Have we, on some occasions, realized that the opinion others have of us simply does not adequately indicate what we know ourselves to be? Such moments hold open to us the possibility of our entering into a whole new way of existing; and yet, we usually revert to the typical routine of allowing past patterns of others' expectations to determine how we view ourselves. Psychoanalysis, though controversial in many respects, at least deserves our admiration for showing us how our early family life unconsciously accompanies us and shapes our attitudes throughout our lives. Many of us can go through an entire lifetime without ever questioning the familial patterns of expectation that gave us our earliest orientation in the world. Because of the power and authority of these familial patterns, any attempt we make at an alternative self-definition may be accompanied by an agonizing sense of guilt and betrayal.

It is instructive to examine the sense of uneasiness that often accompanies the act of departing from the expectations that we think others have imposed upon us. At times, such a departure is, of course, the violation of standards that we are expected to model ourselves on as the basic minimum for human existence. In such a case, genuine feelings of guilt are important to point out to us the error of our ways and to goad us into conforming to the cardinal standards of human conduct. At other times, we need to "violate" certain conventional standards if we think they are an obstacle to the realization of genuine new possibilities of being human to which we sincerely feel called. But we are uneasy before these possibilities as well. It is much easier to be merely conventional in our ethical life than to heed the summons of timeless values that transcend our societal, national or familial ideals.[3]

We may call this sense of dread in the face of new possibilities "anxiety." One meaning of "anxiety" is the awareness of yet unrealized possibilities. It is the intimation that we have other routes of self-definition open to us alongside those that have been so determinative in the past. Our awareness of these unrealized possibilities that would give a new cast to our identity confronts us as a *tremendum*. Unlike the realm of the "actual," the arena of the "possible" is inexhaustible, and so we are reluctant to plunge into its formless, abysmal depths, dreading that the boundaries of our finite existence will be annihilated by the excess of the possible. As Kierkegaard puts

---

3. See Kohlberg, *Philosophy of Moral Development*.

it, our impression of this realm of sheer unrealized possibility may induce in us a "sickness unto death."[4] However, one aspect of the experience of freedom consists precisely of the anxiety evoked in us by our awareness of ever new possibilities, ideals, or values.

An analysis of this anxiety can open us to a deeper understanding of freedom. When we use the term anxiety here, though, we are not referring to something abnormal or pathological. Rather, we are talking about a state of awareness that always accompanies our human existence, whether in a conscious or in an unconscious way. Without it, we would not be human existents at all. In other words, this anxiety is a characteristic aspect of our existence, not something that can be removed pharmocologically or psychiatrically. When psychiatry talks about removing anxiety, it is speaking of a pathological exaggeration or suppression of our "normal" anxiety. And it seriously misleads us if it pretends to cure us of our "existential" anxiety.[5] Nothing can cure us of this anxiety. But such an impossibility need not be the occasion of perpetual unhappiness for us. Instead, it may be seen as an opening to the fulfilling side of freedom.

Existential anxiety may also be understood as the awareness of the fact that our existence is constantly subject to a fundamental and unavoidable threat. Paul Tillich refers to it as the threat of "non-being."[6] The awareness of this threat should be distinguished from fear.[7] Fear is always a response to a specific danger, a definite object of terror. For example, I may fear a rabid animal, an authoritarian teacher, a poor grade on an examination, or the disapproval of parents and friends. And I may combat my fear of these by employing specific strategies. I may shoot the rabid animal, change classes to a more amiable instructor, study harder for an examination, or move away from home. Such strategies are often successful ways of coping with fear. Yet beneath all our specific fears, there is a sustained inkling of a pervasive and ineradicable threat which no evasive action can alleviate. There is at least a vague intuition that our existence is situated precariously over against the threat of "nonbeing."

But what does this discussion of nonbeing have to do with freedom? Strange as it may initially seem, the experience of the threat of nonbeing that I have just described (drawing again from Paul Tillich) is one aspect of the experience of the horizon of freedom. "Nonbeing" is the face that freedom first presents to us as it invites us into its embrace. And difficult as it

4. See Kierkegaard, *Sickness Unto Death.*

5. See Tillich, *Courage To Be,* 64–85.

6. Tillich, *Courage To Be,* 32.

7. Tillich, *Courage To Be,* 36–39.

may be for us to understand, it is by realistically facing rather than running away from this nonbeing that we are liberated from the things that enslave us and drawn toward the fullness of freedom.

Nonbeing is terrifying to us, of course, and so we attempt to avoid it by tying our fragile existence to things that seemingly provide refuge from it. However, since all such things are themselves merely finite and, therefore, also subject to nonbeing, the security they give us is only fragmentary and ultimately illusory. Such precarious security is not truly liberating in the final analysis for it merely constricts our lives by binding us to objects that are too small to help us face existential anxiety. Just as we strive to turn the anxiety of nonbeing into specific objects of fear that we can control, so also we turn to specific objects, persons, events, nations, cults, possessions, etc. in order to anchor our existence against the invasion of nonbeing. Eventually, however, we will be forced to realize that they are mere "idols" that cannot give us the ultimate deliverance for which we really hope. How, then, are we to deal with nonbeing?

The threat of nonbeing can be met adequately only by a courage proportionate to the threat itself. It is through courage that we meet the threat of nonbeing and, in doing so, experience freedom-itself. Indeed, courage may be defined as the "self-affirmation" by which we accept and face up to the anxiety of non-being. The encounter with freedom in the deepest sense, therefore, is inseparable from the experience of courage.[8]

If human freedom has any realistic meaning at all, it cannot mean deliverance from existential anxiety. The quest for freedom is destined for frustration as long as it is undertaken as the search for refuge from nonbeing. This is one lesson that theists can well learn from existentialist philosophers. In what, then, does human freedom consist (freedom in our second sense), if there in no easy escape from fate, death, guilt and the experience of doubt and even meaninglessness? Is human freedom even a meaningful notion, given the fact that our existence is never "free from" existential anxiety?

Humanly speaking, freedom is the awareness that existential anxiety has been conquered rather than simply evaded. It is an awareness that, in spite of the pervasive threat of nonbeing, the core of our existence is always already ultimately secure. Such an awareness delivers us from the obsessive need to secure our existence in particular things and projects. It recognizes the futility of all such enterprises. And it allows for a serenity and peacefulness of existence that transcends the security which comes from our usual possessions.

8. See Tillich, *Courage To Be*, 32–36.

But is such an awareness anywhere an actuality? Are there individuals who have achieved such a state of subjective freedom? I think that we do find such awareness exemplified in the lives of people who exhibit courage. It is not necessary to give examples of such courage here. We see it manifest all around us—in the heroic lives of ordinary people who have themselves been motivated to courageous acceptance of their lives by their participation in the great stories of human courage, passed down from generation to generation, in all cultures and traditions. We have all witnessed the way in which people overcome apparently insurmountable difficulties and emerge as stronger in the process of facing their problems than if they had taken flight from them. This everyday occurrence is, in fact, so commonplace that we hardly notice its utterly "miraculous" character. It is in the lives of such courageous people that we can catch a glimpse of the ultimate horizon of freedom that seeks to liberate our human existence in a decisive way.

Human courage faces and accepts existential anxiety instead of fleeing from it. And in the act of facing it head-on, it gives witness to a transcendent power capable of conquering the threat of nonbeing, providing a solid base for a realistic sense of freedom. We need not construct "proofs" for the "existence" of this power. The evidence for its reality is simply the acts of courage so manifest in the lives of those who accept themselves in spite of the existential anxiety that is part of their concrete existence.[9] In their courageous self-affirmation, we can see evidence of their participation in an objective liberating "power" that conquers nonbeing. In viewing their heroic lives, we can also appreciate the true meaning of human freedom as participation in an ultimate horizon of freedom—call it freedom-itself—which gives them the courage to prevail over the threats of nonbeing. Transparent in such lives of courage is a deep, transcendent freedom which has encircled their lives. Their courage is the "revelation" of an ultimate and abiding freedom that transcends and empowers our existence.

Our finite freedom (freedom in the second sense) is not a negative "freedom from," but rather a participatory freedom, an experience of opening oneself to and being grasped by the encompassing freedom that embraces and conquers the threat of nonbeing. This horizon of freedom of which we partake cannot be comprehended intellectually. It is not a possession and it cannot be controlled by acts of "willfulness" on our part. It can only be experienced by oneself or pointed to as it becomes evident in the courageous lives of human persons. Its reality is felt only in the act of allowing oneself to be grasped by it. For that reason any scientific demonstration of its presence is impossible.

9. See Tillich, *Courage To Be*, 181.

In the concrete lives of heroic people, moreover, we may encounter the *fascinans*, the fulfilling side of freedom; we may get an inkling of the dimension of freedom that corresponds with the "grounding" aspect of our experience of depth; and we may also observe the foundation of what we called hope in the previous chapter.

The name of this ultimately grounding and courage-bestowing horizon of freedom that becomes transparent in acts of courage is—God. That grounding freedom is what the word "God" means. And if that word has not much meaning for you, translate it and speak of the deep freedom for which you yearn, beyond the finite securities you cling to in order to escape existential anxiety. Perhaps, in order to do this, you must forget many things you have learned about "God," perhaps even the word itself. But as long as you open yourself to a courage whereby you realistically accept your existence, you cannot then call yourself an atheist in any meaningful sense of the term. For you cannot consistently maintain that there is no basis in reality for your courage. Even in your uttering such a statement, you would give evidence of your participating in such a power of self-affirmation.

# 4: Beauty[1]

We have seen that the encounter with depth, futurity, and freedom requires an attitude of allowing ourselves to be grasped by them. Our typical response, though, is one of initially shrinking back from entering into the embrace of these horizons (which are really three ways of thinking about a single horizon) while, at the same time, being irresistibly drawn toward them. Rather than allowing ourselves to be immediately comprehended by depth, futurity, and freedom, we try to place them under our control. Such a response is inevitably unsuccessful, however, and we finally realize that our sense of well-being, our happiness, requires that we surrender ourselves to them.

Nowhere is this need to surrender more obvious than in our encounter with beauty. In order for us to experience the beauty of nature, other persons, a great event, or an artistic masterpiece, we have to allow ourselves to be "carried away" by the aesthetic phenomenon. This experience of being grasped by the beautiful is one of the clearest models we have for expressing what is involved in the intuition of the divine. In fact, it is more than a model. We may even say that our ordinary experience of the beautiful is already an encounter with ultimacy.

The experience of beauty is as two-sided as is the religious experience of the sacred. On the one hand, great beauty is overwhelming in its seductiveness and attractiveness. It is a *mysterium fascinans* that compels us and invites us to surrender ourselves to it. At times we have all experienced the seductiveness of the beautiful, especially as it is embodied in other persons, but also in the glories of nature, music, and literature. At the same time, we have felt the pangs of unfulfilled longing that accompany every aesthetic experience. We are implicitly aware of the chasm that lies between the beauty embodied in any particular object of aesthetic delight and the unlimited beauty for which we long in the depths of our desire. This abysmal distance is a *mysterium tremendum* from which we shrink back. Our recoil from ultimate beauty takes the form of a fixation on particular, limited, aesthetic objects; this fixation is accompanied by an anaesthetizing of our deep need for a wider and fuller beauty.

1. The following text is an excerpt. Previously published in Haught, *What is God?*, 69–91. Reprinted with permission.

In short, our quest for beauty is a quest for the divine. That ultimately satisfying beauty which we long for—but continues to elude us—is what the word "God" means. And if that word has not much meaning for you, translate it and speak of the ultimately beautiful for which you are continually searching in the depths of your desire. Perhaps, in order to do this, you must forget much that you have learned about God, perhaps even that name itself. For if you know that God means ultimate "beauty," you already know much about the divine. You cannot then call yourself an atheist, for you cannot think or say, "I am completely indifferent to beauty." If you could say this in complete seriousness, then you would be an atheist; otherwise, you are not. For as long as you have some longing for a wider and deeper beauty than you have experienced thus far in your life, you show that you have already in some way encountered the divine, or rather, that the divine has taken hold of you. Another way to think about God, therefore, is as the horizon of ultimate beauty toward which you are irresistibly drawn.

Scholars of religion rightly make a distinction between religious and aesthetic experience (as we shall call the experience of beauty). Religion, they often say, involves the symbolic sense of a "totally other" dimension that becomes transparent to the believer in the images and objects that stand for and mediate the "sacred." The aesthetic experience, on the other hand, is not explicitly concerned with the symbolic transparency of the aesthetic object. It does not have to understand a beautiful object as standing for any sacred reality "beyond" itself. The beautiful seems sufficient in itself and does not inevitably lead us into another dimension, whereas the religious sense does.[2] To many individuals for whom the "sacred" means nothing at all, the "beautiful" means a great deal. Therefore, some distinction must be made between "the sacred" and "the beautiful."

But can we so neatly set one experience apart from the other? I am uncomfortable with too sharp of a distinction between the aesthetic and the religious experience. To segregate them too crisply seems artificial and out of touch with what actually happens in our encounter with the beauty of reality. For if we carefully ponder what is involved in the experience of concrete beauty, we may think of it as continuous with our encountering the divine. By our tasting the beauty in our ordinary experience, we are already being invited into the realm of ultimacy, although we may not wish to interpret it as such. Nonetheless, the point of the following is to argue that this is indeed the case. An examination of our ordinary encounter with beauty may disclose to us that the beautiful is a *mysterium tremendum et fascinans* too, and that we respond to it with the same

2. See Dupre, *Other Dimension*, 228–42.

ambivalent wavering between repulsion and attraction that the experience of the sacred evokes in *homo religiosus.*

Can we state conceptually what it is that makes things appear to us as beautiful and some things as more beautiful than others? Alfred North Whitehead, whose philosophy is permeated by aesthetic considerations, tells us that beauty is the "harmony of contrasts."[3] What makes us appreciate the beauty of things is that they bring together nuance, richness, complexity, and novelty on the one side, and harmony, pattern, or order on the other. The more "intense" the synthesis of harmony and contrast, the more we appreciate their union. Nuance without harmony is chaos and harmony without nuance is monotony. Beauty involves the transformation of potentially clashing elements into pleasing contrasts, harmonized by the overarching aesthetic pattern of the beautiful object or experience.

An example of such harmony of contrasts may be seen in any great novel. What makes such a novel beautiful is its weaving together into a unified whole the many subplots and characterizations that might have easily led to confusion. A poor novel would be one that was so concerned with overall order that it failed to establish sufficient tension and conflict to bring about the nuanced complexity required by beauty. At the opposite extreme, an inferior novel would degenerate into chaos, failing to bring its details into the unity of a single story. Either lack of harmony or absence of complexity would impoverish the artistic masterpiece. Our appreciation of the work of art, or of anything beautiful, is the result of our implicit sense that the beautiful precariously balances the order and novelty brought together in the aesthetic object.

If we reflect on the elements of the beautiful, however, we are led to the conclusion, also emphasized by Whitehead, that every actuality is, to some degree at least, an aesthetic phenomenon. Every "actual entity" is a patterned synthesis of contrasting elements. In the simplest objects the contrasts are not intense, but they are there at least to some small degree. Nothing would be actual at all unless its ingredients were patterned in some way or other. Whether we are talking about an electron, an artistic creation, a person, a civilization, or the universe as such, these entities would not have any identity whatsoever unless their constituent elements were patterned in a definite way. Their "actuality" corresponds by degrees to the mode and intensity of their synthesizing harmony and contrast. This means that all things are actual to the extent that they are beautiful and all things are beautiful to the extent that they order novelty and complexity into aesthetic contrasts.[4]

---

3. See Whitehead, *Adventures of Ideas,* 252–96.

4. See Whitehead, *Religion in the Making,* 115.

Beauty, therefore, has what philosophers call a "transcendental" nature. This means that "the beautiful" is not any particular thing, but instead a metaphysical aspect of all things (being, truth, unity, goodness, and beauty are the "transcendentals" usually mentioned by metaphysicians). For this reason alone, we may suspect that we cannot casually disassociate any possible encounter with beauty from the experience of the divine, which is said to be the supreme exemplification of the "transcendentals."

We experience beauty in nature, in the physical appearances or personalities of others, in great architecture, art, music, poetry, and other types of literature. But one of the most intense instances of aesthetic experience lies in the spectacle of an heroic story. Since such stories involve the narrative patterning of struggle, suffering, conflicts, and contradictions into a complex unity, they stand out as one of the most obvious examples of beauty. In fact, it is often our being conditioned by the stories of great heroes that determines our whole sense of reality, personal identity, and purpose, as well as the quality of our aesthetic experience in general. From the beginning of human history, it appears that the consciousness of people—their sense of reality, identity, and destiny—has been shaped primarily by their sense of the heroic as it is deposited in the paradigmatic stories of their traditions. In myth, legend, ballad, history, epic, and any other type of story, people have woven around themselves a narrative womb with all the ingredients of ordered contrast that I am here attributing to beauty.

In this light, the seemingly nihilistic dismantling of tradition, history, religion, and story in the "deconstructionist" element of modern criticism may be interpreted as itself a moment of contrast that adds nuance to the wider pattern of beauty for which we remain forever nostalgic. The way in which human consciousness has, at times, been frozen in particular narrative patterns deserves the kind of negative criticism one finds in a deconstructionist philosophy. In spite of its inevitable protests to the contrary, I would suggest that, like Nietzsche, its criticism is directed less at narrative as such than at narrative fixation. Deconstructionists are by no means the most significant threat to the integrity of story. For the demise of story is first of all the result of our childish obsession with particular versions of a dynamic narrative tradition. The attempt to freeze a particular tradition in an absolutely conservative way is already the end of story, the true "nihilism" that prevents the story from remaining alive. Story-fixations bring about the end of story and, with it, the impression of the death of God, long before modern deconstructionists begin their work. Nietzsche himself was well aware of the implicit nihilism buried in the superficial narrative fixation of much Christian theology and spirituality. By bringing the "ending" into narrative view prematurely, by failing to wait in the midst of struggle, and by

narrowing the ending down to dimensions too suffocating to satisfy the human desire for the infinite, story-fixation is itself already the death of narrative. To be properly narrative, the cosmic and human story must remain in
process. To freeze the story artificially is to kill it. Hence, the deconstruction
of story(-fixation) of which we have been speaking is an essential nullifying
operation undertaken for the sake of the survival of narrative itself. The
stories, histories, and cosmologies taken apart by deconstructionists are, in
my view, highly caricatured versions with which some (but by no means
all) believers are uncomfortable anyway. Although its proponents would
undoubtedly deny it, deconstructionism announces not the end of story as
such but rather the end of naive story-fixations. And thus it may be seen as
contributing, in the final analysis, to a wider aesthetic vision.

However, the narrative sense which our critics have rightly tied to the
idea of God is incapable of being absolutely eradicated. Their own writings
display a narrative undercurrent of which they are not always aware. They
themselves tell a story about story. Their tale has a beginning, a period of
struggle, and an end. Deconstructionists envisage themselves as living in
the "final days," when history and narrative have come to an end, when an
eternal "play" of language eschatologically appears.[5] Ironically they usually invoke and transform ancient myths (stories)—like those of Sisyphus,
Eros, Thoth, Prometheus, Zarathustra, and others—to instruct us about
the futility of myth. In the very performance of the deconstruction of narrative, they give evidence of the ineradicably narrative quality of all human
experience and consciousness.

In its announcing the "closure" (which does not necessarily mean
chronological end) of history, self, and narrative, and in its endorsement of
a formless and insignificant play of language, deconstructionism also falls
short of giving us the ultimate aesthetic fulfillment we all long for. In the
final analysis, this philosophy is not a space within which one can live. If it
has any value at all in terms of our aesthetic needs, it is only as a "moment"
in the process of moving toward a wider narrative vision of beauty than is
allowed by our story-fixations. Unfortunately, in its repudiation of the tension intrinsic to narrative, and in its artificial efforts to force the eschaton
of play into the temporal narrowness of the present, it is reduced to one
more version of the gnostic escapes from history to which religious people
are always tempted whenever they grow tired of waiting and struggle. Once
again, it is worth recalling Tillich's words: "We are stronger when we wait

5. See Taylor, *Erring*.

than when we possess."[6] This applies not only to our search for depth but also to our quest for an ultimate beauty.

## The Absence of God

The quest for a completely satisfying aesthetic experience always leaves us with some element of discontent. In the first place, an intense experience of beauty never lasts indefinitely. The most memorable sensations we have of being carried away by beauty are often only instants that quickly fade and that resist adequate repetition. In the second place, there is always a region of our aesthetic longing that remains unfulfilled—even by the most poignant encounters with beautiful persons, music, art, or natural phenomena. It is not difficult for any of us to conjure up examples from our own lives of the elusiveness of beauty. We are seemingly unable to completely control the beautiful, but must instead patiently await the summons to be taken into its grasp.

The experience of never being completely filled up by particular aesthetic experiences is of course frustrating. It might even tempt one to an "absurdist" interpretation of reality. The inability of particular aesthetic manifestations to satisfy the infinity of our desire for the sublime might easily be construed as just another instance of the insuperable incongruity of humans and the universe. And it would be very difficult to offer an empirical refutation of this tragic view.

However, there is another at least equally plausible interpretation of our aesthetic frustration. It stems from our thesis that, ultimately, the beautiful is the divine, a *mysterium tremendum et fascinans*. And if the divine is the beautiful or sublime, then, in keeping with what we have noted in each of the preceding chapters, we should expect not so much to grasp beauty as to allow it to comprehend us and carry us away into itself. However, as we have also emphasized, our initial instinct is usually that of resisting and even denying the gentle envelopment of our existence by the *mysterium*—in this case, the beautiful. Aesthetic frustration, therefore, is not so much a failure on the part of the beautiful to meet us as it is the result of our shriveling our aesthetic sensitivity to restrictive dimensions that "protect" us from the beautiful. The "absurdist" interpretation would insist that our aesthetic frustration is the result of the fact that while we ourselves have an insatiable, even infinite, capacity for experiencing beauty, reality is limited in its ability to satisfy our needs. Hence, absurdism places the source of our frustration in the universe itself instead of in the possible limitedness of our own aesthetic perceptivity.

6. Tillich, *Shaking*, 151.

The view that I am presenting, on the other hand, holds that the "doors" of our perception are possibly too narrow to let in the fullness of the beautiful, while the inner chamber of our consciousness continues to ache in emptiness for a beauty that would fill it and to which our perceptivity is inadequate. Aesthetic frustration stems from the inadequacy of our perceptive faculties to the deep inner need we have for limitless beauty. The absurdist view seems to be based on an unrealistic notion of perception.

Whitehead has shown how an unduly narrow doctrine of perception has dominated most of modern thought, including our understanding of beauty.[7] According to the commonly accepted view of modern, empirically oriented thought, the five senses are the only doors of our perception. If we are to be in touch with the real world, we are instructed to attend primarily to the data given to the mind by the senses of taste, touch, smell, sound, and especially sight (aided of course by scientific instruments of perception). But without denying that our senses do put us in touch with the real world, Whitehead emphasizes that the senses give us only a very abstract and narrow range of the universe. They are inadequate to mediate the full complexity—and beauty—of the world in which we are organically situated. They bite off only a very narrow range of the contemporary world and leave behind the unfathomable temporal depths and aesthetic intensity of the universe as a whole. And so, we typically tend to ignore the wider aesthetic patterning of reality, since it is left out by the clear and crisp impressions given to us by the five senses.

7. See Whitehead, *Process and Reality*, 110–26 and 168–83; Whitehead, *Modes of Thought*, 148–69; and Whitehead, *Symbolism*, 12–59.

# 5: Truth[1]

WHAT DO WE WANT more than anything else? What is our deepest desire? How many of us can honestly respond: the truth? "What we want most is the truth about the universe, about other people, and especially about ourselves"? Is truth what we really want most deeply? Or would we not be better off if we were spared from it? Søren Kierkegaard wrote: "It is far from being the case that men in general regard relationship with the truth as the highest good, and it is far from being the case that they, Socratically, regard being under a delusion as the greatest misfortune."[2] Why is it that we are not always interested in truth and instead often seek refuge in illusions?

Perhaps the reason is that the desire for truth is not the only passion governing our conscious and instinctive lives. Only a little reflection is needed to remind us that we are composed of a morass of drives, desires, longings, cravings, wishes, and hopes. Curiously, the inhabitants of this jungle of desires are often in conflict with one another. One part of us might want sensual gratification, another security, another power, another meaning, and another approval. Furthermore, one desire may be superimposed upon another, so that their disentanglement seems nearly impossible. It is often hard to determine which of the desires is dominant or to which of our various inclinations we should entrust the course of our lives. Often we experiment with a variety of our urges before we commit ourselves to any one of them as our fundamental option. Perhaps a serious pursuit of truth is one of the last of our desires to be accepted as a dynamic force in our lives because there is so much competition from other urges that are quite content to live with illusions.

And yet, the message of our great religious, literary, and philosophical classics is that there is really only one desire that we can completely trust to lead us to genuine happiness, namely our thirst for the truth. Only when we subordinate our other inclinations to the *eros* for truth will we find what we are really looking for. But how dominant is this desire in our own conscious existence? Perhaps the passion to get to the truth has not yet assumed a central role in our lives. "I want the truth" may be only a tentative, barely

1. Previously published in Haught, *What is God?*, 92–114. Reprinted with permission.

2. Kierkegaard, *Sickness Unto Death*, 175.

audible utterance, buried under many layers of longing that are not at all interested in the truth. We may, at times, wonder why the prophets, visionaries and philosophers have made so much of the pursuit of truth, especially if there is little inclination for it in our own lives.

What is the truth? Can it be defined? Or do we not implicitly appeal to it even in trying to define it, so that any attempted definition is circular? It would be an interesting experiment if you would pause at this point and attempt to define "truth." The classical definition of truth is "the correspondence of mind with reality." But what is reality? Can it be defined? The term truth often refers not only to the cognitional stance of one who is in touch with "reality," but it may also be used interchangeably with reality itself. That is, truth may be understood either epistemologically (as referring to the correspondence of our minds to reality) or metaphysically (as the name for that reality our minds are in touch with). In one sense, truth means the attunement of the mind to being, to the real, to the true. In the following, however, I shall use the term "truth" primarily in the metaphysical sense—namely, as "being," the "real," or the "true"—which is intended as the goal of our desire for reality. In other words, I shall use the terms truth, being, and reality interchangeably.

It seems that in the case of truth, we are once again dealing with a "horizon" that evades our efforts at intellectual control and adequate definition. If anything, truth would define us more than we would define it. The encounter with truth is more a case of our being grasped by it than of our actively grasping it.

Perhaps, therefore, we can speak of the truth only in a "heuristic" sense, that is, as something we are seeking but which never allows itself to be completely ensnared by our instruments of discovery. We can speak of truth more as the "objective" or goal of a certain kind of wanting within us than as a possession firmly within our grasp. Yet even though we cannot possess the truth or get our minds around it, we can at least recognize clearly, among the multiplicity of our wants, a desire for the truth, even if it is not yet a powerful impulse. A brief reflection on your own thinking process will confirm the presence of this desire in your consciousness.

You may just now have asked: "Is it really the case that something in me wants the truth?" You need no further or more immediate evidence that you do have some such desire. The simple fact that you ask such a question is evidence enough.

It is in the asking of such questions, indeed of any questions at all, that we have the most obvious evidence of our undeniable longing for the truth. We may call this longing simply the desire to know. It may not yet be highly developed within us. It may be only a whisper that is easily ignored, an occasional impulse readily repressed. And yet, it may well be the deepest and most ineradicable part of ourselves, the very essence of our being. It may turn out that of all our longings and wild wishings our desire to know is the only one whose ardor we can give into with completely trusting abandonment. Maybe only an uninhibited following of our desire to know the truth can bring us into a genuine encounter with depth, future, freedom, and beauty.

And yet we may already have given up the quest for truth, saying to ourselves: "There is no final truth; truth is relative to each person's subjective preferences; truth is a useful social convention; truth cannot be found." If we have been tempted to such conclusions, we may perhaps take comfort in the fact that some famous philosophers have also taught these same "truths." But we must also note that other great minds—most of them, in fact—have demonstrated the self-contradiction in such dogmas.

Suppose, for example, someone says that it is not possible to know the truth. This translates into: "It is a truth that it is not possible to know the truth." Such a statement is self-contradictory because it appeals to our capacity to know the truth (at least the truth of the above statement) even in the very act of denying that we have such a capacity. It overlooks the fact that we implicitly appeal to our trust in the truth every time we raise a doubt about something or every time we say: "It is the case that such and such is so." We could never hope to convince others even that relativism is a truthful philosophical position unless we assumed in advance that these others were capable of recognizing the "truth" of our skepticism. Hence, even if we may at times have explicitly despaired of ever finding the truth, we have not been able to eradicate either our desire for it or our implicit appeal to criteria of truth every time we use the verb "to be."

Every act of judging or questioning presupposes the possibility of our finding the truth. Without an implicit "faith" that intelligibility and truth can be found, we would not have the courage either to seek understanding or to make judgments about the world around us. If deep within us some cynical voice dominated our consciousness by saying "there is no intelligibility or truth to be found in the world or yourself," then we would never even so much as ask a question. Yet by the fact that we do ask questions and make judgments (even, for example, "it is a truth that there is no intelligibility or truth") we give ample evidence that we cannot eradicate our primordial trust in the intelligibility and truth of reality. Like it or not, we are irremediably tied to truth—even as we take flight from it. We have already seen that the same applies in our relation to depth, futurity, freedom, and beauty.

I stated earlier that the direct evidence for the fact of your having a desire to know lies in the simple fact that you find yourself spontaneously asking questions. If you find yourself questioning this, then it is because you have a desire to know. If you are asking what the meaning of these peculiar reflections is, or if there is any truth to them, then this spontaneous questioning is also evidence of your desire to know. You have a desire to know the truth, and it sharply reveals itself in your asking of these simple questions.

But there are different types of questions. Some of our questions inquire as to what a thing is or ask about its meaning, intelligibility, or significance. This type of questioning is resolved when we are given an "insight" into the essence of something. If you find yourself asking what the author of this book is trying to get across in these sentences, then this is an example of the first type of question. It may be called a "question for understanding." It will reach its goal when you find yourself saying: "aha, I now see the point."

But the gaining of understanding is not the end of the questioning process. Not every insight is in touch with reality; there can be illusory along with realistic understanding. So a second type of question spontaneously arises, leading you to ask whether your insights or those of others are true. For example, in reading this chapter, if you reach the point of saying, "I see the point the author is trying to make," an uneasiness will eventually emerge that will be given expression in this fashion: "Yes, I see the point, but is the point well taken? Is it faithful to the facts of my own experience? Is it based in reality? Is it true?" This type of questioning provides evidence that you are not content with mere insight and understanding. You want truthful insight and correct understanding. Thus you ask: is it really so? Does this or that viewpoint correspond with reality? Is it a fact?

We may call this second type a "question for reflection" or simply a "critical question." It is especially our critical questions that give evidence of our desire to know and of our fundamental discontent with mere understanding. We want to make sure that our insights, hypotheses, and theories are true to reality. Otherwise we remain unsatisfied with them. This restlessness in the face of mere "thinking" leads us to undertake "verificational" experiments, in order to test whether our insight and understanding fit the real world or whether perhaps they are out of touch with reality. Our discontent with mere thinking—no matter how ingenious such thinking may be—is what leads us toward "knowledge." Our sense that knowing is more significant than simply thinking is the result of our allowing ourselves to be motivated by a "desire to know."[3]

We have all had the experience of listening to very clever people and of reading very learned books. We often assume that their brilliance amounts to veracity and so we sometimes fail to raise further questions about them. It

3. See Lonergan, *Insight*.

is very easy to be overwhelmed by the genius of an argument or the bright-ness of an idea. But if our critical sense is sufficiently awakened, we realize, as Bernard Lonergan puts it, that "not every bright idea is a true idea."[4] There is always the need to ask whether "bright ideas" are in touch with reality. We must heed the imperative in our mind that tells us: "be critical; do not settle for mere understanding." Science is perhaps the most obvious example of this need to challenge hypothetical insight with critical questions.

Again, it takes only a little reflection on our own experience to no-tice how difficult it can be at times to follow this critical imperative and wean ourselves away from fallacious or shallow understanding. This is the case with respect to our knowledge of others and of reality in general, but especially with respect to self-knowledge. Because the desire to know is not the only motivation in our conscious lives (and perhaps not even the dominant one), we may easily allow some other impulse to construct self-images that have little to do with what we really are. And we may find these fictitious self-images so appealing to our desire for power, gratifica-tion, or approval that they divert us from attaining appropriate insight into ourselves.

Our propensity for self-deception is one of the most interesting and most philosophically troubling characteristics of our human nature. Why should conscious beings, whose questions constantly reveal the fact of an underlying desire to know as an ineradicable aspect of their conscious-ness, also have such a tendency to repress this desire to know when it seeks self-knowledge?

At least part of the reason for the flight from insight into ourselves lies in the fact that, in addition to having an ineradicable desire to know, we also need acceptance and approval. And it appears at times that we will pay almost any price to be held in high, positive regard by significant others. We will go to the point of denying even to ourselves those aspects of our lives and characters that we suspect might not be approved of by others. And so we will hide these "unacceptable" features not only from them but from ourselves as well. Self-deception occurs when, in trying to fulfill criteria of worth established by our immediate social environment, some part of us simply fails to live up to its standards. Rather than admit the presence in us of an "unsocialized" component, we often deny its presence and pretend that we fit comfortably within the circle drawn by familial, national, academic, ecclesiastical, or other societal conditions of self-esteem. The "unacceptable" side of ourselves does not simply go away, however, and our latent interest in the truth feebly attempts to bring it into explicit recognition. But our need

4. Lonergan, "Cognitional Structure," 221–39.

for immediate approval provokes us to take strong internal measures to keep it out of explicit consciousness. Thus, in the context of social conditions of personal value, our pure desire to know comes into conflict with our desire for acceptance when the area of knowledge to be explored is that of the self. This divided condition makes us wonder, then, whether we can find truth at all without first giving up our desire for approval by others.

Are these two desires—the desire for acceptance and the desire for truth—condemned to perpetual mutual combat, or is there not some way in which they can be reconciled? Is there any sense in which the need to be loved can coexist with our need to know the truth?

Some philosophers, both ancient and modern, have despaired of such a union. They tell us that if we honestly follow our desire for the truth, we will ultimately have to admit that reality as such is either hostile or indifferent to us. They point especially to the facts of suffering and death as evidence that, in the final analysis, we are not cared for.[5] They admit that we have a powerful longing for affection and love, but they also advise us to reach some compromise between the demand for acceptance and the ultimate opaqueness of "reality" to any such desire. This view may be called "absurdist" since it sees an irrational flaw at the heart of reality, dividing it dualistically into two incommensurable elements: human consciousness, with its desire for acceptance, on the one side, and the universe, with its refusal to satisfy this desire, on the other. The incongruity of these two sides of reality—namely humans and the universe—means that reality as a whole does not make sense. It is absurd.[6]

One must question, then, whether our deep need for a sense of self-worth can ever be satisfied as long as our sense of reality is an absurdist one. One must also ask, if we truly believe that the universe is, in its depths, unaccepting toward us, can our desire to know ever really emerge as the dominant motivational force in our lives? The absurdist reply is that the hostility of the universe toward us is the very occasion for our exercising an honesty and courage, which gives us an even deeper sense of self-esteem than we could have had in a beneficent universe. Facing the challenge of living without hope requires a heroism which allows us to feel better about ourselves to the extent that we face courageously the insurmountable challenge of an absurd universe. Thus, in order for us to be honest about ourselves, there is no need for an ultimate or transcendent

5. See Freud, *Civilization and Its Discontents* and Camus, *Myth of Sisyphus*.

6. For the most explicit formulation of an "absurdist" perspective, see Camus, *Myth of Sisyphus*.

context of love. All we need is to summon up from within ourselves the courage to "face the facts."

The tragic or absurdist interpretation which holds that our courage comes only from "within" us is a position which promotes itself as the only honest interpretation of the facts of human existence. Its apparent heroism and honesty has made the tragic vision an attractive one, for at least some people, for centuries. On the surface, it seems to be an exemplary instance of following the desire for truth, no matter how much it hurts. At first sight, this "tragic" interpretation appears to avoid self-deception and to face the truth by renouncing the need for love, approval, and acceptance. The self can stand on its own in complete lucidity about its situation in the world without the support of the universe or even of other people.

And yet, on closer examination, the tragic alternative, in its denying the basic dependency and interdependency of all things, is itself also condu-cive to self-deception. It seems to fall short of complete honesty inasmuch as it fails to acknowledge the necessity of sources of courage beyond the individual's own heroism. The tragic hero who announces the absurdity of the world stands up courageously against the alleged hostility of society and the universe, which often explains the appeal tragic heroes have to the rebellious tendencies within us. But the absurdist hero is oblivious to the sustenance our courage receives from our environment, and this is where a certain dishonesty begins.

# 6: Mystery[1]

THE MOST IMPORTANT WAY of responding to the question, "what is God?" is of course to say that, essentially, God is mystery. For many believers, the term "mystery" is resonant with the depth, future, freedom, beauty, and truth to which I have pointed in this book. And undoubtedly, for many such individuals, the term "mystery" is more religiously appropriate than any of the five notions that I have used. Rudolf Otto considered *mysterium* to be the very essence of the sacred and theological reflection may no more casually abandon use of the term "mystery" than the word "God."[2] The notion of mystery is indispensable to our discourse about the divine.

Therefore, we must come back to this word "mystery" at the end of our obviously unsatisfactory attempts to verbalize the "whatness" of God. To say that God is ultimately mystery is the final word in any proper thinking about the divine. Recourse to the notion of "mystery" is essential in order to accentuate the utter inadequacy of any thoughts we may formulate about God. And it is also necessary to evoke in us a cognitive "feeling" of the inexhaustibility we have pointed to by way of our five metaphors.

None of the five notions I have employed can be substituted for that of mystery. My objective in resorting provisionally to them has been simply to provide several avenues leading up to the idea of mystery as the most appropriate designation for the divine. In the esoteric language of theology, it might be said that my purpose in writing this little book has been to provide a simple "mystagogy," that is, an "introduction to mystery."[3] We live in an age and culture in which there reigns an "eclipse of mystery." And the difficulty people have in connecting their experience with the word "God" is, for the most part, a consequence of the lack of a sense of mystery in their lives. Mystagogy would not be necessary if we could presume that people were universally in touch with the encompassing horizon of mystery in their lives and in the world around them. Books on the problem of God would not be so abundant if mystery were self-evident in our cultural experience. For

---

1. The following text is an excerpt. Previously published in Haught, *What is God?*, 115–131. Reprinted with permission.

2. See Otto, *Idea of the Holy.*

3. See Bacik, *Apologetics*, 3–64.

ultimately, "God" means mystery, and the prevalence of a sense of mystery would render books like this one superfluous.

Unfortunately, the dimension of mystery, though never absent from the experience of any of us, has been lost sight of by our theoretical consciousness. It still hovers around the fringes of our spontaneous involvements in life, in our relations to nature, other persons, and ourselves. And it is intimated in the symbols and stories that inform our consciousness. But in a world where the mastering methods and techniques of science have become so dominant, the cognitive surrender that a sense of mystery requires of us has often been subordinated to an "epistemology of control."[4] That is, the handing of ourselves over to mystery has become almost impossible whenever knowledge has been understood in terms of power. Confrontation with the uncontrollable domain of mystery often leaves us feeling insecure, restless, and even hostile. So we strive to suppress the unmanageable horizon of mystery and vanquish the need for any surrender of self to it.

In the face of this eclipse of mystery, the very possibility of speaking meaningfully about God has likewise diminished, even to the point of almost vanishing. And yet mystery cannot be completely suppressed. It still functions as the silent horizon that makes all of our experience and knowledge possible in the first place. In its humility and unobtrusiveness, it refuses to force itself upon us, but nonetheless it graciously undergirds our existence and understanding without making itself obvious. We go through the course of our lives enabled by the horizon of mystery to think, inquire, adventure, and discover, but we seldom become explicitly aware of its encompassing presence-in-absence or extend our gratitude to it for giving us the free space in which to live our lives. My objective in the preceding has been to render this dimension of mystery somewhat more obvious by leading up to it with alternative names. But because of its highly theoretical nature, such an approximation still leaves us only at the doorway of mystery. Only the actual living of our lives—and not the mere reading of a book—can lead us into the realm of mystery. The most that any book like this can do is merely point the reader in a certain direction. It cannot substitute for experience itself.

A theoretical introduction to mystery may not be a necessity to many people for whom the term already possesses a symbolic power sufficiently expansive enough to open up to them the ultimate horizon of their existence. But for countless others, the term "mystery," like the words "God" and "sacred," has also lost its power and meaning, or it has become so trivialized by common usage that it no longer evokes in them any deep sense

---

4. See Smith, *Beyond the Post-Modern Mind*, 83, 88, 114, and 134–35.

of the inexhaustible depths of reality. For some, the notion of mystery has even become altogether empty. For that reason, it is essential today to provide a sort of pedagogy to mystery. I do not in any way consider my own attempts adequate, and I have presented them only as starting points for introducing some small part of what is designated theologically by the notion of divine mystery. At this point, then, it may be well to speak a bit more directly about the word "mystery" as such, if indeed this term is finally the most suitable one we can use in thinking of God.

## Mystery and Problem

The term "mystery" is often misunderstood simply as a gap in our knowledge, a temporary hiatus that might possibly be closed as scientific consciousness advances further. According to this narrow view, as our intellectual mastery of the world progresses, we will find answers to the "mysteries" which remain in principle answerable but in fact are unanswered at the present. Thus the realm of "mystery" will allegedly be gradually diminished and "knowledge" will take its place. As noted psychologist B. F. Skinner has put it, the objective of science is to eliminate mystery.[5]

When "mystery" is understood in this fashion, namely as a gap to be replaced by scientific knowledge, it is little wonder that the word no longer functions to evoke a religious sense of the *tremendum et fascinans*. For in this case, "mystery" is merely a vacuum that begs to be filled with our intellectual achievements and not an ineffable depth summoning us to surrender ourselves completely to it. If such is the meaning of mystery, then it is hardly adequate as a term for the divine.

But the gaps in our present understanding and knowledge would better be called problems than mysteries.[6] "Problem" points to an area of ignorance that is eventually able to be solved by the application of human ingenuity. Perhaps at the present time, a "problem" remains unsolved and even unsolvable by the devices at our disposal, but it should not be called a mystery, for it is at least open to some sort of future solution. For example, a science that connects gravitational, electro-magnetic, and other forces into a unified field theory is at present unavailable. But since such a science will probably emerge at some future time it is better to call this quandary a problem rather than a mystery. A problem is in principle open to a scientific, logical, or

5. Skinner, *Beyond Freedom*, 54.

6. On the distinction between problem and mystery, see Gabriel Marcel, *Being and Having*, 117.

technological solution. It is somehow under our human control and can be mastered by our intellectual or technological powers.

Mystery, on the other hand, denotes a region of reality that, instead of growing smaller as we grow wiser and more powerful, can actually be experienced as growing larger and more incomprehensible as we solve more of our scientific and other problems. It is the region of the "known unknown," the horizon that keeps expanding and receding into the distance the more our knowledge advances. It is the arena of the incomprehensible and unspeakable that makes us aware of our ignorance, of how much more there yet remains to be known. No one to date has shown Socrates to be wrong in his insistence that we are truly wise only when we are aware of the abysmal poverty of our present cognitional achievements. Such an awareness of the lowliness of our knowledge is possible, though, only if we have already been made aware of the inexhaustibility of the yet-to-be-known—that is, of mystery. It is wise for us to emphasize that this state of "learned ignorance" (*docta ignorantia*) is possible only to those whose horizons have expanded beyond the ordinary; in other words, to those who have begun to taste the mysteriousness of reality.

Mystery, in contrast to problems, is incapable of any "solution." Whereas problems can be solved and thus gotten out of the way, mystery becomes more prominent the deeper our questions go and the surer our answers become. Mystery appears to consciousness at the "limit" of our ordinary problem-oriented questions. It reveals itself decisively at the point where we seriously ask what may be called "limit-questions," questions that lie at the "boundary" of our ordinary problem-solving consciousness.[7] For example, while science is dominated by problems for which some resolution or definitive answer is expected, the scientist might find himself or herself eventually asking: Why should I do science at all? Why search for intelligibility in the universe? Is the universe completely intelligible, as scientific questioning seems to take for granted? At this point, the scientist has reached the limit of the problem and has asked a kind of question that explicitly opens up the horizon of mystery. This type may be called limit-questioning since it does not fall within but rather only at the boundary of ordinary scientific inquiry.

---

7. Haught's discussion of limit questions was especially influenced by Tracy, *Blessed Rage for Order*, 91–118. The original notion of "limiting questions" comes from the philosopher Stephen Toulmin, *Examination*, 202–21.

## Naming the Mystery

The question remains, however, why we may call this mystery by the name "God." Is it not sufficient that we simply have a vivid sense of the horizon of mystery? And is it essential that we give it any specific name? I think that in the case of some of us, because of the psychologically unhealthy images evoked by the word "God," it may be better not to use this word at all. There are individuals for whom the word "God" may actually stand in the way of a healthy sense of mystery. However, I would suggest that this is due less to the term itself than to a faulty religious education or trivialization through its usage in self-justifying political and ecclesiastical discourse. When the word has been so misshapen, it is better to abandon it—at least until such time as its usage once again opens us to a sense of mystery.

On the other hand, the word "God" is irreplaceable in theistic religion, and it cannot be dropped completely from our Western vocabulary for naming the mysterious dimension of our existence. Furthermore, the word "God," if it is understood according to the symbolic and narrative way in which it originally came into religious consciousness, specifies and adds an element of meaning to the notion of mystery that the latter term itself may not immediately suggest. We may call this added dimension of significance simply the "graciousness" of mystery. It is in order to accentuate the gracious, self-giving nature of mystery that we use the term "God" in referring to it.[8]

We might say that there are only two major "truths" that a genuine religious sense requires from us.[9] All other "doctrines" of religion are derivatives of these two truths; if we keep this in mind, religion will not have to be as cumbersome or complicated an affair as it sometimes seems to be. The first of these truths, as I have been trying to show, is simply that our lives are embraced by mystery. The second major truth is that this mystery is gracious. All religions try to give their devotees some sense of mystery, and this fact alone should be sufficient to establish a sense of community and solidarity among all the various religious traditions today, especially in the face of the contemporary suppression of mystery by cultures built on the ideal of domination. The graciousness of mystery is also enunciated by all the religious traditions, in markedly diverse ways of course, but with a sense of unanimity that mystery is trustworthy and that our fulfillment lies only in a surrender to it. One of the most explicit formulations of the

8. See Rahner, *Theological Investigations*, 67–73.

9. Rahner speaks of three central mysteries in Christian faith. Speaking of religion in a general sense, Haught believes it is consistent with Rahner's thought to only speak of two.

graciousness of mystery is the one which maintains that the mystery gives itself away completely, in self-emptying love, to the world which it embraces.[10] It is especially because of this graciousness that we may call the mystery by the name "God."

From these two propositions—that we are circumscribed by mystery and that this mystery, referred to as God, gives itself completely to us—can be derived all the other important ideas of religion. Religion has been made entirely too complicated and forbidding at times and, in the morass of doctrines and practices that it inevitably generates, its two foundational insights may easily be lost sight of. Obviously, the sense of mystery and its graciousness have to be mediated in particular forms of speech, narrative, and activity corresponding to different cultural and historical habits of thought. So we must be tolerant of the diversity of religions and not seek the monotony of a homogeneous, all-encompassing religious format. But amidst the diversity of religious ideas and practices, it is helpful to keep before us their common grounding in an appreciation of mystery and its gracious intimacy with the universe. Seeing through the jungle of concrete religious life to these two central tenets of religion should prevent us from making hasty condemnations of others' religious ideas and practices. For beneath their apparent peculiarity and needless extravagance, there may lie a deep and simple sense of mystery and its goodness.

At the same time, however, our keeping the two "truths" constantly before us provides us with criteria to evaluate and criticize the actual religious lives of others and ourselves. For there is no doubt that religious traditions which have their origin in a decisive encounter with mystery and its graciousness can themselves deviate from their founding insights and end up participating in the eclipse of mystery. Religions can become entangled in the pursuit of domination or the legitimation of oppression and thus themselves become an obstacle to the sense of liberating mystery. Hence they should constantly be evaluated in accordance with the criteria of mystery and its graciousness.

It should not be either embarrassing or surprising to us that the human experience of the nearness and graciousness of mystery would often come to expression in a religious language heavily loaded with personalistic imagery. Although the mystery is not exhausted by its representation as a "person," the disclosure of its intimacy to human subjects endowed with intelligence, will, and feelings could scarcely be possible unless it were itself presented to them as having analogously personal attributes. It is doubtful that something less than personal could inspire us deeply to trust

10. See Rahner, *Theological Investigations*, 67–73.

and surrender. To persons the mystery must at least be personal itself. It is difficult to find precise language with which to interpret the relationship of divine personality to divine mystery. Is the mystery really personal, or is personality merely one of the projective ways in which we creatively go out to meet the mystery that summons us toward itself? We have already admitted that our religions are inevitably imaginative, projective, and that there is always some level of illusion in our actual religious consciousness, owing to the infantilism of desire that we can never completely eradicate. Is the propensity to think of God as personal still perhaps more a manifestation of our immaturity than a realistic appreciation of the inexhaustible mystery of reality?

Without denying that our images of a personal God always have a projective aspect to them or that these images do not exhaustively represent the mystery of our lives, we may still view "divine personality" as an indispensable symbol of the proximity to us of mystery. All of our language about this mystery necessarily has a symbolic character. Because of mystery's unavailability, we cannot discuss it directly or literally. We tend to speak of it, if we speak of it at all, in terms of those places and events where it breaks through to us most decisively and intensely. For most of us, the most intense disclosure of mystery probably occurs in our encounter with other persons. The child's earliest encounter with mother and father, for example, is an experience of such overwhelming "numinosity" that it remains a permanent layer of all of our involvements. And the meeting with a truly accepting and caring person is often the occasion for our experiencing the depth and graciousness of life's mystery in a decisive way. The human face itself has often been experienced as deeply mysterious, as causing us to turn away in fear or as attracting us with its enchanting power. Human personality is often the occasion for our experiencing the *mysterium tremendum et fascinans*.

Inasmuch as human personality is especially transparent to the horizon of mystery and its graciousness, it is not surprising, then, that personalist imagery would cling to our discourse about God. Since we often perceive the mystery most clearly as it shines through the lives of other persons, we can never completely separate our experience of God from the experience of personality. To do so would again be an unnecessary reduction of the mystery. The freedom and unmanipulability of other persons gives us a sense of the unavailability of the mystery that is their depth. To remove the personal face of mystery is to lose access to it. Through the medium of personality, the depth of reality is "revealed" in such a complete way that we must speak of God as personal. God is the depth and ground of all personality.[11]

11. This formulation is, of course, a Tillichian one.

# 7: Religion[1]

"There is communion with God, and communion with
the earth, and communion with God through the earth."

—PIERRE TEILHARD DE CHARDIN[2]

IF NATURE IS NOT all there is, then what else is there, and how do we know
about it? Religions are convinced that there is more, indeed infinitely more,
but they tell us we can know about it only if we are disposed to receive it. The
infinitely "more" cannot be known in the same way that ordinary objects are
known. In fact, religion is less a matter of knowing than of being known. It
is a state of being grasped rather than of grasping. Not every person is ready
for religion, and even self-avowed religious believers cannot truthfully
claim to be ready for it most of the time. Indeed, much of what we usually
call religious life consists of avoiding or running away from the demands of
religion. Religious understanding—as most theologians see it—is impossible without surrender, worship, and prayerful waiting, along with struggle
and frustration. Yet, to those who wait, the rewards can be peace and joy, as
well as profound intellectual satisfaction.

Religion, at least in any conventional sense, cannot get along with scientific naturalism, but it can get along quite well with science. Science deals
with what can be sensed or, at least, what can be inferred from sensation.
Religion is based in experience too, but of a different kind from science. Religious people testify to having felt, beneath all sensible appearances, the very
real presence of an elusive mystery that takes hold of them, invites them,
sometimes unsettles them, and often reorients their lives. They profess to
having been carried away, as it were, by something "more" than nature. Their
sense of a mysterious presence beyond the world, beneath the surface of life,
or in the depths of the universe, evokes responses of vague anxiety sometimes mixed with overwhelming excitement and the impulse to worship.

1. Previously published in Haught, *Is Nature Enough?*, 21–31. Reprinted with
permission.
2. Teilhard de Chardin, *Writings in Time of War*, 14.

69

Religion often also involves the encounter with unseen agents, powers, and personalities, but these are experienced as emerging out of the background of a more fundamental transcendent mystery. Religion, taken here in a very broad sense, is a *conscious appreciation of and response to the mystery that grounds, embraces, and transcends both nature and ourselves.* There are other ways of defining religion, of course, but the issues raised by scientific naturalism have to do especially with religion's bold claims that there is *more* than nature. A good name for this *more* is "mystery."

Religion, therefore, means that the universe available to science and ordinary experience is *not* all that is, all there ever was, and all there ever will be. To most religious persons, there is something *other* than the physical universe. This mysterious presence is not separate from the universe, but it is not identical with it either. It simultaneously penetrates, encircles, grounds, and enlivens nature without being reducible to nature. Religions are convinced that reality does not end at the limits of nature, but instead includes an incomprehensible dimension that extends beyond the scientifically knowable world. The infinite scope of mystery provides religious devotees a permanent reason for hope and a sense of freedom. It allows for limitless breathing room in the face of nature's obvious constraints and ultimate perishability.

It is especially those whose thoughts and passions reach toward infinite mystery who are most prone to feel imprisoned by naturalistic doctrine. Religious believers, unlike naturalists, do not look to nature for either ultimate fulfillment or ultimate explanation. Still, a wholesome communion with ultimate reality can take place *through* nature. Healthy religion is gratefully aware of the riches of life and the resourcefulness of the natural world. It is appreciative of science as well. But it also senses that nature imposes obvious limits on life, most notably suffering and death. Religion, then, is a kind of route-finding that looks for pathways beyond the boundaries that nature places on life.[3]

It is imperative that naturalists be fully sensitive to this point even if they vehemently disagree with it. Religious persons may turn out to be wrong, but clearly they are seeking ways to get beyond what they take to be the natural limits on life. This does not mean that they have to despise the world—although in some cases they do—but that they relativize it. They neither take nature to be ultimate nor do they see science as ultimate explanation. Characteristically, no matter how large science has shown the universe to be, religious people look upon the claim that "nature is enough" as itself an arbitrary confinement that they must get beyond.

3. See Bowker, *Is Anybody Out There?*, 9-18 and 112-43.

To religious ears, including those attuned to the monumental scale of contemporary cosmology, the assertion that "nature is enough" sounds like a prison sentence. This is because religious awareness generally involves a sense that the human mind (or spirit) has already transcended the limits of nature, not finally or decisively, but at least by *anticipation*. In the next chapter, I will show that human intelligence, in spite of all attempts to understand it naturalistically, extends itself beyond the limits of nature in every act of questioning, understanding, and judging. Religion is inseparable from the intellect's anticipation of an infinite fullness of being. In biblical circles, religious anticipation of this fullness of being takes the form of *hope*. And so, to those who hope for final transcendence of death and suffering, naturalism is the most dreary and suffocating of dogmas. Instead of limitless horizons, naturalism offers only an ultimate captivity, unbearable to those who sense that at the core of their being they are *capax infiniti*—open to the infinite.

Of course, to the naturalist, religion is fully part of nature and, like everything else, it must submit to being explained naturalistically. There must be a purely scientific answer to the question of why so many humans have longed for the infinite and thereby experienced nature as a limit. To many naturalists these days, it is evolutionary biology that seems best equipped to provide the deepest account of humanity's persistent religious tendencies. If evolutionists can come up with a purely natural explanation of the habit religious believers have of looking toward limitless horizons, then this will supposedly expose infinite mystery itself as empty fiction rather than ultimate reality. Therefore, the most efficient way to disabuse religious people of the illusion that there is anything beyond the limits of nature is to explain, in purely scientific terms, how that illusion could have arisen in the first place. Nowadays, Darwin's idea of natural selection, brought up to date by genetics, seems to provide the best, perhaps even the ultimate, explanation of the human conviction that reality overflows nature's boundaries.

Naturalists today often attempt to explain not only religion but also morality in Darwinian terms. There was a time not long ago when the moral instincts of people seemed to be the best evidence for God's existence. Indeed, moral aspiration was a clear indication of the direct imprint of a transcendent, divine goodness on each soul; conscience was the stamp of God's will on the inner core of each personality. Hints of an infinite perfection could be found in the insatiable anticipation of the goodness, truth, and beauty that drives the questing human heart. Humans were said to be restless only because an infinite goodness, truth, and beauty had already made itself tacitly present to their moral, intellectual, and aesthetic sensibilities.

The scientific naturalist, however, will have none of this, at times even rebuking religious people for being so "greedy" as to look for fulfillment

beyond the limits of nature. In a book whose every page chastises those
of us with cloudier images of reality than his own, the philosopher Owen
Flanagan asserts that there is nothing beyond what scientific naturalism is
able to discern. How he knows this he does not say, but he is certain that
people who look beyond nature for fulfillment "are still in the grip of illusions." "Trust me," he says, "you can't get more. But what you can get, if you
live well, is enough. Don't be greedy. Enough is enough."[4]

My own work brings me into contact with many good scientists and
philosophers from all over the world. Some are religious, but many others are naturalists like Owen Flanagan. Naturalism is now so entrenched
in science and philosophical faculties around the globe that it constitutes
one of the most influential "creeds" operative in the world today. Scientific
naturalists are still a small minority in the world's overall population, but
their influence is out of proportion to their numbers. Generally speaking,
their beliefs quietly determine what is intellectually acceptable in many of
our universities. Naturalism has now spread from science and philosophy
departments into social studies and the humanities. Even departments of
religion are no longer immune.

The academic world now harbors numerous scientific naturalists who
prefer to keep a low profile in order to avoid controversy wherever religion
is considered important. Flanagan wants them to come clean. Likewise,
the Pulitzer Prize winning science writer Natalie Angier believes that most
scientists are closet naturalists, but are reluctant to state openly what they
really think about religion and theology. In a recent issue of *The American
Scholar*, she cites studies showing that as many as 90 percent of the members
of the elite National Academy of Sciences are nontheists, and less than half
of other scientists believe in a personal God. She upbraids scientists for not
being more vocal in criticizing the "irrationalities" of religion in all of its
forms. Most scientists are no longer afraid to state publicly that Darwinism
has made creationism obsolete, but Angier is annoyed that they pass over in
silence the larger body of religious illusions. In her own opinion, the entire
history of human religiousness is a preposterous mistake—since there is no
scientific evidence for its empty musings. And so she is agitated that most
scientists refuse to wear their *de facto* naturalism on their sleeves.[5]

It is annoying to scientific naturalists such as Flanagan and Angier
that religious people can't come up with "evidence" for what they take to
be more than nature. But to religious experience, this "more" will always
be something that grasps us rather than something we can grasp. We can

---

4. Flanagan, *Problem of the Soul*, 319.

5. See Angier, "My God Problem," 131–34.

know it only by surrender, not possession. It will never have the clarity of scientific evidence, nor should it be presented as an alternative to science. The most immediate "evidence" for it is the fact of our own anticipation of more truth, deeper goodness, and wider beauty, an insatiable reaching out toward a fullness of being that is by no means illusory, but instead the very core of our rationality. Biblical religions refer to this transcendent dimension as God. They think of God as possessing the most noble of attributes: infinite goodness and love, unsurpassable beauty and splendor, the fullness of being and truth. God is also the epitome of fidelity, creativity, freedom, healing, wisdom, and power. As one who allegedly makes and keeps promises, this God is understood to be "personal" as well, since only persons can love and make promises.

Naturalists, on the other hand, consider such a belief untenable, especially after Darwin. To them, the universe is, at heart, utterly impersonal. Their persistent question is: where is the *evidence* for God in this imperfect world? Religious people, however, do not usually claim to be able to *see* the mystery of God directly—"nobody can see God and live." God is the light that lights up everything else, but one cannot look directly into that primordial illumination without being blinded. Yet, even though the human person cannot grasp God, many people testify to being grasped by God. For them, the powerful sense of being carried away by something of ultimate importance is evidence enough. To take them at their word, they have surrendered their lives and hearts to an irresistible presence and power that receives them into its compassionate embrace. It is not that they have comprehended the overwhelming divine mystery of beauty, goodness, and truth. Rather, they have been comprehended by it. They express their response to this experience in acts of worship, prayer, praise, and gratitude, as well as in distinctive ways of living and relating to the world. That this is not wishful thinking can be demonstrated if it turns out that our longing for the infinite is supportive of what I shall call "the desire to know," the very heart of human rationality.

As Flanagan and Angier illustrate, however, the naturalist ideal is to bring the totality of being out into the clear light of daytime consciousness, so that there is nothing left for religions to talk about. If theology wants to be respected intellectually, so says the naturalist, it must also adduce the right kind of evidence, namely scientific. This does not necessarily mean that all naturalists demand that God show up among the objects available to empirical inquiry. But there must be visible and unambiguous tracks of divine reality in the natural world if scientifically educated people are to pay any attention to theology. If science comes across anything in nature that cannot be fully explained naturalistically, then there might be good reason to invoke the causal powers of a deity. Today, however, naturalists are eager to demonstrate that everything that formerly gave the appearance of being a trace of the divine can now be explained in natural terms. Not only the "apparent" design in living organisms but also the ethical and mystical inclinations of human beings can be "naturalized." And if science can account sufficiently for even the holiest of phenomena, there is no need any more for theology.

## The Outlines of a Response

The goal of scientific naturalism is to explain everything, insofar as it can be explained at all, in terms of natural processes. This would include the mind itself, which is part of nature. Human intelligence arose by way of a natural process that can be accurately laid out in Darwinian terms. But, as we shall see, the actual performance of human intellection (and later I shall include moral aspiration) is such that it will forever overflow the limits of naturalistic understanding, no matter how detailed scientific understanding becomes in the future. I shall propose that the concrete functioning of intelligence cannot, in principle, let alone in fact, be fully captured by the objectifying categories of any science. In other words, the natural sciences cannot account completely for what I shall be calling *critical intelligence*. If this claim turns out to be true, it will be necessary to go beyond naturalism in order to arrive at an adequate understanding of the universe.

In order to present my argument as clearly as I can, I shall be inviting you, the reader, to place yourself in the mindset of the naturalist, even if ordinarily you are not quite at home there. Then I shall ask you, if only as a thought experiment, to try to provide adequate justification *on naturalist premises* for your own mental functioning. I don't believe you can do so in all honesty. As a naturalist, you already claim that your mind is fully part of nature. But your naturalistic worldview, as I hope I can lead you to acknowledge, is too restrictive to account fully for your own cognitional activity. And if your mind and your view of nature do not fit each other, then something has to give. My suggestion is not to abandon scientific explanations of mind but rather to accept them as intermediate rather than ultimate. By itself, science cannot justify the spontaneous trust you have placed in your own mind, even as you seek to arrive at scientific truth. To justify your implicit trust in the possibility of arriving at truth, you will need to look for a wider and deeper understanding of the universe, a more expansive worldview than naturalism has to offer. My proposal is that your own mind's spontaneous and persistent trust in the possibility of reaching truth is itself a hint that the physical universe, at least as naturalism conceives it, is only a small fragment of all that is, all there ever was, and all there ever will be.

# 8: Is Religion Opposed
# to Science?[1]

WHEN WE HEAR THE words "science" and "religion" we immediately think of the stormy history of their relationship. But the chronicle of religion's encounter with science is by no means only one of warfare. Here we shall examine four distinct ways in which science and religion may stand in relation to each other:

1. *Conflict*—the conviction that science and religion are fundamentally irreconcilable;

2. *Contrast*—the claim that there can be no possibility of genuine conflict since religion and science are each responding to radically different questions;

3. *Contact*—an approach that goes beyond the standoff, in which science and religion simply agree not to be enemies, seeking a positive and fruitful correspondence between them;

4. *Confirmation*—a seldom articulated position that shows the ways in which, at a very deep level, religion supports and nourishes the entire scientific enterprise.

A grasp of these four approaches should help us make our way through the thicket of issues that make up the subject matter of this book. Let us now examine each of them more closely.

## I. Conflict

Many scientific thinkers are quite certain that religion can never be reconciled with science. If you are a scientist, they say, it is hard to imagine how you could honestly also be religious, at least in the sense of believing in God. Their main reason for drawing this conclusion is that religion apparently cannot demonstrate the truth of its ideas in a straightforward way, whereas science can. Religion tries to sneak by without providing any concrete

1. The following text is an excerpt. Previously published in Haught, *Science & Religion*, 9–26. Reprinted with permission.

evidence of God's existence. Science, on the other hand, is willing to test all of its hypotheses and theories against "experience." Religion cannot do this in a way that is satisfying to an impartial witness. Thus, there is a "conflict" between the scientific and the religious ways of understanding.

Both historical and philosophical factors seem to substantiate such a grim verdict. Historically, we need only to recall the obvious examples: the Church's persecution of Galileo in the seventeenth century and the wide-spread religious aversion to Darwin's evolutionary theory in the nineteenth and twentieth. The slow pace by which religious thought comes to terms with science, and the fact that many theists still have a distaste for it, suggest that religion will never get along with science. Since so many believers in God have resisted the findings of astronomy, physics, and biology, is it any wonder that religion comes across as inherently hostile to science?

More important than these historical considerations, however, are the imposing philosophical (specifically epistemological) obstacles that religion and theology present to scientific skeptics. The main problem here is that religious ideas seem to be experientially untestable. That is, they exempt themselves from the rigors of public examination, whereas science always submits its ideas to open experimentation. If empirical scrutiny shows a scientific hypothesis to be mistaken, then science will-ingly discards it and tries out alternatives, subjecting these also to the same rigorous process of inspection.

But can you do the same with religious teachings? Don't they dodge all attempts to demonstrate their truth observationally? Don't theists, for example, go on believing in God no matter what they observe in the world, including enormous suffering and evil? Doesn't Judaism, for example, say of its Lord: "Even though He slay me, yet shall I trust in Him"? Isn't the "reli-gious hypothesis," if we may use this expression, completely impervious to, and fundamentally unaffected by, the things we actually experience?

Putting this another way, it seems to skeptics that religious teachings are "unfalsifiable." After all, the renowned philosopher Karl Popper argued that genuine science strives to come up with evidence that will show its ideas to be wrong. That is, science has the fortitude to risk the "falsification" of its own claims.[2] For example, since relativity theory predicts that light waves will always bend in the presence of gravitational fields, then scientists should look for possible instances in which this prediction might *not* be true. Then, if they cannot find any evidence to the contrary, this means that relativity is a pretty strong theory for weathering all attempts at falsification. Falsifiability is the mark of a theory's scientific status. A willingness to allow

2. See Popper, *Conjectures and Refutations*, 33–39.

its ideas to be falsified purifies science and shows it to be a truly open and honest way of learning about the nature of things.

But can religion display a comparable openness? Scientific skeptics (i.e. those who reject religion in the name of science) think that religion lacks the robust probity of science. The God-hypothesis, for example, seems to be completely beyond falsification, so it cannot pass muster before the courts of science. Religion is based, skeptics claim, on a priori assumptions, or "faith," whereas science takes nothing for granted. In addition, religion relies too heavily on the imagination, whereas science sticks to observable facts. Religion is highly emotional, passionate, and subjective, whereas science strives to remain disinterested, dispassionate, and objective. These antitheses seem to add up to nothing less than an insuperable mutual hostility between science and religion.

Whenever scientific ideas do not correspond with the letter of the Bible (which is quite often), biblical literalists argue that science must be wrong and religion right. This is especially the case regarding evolution, but also with miracles, the creation of the universe, the origin of life, and other issues. Many Christians in the USA and elsewhere maintain that the Bible teaches the "true" science and that secular science should be rejected if it does not correspond with the letter of Scripture.

In addition to biblical literalists, there are other critics who think that science is the enemy of religion. They argue that it was the coming of science that produced the emptiness and meaninglessness of modern experience. When science separated the experience of "facts" from our human need for eternal "values," they argue, it emptied the cosmos of any real meaning. And since the main business of religion is to teach us the meaning of things, it cannot be reconciled with science. We would have been better off if the scientific revolution had never occurred.

In a controversial new book, for example, the British journalist Bryan Appleyard passionately argues that science is "spiritually corrosive, burning away ancient authorities and traditions."[3] Science, he insists, is inherently incapable of coexisting with religion. It is not a neutral way of knowing at all, but a subversive and demonic force that has evacuated our culture of its spiritual substance. It is impossible, he goes on to say, for anyone to be both religious and scientific in any honest, straightforward way.

Appleyard's contention that science is "absolutely not compatible with religion" is confirmed from the other side by scientific skeptics, although, for them, science brings about the liberation rather than the emptying of culture. While they are certainly aware that many religious believers see

3. Appleyard, *Understanding the Present*, 8–9.

no conflict between religion and science today, and that many theists are admittedly good scientists, skeptics claim that both the logic and the spirit of science are nevertheless fundamentally incompatible with any form of theistic religion. As the Cornell historian of science William Provine puts it, we have to "check our brains at the church house door" if we are to be both scientist and believer.[4] More specific reasons for this judgment will be offered in each succeeding chapter.

## II. Contrast

Many other scientists and theologians, on the other hand, find no such opposition between religion and science. Each is valid, they argue, though only in its own, clearly defined sphere of inquiry. Religion cannot be judged by the standards of science, nor vice-versa, because the questions each asks are so completely disparate and the content of their answers so distinct that it makes no sense to compare them with each other. If religion and science were both trying to do the same job, then they might be incompatible. But as they have radically dissimilar tasks, if we just keep them in their separate jurisdictions, preventing them from invading each other's territory, there can never be any real "problem" of science and religion.

According to this "contrast" approach, the impression that religion conflicts with science is almost always rooted in a previous confusion or "conflation" of science with religion or some other belief system. To avoid conflict, then, we must first avoid any mindless melding of science and belief into an undifferentiated smudge. It was, after all, the inability of medieval theology to distinguish religion's role clearly from that of science that made Galileo's ideas seem so hostile to believers in the sixteenth century.

In fact, it is nearly always a prior conflation of science with religion that leads eventually to the sense that there is a conflict between them. The uncritical mixing of science with religion before the scientific era is what led to the lamentable condemnation of Galileo by the Church and to the hostility that many scientists still feel toward religion. Now, however, we should know better: religion and science have no business meddling in each other's affairs in the first place. To avoid conflict, therefore, our second approach claims that we should carefully *contrast* science with religion. They are such completely independent ways of understanding reality that it is meaningless to place them in opposition to each other.

Conflation, in this view, is an unsatisfactory attempt to avoid conflict by carelessly commingling science with belief. Instead of respecting the

4. Provine, "Evolution and the Foundation of Ethics," 261.

sharp differences between science and religion, conflation weaves them into a single fabric where they fade into each other, becoming indistinguishable. Today, for instance, some conservative Christians argue that the biblical stories of creation give us the best *scientific* information about the beginnings of the universe and life. They call their fusion of science and belief "creation science," an amalgamation that renounces the Darwinian theory of evolution in favor of a literalist interpretation of the biblical accounts of the world's creation. It insists that the biblical stories are "scientific" and that they should be taught in public schools as the best alternative to evolutionary biology.

Another common brand of conflation is "concordism." Rather than rejecting modern science outright, concordism forces the biblical text to correspond, at least in a loose way, with the patterns of modern science. In order to salvage the literal truth of the biblical book of Genesis, for example, some religious scientists match the six days of creation with what they consider to be six corresponding epochs in the scientific account of cosmic evolution. Religion, in this interpretation, must be made to look scientific at all costs if it is to be intellectually respectable today. In his book *Genesis and The Big Bang*, physicist Gerald Schroeder, for example, argues that relativity theory, with its challenge to the common sense notion of absolute simultaneity, once again allows us to take literally the six-day sequence of creation as depicted in the Bible. He attempts to show that what from one frame of reference appears as a single day may be billions of years from another. So the Bible agrees with science after all and physicists can now embrace religion![5]

This conflation of science and religion is born out of a very human craving for unity in our understanding of the world. Because it seems to harmonize science and religion so neatly, it appeals to millions of people. At first sight, its blending of religion with science would seem to be a credible way of avoiding conflict. However, history shows that eventually the incommensurate strands of science and religion will begin to unravel, and a sense of conflict will take the place of superficial agreement. New developments in science, such as in evolutionary biology, geology, or astrophysics, put an end to easy alliances of the Bible and scientific interpretations of nature. Avoiding conflict by ignoring the vast differences between science and religious scriptures leads inevitably to fruitless confrontations. Unfortunately, these are what the mass media focus on, giving many people the impression that science and religion are perpetual enemies. The "contrast" approach proposes a very simple way of heading off any such appearance of conflict.

5. See Schroeder, *Genesis and the Big Bang*.

## III. Contact

The method of contrast may be an important step toward clarity, but it still fails to satisfy those who seek a more unified picture of reality. As Ian Barbour might say, it is a helpful first approximation, but contrast leaves things at a frustrating impasse.[6] The urge to discover the coherence of all of our ways of knowing is too powerful for us to suppress indefinitely, so I suggest here that we consider a third approach—one that I shall simply call *contact*.

This way of relating religion to science is not content to leave the world divided into the two realms defined by the contrast position. Yet it also does not wish to revert to the superficial harmony of conflation either. It agrees that science and religion are logically and linguistically distinct, but it knows that, in the real world, they cannot be easily compartmentalized, as the contrast position supposes. After all, religion in the West has helped shape the history of science and scientific cosmology, in turn, has influenced theology. It is impossible to separate them completely, even though we can try to make clear logical distinctions in our definitions of them.

In addition, it seems unlikely that just any old cosmology will be compatible with just any old theology, as the contrast position would seem to allow. The kind of world described by evolutionary biology and big bang physics, for example, cannot peacefully coexist with the picture of God that Newton, Descartes, and perhaps even Thomas Aquinas idealized. Whether they are aware of it or not, theologians always bring at least implicit cosmological assumptions to their talk about God. But it often happens that these assumptions are scientifically out of date. The contact approach, therefore, is concerned that theology always remain positively "consonant" with cosmology.[7] Theology cannot rely too heavily on science, but it must also pay attention to what is going on in the world of scientists. It must seek to express its ideas in terms that take the best of science into account, or else it will become intellectually irrelevant.

For that reason, the contact approach looks for an open-ended conversation between scientists and theologians. The word "contact" implies coming together without necessarily fusing. It allows for interaction, dialogue, and mutual impact, but forbids both conflation and segregation. It insists on preserving differences, but it also cherishes relationships.

Contact proposes that scientific knowledge can broaden the horizon of religious faith and that the perspective of religious faith can deepen our

---

6. Barbour, *Religion in an Age of Science*, 15.

7. The search for "consonance" between theology and science has been advocated by Ernan McMullin, Ted Peters, and Robert Russell, among others. See Peters, *Cosmos as Creation*.

understanding of the universe. It does not hope to prove God's existence from science but rather is content simply to interpret the latter's discoveries within the framework of religious meaning. The days in which scientific ideas could be used to seal arguments for God's existence are over. So this third approach will not attempt to shore up religious doctrines by appealing to any scientific concepts that may on the surface seem to require a transcendent grounding. Nevertheless, it considers it fruitful to survey and interpret the results of science with a sensitivity and consciousness that has already been shaped by religious faith.

The kind of religion we are discussing in this book, for example, characteristically strives to instill in its followers a special way of looking at things. Rooted in the story of Abraham, the prophetic faith traditions invite their followers to look for the *promise* that lies in all things. Judaism, Christianity, and Islam think of genuine "faith" as a confidence that new life and undreamed of possibilities are latent even in the most desperate of situations. The authentic religious attitude, then, is a steadfast conviction that the future is open and that an incalculable fulfillment awaits the entire cosmos.

At first sight, such a hopeful orientation of consciousness would seem to be anything but compatible with the "realism" that science demands of us. And yet, as we shall note often in the following chapters, many religious thinkers have found what they consider to be a remarkable accord between a faith-perspective shaped by a sense of reality's promise, and the universe now coming to light as a consequence of new developments in science.

It is probably in the area of "contact" that the most interesting conversations between scientists and theologians are occurring today. Admittedly, these conversations sometimes resemble high-wire acts and the participants occasionally plunge back down into either conflation or contrast. Contact is much more difficult to stabilize than the other approaches. To avoid burning up in the fire of conflation or being frozen in the ice of contrast, it assumes, at times, a rather fluid and even turbulent character. Its efforts to find coherence are interesting and promising, but seldom completely conclusive.

Nevertheless, according to the contact position, though scientific "facts" are always in some sense our own constructs and are inevitably theory-laden, they are not simply wild guesses that have no reference to a real world existing independently of our preferences. This appreciation of the mind's capacity to put us in touch with the real world—in an always provisional way—is known as "critical realism." Critical realism maintains that our understanding, whether scientific or theological, may be oriented toward the real world; but precisely because the world is always too big for the human mind, our thoughts are also always open to correction.[8]

Science and religion make meaningful contact with each other, especially when they decide to play by the rules of what we are calling critical realism. Accordingly, good science hopes more or less to approximate the way things are, but it is always willing to be critical of its contemporary ways of representing the world. And in the case of religion, the same critical realism allows that though our religious symbols and ideas need constant correction, they may nonetheless reflect—in an always limited way—a Transcendent Reality which is truly "there" and which always necessarily transcends our subjective narrowness.

Scientific theories and religious metaphors, in this epistemological setting, are not just imaginative concoctions, as much modern and postmodern thought asserts. Rather, they bear an always tentative relationship to a *real* world and its ultimate ground. This world beyond our representations is always only incompletely grasped, and its presence constantly "judges" our hypotheses, inviting us continually to deepen our understanding in both science and religion. It is their mutual sharing in this critical openness to the real that provides the basis for genuine "contact" between science and religion.

## IV. Confirmation

While it would be quite fruitful to leave our discussions in science and religion at the stage of contact, I would personally prefer to go even further. I appreciate all the efforts to discover consonance between science and religion, but I envisage an even more intimate relationship of religion to science than any of the first three approaches has yet explicitly acknowledged. I propose that religion is supportive—in a very deep way—of the entire scientific enterprise.

Religion, of course, should not be solicited to reinforce the dangerous ways in which scientific knowledge has often been applied in practice. My suggestion is simply that religion essentially fortifies the humble desire to know that gives rise to science in the first place. I call this approach "confirmation," a term equivalent to "strengthening" or "supporting." It holds that religion, when carefully purged of idolatrous implications, fully endorses and even undergirds the scientific effort to make sense of the universe.

I am aware that science has come under heavy criticism today. Many critics even think that it is responsible for most of the ills of the modern

8. See Peacocke, *Intimations of Reality.*

world. Were it not for science, they say, we would have no nuclear threat, no global pollution of the air, soil, and water. We and our planet would probably be better off without it. Science, they claim, is at root an assault upon nature, a crushing exercise in control. It is a Faustian effort to wrest all mystery from the cosmos so that we can become masters of it. Some even argue that science is inherently patriarchal, an exploitation of nature closely tied to our culture's oppression of women.

Obviously theology would not wish to endorse science if it were inherently connected to these evils. But I suspect that much criticism of science mistakenly identifies it with trends and motives that can, at least in principle, be clearly distinguished from science itself. *Essentially* speaking, I consider science to be a modest but fruitful attempt to grasp, with mathematical clarity, some small part of the totality of reality. Any pretensions to omniscience, such as we find in scientism, are not a part of science at all—a point that Appleyard cannot accept, but one that the contrast position rightly clarifies in its protest against conflation.

Most criticisms of science fail to distinguish the humble desire to know that constitutes its basic dynamism from other human desires—such as the will to pleasure, to power, or to security—that place science in servitude to impulses that have nothing to do with truth-seeking. When I say that religion supports science, therefore, I am not arguing that it favors all the twisted ways in which science is exploited and conflated. I am simply saying that the disinterested desire to know, out of which science grows and flourishes, finds its deepest confirmation in a religious interpretation of the universe.

Such an approach does not look for or expect in return any scientific endorsement of religion. Rather, it simply maintains that a religious vision of reality can actually foster the scientific exploration of the cosmos. The contrast approach wisely points out how dangerous it is for religion to seek support for its teachings in any particular scientific theories, since currently accepted scientific ideas may easily be discarded by the next generation of explorers. But science has nothing to lose—and everything to gain—by rooting itself in religion's fundamental premise that reality is intelligible or that the universe is grounded in an ultimately trustworthy reality, one to which the followers of Moses, Jesus and Muhammad give the name "God."[9]

This, again, is not to argue that religion provides scientists with any information about the universe of the sort that science can gather all by itself. Religion has no special insights to dish out about particle physics or

9. As stated in the Introduction, "religion" in this book refers to "theistic" religion, but, as we shall see later, the meaning of "theism" will be inevitably affected (and often considerably revised) by its contact with science.

the genetic code. Its confirmation of science in no way involves any conflation or fusion with particular scientific hypotheses and theories. Rather, its
support of science goes much deeper, though it is seldom noticed either by
scientists or theologians.

The *confirmation* approach may be stated as follows: religion's claim
that the universe is a finite, coherent, rational, ordered totality grounded in
an ultimate love and promise of fidelity provides a general vision of things
that consistently nurtures the scientific quest for knowledge and helps to
liberate science from association with imprisoning ideologies.

Science, for example, cannot even get off the ground without rooting
itself in a kind of a priori "faith" that the universe is a finite, coherent,
rational, ordered totality. Scientists always rely on a tacit faith (which they
seldom reflect on in an explicitly conscious way) that there is a real world
"out there," that this real world hangs together intelligibly, that the human
mind has the capacity to comprehend at least some of the world's intelligibility, and that, no matter how far we probe, there will still be further
intelligibility to uncover. Without this kind of trust, there could be no
incentive to look for the order present in nature or to keep looking deeper
into the specifics of this order.

Even in the mind's spontaneous quest for insight, coherence, and truth,
there is a dynamism that is not far removed from what we may call "faith."
As we see plainly in modern physics, but also in other fields, a fundamental
objective of the scientific quest is to find whatever it is that unifies or holds
together the universe that we are exploring. Science, no less than religion, is
borne along by this quest for a unifying knowledge. But at the roots of this
irrepressible desire to make sense of things, there lies a basic confidence,
nothing less than a "faith," that reality will eventually yield to our desire to
find in it the unity of some kind of order.

Thus faith, in the sense of a basic trust in the limitless rationality of
the real, is not opposed to science but rather is its very wellspring. Science,
like all human knowing, has what Michael Polanyi calls a "fiduciary" aspect
(from the Latin *fideo*, to trust). Without this element of trust there would be
no incentive to pursue the truth through science in the first place.

What then is the precise connection of religion to this prerequisite trust?
We must be careful not to let religion intrude into the actual work of science,
but it is my conviction that religion does provide *confirmation* of the trusting
that inevitably underlies science. Religion, I repeat, cannot add anything to
the list of scientific discoveries. It is not in the business of disclosing things
about nature that science can arrive at on its own. Rather, religion, by its very
nature, is concerned that we put our trust in reality's over-all rationality. In
this sense, religion is much more intimately connected to the epistemological

*roots* of scientific inquiry than the other approaches have enunciated. Religion, taken as a confirmation of the faith assumptions out of which science springs, and not as an alternative source of scientific hypotheses, will not obstruct but rather only promote the work of science.

Religion comes about in human culture because of our awareness of the fact that trust can fail. Religion's central mission is continually to revive this trust. It does not initiate our trust, since we are born with a capacity to trust in reality, but instead functions to revive our confidence when it fails. Religion, Schubert Ogden correctly notes, is best understood as "reassurance," a replenishing of the basic confidence we may have lost in the course of living.[10] Religion exists because our trust in reality is subject to constant erosion by the pain, tragedy, hostility, absurdity, and death with which the world confronts us.

There are any number of experiences that can lead us to doubt the intelligibility of the universe. The point of religion, though, is to encourage us to trust anyway. It seeks to restore our hope in the face of despair, to help us cling to the conviction that there is a final meaning, a vision of things that can eventually light up even those experiences that seem to make the universe absurd. The word "God" points to that mysterious dimension in the depths of reality that guarantees its ultimate trustworthiness.

Religious symbols, stories, and teachings persuade us that there is an infinitely wider perspective than our own and that our own minds are not encompassing enough to take in the whole horizon of being at any given moment, but, nonetheless, that things do make sense in terms of an ultimate frame of reference. Religion implies that we need to continually press onward, beyond the narrowness of current understanding, and go in search of this transcending breadth and depth. Such an impetus, I am saying, can also quietly energize the enterprise of scientific discovery. Scientists can be theists, in other words, because their discipline thrives on the conviction that the world does finally make sense.

The four positions I have just summarized set the pattern for the conversations in the following chapters. Under the headings of conflict, contrast, contact, and confirmation, each chapter will ask you to picture representatives of the several stances appealing to you in the first person plural. They will each try to convince you of the comparative merits of their respective points of view. Obviously, no single chapter can provide more than a sampling, but, as the book proceeds, the fragments should begin coming together into a fuller picture of each way of responding to the central questions in science and religion.

10. Ogden, *Reality of God*, 32.

As we shall see more clearly . . . [later], all of the issues we shall be examining finally converge on the large, perhaps too large, question of whether—in the light of modern science—we can any longer plausibly maintain, as did most of our ancestors, that there is some "point" to the universe. It is out of an implicit preoccupation with cosmic purpose that we ask about such things as evolution and God, Einstein and God, chaos and God, the universe and God. It is to the issue of cosmic purpose that we shall return at the end of our expedition.

# Part II: God, Evolution & Darwin

# 9: Does Evolution Rule Out God's Existence?[1]

In 1859 Charles Darwin published *On the Origin of Species*, his famous treatise on "evolution." It is one of the most important books of science ever written, and experts today still consider it to be largely accurate. Theologically speaking, it caused a fierce storm of controversy, and we are still wrestling with the question of what to make of it. Does Darwin's theory perhaps put the final nail in religion's coffin? Or can there be a fruitful encounter of religion with evolutionary thought?

For many scientists, evolution means that the universe is fundamentally impersonal. In fact, Steven Weinberg asserts that evolution refutes the idea of an "interested" God much more decisively than physics does. Only a brief look at Darwin's theory will show why it disturbs the traditional religious belief in a loving and powerful God.

Darwin observed that all living species produce more offspring than ever reach maturity. Nevertheless, the number of individuals in any given species remains fairly constant. This means that there must be a very high rate of mortality, since more young are produced than ever reach maturity. To explain why some survive and others do not, Darwin noted that the individuals of any species are not all identical: some are better "adapted" to their environment than others. It appears that the most "fit" are the ones that survive long enough to produce offspring. Most individuals and species lose out in the struggle for existence, but, during the long journey of evolution, there emerge the staggering diversity of life, millions of new species, and eventually the human race.

What, then, is so theologically disturbing about the theory? What is there about evolution that places in question even the very existence of God? It can be summarized in three propositions:

1. The variations that lead to differentiation of species are purely *random*, suggesting that the workings of nature are "accidental" and irrational. Today, the source of these variations has been identified as genetic

1. The following text is an excerpt. Previously published in Haught, *Science & Religion*, 47–71. Reprinted with permission.

mutations. Most biologists today follow Darwin in attributing them to "chance."

2. The fact that individuals have to *struggle* for survival, and that most of them suffer and lose out in this contest, points to the basic cruelty of the universe, particularly toward the weak.

3. The mindless process of *natural selection*, by which only the better adapted organisms survive, suggests that the universe is essentially blind and indifferent to life and humanity.

These three ingredients—randomness, struggle, and blind natural selection—all seem to confirm the strong impression of many scientific skeptics today that the universe is impersonal, utterly unrelated to any "interested" God. Darwin himself, reflecting on the "cruelty," randomness, and impersonality in evolution, could never again return to the benign theism of his ancestral Anglicanism. Though he did not completely lose his religious faith, many of his scientific heirs have been much less hesitant to equate evolution with atheism.

From the middle of the last century up until today, prominent thinkers have welcomed Darwinian ideas as the final victory of skepticism over religion. T. H. Huxley, Darwin's "bulldog," as he was known, thought evolution was antithetical to traditional theism. Ernst Haeckel, Karl Marx, Friedrich Nietzsche, and Sigmund Freud all found Darwin's thought congenial to their atheism, and numerous others—in our own time—closely associate evolution with unbelief. Given this coalition of evolution and hostility to theism, it is hardly surprising that the idea has encountered so much resistance from some religious groups.

Darwin himself, however, did not envisage so unambiguous a union between evolution and skepticism. If he moved toward unbelief at all, it was not before undergoing a great deal of personal anguish and mental reservation. In 1860, a year after the publication of *Origin*, he wrote:

> There seems to me too much misery in the world. I cannot persuade myself that a beneficent and omnipotent God would have designedly created the Ichneumonidae with the express intention of their feeding within the living bodies of caterpillars, or that cats should play with mice. Not believing this, I see no necessity that the eye was expressly designed. On the other hand, I cannot anyhow be contented to view this wonderful universe, and especially the nature of man, and to conclude that everything is the result of brute force. I am inclined to look at everything as resulting from designed laws, with the details,

whether good or bad, left to the working out of what we may call chance.[2]

Yet, we must ask here whether the Darwinian or neo-Darwinian picture of nature in evolution is after all compatible with religion, and if it is, in what sense? Answers to this question generally fall into the four categories we are following throughout this book. Here is a brief summary of what each has to say on the topic of evolution and religion.

## Conflict

Is it any wonder that we skeptics find the most compelling scientific basis for rejecting theistic religion in evolution? The three features of chance, struggle, and blind natural selection are so antithetical to any conceivable notion of divine providence or design that we find it hard to understand how any scientifically educated person could still believe in God.

Richard Dawkins, a British biologist, presents our position handily in his book *The Blind Watchmaker*. His thesis is that chance and natural selection, aided by immensely long periods of time, are enough to account for all the diverse species of life, including ourselves. Why would we need to invoke the idea of God if chance and natural selection alone can account for creativity in the story of life? Before Darwin, we concede, it may have been difficult to find definitive reasons for atheism. The order or patterning in nature seemed to beg for a supernatural explanation, so the design argument for God's existence may have made some sense then—but this is no longer the case. Evolutionary theory, brought up to date by the discoveries of molecular biology, has demolished the divine designer that most educated people believed in before the middle of the last century. Evolution has once and for all purged any remaining intellectual respectability from the idea of God.[3]

In his book *Natural Theology*, which set forth the standard academic and theological wisdom of the early nineteenth century, William Paley compared nature to a watch.[4] If you chanced upon a watch lying alone on the ground, he wrote, and then examined its intricate structure, you could not help concluding that it had been made by an intelligent designer. It couldn't possibly be the product of mere chance. And yet, the natural world exhibits much more complex order than any watch. Thus, Paley

2. Greene, *Darwin and the Modern World View*, 44.

3. See Dawkins, *Blind Watchmaker*, 6.

4. See Paley, *Natural Theology*.

concluded, there has to be an intelligent designer responsible for nature's fine arrangement. This designer, of course, would be none other than the Creator God of biblical religion.

Even though David Hume and other philosophers had already severely battered the design argument for God's existence, Dawkins thinks that only Darwin's theory of natural selection provided a fully convincing refutation of natural theology. "Darwin made it possible to be an intellectually fulfilled atheist."[5]

## Contrast

Our position, you will recall, is that science and religion are such disparate ways of looking at the world that they cannot meaningfully compete with each other. This means that evolution, which may be quite accurate as a scientific theory, bears not the slightest threat toward religion. "Conflict" arises not from evolution itself but rather from the unnecessary conflation of evolutionary theory with scientific materialism (in the case of skeptics), and the confusion of the biblical accounts of creation with "science" (in the case of scientific creationists).

Here we shall examine "scientific creationism" and follow up with a critique of materialist evolutionism. We would like to emphasize, though, that we are in no way attacking *scientific* theories of evolution; at the end of our presentation, we shall even show how our theology is logically consistent with the three items that our adversaries find antithetical to religion—namely, chance, struggle, and natural selection.

The opposition that scientific creationists see between evolution and theism follows from their attempts to wrest pure science out of the biblical texts. Creationists take *Genesis* not only as a religious tract but also as a compendium of scientifically accurate information. So we should not be surprised that conflict appears as soon as an alternative set of scientific ideas, such as those of Darwin, becomes established. Creationists simply assume that the Bible is scientifically accurate, while evolutionists think of it as scientifically inaccurate. Both sides, however, treat it as though its intention were to give us scientific understanding. One side (creationism) views it as good science; the other (evolutionary skepticism) sees it as bad. But both implicitly conflate science with the Bible, an alliance that inevitably leads to conflict.[6]

5. Dawkins, *The Blind Watchmaker*, 6.

6. Evolutionary scientists, in their dialogue with "religion," often assume that all theologians are "creationists," unaware that the idea of "creation" is a highly nuanced

So-called "scientific creationism" is objectionable in the first place because, from the point of view of good science, it refuses to look at the relevant data. The scientific evidence in favor of evolution is overwhelming. Geology, paleontology, the fossil record, radio-carbon dating, comparative anatomy, and embryology—all of these and many broader features of current cosmology—now converge to support some version of Darwin's theory. Although evolutionary theory is certainly not unrevisable, as there are apparent gaps in the fossil record as well as other problems yet to be resolved, this does not mean that the world and life did not evolve. All it means is that science still has a long way to go in clarifying our understanding of the details of evolution. We fully support scientific efforts to learn more about how evolution works.

In the second place, however, scientific creationism is *theologically* embarrassing. It trivializes religion by artificially imposing scientific expectations on a mythic-symbolic text. It completely misses the Bible's religious point by placing the text of Genesis in the same arena with science, as an alternative "scientific" account.

In the third place, scientific creationism is historically anachronistic. Creationists ironically situate the ancient biblical writings within the time-conditioned framework of modern science. They refuse to take into account the social, cultural, and historical conditions in which the books of the Bible were fashioned over a period of two millennia. In doing so, they close their eyes to modern historical awareness of the time-sensitive nature of all human consciousness, including that expressed in the sacred texts of religion. They are unable to discern the different types of literary genre—symbolic, mythic, devotional, poetic, legendary, historical, creedal, confessional, etc.—that make up the Bible. And so they fail to read them in their proper context.

Our contention is that humans cannot learn the nature of ultimate reality simply by pondering purely natural laws and occurrences. We too reject Paley's narrowly conceived "natural theology" since it seeks to know God independently of God's self-revelation. Nature itself provides evidence neither for nor against God's existence. Something so momentous as the reality of God can hardly be decided by a superficial scientific deciphering of the natural world. Hence we are in no way troubled by evolutionary theory.

---

notion in most theology. See Eldredge, *Monkey Business*, 132–35.

## Contact

We allow that the contrast approach has the merit, at least, of shattering the facile fusion of faith and science that underlies most instances of conflict. Its sharp portrayal of the ideological biases in both creationism and evolution-ism is very helpful. Contrast may be an essential step in the process of think-ing clearly and fruitfully about the relationship of evolution to religion.

But for many scientists and religious thinkers contrast does not go nearly far enough. Evolution is more than just another innocuous scien-tific theory that theology can innocently ignore. We need to do more than just show that evolution does not contradict theism. Evolution, in our judgment, may very well be the most appropriate framework we have ever had through which to express the true meaning of our religious convic-tions. Evolutionary science helps deepen our understanding not only of the cosmos but also of God.

Unfortunately, many theologians have still not faced the fact that we live in a world after and not before Darwin, and that an evolving cosmos looks a lot different from the world-pictures in which most religious thought was born and nurtured. If it is to survive in the intellectual climate of today, therefore, our theology requires a fresh expression in evolutionary terms. When we think about religion in the post-Darwinian period, we cannot have exactly the same thoughts that Augustine, Aquinas, or, for that matter, our parents and grandparents had. Today, we need to recast all of theology in evolutionary terms.

Without fusing science with religion, theology is making fruitful con-tact with the same Darwinian ideas that evolutionists consider antithetical to God's existence. In fact, for many of us, evolution is an absolutely es-sential ingredient in our thinking about God today. As the Roman Catholic theologian Hans Küng puts it, evolutionary theory now makes possible:

1.  a deeper understanding of God—not above or outside the world but in the midst of evolution;

2.  a deeper understanding of creation—not as contrary to but as making evolution possible; and

3.  a deeper understanding of humans as organically related to the entire cosmos.[7]

In other words, if the world is to be anything distinct from God, it has to have some scope for meandering about, for experimenting with different ways of existing. In their relative freedom from divine coercion, some of

7. Küng, *Does God Exist?*, 347.

the world's evolutionary experiments may work and others may not. But divine love does not interfere. It risks allowing the cosmos to exist in relative liberty. In the evolution of life, the world's inherent quality of being uncompelled manifests itself in the form of the random variations or genetic mutations that comprise the raw material of evolution. Thus a certain amount of chance is not at all opposed to the idea of God.

Some of us believe that a God of love influences the world in a persuasive rather than coercive way and this is why chance and evolution occur. It is because God is love rather than domineering power that the world evolves.[8] If God were a magician or a dictator, we might expect the universe to be finished all at once and remain eternally unchanged. If God were in total control of things, we might not expect the weird organisms of the Cambrian explosion, the later dinosaurs and reptiles, or the many other wild creatures that seem so alien to us. We would want our divine magician to build the world along the lines of our own narrowly human sense of clean perfection. But what a pallid and impoverished world that would be. It would lack all of the drama, diversity, adventure, and intense beauty that evolution has produced. It might have a listless harmony to it, but it would have none of the novelty, contrast, danger, upheavals, and grandeur that evolution has brought about over billions of years.

## Confirmation

We fully endorse the attempts to construct an evolutionary theology. However, we would go even further in establishing the close connection between theism and evolution. Our view is that religious ideas provide much of the soil in which Darwinian ideas have taken root in the first place. There are a number of recent studies that demonstrate theism's fundamental "confirmation" of evolutionary thinking—we cannot discuss them all here.[9] But one point we should make is that evolutionary theory could hardly have originated and thrived outside of a cultural context shaped by the biblical understanding of God and its correlative picture of the nature of time.

The Bible understands time in terms of God's bringing about a new and surprising future. When, through biblical faith, we became aware of a *promise* that seemed to be offered to us by a God who appears out of the future, we began to experience time in a new way. As the promised new creation beckoned us, we no longer felt the compulsion to return to a golden age in the past. Time became directional and irreversible at a very deep

8. For a discussion of this approach, see Haught, *Promise of Nature*.

9. See Benz, *Evolution and Christian Hope*.

level of our awareness. Even in the modern period, when the idea of God dropped out of the intellectual picture of the cosmos, the feeling of time as directional and irreversible remained deeply lodged in our sensibilities, including that of secular scientists. It is an originally biblical perception of temporality that made it possible for Western science to embrace an evolutionary picture of the universe.

In contrast to this linear-historical sense, most non-biblical religions and cultures have understood time as a repeating circle. Time's destiny, in both primal and Eastern religious traditions, is not something radically new but instead a return to the purity and simplicity of cosmic origins. The Bible's emphasis on God as the source of a radically new future, on the other hand, breaks open the ancient cycle of time. It calls the whole cosmos, through the mediation of human hope, to look forward in a more linear way for the coming of God's kingdom, either in the indefinite future or at the end of time.

Only on the template of this stretched out view of irreversible duration could evolutionary ideas have ever taken shape. Even though evolution does not have to imply a vulgar notion of "progress," it still requires an eschatological, future-oriented understanding of time as its matrix. This view of time, we would like to emphasize here, originally came out of a *religious* experience of reality as promise.

However, there is an even deeper way in which faith in God nourishes the idea of evolution. The central idea of theistic religion, as Karl Rahner (among others) has clarified, is that the Infinite pours itself out in love to the finite universe.[10] This is the fundamental meaning of "revelation." But if we think carefully about this central religious teaching, it should lead us to conclude that any universe related to the inexhaustible self-giving love of God must be an evolving one. For if God is infinite love, giving itself to the cosmos, then the finite world cannot possibly receive this limitless abundance of graciousness in any single instant. In response to the outpouring of God's boundless love, the universe would be invited to undergo a process of self-transformation. In order to "adapt" to the divine infinity, the finite cosmos would likely have to intensify, in a continuous way, its own capacity to receive such an abounding love. In other words, it might endure what we know scientifically as an arduous, tortuous, and dramatic evolution toward increasing complexity, life, and consciousness. In the final analysis, it is as a consequence of the infusion of God's self-giving love that the universe is stirred into a movement of self-transcendence—that is to say, evolution.

10. See Rahner, S.J., *Hominization*.

Viewed in this light, the evolution of the cosmos is more than just "compatible" with theism. Faith in a God of self-giving love, it would not be too much to say, actually anticipates an evolving universe. It would be very difficult for us to reconcile the religious teaching about God's infinite love with any other kind of cosmos.

# 10: Darwin's Dangerous Idea[1]

ACCORDING TO THE PROLIFIC American philosopher Daniel Dennett, Charles Darwin's theory of evolution by natural selection is a "dangerous idea."[2] It is particularly threatening to religious believers because it wrecks any hope that the universe is here for a reason. Evolutionary science has shattered every pious illusion that life and human existence were planned from all eternity. It contradicts all the traditional religious intuitions that our universe is guided by divine wisdom and that a glorious destiny awaits it.

Consequently, most of us, Dennett insinuates, will be afraid to look squarely at this "dangerous idea." Even when we think we have understood it, we probably have not really countenanced its appalling depths. Obviously theologians have not examined it closely, or else they would have abandoned their trade long ago. But, annoyingly, even many scientists carry on as though Darwin had not completely pulverized their pictures of an intelligently governed universe. Still clinging implicitly to the stories of meaning that beclouded our ignorant ancestors, some of our best naturalists, Dennett complains, refuse to face the darker implications of evolutionary science.

In laborious detail, Dennett argues that Darwin and his true followers have now demonstrated conclusively that biological evolution is an inherently meaningless process. It is only the working out of impersonal physical laws. The story of life on Earth requires nothing more than purely random genetic mutations, the deterministic laws of "natural selection," and enormous spans of time. There is no need for supernatural "skyhooks" to explain even nature's most impressive creations. The various animate forms result, one and all, from a very gradual and purely mechanical kind of causation, lifting only from below.

Mathematically speaking, evolution takes place, Dennett goes on to say, in an open-ended "Design Space" composed of all the logically possible forms of life. It meanders through "virtual" archives, containing every conceivable arrangement of DNA, segments of which we call "genes." Within this "Library of Mendel," evolution toys with countless possibilities until it chances upon those that actually "work." The workable or "fit" genetic

---

1. Previously published in Haught, *God After Darwin*, 11–24. Reprinted with permission.

2. See Dennett. *Darwin's Dangerous Idea.*

combinations are those that happen to be adaptive to their environments and thus are able, by way of the living organisms that unknowingly transport them, to survive and reproduce. Through selection of minute adaptive changes in organisms over a period of several billion years, this totally blind process can bring about all the diversity of life on our planet, including beings endowed with sight and consciousness. Even the human mind is an eventual—and perhaps inevitable—outcome of an utterly mindless sequence of physical occurrences.[3] The point is, there is no need for an "intelligent designer" to supervise the process.

This, according to Dennett, is the most "dangerous" implication of Darwin's idea, especially in its contemporary neo-Darwinian form. (Neo-Darwinism, once again, is essentially Darwin's original theory of selection, clarified and brought up-to-date by our more recent discovery of genes and the molecular constituents of life, of which Darwin himself knew nothing.) If we had the fortitude to look closely at what this revised version of evolution tells us about life, we could have no doubt, Dennett insists, that any notion of divine influence in nature is cognitively empty. Therefore, those biologists "who see no conflict between evolution and their religious beliefs" are refusing to face incontestable scientific facts.[4] If they took evolution seriously, they would see clearly that the natural world does not conform to humanity's traditional mythic, religious, or philosophical depictions. The cosmos, in no sense, bears the inscription of a cosmic orderer. If evolution has any message at all, it is that the universe is devoid of any message. The cosmos as a whole has no explanation—it "just is"—and the stream of life that accidentally appears and evolves within it has no goal of purpose. No deity has ever "planned" for our own existence either.

Hailed by Marvin Minsky as "our best current philosopher" and the "next Bertrand Russell," Dennett clearly holds a position of respect among contemporary American thinkers.[5] Even though many other scientists and intellectuals quietly share his reading of evolutionary science, Dennett's voice seems much louder than most others. He clearly relishes exhibiting what he takes to be the atheistic underside of Darwin's revolution.[6] The sheer vehemence of his writing almost forces one to pay attention. For our purposes, his work has the advantage of spotlighting some of the suspicions that many other evolutionary biologists harbor but are usually reluctant to flash so publicly.

3. Dennett, *Darwin's Dangerous Idea*, 266.

4. Dennett, *Darwin's Dangerous Idea*, 310.

5. Dennett, "Intuition Pumps," 181.

6. See also Dennett's more recent book, *Breaking the Spell*.

Dennett's depiction of evolution closely follows that of the well-known British zoologist and evolutionist Richard Dawkins. In *The Blind Watchmaker* and, more recently, in *River Out of Eden* and *Climbing Mount Improbable*, Dawkins has argued that blind chance and natural selection, working over long periods of time, can account for life's creativity all by themselves.[7] The fundamental players in the game of life are not individual organisms or populations of organisms, as some Darwinians have held, rather, they are genes—coded segments of DNA. Evolution is primarily about "selfish" genes "trying" to survive and only secondarily about the organisms and populations by which they perpetuate themselves. According to Dawkins, it is the nature of genes to maximize opportunities for survival and reproduction. Genes are driven by an impersonal, physical necessity to secure their immortality, so they fashion individual organisms and a diverse array of species to function as "vehicles" that will carry them on to future generations. Even if it means invading innocent organisms and exploiting them in devious and destructive ways, the "selfish" genes must do all they can to endure indefinitely. It is this blind necessity, in combination with random genetic variations, that carries evolution along and allows it to execute all of its apparent magic.

Such a picture, Dawkins readily admits, "is not a recipe for happiness. So long as DNA is passed on, it does not matter who or what gets hurt in the process. It is better for the genes of Darwin's *ichneumon* wasp that the caterpillar should be alive, and therefore fresh, when it is eaten, no matter what the cost in suffering. Genes don't care about suffering, because they don't care about anything."[8] Maximization of the "utility function" of DNA survival can account for all outcomes of evolution.[9] Life, therefore, has no need for an intelligent designer to provide it with its various profiles. The same impersonal momentum that rules atoms and stars also governs the selfish genetic units of evolution. Genes will seek to survive at all costs and by whatever means available. They will even invent intelligent beings as vehicles to carry them on, unknowingly, to subsequent generations.

According to Dawkins, atheism has found in Darwin's ideas the firmest intellectual foundation it has ever had.[10] Dennett fully agrees. He flaunts the gene's-eye interpretation of Darwinian selection as the definitive "scientific" refutation of theology. In this respect, his work is an obvious challenge to all

---

7. See Dawkins, *Blind Watchmaker; River Out of Eden;* and *Climbing Mount Improbable.*

8. Dawkins, *River Out of Eden,* 131.

9. See Dawkins, *River Out of Eden,* 95–133.

10. Dawkins, *Blind Watchmaker,* 6.

of us who are happy to accept modern science but who continue to embrace a religious vision of the universe. Ever since Darwin, of course, scientifically educated religious thinkers—especially the many who never interpreted their scriptures too literally in the first place—have talked approvingly and at times even lyrically about evolution. But have they ever looked closely at evolution's most "dangerous" features? If they had done so, Dennett claims, their theology could never have endured.

As I have already noted, Dennett's is by no means a lone voice. William Provine, a Cornell professor of the history of science, comes even closer than Dawkins and Dennett to equating evolution with atheism. He allows that, prior to the "modern synthesis" of Darwinism and genetics, theological interpretations of evolution may have seemed plausible, but once science became aware of the imperial role of genes and molecular structures in the story of life, no room remained anywhere for the work of an ordering deity. Consequently, those evolutionary scientists who continue to think they can find room for God alongside of natural science must "check their brains at the church-house door."[11]

Dennett and Dawkins, in particular, have given fresh verbalization to a position that is by no means new, so there has been no lack of response to it. Some rebuttals have taken the approach of insisting that Darwinian ideas are simply wrong, whereas others, in spite of Darwinian complications, have looked for ways to rehabilitate old arguments for intelligent design. I believe, however, that such theological strategies are generally misdirected and apologetically fruitless. My own preference is to concede from the outset the general integrity of Darwinian science (which I would distinguish carefully from the materialist ideology in which it is often packaged). Certainly, Darwinian ideas are not perfect. That evolutionary theory will continue to undergo revision, I have no doubt. Even today, there is some discontent with neo-Darwinism in the scientific community. But out of respect for the thinking of most contemporary scientific experts, especially the majority of biologists, I shall take Darwin's version to be a reasonably close, though incomplete and abstract, approximation of the way life has developed on Earth.

In its conversations with science, theology should, I think, deal with all the untidiness of the Darwinian picture of life and not work with cleanly edited versions of it. For this reason, I have chosen to focus here on the rather extreme views of Dawkins and Dennett. It is true, of course, that many biologists would themselves insist that these two neo-Darwinians exaggerate the role of genes and adaptation in the evolutionary construction

11. Provine, "Evolution and the Foundation of Ethics," 261.

of the forms of life. Both authors, I would also agree, have produced cleverly written books that make evolution look much simpler than it really is, and they do not by any means speak for all mainstream scientists. Nevertheless, even if their renditions of Darwinism are one-sided, they highlight aspects of evolution—especially its apparent randomness, blind experimentation, and impersonality—that are present (at least to some degree) in most other contemporary scientific renderings of the story of life. It is just these troublesome features that a theology in conversation with science must address today, more carefully than it has done previously. Moreover, theology must grapple with the more extreme Darwinist interpretations simply because of their high public visibility and the shrillness of their assaults on the notion of God. For theologians simply to ignore these voices could be construed as an implicit submission to the apparent "deathblow" that Dawkins and Dennett think Darwin's science has dealt to religion.

## The Sufficiency of Darwinism?

Has it, then, been conclusively established that Darwinian evolution rules out the existence of God? Is evolution inconsistent with the sense of cosmic purpose posited by many religions? Is the evolution of the universe and of life determined solely by a blind and mindless set of mathematical rules? Does the impersonal notion of "natural selection" provide us with a *sufficient* explanation of life's creativity? Is there no discernible directionality to evolution? Does evolutionary science adequately explain human existence, our place in the universe, and the reasons for our moral and religious behavior? Does neo-Darwinian biology give us the "ultimate" explanation of life?

If we listen to Dawkins and Dennett, we are led to believe that Darwin's scientific legacy provides so total an account of life that it removes any need for appeal to theological explanation *at any level* of understanding. Religious faith's intuition that a mysterious but infinitely intelligent creativity underlies biological process is now considered unacceptable not so much because we can prove it is not there but because science has apparently shown it to be superfluous. Before Darwin, there may well have been logically sound reasons for invoking the idea of a divine designer, as even Dawkins agrees. But after Darwin, it appears that blind natural selection deployed over the course of immense epochs of time is enough to account for the adaptive order in living beings, including the physiological and neurological complexity underlying human consciousness and behavior. Why seek multiple complex explanations when a single, simple explanation—the Darwinian one—suffices? Why appeal to an "extraneous" notion of divine causation if nature can so autonomously create itself, and if science can now tell us precisely how?

Evolutionary theory, at least to the scientific thinkers I have been considering here, provides a comprehensive account of life, of mind, and—especially in E. O. Wilson's writings—of morality and religion.[12] Theology, therefore, even if it still gives comfort to the scientifically ignorant, must appear cognitionally inane to those who take Darwin's science as ultimate explanation seriously, especially many of the experts in our universities. "At least in the eyes of academics," Dennett contends, "science has won and religion has lost. Darwin's idea has banished the Book of Genesis to the limbo of quaint mythology."[13]

Adequately understanding evolution, according to Dennett, requires an uncompromising naturalism—that nature is all there is and that any talk of supernatural guidance or intervention is superfluous. What need is there for God if nature, when given enough time, can do the work of designing life all by itself? In his revolutionary book, *On the Origin of Species*, Charles Darwin had already portrayed natural selection as a pitiless but nonetheless effective engineer of life's creations. Although for a time he was perhaps somewhat tormented by his findings, Darwin eventually arrived at the conclusion that the older theological notion of "creation by design" no longer had explanatory serviceability. Nature allows only those organisms to survive and reproduce that *by sheer chance* happen to possess physical variations and features that are more adaptive than "weaker" ones. In evolution, the feeble lose out and the reproductively fit survive. Mindless though the process may be, it has seemed to Darwin and many of his followers quite sufficient to account for the many different kinds of life and eventually mind as well. Thus, the notion of an ordering and creative "God" loses out to a more elegant and parsimonious explanation.

Genetics and molecular biology have by now brought Darwin's "dangerous idea" into even sharper focus. Although the essentials of his vision may have been a good start for evolutionary science, they do not go far enough on their own. Darwin knew nothing about DNA or genes, so he could understand evolutionary selection only in terms of organisms and populations. But for many evolutionary scientists today, the capacity of some organisms to survive and reproduce in any given environment can be explained more exactly if we also take into account the changes in gene frequencies within a given population. The neo-Darwinian joining of genetic knowledge to the implacably rigid law of natural selection is what biologists usually have in

12. See Dennett, *Breaking the Spell*.
13. Dennett, "Intuition Pumps," 187.

mind today when they refer to the "Darwinian" picture of nature. Thus, unless otherwise indicated, I shall follow the contemporary scientific practice
of using Darwin's name in these pages as shorthand for what is now known
more technically as the "neo-Darwinian synthesis."

In any case, the latest versions of Darwinism may seem even more
religiously lethal than the master's original. According to Darwinian science, some individuals or groups in any given population of organisms
can adapt to the challenges of their environment more readily than others.
Out of this inequality, nature selects those whose genotypes are the most
"fit"—in the sense of possessing the highest probability of surviving and
reproducing. Since only a few organisms will prove to be "fit" in this reproductive sense, nature will ruthlessly eliminate all the others. Mindless
though this mechanism is, it appears to have been enough to bring about all
of the rich diversity and complexity we see in the fossil record and in living
species today. And so, if nature is, in this sense, so *self*-creative, where is the
need for a transcendent intelligence to act or intervene in evolution? Hasn't
Darwin demonstrated that nature is inventive enough on its own, in need of
no extrinsic "supernatural" support or ordering principle?

Whether in textbooks or philosophical essays on evolution, it is becoming increasingly routine for biologists and scientific thinkers in general
to claim that all the diverse phenomena of the life-world can be explained
in sufficient depth through the purely naturalistic concepts of evolutionary science. For example, in his latest book, the revered Harvard zoologist
Ernst Mayr repeatedly refers to neo-Darwinian science as the "ultimate"
explanation of life.[14] Philosopher Gary Cziko claims that it is natural selection *rather than* divine providence that explains why living organisms have
their various physical characteristics, such as ears, eyes, and brains.[15] Much
earlier, in a major article for *Encyclopedia Britannica*—where one might
have expected more neutrality—Gavin de Beer even argued that Darwinism emphatically rules out the idea of God. "Darwin," his article concluded,
"did two things: He showed that evolution was a fact *contradicting* scriptural
legends of creation and that its cause, natural selection, was automatic *with
no room for divine guidance or design*."[16]

In a lucid summary of the Darwinian revolution, the noted biologist
Francisco J. Ayala—who has, incidentally, authored the article on evolution in a more recent version of the same encyclopedia—also states that

14. Mayr, "Evolution," 50.

15. See Cziko, *Without Miracles.*

16. Beer, "Evolution." This reference was brought to my attention by Rolston, *Science
and Religion*, 106.

evolutionary science "excludes" the influence of God. If he had said, more explicitly, that evolutionary science *methodologically* excludes any reference to God, there would be nothing controversial about such a statement. Indeed, science simply makes no appeal to supernatural explanations. But Ayala writes that "it was Darwin's greatest accomplishment to show that the directive organization of living beings can be explained as the result of a natural process, natural selection, without any need to resort to a creator or other external agent. The origin and adaptation of organisms in their profusion and wondrous variations were thus brought into the realm of science."[17] If we take Ayala literally here, his wording seems to imply that an adequate understanding of life has no need for any additional, nonscientific explanations—at any level of understanding—although this may not be his intention. After Darwin, Ayala writes:

> the origin and adaptive nature of organisms could now be explained like the phenomena of the inanimate world, as the result of natural laws manifested in natural processes. Darwin's theory encountered opposition in religious circles, not so much because he proposed the evolutionary origin of living things (which had been proposed many times before, even by Christian theologians), but because his mechanism, natural selection, *excluded* God as accounting for the obvious design of organisms.[18]

Does this mean, then, that the concept of God can have no explanatory value at all, as far as the evolution of life and its diverse patterns are concerned? It is not entirely clear, at least from the wording here, whether Ayala would allow for or exclude theological explanation at some other level of understanding. But at the end of his essay, he gives readers at least the appearance of subscribing to a purely naturalistic account of evolution: "This is the conceptual revolution that Darwin completed—that everything in nature, including the origin of living organisms, can be explained by material processes governed by natural laws. This is nothing if not a fundamental vision that has forever changed how mankind perceives itself and its place in the universe."[19]

If Darwin had merely changed our understanding of life, this would itself have been compelling enough. But apparently, according to Ayala's understanding, the Darwinian revolution has gone much further than this: it has altered, once and for all, our standards of what should count as an *adequate* explanation of life. Copernicus and other scientists had shown

17. Ayala, "Darwin's Revolution," 4.

18. Ayala, "Darwin's Revolution," 5.

19. Ayala, "Darwin's Revolution," 4.

already that blind, mechanical causation is sufficient to understand inanimate nature, but, before Darwin, we had been reluctant to apply the impersonal methods of science to the realm of living beings. Now we should know better. To understand life, there is no need ever to fall back on regressive religious explanations again. Science alone suffices.

## Contingency, Law, and Time

Many biologists now share the view that Darwinian science leaves no room at all for theological attempts at explanation. Apparently only three ingredients are needed for evolution to cook up the wide diversity of living beings: first, accidental, random, or *contingent* occurrences. These include, for example, the highly improbable chemical coincidences required for the very origin of life, the chance genetic mutations that make possible the diversification of life, and many other unpredictable events in natural history that shape the course of evolution (for instance, ice ages, volcanic eruptions, plate movements of the Earth, asteroid impacts, or the influence on populations by famines, earthquakes, floods, etc.). The second generic constituent of evolution is the determinism or so-called *necessity* implied in the "law" of natural selection and in the inflexible dictates of chemistry and physics that pertain throughout the universe. These remorseless rules lay out the boundaries within which life's contingencies can occur. They thicken what would be too thin a stew if evolution were only a matter of chance events. Lawfulness "constrains" randomness, placing it within limits, thus contributing order and consistency to life. Third and finally, biological evolution requires a stupendous span of *time*. Without a vast amount of temporal duration, the many improbable products of evolution could never have come about. In the absence of an intelligent designer, after all, an enormous expanse of time is required to provide ample scope for the accidental emergence of those few genetic combinations that will permit survivable evolutionary outcomes.

According to many influential neo-Darwinians, the mixing and brewing of elements and occurrences bearing these three features—let us call them contingency, law, and time—are sufficient to account for the entire evolutionary stew. What explanatory enhancement, then, could religion or theology possibly add to this most economical of recipes?

## The Problem of Suffering

Before I undertake a theological response to claims about Darwinian science's explanatory adequacy, I should take more careful notice of evolution's insensitivity to the pain of living beings, a fact that also seems logically incompatible with belief in the compassionate God to which many religions refer. "If Nature were kind," Dawkins writes, "she would at least make the minor concession of anaesthetizing caterpillars before they are eaten alive from within." Instead, he continues, "nature is neither kind nor unkind. She is neither against suffering nor for it. Nature is not interested one way or the other in suffering, unless it affects the survival of DNA . . . The universe we observe has precisely the properties we should expect if there is, at bottom, no design, no purpose, no evil, and no good, nothing but blind, pitiless indifference."[20]

Darwin, then, has done nothing to quiet the powerful complaint sensitive people have always aimed at the idea of God. How could a powerful and compassionate creator permit all the suffering, aimless wandering, and obscene waste that we behold in surveying the millennia of evolution? How could a lovingly concerned God tolerate the struggle, pain, cruelty, brutality, and death that lie beneath the relatively stable and serene surface of nature's present order?

Previous ages were not unaware of suffering, of course, but they had no sense of the millions of years of it that Darwin and his scientific progeny have uncovered, and which many of us have still not integrated fully into our benign cosmic visions. It is instructive, then, to feel the anguish of one whose religious feelings have been wounded so deeply by the Darwinian picture of life that belief in God is no longer an option:

> Could an Almighty God of love have designed, foreseen, planned, and created a system whose law is a ruthless struggle for existence in an overcrowded world? Could an omnipotent, omniscient, and omnibenevolent God have devised such a cold-blooded competition of beast with beast, beast with man, man with man, species with species, in which the clever, the cunning, and the cruel survive?

> How could a loving God have planned a cruel system in which sensitive living creatures must either eat other sensitive living creatures or be eaten themselves, thereby causing untold suffering among these creatures? Would a benevolent God have created animals to devour others when he could have designed

---

20. Dawkins, *River Out of Eden*, 133.

them all as vegetarians? What kind of deity would have designed the beaks which rip sensitive flesh? What God would intend every leaf, blade of grass, and drop of water to be a battle ground in which living organisms pursue, capture, kill, and eat one another? What God would design creatures to prey upon one another and, at the same time, instill into such creatures a capacity for intense pain and suffering?[21]

These are the words of a former Christian clergyman who eventually came to be persuaded by Darwinian evolution that atheism is really the only honest response one can make to it. I could cite many such testimonies, and there can be no doubt that similar sentiments have at least occasionally crossed the minds of more than a few scientifically educated religious believers. Evolution not only threatens to make divine creativity an intellectually superfluous idea but also challenges us to confront more deliberately than ever the most intractable question of every age: how can we make sense of the universe, given the facts of suffering and eventual death? In a century that anyone aware has witnessed the Holocaust, widespread warfare, genocides, political purges, and the prospect of ecological catastrophe, evolutionary science is hardly going to add much to what is already the most pestilent of all human and religious concerns, the problem of innocent suffering. However, even if it fails to deepen the wound, evolution clearly seems to widen it.

It is true that evolution is not just about competition and wasteful struggle. Evolution is also, as we are now beginning to realize more clearly, a story of cooperation among many diverse layers of organisms. Moreover, there is an inspiring beauty in the life-story that we can overlook too easily if we focus only on the vulnerability of living beings to pain and death. Nevertheless, Darwin has extended the story of life's innocent suffering considerably, leading us down pathways of pain and bloodletting that stretches back through many millions of years. His "dangerous idea" has uncovered regions of terror and torture that we had never known about before. The picture of life he left us only fuels our perennial religious revolt against what seems to be God's indulgence of undeserved agony. By expanding the horizons of life's travail, Darwin gives unprecedented breadth to our sense of the tragic. His disquieting account of evolution intensifies our outrage at suffering and only adds to our consternation at the silence of God.

Nevertheless, Darwin's challenge turns out to be a great gift to theology. It spreads out before us a panorama of life that can pilot us away from cheap and easy representations of the sacred such as that implied in a

21. Mattill Jr., *Seven Mighty Blows to Traditional Beliefs*, 32.

one-sided commitment to the notion of "intelligent design." The story told by evolutionary science may frighten or confuse us, but we cannot deny what Darwin referred to justifiably as the "grandeur" of its vision.[22] Those who prefer simple stories with fairy-tale endings will not relish the new narrative of life's troubled but creative journey here on Earth. If they are pious, they may plug up their ears when scientists speak and if they are skeptics, such as Dawkins and Dennett, they will flourish the facts of evolution before us as the definitive proof of religion's intellectual emptiness. But we shall see that Darwin's portrayal of the way the universe works actually invites us to think about God, once again, in a meaningful and truly inspiriting way.

22. Darwin, *Origin of Species*, 649.

# 11: Darwin[1]

I had no intention to write atheistically . . . I can see no
reason why a man or other animal may not have been ab-
originally produced by other laws; that all these laws may
have been expressly designed by an omniscient creator,
who foresaw every future event and consequence. But the
more I think, the more bewildered I become.[2]

—CHARLES DARWIN, "LETTER TO THE HARVARD
BOTANIST ASA GRAY," MAY 1862

Formerly I was led . . . to the firm conviction of the existence
of God and of the immortality of the soul. In my Journal I
wrote that whilst standing in the midst of the grandeur of a
Brazilian forest: "It is not possible to give an adequate idea
of the higher feelings of wonder, admiration, and devotion,
which fill and elevate the mind." I well remember my conviction that there is more in man than the mere breath of
his body. But now the grandest scenes would not cause any
such convictions and feelings to rise in my mind.[3]

—CHARLES DARWIN IN 1870

AT THE YOUTHFUL AGE of twenty-two, Charles Darwin began his famous,
five-year sea voyage (1831–1836). It turned out to be one of the most
important travel adventures anyone on earth has ever undertaken. Our

1. Previously published in Haught, *Making Sense of Evolution*, 1–10. Reprinted
with permission.

2. Darwin, *Correspondence*, 224.

3. Darwin, *Autobiography*, 65.

world has not been the same since. Even those millions of people who refuse to accept what Darwin discovered still feel the impact of his work. You would not be reading this book unless his writings had given rise to important theological controversies. You would not be wondering, along with me, what difference Darwin makes when it comes to such important questions as who we are, where we came from, where we are going, and what we should be doing with our lives.

Darwin's breakthrough book was originally titled *On the Origin of Species by Means of Natural Selection, or the Preservation of Favoured Races in the Struggle for Life.* First published in 1859, by the time the sixth edition arrived the title had been mercifully elided. I shall be citing this latest edition (1872) and referring to it simply as the *Origin of Species.*

Darwin's masterpiece launched an intellectual and cultural revolution more sensational than any since Galileo. The revolution is not over. The discovery that the earth is a planet moving around the sun was disturbing enough when common people, philosophers, and popes first heard about it. Galileo's sun-centered cosmology destroyed the ageless belief that the superlunary world is fixed in unchanging perfection. "'Tis all in pieces, all coherence gone," the poet John Donne had written about his impressions of nature in 1612, two years after Galileo had published science's first bestseller *The Starry Messenger.*[4] But Galileo and the emerging scientific revolution did not lead Donne to question his Anglican creed, and the new cosmology caused few people to lose their faith in God. The same cannot be said of Darwin's new picture of life.

The *Origin of Species* sold out on the first day of publication and with its appearance science entered a brand-new age. Not only did the biological sciences begin to undergo a dramatic transformation, but eventually other disciplines, from anthropology to economics, would also begin to follow the Darwinian drift. Nowadays, the ideas forged at Down House, Darwin's home in the English countryside, are having more influence in the intellectual world than ever. What is most intriguing for theologians is that countless people think this influence includes a decisive debunking of religion. In the United States, a good percentage of the religious population associates "Darwinism" with atheism, and many scientists and philosophers do too. Evolution, they say, makes the most sense if we assume that the universe is godless. After Darwin, as the renowned evolutionist Richard Dawkins exclaims, atheism rests on a more-solid intellectual foundation than ever before.

4. Donne, "Anatomy of the World."

Darwin himself never came close to drawing such conclusions from his theory. In spite of his doubts about some Christian teachings, especially the ideas of hell and divine providence, he remained close to the Anglican Church in Downe. He had his children baptized there and took on a leadership role in some of its charitable missions. He was involved in the life of the church to the point of expressing annoyance at the laxity of several clerics assigned to the parish after the departure of his close friend, the Reverend J. B. Innes. Innes was to say of Darwin in 1878:

> I have the pleasure of the intimate friendship of one of the very first Naturalists in Europe. He is a most accurate observer and never states anything as a fact which he has not most thoroughly investigated. He is a man of the most perfect moral character, and his scrupulous regard for the strictest truth is above that of almost all men I know. I am quite persuaded that if on any morning he met with a fact which would clearly contradict one of his cherished theories he would not let the sun set before he made it known. I never saw a word in his writings which was an attack on Religion. He follows his own course as a Naturalist and leaves Moses to take care of himself.[5]

## The Theory

Eventually someone else would have let the evolutionary cat out of the bag, but let us give credit to Darwin. Other scientists had already begun to realize that nature, ranging from rocks to rodents, changes over time. Still, it was Darwin and Alfred Russel Wallace, a younger contemporary of Darwin, who first illuminated what had been called the "mystery of mysteries": the puzzle of how new species can emerge in natural history. Wallace should be given his due as a codiscoverer of natural selection, but, in the present work, the spotlight is on Darwin, the more famous and more theologically interesting of the two. The modest Wallace, who considered the *Origin of Species* to be as important in the history of science as the works of Isaac Newton, would not have objected to our centering on Darwin's work.

Darwin's scientific ideas about life's common descent, together with the mechanism of change that he called "natural selection," still make up the core of what has come to be called "evolutionary theory." But Darwin needed help to become as influential as he is today. His theory lacked a good explanation of how physical traits can be inherited, and it was only after he

5. Innes, "1 December 1878."

died that the science of genetics arrived to account for variation and heredity, thus rescuing the theory. Already in Darwin's lifetime, the Austrian Monk Gregor Mendel had demonstrated that traits are passed on from one generation to the next in discrete units now called genes, but unfortunately Darwin knew nothing of Mendel's work. Eventually, the discovery of genes would become an essential part of evolutionary theory, and the fruitful marriage of Darwinian theory with the science of genetics is now known as the "Modern Synthesis" or "neo-Darwinism."

Even without Darwin, we would all have heard about evolution by now, and this entirely new way of looking at life would possibly have made just as big a splash. However, a distinctively Darwinian seasoning still flavors the idea of evolution. The theory has never worked itself completely free of its originator's assumptions, just as Darwin himself never fully shed his own theological preoccupations. Contemporary interpretations of evolution still feel Darwin's personal touch, and the theological controversies that the *Origin of Species* stirred up in the nineteenth century continue to surround the most popular presentations of evolution today. In the Western world, at least, it is hard for anybody—atheist, agnostic, or theist—to think about evolution without also thinking about God. It should prove helpful, therefore, to trace the steps of the theory's gradual emergence in the life and mind of the man most renowned for its discovery. We shall see that along with the voyage of the *Beagle*, the ship that carried Darwin around the earth, there is an even more adventurous journey of one man's soul as it drifts slowly away from its frail theological moorings toward the shoals of agnosticism. It is especially the latter voyage that will interest theologians.

In the case of Darwin, the theologically interesting itinerary began in a life shaped by a traditionally Christian belief system and, in the end, it came close to the quite modern creed known as *scientific naturalism*. This is the name Darwin's friend T. H. Huxley gave to the relatively new belief that, as far as science is concerned, nature is all there is and that the search for supernatural explanations is not part of scientific inquiry. Since so many other educated people over the last century and a half have made a similar pilgrimage—from an unquestioning childhood faith in God to the new creed of scientific naturalism—it is instructive to watch how some of Darwin's own theological convictions, never very fervent to begin with, began to fall overboard and eventually vanish in the *Beagle's* wake.

## The Voyage

Charles Robert Darwin was born in Shrewsbury, England, on February 12, 1809, a birthday he shares with Abraham Lincoln. He died in Downe, England, on April 19, 1882, and was laid to rest in Westminster Abbey. His father, Robert, was a successful and wealthy physician whose financial resources would subsidize Charles throughout his lifetime. Robert's famous father, Erasmus Darwin (1731–1802), had already portrayed life in evolutionary terms, although it is doubtful that his views had much influence on Charles, apart from vaguely suggesting the descent of later forms of life from earlier forms.

Charles's mother died when he was only eight, an event whose effect on his character must have been profound, but which is hard to measure. Later, the death of his own daughter Annie, at the age of ten, would prove to be more of a factor in Charles's abandonment of the idea of a beneficent deity than would the idea of natural selection. As a youngster, Darwin's preferred pastime was collecting rocks, shells, coins, and insects, and this activity may have helped him cope with his grief, just as a determined return to scientific work would later blunt the pain he felt at the death of his daughter. At any rate, Charles's youthful delight in collecting things certainly helped to shape the exceptional observational talents that would eventually fit him for the life of a scientist.

When Charles was nine, his father enrolled him in a boarding school with his older brother Erasmus. Throughout his formal education, Charles could generally be described as an average student, both in drive and achievement. At the age of sixteen, he followed his brother to Edinburgh University, after being persuaded by his father to prepare for the medical profession. However, this Edinburgh experiment was to prove unsuccessful. Charles found the academic lectures, at least those he bothered to attend at all, tediously dry. But it was his witnessing the unspeakable pain of surgeries during medical demonstrations—performed on patients without anesthesia—that turned him away from following in his father's footsteps. Overcome by the howls of agony in two such cases, one involving a child, he later wrote in his autobiography: "I rushed away before they were completed. Nor did I ever attend again, for hardly any inducement would have been strong enough to make me do so; this being long before the blessed days of chloroform." Then he adds: "The two cases fairly haunted me for many a long year."[6]

6. Darwin, *Autobiography*, 12

On a brighter note, during his brief stay at Edinburgh, Charles began to share the interests of several other young naturalists, and with them he thoroughly enjoyed scouring the Scottish countryside for specimens. During the same period, he also befriended an expert taxidermist of African descent, from whom he began to learn the technique of preserving the cadavers of birds and animals slaughtered for the sake of science. This know-how would later come in handy on his sea voyage when he had to prepare the remains of diverse species to send or take back to England for closer study.

Having failed at medicine, Charles accepted the advice of his disappointed father and enrolled in Cambridge University, where he remained from 1828 to 1831. The expectation was that Darwin might there prepare for holy orders. He had never been particularly devout, but this deficit of piety did not seem to bother either him or his father, who also had little interest in matters of religious faith. They both fancied that Charles could best indulge his naturalist propensities if he were ensconced in a parsonage somewhere in the countryside. Yet such a languid dream was not to become reality either. Circumstances were about to point the young Darwin in a direction that would change not only his own life dramatically but also the wider world of thought and culture.

During his period at Cambridge, Darwin studied the widely influential works of Archdeacon William Paley (1743–1805), including Paley's important book *Natural Theology* (1802). Paley was renowned for his "watchmaker" argument for God's existence. He had reasoned that the orderly and adaptive arrangements in living organisms, on the analogy of a watch's complexity, provide evidence of a designing deity. Impressed by Paley's logic and eye for detail, the young Darwin accepted the conventional observation that organisms are adapted exquisitely to their diverse environments. This remarkable fact, Darwin agreed at the time, could only be explained by reference to the existence of an eminently intelligent and benign creator. Later, however, Darwin's own discoveries would persuade him and many of his scientific and philosophical followers to replace Paley's theological explanation of design with a purely natural account of adaptation.

By his own admission, Darwin's formal studies at Cambridge could scarcely compete with his enthusiasm for riding, shooting small animals, and collecting beetles. Still, during the latter part of his Cambridge period, he won the patronage of two instructors, John Stevens Henslow and Adam Sedgwick, both of them clerics as well as scientists. Their own love of nature, along with their kindness and encouragement, aroused in the young

Charles "a burning zeal to add even the most humble contribution to the noble structure of Natural Science."[7]

Eventually, after an intense period of cramming, Charles passed his exams quite handily and acquired a degree from Cambridge. At this juncture in his life, however, he was uncertain about his future, still pondering the possibility of ordination. Then an invitation arrived (by way of his instructor Henslow) from the highly esteemed Captain Robert Fitzroy for Charles to accompany him aboard *HMS Beagle* on what was originally intended to be a three-year journey to survey the coast of South America for commercial purposes. Fitzroy, an accomplished naturalist himself, was looking for a companion with similar interests to travel along and serve as a conversation partner, someone to help ease the maddening loneliness of an interminable sea excursion. Having overcome the initial objections of his father, Charles gratefully accepted Fitzroy's offer and, after exhaustive preparations, set sail in 1831 on what would turn out to be, not just a three-year cruise, but an arduous and endlessly fascinating five-year voyage around the globe. It was a passage that would give surprising new direction to Charles's own life and also provide information about nature that would agitate the religious and ethical sensibilities of many Christians and other people ever since.

Aboard the *Beagle*, Darwin had ample time, when he was not completely immobilized by seasickness, to read Charles Lyell's *Principles of Geology*. Lyell recognized that the earth's geological features had changed significantly over time, but that these changes had occurred only gradually rather than simply by occasional upheavals. Previously, geology had generally endorsed catastrophism, the belief that geological changes, such as the carving out of great canyons, had occurred abruptly rather than over long spans of time. To make room for a literal acceptance of the biblical account of Noah and his ark, as well as the assumed short age of the earth, geological catastrophists had attributed startling formations on the earth to occasional, God-sent disasters, such as floods and earthquakes.

Darwin, however, was convinced by Lyell's work that many geological features are the outcomes of long-drawn-out, gradual change. Reading Lyell's captivating work helped prepare Darwin's mind to theorize that the story of life on earth was also one of incremental change over a long period of time. Whenever the *Beagle* dropped anchor, as it did for extended periods during its voyage, Darwin would eagerly explore the countryside. Among his many new discoveries, he found what he took to be reliable evidence of Lyell's uniformitarian theory. Increasingly, his newly confirmed sense of

7. Darwin, *Autobiography*, 24.

geological gradualism would provide a firm foundation for his theory of the prolonged transformation of life on earth as well.

In the Galapagos Islands, and at numerous other sites during his lengthy journey, Darwin kept meticulous notes on geological features, flora, fauna, and fossils in the places he explored. All the while, he kept sending specimens and many pages recording his observations back to England for other naturalists to ponder. Hence, it was during the *Beagle's* voyage that his name began to become respected in scientific circles.

Among the many questions that Darwin and other naturalists who later studied his specimens began to ask was: why do small but distinct variations (as recorded most famously in his observations in the Galapagos archipelago) appear among geographically distributed species of birds and other animals? After returning home, Darwin's own earlier belief in the special divine creation of each distinct species gave way to a strong suspicion that the origin of different living species had occurred gradually, in a purely natural way. Specific differences, Darwin began to suppose, could be accounted for without divine special creation if there had been minute, geographically conditioned, and cumulative changes in living organisms over an immensely long time.

Darwin began to doubt that a wise and intelligent deity would be so fastidious as to separately fashion each minute variation in distinct species of finch, iguana, or tortoise in an initial act of creation. The young naturalist became increasingly convinced that Lyell was correct in surmising that habitats had changed gradually over the course of time. So it was not a great leap to suppose that life had adapted to these new habitats gradually as well. It is possible that even during the latter part of his travel on the *Beagle*, Darwin was already beginning to turn away from conventional Christianity's belief in special creation. At this time, his theological sensibilities may have started to move, almost imperceptibly at first, toward a rather dispassionate agnosticism that would never reach the extreme of atheism.

## Back Home

After returning to England, Darwin began to feel the need for a more settled style of life. In 1839 he married his cousin Emma Wedgwood and, in 1842, the couple moved from London to a home in Down (later known as Downe) in the nearby Kent countryside. Plagued by nearly constant illnesses for the remainder of his life, Darwin helped raise a large family, but still found opportunities to engage in biological research and write prolifically until his death. Fortunate to have inherited ample income, he could spend most of his days at home. There, even amid almost constant physical and more than occasional mental suffering, he undertook meticulous experiments, produced volumes of very readable scientific publications, and wrote thousands of letters to friends and fellow scientists.

As early as 1838, Darwin was already outlining his famous theory of "transmutation," later named "evolution." More than twenty years before the actual publication of the *Origin of Species*, he had already laid out the core elements of his theory of "natural selection." One evening, after reading Thomas Malthus's popular book, *An Essay on the Principle of Population* (1798), the thought occurred to Darwin that the restrictions on human population growth, on which Malthus was a recognized expert at the time, applied in some manner to the nonhuman world of living beings as well. Malthus had theorized that the growth in human numbers is limited by the amount of food and other resources available. Given these constraints, Malthus argued, a struggle for the relatively scarce amount of sustenance available has to take place, and, unfortunately, only a finite number of human beings can survive while others will lose out in the competition. The stronger will survive and the weak will be eliminated.

Darwin began to speculate, correspondingly, that a ruthless principle of selection and a similar "struggle for existence" have always been operative among all species of life. In this way, natural selection could account for the gradual evolution and diversification of species over time. The "mystery of mysteries" would be solved. All organisms and species living today, he reasoned, have descended with modification from a common ancestor, and the various forms of life still extant could be accounted for by "natural selection." Natural selection is a mechanism by which nature "selects" the more adaptive organisms to survive and reproduce while eliminating nonadaptive organisms—and even entire species—over the course of time. Natural selection also explains how new species can come into existence periodically without special divine creation. Darwin would later supplement his theory of natural selection with that of "sexual selection."

In later chapters I shall have occasion to flesh out Darwin's idea of natural selection and its implications more fully. At present, I simply want to point out how puzzling it is that after Darwin arrived at his theory, he waited another twenty years before publishing the *Origin of Species* in 1859. Only after learning that a nearly identical and well-researched interpretation of life by his younger contemporary, Alfred Russel Wallace, would soon appear, was he finally persuaded to publish his own version. One might suppose that, as a good scientist, Darwin waited so long because he was simply being cautious, but he was also aware that several previous works by other writers on life's evolutionary descent had stirred up considerable debate and much hatred as well. So the postponement of publication may have been due, in part at least, to Darwin's reluctance to introduce ideas that he must have known would cause anguish to many religiously sensitive people, including his wife, Emma.

Pressured by friends, other scientists, and his publisher, Darwin finally agreed to publish his work. After appearing in print, the *Origin of Species* became an immediate sensation, and deservedly so. Everything about life now looked different. In the following chapters, therefore, my objective is to dwell on the main theological questions about life that Darwin's work stirred up. I shall be dealing henceforth not so much with the historical person and preoccupations of Darwin the man, but mostly with what might be called the Darwinian specter, the set of ideas that he let loose that, in scientifically updated form, continue to call for theological comment. I intend these compact reflections to be only starting points for the reader's own theological meditation on themes central both to Darwin and contemporary evolutionary biology.

# 12: Theology Since Darwin[1]

EVEN THOUGH THE "SEPARATISTS" have no objections to neo-Darwinian science, as long as its followers stay out of metaphysics, their theological method holds evolution at arm's length. Separatism provides an essential moment of clarification, perhaps, but it does not give us an evolutionary theology. It tolerates evolution but does not celebrate it. A third family of theological responses to Darwin, on the other hand, after accepting the separatists' clear distinction of science from ideology, argues for the "engagement" of evolutionary science and theology. It refuses to hold Darwin's supposedly "dangerous idea" apart from theological understanding, but instead takes evolution into the very center of its reflections on the meaning of life, of God, and of the universe.

Generally speaking, Darwin's impact on this adventurous theology has been twofold. It has caused a noticeable shift in the character of "natural theology," an approach that looks for evidence of God in the natural world, and it has stimulated the emergence of what we may call "evolutionary theology," a radical reinterpretation of classic religious teachings in terms of Darwinian concepts. I shall say only a brief word about the first and then go on to treat the second dimension at length.

## Post-Darwinian Natural Theology

Before Darwin, as even Dawkins agrees, the best explanation for the ordered and adaptive features of living organisms seemed to be that of divine "intelligent design," the position William Paley made famous in his watchmaker analogy.[2] Suppose that while walking across a patch of ground you kick up a stone. Upon examining it, you would not find it very remarkable. But suppose that you then stumble across a watch in the same setting. Upon opening up the timepiece and examining its interior structure, Paley observed, you would undoubtedly conclude that it was purposefully designed. Analogously, you should be able to understand that the even more intricate design in living organisms must also point toward creation by an intel-

1. The following text is an excerpt. Previously published in Haught, *God After Darwin*, 25–48. Reprinted with permission.

2. See Paley, *Natural Theology*.

ligent designer, the One whom theists readily identify as the creator God of biblical religion. However, Darwin seems to have provided an adequate explanation of the design in living beings without resorting to theology at all. Natural selection of random variations, now called mutations, can explain life's "design"—that is, if you give it enough time. Scientists today think that life originated as long as 3.8 billion years ago, leaving more than enough opportunity for the seemingly improbable design in living beings to come about gradually in a purely naturalistic way. So the story of life does not require any special *ad hoc* interventions of the supernatural and we can discard the design argument of natural theology.

## Evolutionary Theology

A second and more important form of "theological engagement" with neo-Darwinism is "evolutionary theology." Evolutionary theology claims that the story of life, even in its neo-Darwinian presentation, provides essential concepts for thinking about God and God's relation to nature and humanity. However, it also agrees with Polkinghorne and others that all serious theological reflection on biological evolution today must be situated in the more expansive context of "cosmic evolution." It would be artificial in the extreme to relate theology to neo-Darwinian evolution without taking into account the entire physical universe that has sponsored the emergence of life.

Evolutionary theology, unlike natural theology, does not search for definitive footprints of the divine in nature. It opposes "intelligent design," not only because it is scientifically useless but also because such a notion is entirely too lifeless to capture the dynamic and disturbing way in which the God of biblical religion interacts with the world. Instead of trying to prove God's existence from nature, evolutionary theology seeks to show how our new awareness of cosmic and biological evolution can enhance and enrich traditional teachings about God and God's way of acting in the world. In other words, rather than viewing evolution simply as a dangerous challenge that deserves an apologetic response, evolutionary theology discerns in evolution a most illuminating context for our thinking about God today. Here, we may sample briefly some ways in which the Darwinian vision has already affected theological understanding of the notions of creation, eschatology, revelation, divine love (or "grace"), divine power, and redemption.

# Creation

The notion that God creates the world is, of course, central to the faith of millions. Traditionally, Christian theology spoke of three dimensions of God's creative activity: original creation (*creatio originalis*), ongoing or continuous creation (*creatio continua*), and new creation or the fulfillment of creation (*creatio nova*). Prior to the scientific discoveries of cosmic and biological evolution, however, the latter two notions were usually eclipsed by the first. "Creation" meant primarily something that God did in the beginning. But even in the late nineteenth century, a few theologians had already recognized that evolution implicitly liberates the notion of creation from its confinement to cosmic origins.[3] Although today discussions between scientists and theologians about God and the big bang often assume that "creation" is only about cosmic beginnings, the idea of evolution forbids such narrowing of so powerful a notion.[4]

Indeed, the fact of evolution now allows theology to realize more palpably than ever that creation is not just an "original" but also an ongoing and constantly new reality. In an evolving cosmos, creation is still happening, no less in the present than "in the beginning." The big bang universe continues to unfold, so every day is still the "dawn of creation." As Teilhard de Chardin puts it, in an evolving universe, "incessantly even if imperceptibly, the world is constantly emerging a little farther above nothingness."[5]

Moreover, evolution has allowed theology to acknowledge at last that the notion of an originally and instantaneously completed creation is theologically unthinkable in any case.[6] If we could imagine it at all, we would have to conclude that an initial creation, one already finished and perfected from the beginning, could not be a creation truly distinct from its creator. Such a "world" would simply be an appendage of God, not a world unto itself; nor could God conceivably transcend such a world. It would be a world without internal self-coherence, a world without freedom or a future, and, above all, a world devoid of life. By definition, living beings must continually transcend, or go beyond, themselves. As Henri Bergson said long ago, life is really a cosmic *tendency* rather than something rounded off and complete.[7] An unfinished or evolving universe is the essential context for this tendency's actualization.

---

3. See Pannenberg, "Human Life: Creation Versus Evolution?" 138–139.
4. See Hawking, *Brief History of Time*, 140–141 and Davies, *Mind of God*, 66.
5. Teilhard de Chardin, *The Prayer of the Universe*, 120–121.
6. Teilhard de Chardin, *Christianity and Evolution*, 239.
7. Bergson, *Creative Evolution*, 13, 96.

But if the universe is still unfinished, then we cannot demand that it should here and now possess the status of finished perfection; if the universe is not perfect, then this can mean only that it is now imperfect. Moreover, if ours is an imperfect world, the appearance of evil (including the suffering and struggle depicted by Darwinian science) is not inconceivable. Evil and suffering could be thought of as the dark side of the world's ongoing creation.[8] To say that suffering is a logical possibility in an evolving universe, however, is not to claim that it is morally tolerable. For this reason, faith and theology cry out for the completion of creation (*creatio nova*). This brings us to the question of the meaning of eschatology in an evolving universe.

## Eschatology

Biblical faith is concerned especially with what we humans may hope for, that is, with what awaits us as our final destiny and ultimate fulfillment. This branch of theology is known as eschatology (from the Greek word *eschaton*, which means "edge," or what is "last" or "final"). In an evolutionary context, however, our own human hope for final fulfillment must be situated within the wider context of the ongoing creation of the cosmos. The scientific epic of evolution invites us to extend our human hope outward and forward to embrace the entire cosmos, thus retrieving an often lost theme in the biblical wisdom literature and in the writings of Saint Paul, Saint Irenaeus, and many other religious thinkers who have also sought to bring the entire universe into the scheme of salvation.

The Jesuit scientist Teilhard de Chardin often pointed out that as long as nature seemed static or eternal, it had no future of its own. Human hope for what is truly new and fulfilling, therefore, could lead us only to withdraw from the natural world in order to arrive, decisively after death, at an entirely different (supernatural) world, situated "up above." But after Darwin and other recent scientific developments, the cosmos began to be perceived as itself moving; slowly perhaps, but nonetheless moving. The horizon of human expectations could begin to shift toward a future that includes the universe and the entire sweep of its evolution. In this way, evolutionary science has provided theology with a great opportunity to enlarge upon the ancient religious intuition—expressed so movingly by Saint Paul—that the *entirety* of creation "groans" for ultimate fulfillment (Rom 8:22). After Darwin, we may speak more assuredly than ever about the inseparability of cosmic and human destiny.

---

8. See Teilhard de Chardin, *Christianity and Evolution*, 131–132.

Correspondingly, the sense of where the reality of God is to be "located" can also begin to shift from the One who abides vertically "up above" to the One who comes into the world from "up ahead," out of the realm of the future.[9] This new understanding of divine transcendence, as it turns out, actually corresponds to the God of the Bible more closely than pre-evolutionary conceptions of the supernatural—where God is the One who "goes before" the people, leading them to liberty. This is the God who turns the eyes of faith toward the future and "who makes all things new," as depicted by Second Isaiah and the Book of Revelation (Isa 43:19 and Rev 21:5). The evolutionary portrait of life and the universe fits quite comfortably into the framework of biblical eschatology and, in doing so, gives it even wider compass than the biblical authors could have envisaged.

## Revelation

Evolution also helps theology understand what is implied in the idea of "revelation" more clearly than before. Indeed, as Catholic theologian Karl Rahner has suggested, the notion of revelation already logically anticipates an evolving cosmos.[10] Revelation is not fundamentally the communication of propositional information from a divine source of knowledge. Rather, it is at root the communication of *God's own selfhood* to the world. According to Rahner, the central content of Christian faith is that the infinite mystery of God pours itself generously, fully, and without reservation into the creation. Put in simpler terms, the infinite gives itself away to the finite. But the fullness of divine infinity cannot be received instantaneously by a finite cosmos. Such a reception could take place only incrementally or gradually. A finite world could "adapt" to an infinite source of love only by a process of gradual expansion and ongoing self-transcendence, the external manifestation of which might appear to science as cosmic and biological evolution.

## Grace

Reflection on evolution has helped some theologians, beginning in the last century, to illuminate the theme of divine love (or grace) and, along with it, the world's response to this grace. At the same time, a theology of grace can make intelligible the randomness, natural selection, and eons of time

9. See Moltmann, *Experiment Hope* and Bloch, *Principle of Hope*. Teilhard de Chardin, Wolfhart Pannenberg, and Karl Rahner also think of God as essentially future. I shall take up this theme of the futurity of God more explicitly later.

10. See Rahner, *Foundations of Christian Faith*, 78–203.

for experimentation that form the core of the Darwinian understanding of evolution. The doctrine of grace claims that God loves the world and all of its various elements fully and unconditionally. By definition, however, love does not absorb, annihilate, or force itself upon the beloved. Instead, it longs for the beloved to be self-actualizing, so as to become more and more "other" or differentiated. Along with its nurturing and compassionate attributes, love brings with it a longing for the independence of that which is loved. Without such "letting be" of its beloved, the dialogical intimacy essential to a loving relationship would be impossible.

Consequently, if there is any truth to the central religious intuition that God loves the world with an unbounded love, then God's "grace" must also mean "letting the world be itself." God's love would refrain from forcefully stamping the divine presence or will upon the world, much less dissolving the world into God. Indeed, this love might even take the form of a self-withdrawal precisely as the condition for allowing the world to emerge on its own in order to attain the possible status of being capable of a deep relationship with God. However, this "self-withdrawal" must not be construed in any sense as an abandonment of the world, such as historians associate with the God of deism. Rather, God forgoes any annihilating "presence" to or compelling of the world in order, paradoxically, to be nearer to it. What is "withdrawn" is not at all God's "loving kindness" or God's intimate involvement with the world, but instead any coercive or obtrusive presence that might suppress the autonomy of the beloved. God is present in the mode of "hiddenness," not abdication.

Nicholas of Cusa, in praying to God, asked: "How could you give yourself to me unless you had first given me to myself?"[11] It must be likewise with God's relation to the entire cosmos. Only a relatively independent universe, a universe allowed to "be itself," could be intimate with God. Theologically interpreted, therefore, the epic of evolution is the story of the world's struggle—not always successful or linearly progressive—toward an expansive freedom in the presence of self-giving grace.[12]

Evolution, in all of its wandering, struggling, and temporally drawn out self-creating—as described by the neo-Darwinian accounts—is perfectly consonant with this notion of divine grace understood as God's "letting be" of the world. Indeed, if we reflect on cosmic process in the light of faith's assumptions about the selfless character of divine grace (impressed on Christians, for example, through the image of a crucified Goodness), we should *expect* to find a world percolating with contingency rather than

---

11. O'Donnell, *Hans Urs Von Balthasar*, 73.

12. See Pannenberg, *Systematic Theology*, 127–136.

one rigidified by necessity. Even Saint Thomas Aquinas argued that a world devoid of chance or contingency could not really be distinct from its God. The world has to have aspects of nonnecessity or contingency in order to be a world at all: "It would be contrary to the nature of providence and to the perfection of the world if nothing happened by chance."[13] Thus, the randomness and undirected features of evolution are not just "apparent," as some of the "separatists" would argue. They are, in fact, essential features of any world created by a gracious God.

## Divine Power

Belief that the world can be finally redeemed from the evil and suffering that accompany its evolution requires special theological concentration on the notion of divine power. And of all the varieties of contemporary religious reflection on this doctrine of faith, it seems to me that "process theology" has been the most attentive to evolution. It seeks, more directly than other kinds of theology, to show how God can be deeply involved with a world wherein life meanders, experiments, strives, fails, and sometimes succeeds. Using concepts of Alfred North Whitehead and his philosophical followers, process theology seeks to interpret the teachings of biblical religion about God's creative and redemptive power in terms consistent with the dynamic, evolutionary character of the world.[14] Evolution, according to process theology, occurs in the first place only because God's power and action in relation to the world take the form of persuasive love rather than coercive force. In keeping with the notion of grace mentioned immediately above, divine love does not compel, but invites. To compel, after all, would be contrary to the very nature of love.

But isn't the use of persuasion a sign of weakness rather than power? After Darwin, can theology still hold that God is a God of "power and might"? Process theology responds that if power means "the capacity to influence," then a persuasive God is much more powerful than a hypothetical deity who magically forces things to correspond immediately to the divine intentions. A coercive deity—one that an immature religiosity often wishes for and that our scientific skeptics almost invariably have in mind when they assert that Darwin has destroyed theism—would not

13. Mooney, SJ, *Theology and Scientific Knowledge*, 162.

14. The philosophy of Charles Hartshorne has also been influential in shaping the ideas of many process theologians. A useful summary of process theology can be found in Cobb and Griffin, *Process Theology*. I have discussed some of the contributions of process thought to evolutionary theology more fully in Haught, *Cosmic Adventure*.

allow for the otherness, autonomy, and self-coherence necessary for the world to be a world unto itself. Such a stingy and despotic forcefulness, by refusing to favor the independence of creation, would clearly be less influential in the final analysis than a God who wills the independence of the world. A world given lease to become more and more autonomous, even to help create itself, eventually attaining the status of human consciousness and freedom, has much more integrity and value than any conceivable world determined in every respect by an external "divine designer." If something greater than a puppetlike universe is permitted to come into being by persuasion rather than coercion, then we can say that persuasive power is more influential than brute force.

A coercive divine power, furthermore, would be incompatible not only with human freedom but also with the prehuman spontaneity that allows the world to evolve into something other than its creator over the course of billions of years. Thus, process theology finds nothing religiously peculiar in the spontaneity manifested at the levels of quantum indeterminacy or in the undirected mutations in biological evolution that Darwinians refer to as random. Its conception of God is neither inconsistent with all the other contingencies in life's open and undetermined history nor in the capacity for free choice that emerges during the human phase of evolution. Theologically speaking, process theology suggests that we should logically foresee, rather than be surprised, that God's creation is not driven coercively, that it is widely experimental, and that it unfolds over the course of a considerable amount of time. To those who object that process theology is hereby illegitimately redefining the idea of God's power in order to contrive a fit with neo-Darwinian theory, the reply is simply that no other conception of power is more consistent with the quite orthodox religious belief that God is infinite love. Neo-Darwinian evolution does not require that we abandon or modify the ancient biblical teachings about the unbounded generosity and compassion of God, but that we return to them more earnestly than ever.

Evolution occurs, according to process theology, because a God of love is the source not only of order but also of novelty. It is the introduction of novelty into the world that makes evolution possible. Thus, the obsession by creationists, ID proponents, and scientific skeptics with the idea of God as an "intelligent designer" is entirely too narrow for—and in great measure irrelevant to—a genuine engagement of theology and science on the issue of Darwinian evolution. ID shares with mechanistic biology the trait of abstracting from the concrete reality of *life*. As the ultimate source of novelty in evolution, God must also be the cause of instability and disorder, conditions essential to life. There can, after all, be no process of ordering or reordering, such as that exhibited by evolutionary transformations, that does not also include aspects of instability or disorder. So it is simply inappropriate to think of God exclusively as a source of order (a distortion shared by much natural theology and scientific skepticism). God is also the source of novelty, so God is also the reason for some disorder—and hence for the possibility of life.

According to process theology, evolution occurs because God is more interested in adventure than in preserving the status quo. "Adventure," in Whiteheadian terms, is the cosmic search for more and more intense versions of ordered novelty, another word for which is "beauty." God's will, apparently, is for the maximization of cosmic beauty.[15] The epic of evolution, then, is the world's response to God's own longing that it strive toward ever richer ways of realizing aesthetic intensity. By offering new and relevant possibilities to the cosmos in every period of its becoming, God "acts" not only to sustain but also to create the world continually. I shall develop this point in more detail later.

## Redemption

Finally, process theology also rightly highlights the hope for redemption that perennially lies at the heart of human longing and that comes to its most explicit expression in the world's religious traditions. But how can it conceive of redemption in a world of evolution, given the perpetual perishing that goes along with cosmic process? According to process theology, the answer is the same as that given in biblical and other traditions, namely, that God is infinitely *responsive* to the world as well as creative and nurturing of it. Following the pattern of love, God intimately "feels" the world, as the biblical narratives affirm over and over. A truly compassionate God, it would seem, is influenced deeply by all that happens in the evolutionary process. Everything whatsoever that occurs in evolution—all of the suffering and tragedy as well as the emergence of new life and intense beauty—is "saved" by being taken eternally into God's own feeling of the world. Even though all events and achievements in evolution are temporal and perishable, they still abide permanently within the everlasting empathy of God. In God's own sensitivity to the world, each event is redeemed from absolute perishing, receiving the definitive importance and meaning that religions encourage us to believe in—always without seeing clearly. That we abide in darkness on something of such ultimate concern is itself consistent with the fact that we live in an

15. See Whitehead, *Adventures of Ideas*, 252–296 and Cobb and Griffin, *Process Theology*, 57–79.

unfinished, imperfect universe; in other words, the only kind of universe consistent with the idea of an infinitely loving and active God.

# 13: Darwin's Gift to Theology[1]

THE DARWINIAN PICTURE OF life's long struggle and travail gives unprecedented breadth to the so-called problem of theodicy—that is, how to "justify" God's existence given the fact of suffering and evil. How could a powerful and compassionate God permit all the agony, aimless wandering, and waste that scientific portrayals of evolution have laid out before us? In addressing this issue, I should stress once again that evolution is not unambiguously malign. In fact, as contemporary evolutionary science is bringing out more clearly all the time, the story of life on Earth is less one of competition among species and more one of their cooperation and interdependence than we used to think. Generally, neo-Darwinian models have failed to give sufficient attention to the ecological richness of the life-process.

Nevertheless, we cannot remain untroubled by the innocent suffering that evolution brings along with it. Because of the enormity of this suffering in nature, it seems to me that recent efforts to confront the challenge of evolution by simply restating or revising arguments for "intelligent design" are both apologetically ineffective and theologically inconsequential. One-sided appeals to the idea of God as an "intelligent designer" render the issue of theodicy all the more intractable. They lead us to ignore the more theologically challenging aspects of evolution. Rather than attuning theology and human life to the restlessness and ambiguity of an unfinished universe, advocates of "intelligent design" typically ignore the contingency, randomness, and struggle in evolution. But it is precisely the latter that a theology of evolution needs to take into account.

The idea of "intelligent design" is too restrictive, theologically speaking, to capture the deeper and ultimately more compelling meaningfulness that a robust theological vision may discern in an evolving universe. A reactionary focus on design filters out the tragic aspects of life. Fixation on nature's rational orderliness blunts our religious sense of the divine pathos. It ignores the "irrational" and anguished intimacy in God's whole long affair with the cosmos.

I suspect that only a theology that looks for concepts other than "design" and "order" can open us up—painfully, perhaps, but also salvifically—to the

1 The following text is an excerpt. Previously published in Haught, *God After Darwin*, 45–56. Reprinted with permission.

messiness, novelty, and chaos in Earth's life-story. An innocent preoccupation with design can obscure the theological riches we might recover by contemplating Darwin's "dangerous idea" in its rawness as well as its grandeur. Our facing openly and honestly the disquieting scientific accounts of life's evolution can expose us to the passionate and creative divine depths of nature much more nakedly than can a shallow skimming of isolated samples of order off of life's surface.

It is especially in this sense that the challenge by Darwin to theology—and I speak here from within a Christian context—may prove to be not so much peril as gift. Reflection on the Darwinian world can lead us to contemplate more explicitly the mystery of God as it is made manifest in the story of life's suffering, the epitome of which lies for Christians in the crucifixion of Jesus. In the symbol of the cross, Christian belief discovers a God who participates fully in the world's struggle and pain. The cruciform visage of nature reflected in Darwinian science invites us to depart, perhaps more decisively than ever before, from all notions of a deity untouched by the world's suffering.[2] Evolutionary biology not only allows theology to enlarge its sense of God's creativity by extending it over measureless eons of time; it also gives comparable magnitude to our sense of the divine participation in life's long and often tormented journey.

Hence Darwin's idea will indeed prove to be dangerous after all—dangerous not to theology as such but certainly to all the shallow theologies of order that ignore the divine attribute of co-suffering, or com-passionate involvement, in the life-process. After Darwin, we may still think of God as powerfully effective in the natural world, but we will have to do so in a manner quite distinct from that implied in much pre-evolutionary theology. Of course, in order to possess theological integrity, our thoughts about God after Darwin must be continuous with the authoritative scriptural and traditional sources of faith. But our attending to the details of evolution invites us to appropriate these sources in a fresh manner today.

## The Theological Task

How, though, can we accomplish such an objective in view of the position represented by Dawkins and Dennett on the one hand, and the reserve with which so many Christians and other religious believers have approached the topic of evolution on the other? Can theology after Darwin, instead of retreating from or only reluctantly accommodating Darwinian ideas, actually embrace them with enthusiasm?

2. See Rolston, *Science and Religion*, 144–146.

Here I shall propose that the central and original content of Christian faith provides us with an image of God that is not only logically consistent with but also fruitfully illuminative of the Darwinian picture of life. I must emphasize once again, of course, that when I use the term "Darwinian," I do not mean it in the materialistic sense often associated with it. Contrary to both Stephen Jay Gould and Phillip Johnson, I think it is quite possible to distinguish evolutionary science from the obsolete materialism that cripples both Darwin's and many of his followers' public presentations of it. Indeed, I would go so far as to say that when we look at evolutionary data in light of the biblical image of God, the life-process can make much more sense than when interpreted against the backdrop of materialist metaphysics. The undirected mutations, the process of natural selection, and the vastness of time required for the still unfolding story of life do not mandate the mechanistic conceptualization that Darwinians inherited from Newton and Descartes. Instead, the data of evolutionary science can be more intelligibly situated within a theological metaphysical framework centered around the biblical picture of "the humility of God."

The image of a vulnerable, defenseless, and humble deity may seem shocking to some, but it is crucial to the primordial Christian sense of the nature of ultimate reality. It is in a God who submits to crucifixion that Christian faith invites us to put the fullness of our trust. The portrait of God as a self-giving rather than self-aggrandizing mystery has always been implicit in the symbols of Christian faith. In fact, through its Trinitarian doctrine, Christianity has clearly made the crucifixion of Jesus an inner dimension of God's experience rather than something external to deity. But theologians and religious educators have often fled from this disquieting and revolutionary idea. When Christianity entered Western culture, as Alfred North Whitehead rightly indicates, the image of Caesar rather than that of the humble shepherd of Nazareth became the regnant model of God.[3] This specter of divinity as potentate still hovers over ideas about the "intelligent designer," whose existence is so tediously debated by creationists and evolutionary materialists.

Meanwhile, however, the ancient Christian sense of God's humility and vulnerability has once again begun to emerge more explicitly in contemporary theology. It has by no means penetrated the sensibilities of all believers and it is completely absent from scientific skeptics' typical caricatures of "God"—but today a good number of theologians consider it fundamental to Christian faith.[4] The image of a self-effacing God, although

3. See Whitehead, *Process and Reality*, 342.
4. Richard Dawkins, for example, has repeatedly asserted that the only real issue

always resident implicitly in Christology, is now—at least in the best of our theologies—beginning to supplant the specter of an invulnerable, immobile, and essentially nonrelational God that seems so antithetical to the world's evolutionary becoming and self-creativity.[5]

At the center of Christian faith lies a trust that, in the passion and crucifixion of Jesus, we are presented with the mystery of a God who pours the divine selfhood into the world in an act of unreserved self-abandonment. The utter lowliness of this image has led some theologians in our century to speak carelessly of God as "powerless." Dietrich Bonhoeffer, for example, wrote from prison that only a "weak" God can be of help to us.[6] Some process theologians, in their effort to avoid crude notions of divine omnipotence, also speak of a powerless God. The Roman Catholic theologian Edward Schillebeeckx, however, rightly argues that it is theologically unnecessary for us to deny God's power when we acknowledge the divine participation in the world's suffering. The image of God's humility does not imply weakness and powerlessness but rather a kind of "defenselessness" or "vulnerability." These attributes, as Schillebeeckx claims, can powerfully and effectively disarm evil. Paradoxically, it is through divine humility that the power of God becomes most effective. Since "power" means the capacity to bring about significant consequences, the concept need not be abandoned, but is instead endowed once again with the meaning given to it by the properly Christian sense of God. Schillebeeckx writes that "the divine omnipotence does not know the destructive facets of the human exercising of power, but in this world becomes 'defenceless' and vulnerable. It shows itself as a power of love which challenges, gives life, and frees human beings, at least those who hold themselves open to this offer."[7] Theological reflection on this image of divine defenselessness (which, I repeat, is not identical with powerlessness) can also help faith make sense of the ways of evolution, especially as these are depicted by neo-Darwinian biology.

The image of a self-emptying God lies at the heart of Christian revelation and the doctrine of the Trinity.[8] It is just this surprising portrait of the divine mystery that allows us to situate intelligibly the process of the world's creation and evolution. Theologian Jürgen Moltmann, influenced by Jewish Kabbalistic speculation, as well as classic Christian thought, argues that the

---

in the question of God and evolution is whether Darwin has destroyed the notion of a designing deity. See Dawkins, *River Out of Eden*, 59–93.

5. See Dawe, *Form of a Servant*.

6. See Bonhoeffer, *Letters*.

7. Schillebeeckx, *Church*, 90.

8. See Jüngel, *Doctrine of the Trinity*.

creation of the universe itself is not so much a display of divine might as the consequence of God's self-restraint:

> [God's] creative activity outwards is preceded by his humble divine self-restriction. In this sense, God's self-humiliation does not begin merely with creation . . . It begins beforehand, and is the presupposition that makes creation possible. God's creative love is grounded in his humble, self-humiliating love. This self-restricting love is the beginning of that self-emptying of God which Philippians 2 sees as the divine mystery of the Messiah. Even in order to create heaven and earth, God emptied Himself of his all-plenishing omnipotence, and as Creator took . . . the form of a servant.[9]

Moltmann is referring here to Saint Paul's appreciation of the paradox that Jesus Christ, the Lord of all, "emptied himself" (*ekenosen seauton*) and became the servant of all. Jesus's selfless submission to death is the main theme in a very early Christian hymn interpolated into chapter 2 of Paul's letter to the Philippians. Subsequent theological reflection on this hymn has led many theologians to conclude that it is ultimately God's own being that undergoes "kenosis," or "emptying."[10]

In faith's response to this self-emptying or "kenotic" image of God, there lurks, I think, a way of bringing new meaning not only to our perplexity at the broken state of social existence or individual human sufferings but also to our more recent bewilderment over the unfathomed epochs of wandering experimentation, struggle, apparent waste, and suffering that occur in the larger story of life as the result of evolution by natural selection.

The ways of nature take on a distinctively new definition when we view them in light of the vulnerability of God. In their apologetic response

9. Moltmann, *God in Creation*, 88.

10. Readers who may suspect that my focus here on the divine self-emptying is theologically novel or marginal may note that Pope John Paul II, in his recent encyclical "*Fides et Ratio*," also places the theme of God's *kenosis* at the center of theology: "The chief purpose of theology is to provide an understanding of Revelation and the content of faith. The very heart of theological enquiry will thus be the contemplation of the mystery of the Triune God. The approach to this mystery begins with reflection upon the mystery of the Incarnation of the Son of God: his coming as man, his going to his Passion, and Death, a mystery issuing into his glorious Resurrection and Ascension to the right hand of the Father, whence he would send the Spirit of truth to bring his Church to birth and give her growth. From this vantage-point, the prime commitment of theology is seen to be the understanding of God's kenosis, a grand and mysterious truth for the human mind, which finds it inconceivable that suffering and death can express a love which gives itself and seeks nothing in return" (John Paul II, "*Fides et Ratio*").

to evolutionary materialists, theists who focus exclusively on evidence of nature's design or order overlook the remarkable religious insight that divine
influence characteristically manifests itself in "weakness"—ways that do not
correspond to conventional views of power. Therefore, a truly responsive theology of evolution must bring to the fore faith's sense of the self-outpouring
God who lovingly renounces any claim to domineering omnipotence. The
same self-withdrawal of God that, according to Moltmann's interpretation,
makes creation initially possible (*creatio originalis*) also allows for the ongoing
creation (*creatio continua*) of the world through evolution.

A theology of evolution need not lose sight of other aspects of revelation, but it will make central the theme of divine suffering love. Biblical
teachings about God's word and promise, exodus, redemption, covenant,
justice, wisdom, the Logos made flesh, the Spirit poured out on the face
of creation, and the Trinitarian character of God are all indispensable to
Christian theology. But they disclose to us the nature of God only when
they are joined closely to the theme of divine vulnerability, which, for
Christians, assumes its most explicit expression in the life, death, and resurrection of Jesus.

The picture of an incarnate God who suffers along with creation is offensive to our customary sense of what should pass muster as ultimate reality.
But perhaps this image can be called "revelatory" precisely because it breaks
through the veil of our pedestrian projections of the absolute in such a way
as to bring new meaning to all of life's suffering, struggle, and loss. This new
meaning consists, in part at least, of the intuition that the agony of living
beings is not undergone in isolation from the divine eternity, but is taken up
everlastingly and redemptively into the very "life-story" of God.

Both scientific skeptics and anti-Darwinian Christian theists assume that the concept of the almighty as an "intelligent designer" scarcely
permits such participatory, empathetic association with the messiness
of nature. Though on opposite sides of the question of God's existence,
they share the assumption that an ordering deity is incompatible with a
universe in which the evolution of life occurs by way of natural selection.
Both sides, however, refuse to grant that "belief in the divine self-emptying
or condescension in Christ" is, in the words of theologian Donald Dawe,
"basic to Christian faith"[11]:

> God, in his creation and redemption of the world, accepted the
> limitations of finitude upon his own person. In the words of the
> New Testament, God had 'emptied himself, taking the form of a

11. Dawe, *Form of a Servant*, 13. I have dealt with the notion of God's humility at
greater length in Haught, *Mystery and Promise*, 199–214.

servant.' God accepted the limitations of human life, its suffering and death, but, in doing this, he had not ceased being God. God the Creator had chosen to live as a creature. God, who in his eternity stood forever beyond the limitations of human life, had fully accepted these limitations. The Creator had come under the power of his creation. This the Christian faith has declared in various ways from its beginning[12]

An evolutionary theology, it goes without saying, expands this picture of God's suffering so as to embrace also the struggles of the entire universe—and not just the brief history of our own species. God's empathy enfolds not just the human sphere but the whole of creation; this can mean only that the vast evolutionary odyssey, with all of its travail, enjoyment, and creativity, is also God's own travail, enjoyment, and creativity. Nothing that occurs in evolution can appropriately be understood by faith and theology as taking place outside of God's own experience.

In the words of Saint Paul, of course, such an understanding of God and God's ways amounts to "foolishness" in contrast to our conventional wisdom (1 Cor 1:25). How strange an idea the "humility of God" is in the history of human attempts to understand the absolute. John Macquarrie comments:

> That God should come into history, that he should come in humility, helplessness, and poverty—this contradicted every-thing—this contradicted everything that people had believed about the gods. It was the end of the power of deities, the Marduks, the Jupiters . . . yes, and even of Yahweh, to the extent that he had been misconstrued on the same model. The life that began in a cave ended on the cross, and there was the final conflict between power and love, the idols and the true God, false religion and true religion.[13]

We continue to resist this image of God's humility, even though, as Karl Rahner asserts, "the primary phenomenon given by faith is precisely the *self*-emptying of God," the divine kenosis.[14] Evolutionary science invites us, however, to appropriate more solemnly than ever this way of thinking about the divine mystery.

The real stumbling block to reconciling evolution with faith is not the "dangerous" features of evolution that Dennett dwells upon, but the scandalous image of God's humility that comes right from the heart of religious

12. Dawe, *Form of a Servant*, 13.
13. Macquarrie, *Humility of God*, 34.
14. Rahner, *Foundations of Christian Faith*, 222.

experience and not from the logic of design arguments. In debates about "God and evolution," theologians have usually focused on the question of how to reconcile God's "power" and "intelligence" with the autonomous, random, and impersonal features of nature's evolution. Too seldom have we entered into such reflection by thinking first of nature in terms of how it might appear if the creator of all things is, in essence, suffering love. In its encounters with evolutionary science, theology has generally preferred to assume a typically dictatorial concept of divine power. This bias has only led it to overlook or disavow those features of evolution that skeptics like Dawkins and Dennett consider to be most theologically lethal.

The reason, of course, that theology has resisted thinking of evolution in terms of the revelatory image of God's humility is that such an image seems to imply that God has too little power, perhaps even no power at all, to act in nature. And since any coherent faith or theology rightly demands that God be actively involved in the world, such a vulnerable and defenseless God does not seem capable of providing an adequate foundation for our hope in redemption, resurrection, and new creation. Perhaps it is for this reason, as Macquarrie observes, that "the God of Jesus Christ, like Yahweh before him, has been turned back again and again into a God of war or the God of the nation or the patron of a culture."[15]

So we cannot help asking again: is the Christian story of God's vulnerability really adequate for the religious need of a God whose power not only serves as the ultimate explanation of nature and its evolutionary creativity but also works to redeem an evolving world? Faith, it bears repeating, requires a God who is actively involved in the world. Yet our scientific understanding of the autonomously creative resourcefulness of natural selection, working over the course of immense periods of time, raises serious questions about how and whether God could be effectively operative in nature as science now understands it.

Why, we might ask with the Darwinians, do we need to posit any divine action at all if nature can create itself autonomously? After all, the main support for Dawkins and Dennett's atheism is the impression evolution gives them that life's astonishing creativity can be accounted for fully by the mindless filtering process known as "natural selection." And if nature is so self-creative, there is apparently no room for a providential, personal, and intelligent God to act or intervene in nature. In support of this conclusion, the skeptic might elicit even further confirmation from other branches of recent science, especially the new studies of complexity and chaos, which also feature the spontaneously "self-organizing" character of natural processes.

15. Macquarrie, *Humility of God*, 34.

However, theology may still provide an *ultimate* explanation of why evolutionary creativity occurs in the spontaneous and self-creative manner that it does. For if ultimate reality is conceived of neither as mindless and impersonal "matter," as materialism sees it, nor simply as an "intelligent designer," but fundamentally as self-emptying, suffering love, we should already anticipate that nature will give every appearance of being, in some sense, autonomously creative (autopoietic). Since it is the nature of love, even at the human level, to refrain from coercive manipulation of others, we should not expect the world that a generous God calls into being to be instantaneously ordered to perfection. Instead, in the presence of the self-restraint befitting an absolutely self-giving love, the world would unfold by responding to the divine allurement at its own pace and in its own particular way. The universe, then, would be spontaneously self-creative and self-ordering and its responsiveness to the possibilities for new being, offered to it by God, would require time—perhaps even immense amounts of it. The notion of an enticing and attracting divine humility, therefore, gives us a reasonable metaphysical explanation of the evolutionary process as this manifests itself to contemporary scientific inquiry.

Such an "ultimate," theological account of cosmic and biological evolution in no way interferes with purely scientific explanations of evolutionary events. The theological explanation I have just proposed does not seek in any way to supplant the autonomy of scientific discovery, nor to restrict the latter's scope. In fact, it shares with materialist evolutionism the need to place the results of all scientific discovery within at least some general understanding of the nature of reality. To formulate such a general vision is the task of *metaphysics*, some version of which we all carry with us, whether we are aware of it or not. What I am arguing throughout this book is that since we will inevitably situate our scientific understanding within one or another general vision of reality—or metaphysics—a most viable candidate is the theological conceptuality I am setting forth here. In my own opinion, this theological metaphysics is superior to the materialist alternative, both in explanatory power and in its respect for the autonomy of evolutionary science.

Although the theology set forth here will not compete with evolutionary science as such, it will stand in strong opposition to the materialist and scientistic dogmas that so often accompany evolution's public presentation, ironically much to the detriment of the advance of science itself. In subsequent pages, I shall provide a more substantive clarification of this important point.[16]

---

16. In other books, I have shown—in much greater detail—how appropriate

In any case, a theology of divine humility makes room for true novelty to spring spontaneously into being—a feature logically suppressed by deterministic materialist interpretations, as well as by the notion that the universe is simply the unfolding of an eternally fixed divine design or plan. Moreover, God's unobtrusive and self-absenting mode of being invites the world to swell forth continually, through immense epochs of temporal duration and experimentation, into an always free and open future, in the relatively autonomous mode of "self-creation" that science has discerned in cosmic, biological, and cultural evolution. Similarly, when framed by such a theological interpretation, the "irreducible" biochemical complexity that leads Michael Behe to reject Darwinian gradualism, no more demands any special divine creativity than is already present in the self-ordering of atomic entities, crystals, snowflakes, or other instances of "design." Autopoiesis becomes more complex as we move from nonliving to living forms of matter, but there is no need, in the case of the latter, to invoke special metaphysical principles and interventions. The compassionate divine concern for the world's internal integrity would make room for a considerable degree of autonomy and self-creativity on the part of the entire cosmos in increasingly subtle ways and at each new stage of nature's evolution.

Of course, to the empirical eye, within the self-limiting scope of purely scientific "explanation," the whole idea of God will rightly be considered superfluous. Science as such need never resort to the "God-hypothesis." But when we ask the deeper metaphysical question, "Why is nature permitted to evolve in a spontaneous, self-creative way?" a theology has every right to enter its own response as an alternative to materialism and "intelligent design theory." The metaphysics of divine humility, I am arguing, explains the actual features of evolution much more intelligibly than either of the main alternatives.

Consider, for example, the indefinitely extensive reservoir of genetic possibilities that we saw Dennett refer to earlier as Mendel's "library." Viewed against the metaphysical background of an ultimate, self-sacrificing love, this virtual archive is an extravagantly overflowing abundance of possibilities rooted in God's compassionate concern that the world be given full scope to "become itself." Moreover, God's gift of allowing the world to "become itself" is entirely consonant with and, in fact, renders plausible evolution's experimental winding through an endless field of potentialities, its random groping for relevant new forms of being, and the autonomous creativity in the life-process set forth by evolutionary science.

theological explanation in no way interferes with natural or scientific accounts of life and other emergent phenomena. See Haught, *Is Nature Enough?* and Haught, *Deeper Than Darwin.*

Such an understanding of God's love and power is not inconsistent with the existence of pain and struggle in nature and in human existence. There is, I think, no easy answer to the problem of suffering. It is an open sore that theology can never pretend to heal. Inevitably, all theodicies fail. The fact of evolution, however, introduces a dimension that previous responses to the problem did not have available to them. This is the simple fact that the universe is still in the process of being created. It is not yet finished and, if it is not yet finished, it cannot yet be perfect. An evolving universe may aim toward perfection, but at any moment prior to such an unimaginable fulfillment it will have to be not-yet-perfect. If it is not perfect, then we cannot be altogether surprised that imperfection, including the fact of pain, will be a part of it.

As I have pointed out already, the alternative theological notion of a divinely directed, perfectly ordered world that corresponds to our narrowly human notion of "intelligent design" would be theologically incoherent. The only kind of universe compatible with a God who loves—and therefore wills the independence of—the creation is one in which contingency is an essential ingredient. To living finite beings, this contingency can only entail that, along with the thrill of being alive and of having the opportunity for fuller and richer ways of being, there will also exist the possibility of suffering and eventual perishing.

Christian faith's image of a suffering God's eternal restraint, which allows for the world's self-creation, suggests to theology a notion of ultimate reality much more intimately involved with and powerfully effective in the world than a forcefully directive divine agency would be. God acts powerfully in the world by offering to it a virtually limitless range of new possibilities within which it can become something relatively autonomous and distinct from its creator. By giving the divine self away completely to the world, God encourages the world to develop as something radically "other" than the divine. This is how genuine love works. The general picture of evolution that Darwin gives us corresponds intelligibly with a religious vision that sees God as the source and exemplar of selfless love.[17]

If God is essentially compassionate love, however, we must also assume once again that all of the sufferings, struggles, and achievements of

17. God's "self-absenting" is, in fact, an intimate form of presence, after all. Though "withdrawn" from the world—in the sense that God is nonmanipulative of events—God can still be deeply present and effective as the ground of the world's very independence and freedom. God is also involved by being the world's inspiration (source of new possibilities) and redeemer (receiving the world-process into the transforming and enlivening divine experience). Indeed, the self-distancing of God, in the first sense, is a consequence of the intimate involvement of God in the second. On this point, see the perceptive article by Delio, "Humility of God," 36–50.

the evolving world do not take place outside of God's own empathetic care. A vulnerable God, as the Trinitarian nature of Christian theism requires, could not fail to feel intimately and to "remember" everlastingly all of the sufferings, struggles, and achievements in the *entire story* of cosmic and biological evolution. By holding these—and all cosmic occurrences—in the heart of divine compassion, God redeems them from all loss and gives eternal meaning to everything, though in a hidden way that, for us humans, only faith can affirm. Such a theological understanding is not only faithful to religious tradition but also *ultimately* explanatory of the world, as the latter now shows itself in the light of evolutionary science.

# 14: A God for Evolution[1]

TOWARD THE END OF his life, the famous Jesuit paleontologist Teilhard de Chardin (1881–1955) observed that traditional theological reflection has conceived of God's influence on nature too much in terms of Aristotle's notion of a prime mover pushing things from the past (*a retro*). Evolution, Teilhard said, requires that we think of God not as driving or determining events from behind or from the past, but as drawing the world from up ahead (*ab ante*), toward the future. Teilhard goes on to say that "only a God who is functionally and totally 'Omega' can satisfy us." But, he asks, "where shall we find such a God? And who will at last give evolution its own God?"[2]

Almost over half a century later, we still struggle with the same questions. It is not yet evident that theology has thought about God in a manner consistent with the data of evolution. Powerful voices in the religious world continue to hold the idea of an absolute reality as far away from evolution as possible. Even those theologians who have assented notionally to the compatibility of Darwin and theology have often failed to address the difficulties involved in such a novel union of ideas. A complete consummation of Teilhard's hopes for a vision of God deeply resonant with evolution still eludes us.

Probably no modern thinker has been more persistent than Teilhard in seeking to transform our theological sensibilities in a way that takes evolution seriously. Long before most of his fellow believers, he realized that the intellectual plausibility, as well as the renewal, of Christian faith in our day depends upon a sustained encounter with Darwinian ideas. Teilhard himself struggled for many years to spell out what he thought would be the invigorating spiritual outcome of such an engagement. And in terms of sheer inspirational force, it is hard even today to surpass the depth and passion of his own contributions to this venture.

But is Teilhard's religious thought itself adequate to Darwinian science? There have been considerable refinements in the scientific understanding of evolution since his day, especially in the areas of genetics and

1. Previously published in Haught, *God After Darwin*, 81–104. Reprinted with permission.

2. Teilhard de Chardin, *Christianity and Evolution*, 240.

molecular biology. Moreover, his notion of evolutionary "progress" has led some neo-Darwinians to write him off as an outdated ideologue. The late paleontologist Stephen Jay Gould, for example, was so certain that evolution is devoid of the directionality Teilhard discerned in it that he attempted to destroy completely the famous Jesuit's scientific reputation by making him appear to be an accomplice in the notorious Piltdown hoax.[3] Gould's scurrilous attack, incidentally, has been thoroughly debunked; but, to my knowledge, he never publicly retracted his claims, in spite of clear evidence that Teilhard could not have been involved.[4]

What would have led a scientist such as Gould to make such a gratuitous accusation? The renowned biochemist Harold Morowitz wonders "why Stephen Jay Gould decided to do a job on Teilhard de Chardin based on circumstantial evidence, none of which is supported by the latest findings."[5] Although Morowitz does not embrace the famous Jesuit's theology or teleology, he nonetheless professes to being an "admirer of Teilhard's biological writing." In fact, he finds Teilhard's ideas scientifically "insightful and often ahead of their time." Teilhard, for example, anticipated the theory of punctuated equilibrium—without calling it by that name—at a time when those who have since taken credit for it, namely, Gould and Niles Eldredge, were still "in short pants." Surely, though, it could not have been for this reason that Gould decided to pillory Teilhard in such a public way. Another possible explanation might be that Teilhard was a priest, whereas Gould was an agnostic. After all, it has not helped Teilhard's reputation in the scientific community that he was devoutly religious. Still, Morowitz reflects, "it is inconceivable that anyone with Gould's interests in fairness and civil liberties would have fingered a scientist because of his religious beliefs." Gould provocatively referred to Teilhard as a "cult figure." Morowitz asks us, however, to note the "rhetorical device" of representing Teilhard in this manner: "While there are many serious students of Teilhard's thought, they cannot be described as a cult. At the extreme, they form a scholarly association. Gould is not just describing Teilhard, but setting up the reader for the attack."

Daniel Dennett, who is not always sympathetic with Gould on some of the finer points of neo-Darwinian evolution, expresses even more bluntly what Gould may have been trying to say in his attacks on Teilhard. After devoting several pages of *Darwin's Dangerous Idea* to a crude caricature of

3. See Gould, "Piltdown Revisited"; Gould, "Piltdown Conspiracy"; and Gould, "Piltdown in Letters."

4. For a thorough discussion of Gould's charges (and a decisive refutation of them) see King, "Teilhard and Piltdown," 159–169.

5. Morowitz, *Kindly Dr. Guillotin*, 26–27.

Teilhard in order to make him seem scientifically incompetent, Dennett adds: "The problem with Teilhard's vision is simple. He emphatically denied the fundamental idea: that evolution is a mindless, purposeless, algorithmic process."[6]

This is not the place to debate the merits of either Teilhard's scientific reputation or his scientific understanding of evolution, nor is it necessary to do so. Suffice it to say, Gould's and Dennett's charges have been decisively refuted. Teilhard had the reputation in his day of being an excellent scientist. During his scientific career, he was judged to be one of the top geologists of the Asian continent. Had he lived to see the end of the twentieth century, there is no question that he would have kept up with the latest developments in biology.

What is worth talking about here is Teilhard's call for a new metaphysics in which to situate our understanding of evolutionary science. All scientists have at least an implicit metaphysics. Every scientific idea is presented against the backdrop of general assumptions about the nature of reality (which is what "metaphysics" is all about). Even in the case of the "purest" Darwinian accounts, metaphysical convictions are impossible to suppress. Teilhard simply wanted to make sure that the implicit metaphysical beliefs that scientists bring with them to the study of life do not blind them to what is really going on in an evolving universe. Like Bergson and Whitehead, he understood instinctively that the materialist metaphysics that frames the "scientific" ideas of many modern biologists is simply inadequate to the full reality of evolution.

Although science must be distinguished carefully from metaphysics, what scientists actually decide to focus on or leave out of their scientific pictures is deeply determined by their general visions of what is and is not real. Thus, as Teilhard would certainly argue, materialism, instead of leading scientists to see evolutionary data more clearly, actually closes them off to the most obvious feature of evolution—namely, its bringing about new being, or what we shall call "novelty." In the case of Gould and Dennett, both of whose "scientific" thinking is determined in great measure by an a priori commitment to materialist metaphysics, it is not Teilhard's science that really aroused their disdain but rather his demand for an alternative metaphysics. They are disturbed by Teilhard's own "dangerous idea," namely, that metaphysical materialism is incompetent to make full sense of the actual discoveries of evolutionary science. The extravagant lengths to which they have gone in order to distort Teilhard and his ideas is an indication that something much more contentious is occurring here than merely scientific

6. Dennett, *Darwin's Dangerous Idea*, 320.

disagreement. What really repels his materialist critics is Teilhard's suggestion that a metaphysically adequate explanation of any universe in which evolution occurs requires—at some point beyond the limits that science has set for itself—a transcendent force of attraction to explain the overarching tendency of matter to evolve toward life, mind, and spirit.

However, this postulated divine power of attraction, which Teilhard identified with the creative and redemptive God of his Christian faith, was never intended to be taken as a strictly scientific explanation. Teilhard does not introduce the notion of God simply to fill up a "gap" in scientific exploration. Rather, his appeal to a theological metaphysics is undertaken precisely so that our background assumptions, unlike those of materialist evolutionism, will allow all of the data of evolution, and especially the fact of emergent novelty, to stand out.

## A "Metaphysics of the Future"

What Teilhard seemed to be looking for is what we might call a "metaphysics of the future." "Metaphysics" is the term philosophers use to refer to the general vision of reality that one holds to be true. As Teilhard acknowledged explicitly, our religious thought has been dominated by a metaphysics of *esse* (or "being") that has obscured the obvious fact of nature's constant "becoming" and its perpetual movement toward the future. The metaphysics of "being" that we find in Plato and Aristotle was taken over in one form or another by Christian, Jewish, and Islamic theology and still forms the intellectual setting of much religious reflection in the West. An exclusivist preoccupation with "being" may have seemed appropriate to a static cosmos and to the classic hierarchical pictures of the cosmos reviewed in the preceding chapter. But evolution requires that we now entertain an alternative understanding of reality, one that stresses the prominence of the future.

Teilhard called his proposed alternative a "metaphysics of *unire*," that is, a conception of reality in which all things are drawn perpetually toward deeper coherence by an ultimate force of attraction, abstractly identified as Omega, and conceived of as an essentially future reality.[7] Evolution, to put it as directly as I can, seems to require a divine source of being that resides not in a timeless present located somewhere "up above," but rather in the *future*, essentially "up ahead," as the goal of a world still in the making. In this revised metaphysics, the term "God" must once again mean for us, as it did for many of our biblical forbears, the transcendent future horizon that draws the entire universe, and not just human history, toward an unfathomable

7. See Teilhard de Chardin, *Christianity and Evolution*, 237–243.

fulfillment yet to be realized. This, I think, is what Teilhard means when he says that God must become for us less Alpha than Omega.

Teilhard, therefore, surely would have endorsed the contemporary German theologian Jürgen Moltmann's persistent reminder that, in the biblical view of things, the word "God" means, before all else, "Future."[8] And he would have applauded the suggestions by another famous twentieth-century Jesuit scholar, Karl Rahner, who spoke of God as the "Absolute Future."[9] Likewise, he would be sympathetic with the Lutheran theologians Wolfhart Pannenberg and Ted Peters, who think of God as the "Power of the Future."[10] Between Teilhard's own lifetime and today, exegetical rediscovery of the prominent role of hope in biblical religion has made it more theologically appropriate than ever to think systematically of ultimate reality in terms of the dimension of "future."

Nevertheless, in spite of this century's reacquaintance with biblical eschatology and a God who relates to the world primarily in the mode of promise, Christianity's conversion to a metaphysics of the future, implicit in its biblical foundations, is still far from complete. This is the main reason why evolution does not yet have "its own God." After centuries of philosophical domination by Platonic and Aristotelian concepts, a considerable portion of Western theology and spirituality is still ruled by a metaphysics of the "eternal present," according to which the natural world is the always deficient reflection of—if not a perverse deviation from—a primordial perfection of "being" that exists forever in a fixed realm, generally pictured as above creation and untouched by time. In accordance with this traditional "metaphysics of the eternal present," the inevitable "becoming" that occurs in evolution can only be interpreted as meaningless straying from a timeless completeness, rather than as genuinely *new* creation.

Accordingly, when the idea of evolution made its appearance in Europe a century and a half ago, the new historical sense of nature-in-process ran up against a still Platonically sodden mind-set, incapable of accommodating a deep sense of the future. In spite of the biblical hope for new creation, what seems to have dominated our religious preconceptions is a strong suspicion that the future must somehow not be allowed to invade and transform the present. Aside from occasional apocalyptic expressions of hope for radical renewal, Western religious sensibilities still carry at least some residue of the pre-evolutionary prejudice that cosmic time can bring

8. Moltmann, *Experiment Hope*, 48.

9. Rahner, *Theological Investigations*, 59–68.

10. See Pannenberg, *Faith and Reality*, 58–59 and Peters, *God—The World's Future*.

about nothing that has not already been fully realized in a perfection existing from all eternity.[11]

Nostalgia for this lost perfection persists deeply in the souls of all of
us. It is not surprising, then, that evolution is still taken by many theologians as a relatively inconsequential process of becoming. After all, if being is a *fait accompli*, fully realized from all eternity, then evolution, when
interpreted within the classical framework of *esse*, can be relegated easily
to the same order of relative unimportance that pertains to all temporal
occurrence. One must wonder, therefore, whether evolution will ever find
"its own God," as long as theology and spirituality remain hostage to this
brand of metaphysics.

It is worth noting once again that biblical literalists are not the only
ones who cannot make room for evolution in their religious thinking. Intellectually sophisticated devotees of the "perennial philosophy," with their
notion of a "Great Chain of Being," have vehemently denied that evolution can be harmonized with the hierarchical vision of reality essential to
religion. Instead of revising this hierarchical metaphysics, with its static
sense of graded levels of being, proponents of the perennial philosophy
have found it more efficient to ignore, where they have not completely re-
nounced, Darwinian science.[12]

For its part, the typically materialist reading of evolution, following
what might be called a "metaphysics of the past," also logically rules out
the coming of a genuinely new future. Evolutionary materialism locates the
source and substance of life's diversity in the purely physical determinism
that, allegedly, has led, step by fateful step, out of the dead causal past to
the present state of living nature in all its profusion of complexity. Such
a metaphysics no more allows for the emergence of real novelty in evolution than does a religious metaphysics fixated on the eternal present. The
extravagant proliferation of living beings on this planet over the past several billion years—clear evidence of evolution's inclination to bring about
unprecedented novelty—is, for the pure materialist, nothing more than a
reshuffling of lifeless stuff that has always been there. Materialist versions
of neo-Darwinism claim that all events in nature, including the story of life
and mind on Earth, were implicitly coiled up in lifeless primordial cosmic
conditions. Nature needed only to undergo the somewhat incidental drama
of gradually unfurling over the course of time in order for life and mind to
make their unremarkable appearance. Conceived of in this way, the entire

11. For more support of this observation, see Teilhard de Chardin, *Christianity and Evolution*.

12. See Nasr, *Religion and the Order of Nature*, 146.

life-process, rather than being evidence of nature's openness to the arrival of genuine novelty, is only the explication of what was fully latent already in lifeless matter from the time of cosmic beginnings.

It is not hard to find examples of this "metaphysics of the past" in contemporary pessimistic interpretations of evolution. Once again, perhaps the most overt example is Daniel Dennett's convoluted argument that evolution is nothing more than an "algorithmic" process, fully explainable by tracing present outcomes back to their determining physical causes in the past. In order to understand the present, Dennett argues, all we need is to practice a "reverse engineering" of sorts. This is the procedure of figuratively taking apart complex things, such as living beings, piece by piece, in order to disclose how the implacable laws of nature assembled them over the course of time without anticipating any future goal. Reverse engineering will show that the deterministic laws of nature, not any attraction to the future, can fully explain how evolution happens.[13]

I have found Dennett's position especially worth noting in this book not because it has much light to shed on the evolutionary process, but because it so nakedly sets forth the materialist metaphysical assumptions espoused by many distinguished neo-Darwinian scientists.[14] In principle, Dennett's fatalistic vision, not unlike the tragic stoicism that has haunted much modern scientific thought, resolutely prohibits the emergence of true novelty. Dennett, no doubt, would reply that the virtual archive of yet untried genetic combinations is enough to guarantee the perpetual renewal of life. However, the existence of life and the process of evolution requires an informational coefficient that does not itself originate in any past series of mechanical causes and that therefore cannot be accounted for by the method of reverse engineering. By definition, an atomistic, reductive method of inquiry into the past "causes" of life will abstract from the very organizational principles and informational patterns that give living beings their characteristic identities in the first place.[15]

13. Dennett, *Darwin's Dangerous Idea*, 212–216 and 246–250.

14. See Smith, *Did Darwin Get It Right?*

15. In order to undertake reverse engineering, we first must be able to identify an *organizational whole* that allows for such disassembly. But this holistic recognition cannot itself be the consequence of the analytic-particulate method that Dennett takes to be the privileged road to understanding. We always start reverse engineering with what we take to be a meaningfully patterned totality and, as we move our inquiry back into the past, *this pattern itself dissolves*. The reason it dissolves is that it was only there in the mode of being *anticipated* in the first place. Pattern, form, or information is that *toward which* evolving processes move. Information's ontological status is fundamentally future. It is in this sense that Dennett's algorithmic and atomistic approach fails to account for the real novelty without which evolution could not occur.

I would submit here that the novel informational possibilities that evolution has available to it arise from the always dawning future. It is the arrival of the future—and not the grinding onward of an algorithmic past—that accounts for novelty in evolution. Without the persistent coming of an unrehearsed future, the present and the past would have no opening onto the path of transformation. Evolution is rendered possible only because of the temporal clearing made available when the future faithfully introduces relevant new possibilities. The apparent "contingencies" (in the sense of undirected occurrences) in natural history, which appear to shape evolution in all of the serendipitous and unpredictable ways that Gould's writings highlight, are themselves made possible only because of the temporal gift of an open future. Contingent events, then, are not themselves ultimately explanatory of evolutionary novelty, for their own occurrence is itself fundamentally dependent on time's opening toward the future. It is not the occurrence of contingency that brings about the future, rather, it is the arrival of the future that allows events to have the status of contingency—that is, to be more than just the inevitable outcome of past deterministic causes.

Evolutionary materialism's picture of things has attained its intellectual appeal only at the price of abstracting from the concrete actuality of nature in process. What it leaves out is a sense of the "coming of the future" as the fundamental "force" in evolutionary occurrence. Following the ideas of Wolfhart Pannenberg and Ernst Bloch, giving voice to what I think are the sentiments of Teilhard, Rahner, Moltmann, as well as many process theologians, I would argue that we need to situate our understanding of nature's evolution within a "metaphysics of the future."

A metaphysics of the future is rooted in the intuition, expressed primordially in the biblical experience, of what is "really real," that the abode of ultimate reality is not limited to the causal past nor to a fixed and timeless present "up above." Rather, it is to be found most characteristically in the constantly arriving and renewing future. Such a vision, conceptually difficult though it may be, can suitably accommodate both the data of evolutionary biology and the extravagant claims of biblical religion about how a promising God relates to the world.

Let me emphasize, however, that I am not insisting that scientists, insofar as they remain conscious of science's methodological self-limitations, need to take into account explicitly this dimension of the future in their work. Science has every right to leave out any such reference since, as far as scientific method is concerned, a reference to the future would implausibly attribute efficient causation to events that have not yet occurred. Nevertheless, I would argue that the inability on the part of science itself to entertain a metaphysics of the future is a consequence of the abstract nature of scientific work. In saying that science is abstract, I do not mean that science does not deal with concrete reality. What I mean to suggest is that each science has to leave out broad bands of nature's actual complexity in order to say anything clearly at all. The particle physicist as such, for example, has nothing to say about whether Darwinian selection is the only cause of all creativity in the biosphere, or about the function of mitochondrial DNA. A lot has to be left out if science is to achieve any clear results. What I am emphasizing here is that, by focusing on efficient and material causes, science typically abstracts from the futurity of being.[16]

We need a wider vision of reality than science itself can offer, one that makes sense of the most obvious aspects of life's evolution, in particular the fact that it brings about new forms of being. Dennett's mechanistic materialism may seem to provide an appropriate set of background assumptions for explaining some aspects of evolution, but it is too abstract to encompass and account for the novelty that emerges in the life-process. For example, the assumptions of materialist metaphysics can provide no illumination regarding the surprising emergence in evolution of what we all know immediately as the experience of our "subjectivity." Materialist interpretations of evolution have so far shed no light whatsoever on the question of why living beings have developed something like an "inner sense." And it is especially in the ongoing intensification of inwardness that what I am calling "novelty" enters into the material universe.

This inability to take the fact of subjectivity into account is indicative of the more general incapacity of materialism to adjust itself to novelty as such. Materialism is closed a priori to the prospect of there arising truly new being in evolution since, by definition, it has identified being with the mindless "matter" already present prior to life's evolution. Most materialists, of course, will allow that unprecedented arrangements of mindless matter appear in evolution constantly. But the underlying being or reality of all such configurations, including entities endowed with a high degree of subjectivity, consists of lifeless and mindless atomic constituents, rather than of the elusive informational patterns by which they are ordered and in which their novelty is realized.

16. See Polanyi, *Personal Knowledge* and *Tacit Dimension* for a defense of the human need to root all of knowledge in some (faith) commitment or other.

## The Power of the Future

An alternative view of reality, one more commensurate with the evidence provided by evolutionary novelty, is a metaphysics that gives priority to the future rather than to the past or the present. But what exactly do we mean by this oddly named "metaphysics of the future"? I am compelled, in a way, to resist the invitation to clarify. To "clarify" something almost always means—at least in academic circles—to situate it in terms of either the classical metaphysics of *esse* or, in a more modern vein, the metaphysics of the past that hovers over scientific materialism. By definition, the futurity of being cannot be translated into these alien provinces without having its very heart cut out of it in the process.

Let me emphasize, therefore, that the notion of a metaphysics of the future has an irreducibly religious origin. Such an admission will undoubtedly lead anyone committed to either of the other two metaphysical frameworks to judge my commitments as an evasion of "reality." However, I would simply respond that the metaphysics I am espousing here is rooted deeply in the *experience* that people have of something that to them is overwhelmingly and incontestably real, namely, what may be metaphorically called the "power of the future." Of course, it is perhaps only by adopting the religious posture of hope that they have been opened to the experience of this power. But that they are prepared for such an experience by participation in a particular religious tradition, one that encourages them to place their trust in the promise of a surprising future fulfillment, need not be taken a priori as sufficient reason for our suspecting its veracity.

Faith, at least in the biblical context, is the experience of *being grasped* by "that which is to come." Any theology that seeks to reflect such faith accurately, therefore, is required to attribute some kind of efficacy to the future, difficult though this may be to conceptualize clearly. A metaphysics of the future is already implicit in a certain kind of religious experience. Paul Tillich describes it as a sense of being grasped by the "coming order": "The coming order is always *coming*, shaking this order, fighting with it, [both] conquering it and conquered by it. The coming order is always at hand. But one can never say: 'It is here! It is there!' One can never grasp it. *But one can be grasped by it.*"[17]

In the experience of faith, it is the "future" that comes to meet us, takes hold of us, and makes us new. We may call this future, at least in what Rahner calls its "absolute" depth, by the name "God." In biblical circles, the very heart of authentic faith consists of the total orientation of consciousness

17. Tillich, *Shaking of the Foundations*, 27 (emphasis added).

toward the coming of God, the ultimately real. Beyond all of our provisional or relative futures there lies an "Absolute Future." And since our own experience cannot be separated artificially from the natural world to which we are tied by evolution, we are also permitted to surmise that "being grasped" by the Absolute Future pertains not just to ourselves but also to the whole cosmic process in which we are sited. Theology can claim legitimately, along with Saint Paul (Rom 8:22), that the *entire universe* is always being drawn by the power of a divinely renewing future. The "power of the future" is the ultimate metaphysical explanation of evolution.

The sense of being grasped by the power of the future is palpable to religious experience, but it cannot be translated without remainder into scientifically specifiable concepts, precisely because science typically attributes efficacy only to what lies in the causal past. Nevertheless, if we follow Whitehead's pertinent metaphysical reminder that an investigation of human experience provides rich concepts that can be applied (by analogy) to the events that make up the rest of nature, then theology can infer that the same "power of the future" that grasps us in faith also embraces the entire cosmos.

If this all sounds too metaphorical to be scientifically palatable, we may recall here the role that metaphor also plays in scientific explanation. Evolutionary biology in particular has to employ metaphorical language. Even a scientist as reductionistic as Richard Dawkins complains of the "physics envy" among some of his fellow biologists who seek to escape metaphor by collapsing nature's hierarchical structure down to the level of physics, where only mathematics is appropriate.[18] The explanatory success of Darwinian biology, Dawkins insinuates, has occurred *because* of, not in spite of, its reliance on foggy but still illuminating metaphors such as "adaptation," "cooperation," "competition," "survival," and "selection."

To admit that the notion of the "power of the future" is also metaphorical, therefore, is in no sense to diminish its explanatory competence. Accordingly, by a "metaphysics of the future," I mean quite simply the philosophical expression of the intuition—admittedly religious in origin—that all things receive their being from out of an inexhaustibly resourceful "future" that we may call "God." This intuition also entails the notion that the cosmic past and present are in some sense given their own status by the always arriving

18. See Dawkins's critique of "physics envy" in Brockman, "Introduction," 23–24. However, as Niles Eldredge rightly points out, Peter Medawar's label, "physics envy," is no less applicable to Dawkins, who—in spite of his and Dennett's claims that he is not a "greedy" reductionist—borrows from physics the atomistic ideal of explanation and applies it univocally to his "selfish genes," which, for him, are sufficient for explaining life and evolution.

but also always unavailable future.[19] If such an idea at first seems difficult, we need only observe that even our most ordinary experience readily corresponds to this way of thinking about reality. Only a brief reflection suffices to convince us that the past is gone and remains irretrievable while the present vanishes before we can ever grasp hold of it. The "future," on the other hand, is always arriving faithfully at the green edge of each moment, bringing with it the possibility of new being. What has already been consigned to the fixed past is not itself enough to explain the novelty of evolutionary occurrences. We can only look to the future to find the ultimate source from which new life and new species of life arise.

It should not be too hard for us to appreciate, therefore, why a religion that encourages its devotees to wait in patient hope for the fulfillment of life and history will interpret ultimate reality—or God—as coming toward the present and continually creating the world, from the sphere of the future "not-yet." Such an idea, I once again admit, will not make sense to everyone immediately. In fact, many of us think intuitively of the future as quite "unreal," since it has not yet fully arrived. The past and the present may seem to have more "being," in the sense of fixed reality, than the future, which apparently has the character of not-yet-being. So the idea of a *metaphysics* of the future will probably seem confusing, at least at first.

However, perhaps this confusion is the result of our having been bewitched by a metaphysics either of the past or of the eternal present. Modern scientific thinking, which has affected all of us deeply, is not ready to abandon its passionate allegiance to the explanatory primacy of the causal past. Consequently, it seems to scientistic thinkers such as Dennett that everything that occurs in cosmic or biological evolution is simply the unfolding of what has already gone before. We are compelled to acknowledge, I think, that, in such a view of reality, there is no room for the emergence of anything truly new or, in principle, unanticipated. There is something very safe but also very stale, about such a vision of things. It thoroughly suppresses the possibility of any real informational novelty and surprise that might disturb the prospect of complete scientific

19. This formulation is one that I have put together on the basis of my reading not only of Teilhard, but also of Ernst Bloch, Wolfhart Pannenberg, Karl Rahner, and their many followers. See also Hans Küng, *Eternal Life*, 213–214. Küng indicates how deeply indebted Christian theology is to the philosopher Ernst Bloch—and to Bloch's main theological follower, Jürgen Moltmann—for retrieving the futurist orientation of the biblical vision of reality, one that, for centuries, had been buried beneath the metaphysical categories which Christian theology takes from Greek philosophy. See Bloch, *Principle of Hope* and Moltmann, *Coming of God*. In addition, see Williams, *True Resurrection* and Lynch, *Images of Hope*.

prediction or that might challenge us, as part of the evolving universe, to let new creation occur in our own lives.

At the same time, however, I think we must also confess that many of our traditional theologies and spiritualities are equally reluctant to terminate their long affair with the Greek philosophical world's metaphysics of the eternal present, a way of thinking about the real that also forbids the occurrence of anything truly new. The traditional hierarchical vision—according to which all the levels of finite being are held up from above and sacramentally permeated by an eternal, timeless *arche*—is certainly preferable to the modern materialist metaphysics of the past. Materialism, after all, is nothing less than what Paul Tillich and Hans Jonas have perceptively called an "ontology of death," a way of thinking that gives the status of "reality" only to lifeless units of "matter."[20] However, as far apart as the traditional hierarchical view of being is from modern materialist metaphysics, it unfortunately joins with the latter in its cadaverous tendency to nullify the future.

The interior logic of both of these prominent metaphysical options—and indeed what may partially explain their appeal—is their aversion to the future or, in other words, their shared inclination to shut out the disturbing arrival of genuinely new possibilities. Both modern science, with its Newtonian sense of the theoretical reversibility of time, and the traditional hierarchical depiction of the sacred think of what is "really real" in terms that make the passage of time, and hence the coming of a new future, more or less inconsequential. Even though the new studies of complexity and chaos call for an alternative metaphysical horizon for science, there is still enormous resistance to most efforts to supplant the mechanistic worldview.[21]

The Oxford physical chemist Peter Atkins, for example, declares that all the variety in the life-world is merely simplicity *masquerading* as complexity.[22] As this formula implies, the present complex state of nature is mere appearance concealing the lifeless physical simplicity that, for Atkins, is the only true *reality* underneath and temporally prior to the masquerade. Here, the accomplishments of time and the constant arrival of the future are discounted as purely incidental, concealing the harsh truth that only past simplicity is fundamental. Such a way of looking at things ignores the reality of time and implies that the emergent novelty in evolution is only a charade. The limitless possibilities lurking in the future

---

20. Tillich, *Systematic Theology*, 3:9–10.

21. For a scholarly critique of Newtonian assumptions, see Ulanowicz, *Ecology*.

22. Atkins, *2nd Law: Energy, Chaos, and Form*, 200.

are here disregarded, since only physically simple constituents originating in the past can claim to be causally real.

Steven Weinberg's well-received reflections on contemporary physics share the same tendency to abstract from time and the resourcefulness of the future. Weinberg argues that, in the field of particle physics, science is inching ever closer to an irreducibly simple and comprehensive understanding of nature. Once we have acquired a firm hold on the "fundamental" simplicity of which science "dreams" so feverishly, we will be in a position to write a "final theory" of the universe. All that will be left for science to do afterward is merely to describe, in more and more refined detail, how the ultimate simplicity has led to the astounding complexity we see all around us. But the real work of scientific discovery will be over.[23] Along the same lines, science writer John Horgan recently garnered the impression from interviews with several other well-known contemporary scientists that we are at last reaching the end of science.[24] Horgan suspects that science has almost completed the long human quest to understand the makeup of the universe, so science as we know it may be about to disappear. Explanation is going to give way to pure description. As Peter Atkins puts it: "When we have dealt with the values of the fundamental constants by seeing that they are unavoidably so, and have dismissed them as irrelevant, we shall have arrived at complete understanding. We are almost there. Complete knowledge is within our grasp."[25]

That such a thought occurs at all is testimony to the uncritical allegiance some scientific thinkers have had to the imprisoning and depressing "metaphysics of the past" that has governed so much of modern thought. As long as we keep looking "back there" in the cosmic past for what is most "fundamental"—as physicists, biologists, geneticists, astronomers, and other scientists are accustomed to doing—we close our eyes to what is most obvious to all human experience, namely, the arrival of an always unprecedented future; and we inevitably rob science of its own future as well.

As we turn our attention more and more exclusively to the cosmic past, we find that our search for the world's intelligibility will always elude us since everything back there eventually fades out into the incoherence of a primordial multiplicity. The sense of coherence that we associate with intelligibility can be discerned only by our looking toward the world's ultimate future, not by dwelling on the atomic diffusion of the universe's remotest past. Hence a disposition of hope may be essential to any truly

23. See Weinberg, *Dreams of a Final Theory*, 18 and 51–64.

24. See Horgan, *End of Science*.

25. Atkins, *Creation Revisited*, 157.

radical quest for understanding what the universe is all about. In this vein, Teilhard writes:

> Like a river which, as you trace it back to its source, gradually diminishes till in the end it is lost altogether in the mud from which it springs, so existence becomes attenuated and finally vanishes away when we try to divide it up more and more minutely in space or—what comes to the same—to drive it further and further back in time. The grandeur of the river is revealed not at its source but at its estuary.[26]

For this reason, I would suggest that a metaphysics of the future not only allows scope for the hopes of religion but also provides an open-ended and more realistic framework for the ongoing adventure of scientific discovery. For our purposes here, such a metaphysics allows us to make better sense of Darwinian science than the purely mechanistic framework that typically swamps, distorts, and deadens much of the novel information that we associate with evolution.

## An Ultimate Explanation of Evolution

Once again, I would not deny that a serious commitment to the metaphysical primacy of the future may be possible only if we first learn personally to dwell within a tradition or a faith community that enables us to develop the skills of seeing things in a hopeful rather than pessimistic way. Obviously, those who idealize a kind of knowing allegedly devoid of any such commitment will claim that a consciousness attuned to the sense of reality's promise is hopelessly subjective and incapable of being "objective." However, as I have noted already, commitment to a metaphysics of the past or to a metaphysics of the eternal present is no less a matter of belief than is the one that I am defending here. Honesty compels us to acknowledge the inevitably personal, fiduciary, and passionate commitments that underlie all of our knowing, including the alleged "realism" of modern scientific materialism. I am merely proposing that, with respect to contextualizing evolutionary phenomena, the sense of promise in which biblical religion seeks so earnestly to implant our hearts, and by which it also seeks to orient our lives and thoughts, entails a vision of the real that can claim a legitimacy far exceeding the conventional alternatives. In addition, I would argue that it is precisely the implied metaphysics of the future that can best account

---

26. Teilhard de Chardin, *Hymn of the Universe*, 77.

for the three cosmic qualities—chance, lawfulness, and temporality—that allegedly provide the raw stuff of biological evolution.

No doubt there is a risk involved in the kind of commitment I am proposing here as the appropriate framework for understanding evolution. But it is only by allowing ourselves to be imprinted by the sensibilities of a specific religious tradition—and not by remaining safely uncommitted and, in turn, allegedly neutral or presuppositionless—that we can gain an appreciation of the ultimate futurity of being. We may never experience fully the ontological power of the future without first "indwelling" a specific narrative history, wherein a saving future invades the present unpredictably and opens up the world to previously undreamed possibilities. When the Bible speaks of the dramatic action of God in the world, it is giving expression to generations of human experience in which an unpredictable and surprising future has often interrupted the normal course of events, confounding all "realistic" expectations. Our visions of reality today have been so hamstrung by a metaphysics of the past or a metaphysics of the eternal present that we may no longer instinctively feel the competence of the biblical stories to open us up to what is truly new. Indeed, it may even seem irrational, given conventional standards of rationality, for us to allow our consciousness to be enfolded by the biblical narratives of promise and hope.

However, it seems to me that we can get to the point of the biblical narratives, and thus be grasped by their meaning, not when we look at them, as our objectifying intellectual criticism compels us to do obsessively, but only when we look *with* them—in the here and now of our own lives—to a future that may interrupt our own present in as surprising a way as the stories themselves also claim to have happened in the lives of our religious ancestors. Biblical accounts of the "mighty acts of God," whatever judgments we make regarding their historical facticity, are, at least, the clear records of generations of religious openness to clues that point us toward a future coherence that can potentially conquer our own present lostness and confusion. At the same time, these biblical accounts empower us to expect—in a way that goes beyond the predictions of science, without also contradicting them—that the cosmic process will finally be redeemed from the insignificance that alternative metaphysical outlooks logically expect.

It is to such an anticipated but not yet fully actualized coherence that a metaphysics of the future points. And this anticipated integration is the goal and ground not only of our human hopes but also of cosmic and biological evolution. I am convinced that much of the contemporary resistance to situating evolution within a futurist metaphysics is rooted in established beliefs about reality, according to which the natural world is constituted either eternally from above or deterministically *a retro*. In the one case, evolutionary developments provide us only with flashes or reminiscences of a lost eternal and perfect world; in the other, evolution is merely the impersonal unfolding of a mathematical simplicity that first appeared at some remote (and usually unspecified) time, long ago, in nature's past.

If mechanism-materialism makes the cosmic past the crucible in which all present and future states of nature's evolution are fashioned, a religious metaphysics of *esse* is no less inclined to cover up the possible emergence in creation of what is truly new. In both cases, it bears repeating, being is *already* virtually given in full, whether eternally from above or implicitly in the indefinite cosmic past. There is no room in either standpoint for the emergence of real novelty, so both standpoints imply that the future will be inherently barren. In these lusterless conceptions, the future is nothing more than the predictable "outcome" of what has gone on before in time or eternity. In either set of metaphysical beliefs, no cognition, but only *re-cognition*, is possible. Hence, my suggestion that the coming of the future into the present might be the ultimate ground of evolutionary novelty will hardly sit comfortably in the world of conventional religious and scientific thought.

And yet, I am convinced that numerous puzzles that arise in our reflections on evolution will simply fall away as pseudoproblems if we situate the Darwinian picture of things within the framework of a theological metaphysics of the future. Why is nature ordered and yet open to disorder? Why doesn't contingency or chance, so prominent in evolution, prevent order from emerging? Why is natural selection so rigorously lawful and yet open to indeterminate new creation? Why does the world have the temporal character that allows evolution to occur at all? These are all questions that remain without answer when we view them through a metaphysics of the eternal present or the deterministic past. But if we place them within the horizon of the coming of the future, then evolution not only begins to make scientific sense but also—at last—to have "its own God."

I realize, of course, that such a readjustment of our vision of reality may not occur without a certain degree of anxiety, not to mention intellectual bewilderment.[27] The idea that the future, that realm which Ernst Bloch referred to as *not-yet-being*, is what powers evolution will make little sense

27. Some of the philosophical and theological difficulties posed by the notion of a metaphysics of the future have been addressed already in a collection of essays edited by Braaten and Clayton, *Theology of Wolfhart Pannenberg*. In spite of the paradoxes that arise in the context of conventional philosophical discourse—which now mostly embraces natural science's own inclination toward a metaphysics of the past—the Christian theologian must still take seriously and must attempt, conceptually, to unpack (however stumblingly) what it means for a biblically based faith to affirm that God is the "Power of the Future." For an excellent and accessible study of the spiritual, social, and theological implications of this metaphor, see Peters, *God—The World's Future*.

within the framework of the tacit metaphysics underlying current scientific notions of causation and explanation. If the future is not yet available, how can it be explanatory or have metaphysical priority? Isn't the future itself a mode of nonbeing, therefore incapable of grounding the being of nature and its evolution? A metaphysics of the future, and of a God who creates out of the future, seems a contradiction in terms.

Here, though, it may be illuminating to recall ideas I mentioned in previous chapters about the creative and redeeming potency that resides, paradoxically, in the humility of God and the "informational," Taolike character of divine action. I have emphasized already that theology may assume that ultimate reality is informationally effective only by being hidden from the arena of causation familiar to science:

Invisible, it cannot be called by any name.

It returns again to nothingness.[28]

The Taoist intuition is that nature is informationally shaped by the noninterfering effectiveness of ultimate reality. Similarly, as I have proposed along with other Christian and Jewish theologians, it is the "self-withdrawal" of any forceful divine presence and the paradoxical hiddenness of God's power in a self-effacing persuasive love that allows creation to come about, unfolding freely and indeterminately in evolution. It is in God's self-emptying humility that the fullest effectiveness resides.

Consistent with these religious intuitions, a theology of hope also attributes the deepest kind of potency to what is not yet available, in this case, the Absolute Future. We may even speculate that the arena into which God "withdraws" in order to allow for the relatively autonomous self-creation of evolution is that of the unavailable but infinitely resourceful future. We can speak of God's "self-withdrawal" only in terms of a paradox in which the other side of the retracting of divine presence is the most intimate *involvement* of God in the world's evolution. There is nothing remotely deistic about such a proposal. The notion that God is present in the mode of an always arriving future allows us to understand how God can be most intimately involved in the world's continual coming into being without being a datum available to present comprehension.

Because God is the world's future, we cannot discover God by scrutinizing only the past and the present. For this reason, ultimate reality lies off-limits to any scientific verification oriented toward the past alone. But the empirical unavailability of God is consistent with the effectiveness of divine humility and the infinite generosity entailed in the notion of God's

28. Chang, *Tao*, 72.

futurity. In terms of the theological perspective adopted here, to locate the divine reality essentially in the future is not at all to deprive the past and present of the divine presence. However, it is essentially as their future that God becomes present to past and present occurrences. Put otherwise, the past and present are taken continually and forever into the divine future. As such, they never fade into absolute nothingness but are redeemed by being taken up into the novel patterns of beauty that emerge within the horizon— the coming of the Absolute Future.

Once again, I suspect that this biblical notion of God as the world's future may seem novel because our minds have been so thoroughly shaped (or perhaps I should say misshaped) by alternative ways of thinking about the real as either fundamentally past or eternally present. We are not accustomed to envisaging the realm of power as that which lies up ahead rather than behind us or up above us in a timeless place of Platonic perfection. And yet, a metaphysics of the future should not be completely foreign to any of us who have been formed religiously by the traditions that come down from Abraham, the exemplar of all who live out of the future. Arguably, the most distinctive and precious contribution of biblical religion to human life and consciousness is its impression that reality is shaped by promise, a notion that naturally brings the horizon of futurity into view. By urging us to "wait upon the Lord," to live in trust and hope, the biblical vision inevitably locates the fullness of being in an arena that we can only locate "up ahead" and neither "up above" in a timeless heaven of total perfection nor behind us in the fixed routines of past physical causation.

Today, even science seems almost on the verge of a revolutionary shift away from its characteristic understanding of causation only in terms of the impact of the past on the present. Recent scientific descriptions of self-organization, chaos, and complexity in nature often barely conceal the haunting premonition that these occurrences are all *anticipative*. Somehow drawn toward an indeterminate future, these events are more than just the predictable unfolding of a determining past series of causes. Even if chaos is taken to be physically deterministic—in the sense that, from the point of view of physics, chaotic phenomena do not violate the rigid laws of nature—unpredictable novelty can still take up residence in these systems at higher hierarchical and informational levels. Most natural systems are open to indeterminate outcomes without violating the laws of physics and chemistry. In ways that we do not yet understand fully, complex physical systems unfold in time almost as if they "know" where they are going. Their future states, though not yet realized in actuality, exercise a quietly formative effect on them in every moment of their evolution, shaping their trajectories in *absentia*, as it were. Our metaphysics of the future provides an appropriate setting for these phenomena, as well as for Darwinian evolution.

The metaphysical relocation of transcendence into the future—Teilhard's *ab ante*—will neither appeal to those who are satisfied with the way things are nor to those who seek to restore some past epoch in the history of nature, culture, or religion. The horizon of futurity will possibly loom more faintly for those of us who have than for those who *have not*. However, for the destitute and dispossessed, for the wretched of the Earth, for the *anawim* of Yahweh, there remains only the future to sustain their lives and aspirations.

A major part of the message of prophetic religion is that the dreams that arise among the poor are not naive illusions but compelling clues about the true nature of the real. The seeds of our metaphysics of the future are sown in the fields of the fortuneless. Perhaps only by allowing our own lives to be integrated into the horizon of their dreams and expectations, that is, by our own "solidarity with victims," can we too make ourselves vulnerable to the power of the future? Religious infatuation with the past or romantic nostalgia for an ahistorical, eternal present, on the other hand, can all too easily allow us to legitimate the miserable circumstances of the afflicted and thus close us off to the future that their own suffering opens up.

What I am proposing here, then, is that the metaphysics implied in this religious vision of an unsettling but redeeming future also provides a coherent framework for *theologically* locating and understanding the fact of biological and cosmic evolution. The "power of the future" sensed most palpably by the poor and oppressed, the future toward which we also are invited to look for renewal and freshness of being, must—theologically speaking—also be the *fundamental* explanation of nature's evolution.

The prominence of the divine future in shaping our own religious "mentality" provides theology with an inkling of how God relates to the rest of nature as well. Theologically speaking, we may surmise that evolution occurs at all only because, in some analogous sense, all of nature is being addressed by the future that we call God. Evolution happens, ultimately, because of the "coming of God" toward the entire universe from out of an always elusive future. And just as the arrival of God does not enter the human sphere by crude extrinsic forcefulness but rather by participating in it and energizing it from within, we may assume that it does not enter coercively into the prehuman levels of cosmic and biological evolution either. The coming of God into nature, like the nonintrusive effectiveness of the Tao, is always respectful of the world's presently realized autonomy. God's entrance into the present and invitation to new creation may be so subtle and subdued as to go completely unnoticed by a science oriented only toward the temporal past and unappreciated by a philosophical theology that turns us only toward a timeless and already completed plenitude of being.

Our metaphysics of the future can also provide an ultimate explanation for the contingency, lawfulness, and temporality that have sometimes been identified as the "raw ingredients" of Darwinian evolution. Darwinian evolution, as I think most scientists would agree, can occur only in a certain kind of universe, one that already possesses just the right proportions of randomness, regularity, and temporality. The fascinating evolutionary story of life could never have taken place in a world where, for example, chance wiped out all regularity, or where lawfulness allowed no room for contingency, or where sufficient time for adaptational experimentation was not abundantly available. The universe in which evolution has in fact occurred is one that contains a congenial blend of contingency, predictability, and duration. Explaining, in an *ultimate* way, why the universe has these generic features, and why it has them mingled in a way that allows for the evolution of life, is a legitimate function of theology.

## Contingency

Let us look first at nature's contingency, a feature that allows for what evolutionary scientists refer to as random, accidental, or chance occurrences. I would suggest, as others have done previously, that theology can interpret the *contingency* (or nonnecessity) of natural occurrences such as genetic mutations as signals of nature's fundamental openness to new creation.[29] The very same events that appear purely random or absurd when viewed only in terms of a scientific method oriented toward the fixed causal past can be understood theologically as openings to the incoming of an indefinitely renewing future in this presently unfinished and perishable cosmos.

In the Abrahamic religions, one looks toward the future to discover the full meaning of past and present events.[30] Only the coming of a radically new and unpredictable future can give genuine definition to what has gone before. But in order for this identity-bestowing future to come about, the present order has to give way. And so, what evolutionary scientists refer to as random, contingent, or accidental events are—at least from the

---

29. See Polkinghorne, *Faith of a Physicist*, 25–26 and 75–87.

30. This is a point that Wolfhart Pannenberg has often made in his interpretation of biblical eschatology and accounts of resurrection: "By contemplating Jesus's resurrection, we perceive our own ultimate future," he writes, "The incomprehensibility of God, precisely in his revelation, means that, for the Christian, the future is still open and full of possibilities." Pannenberg, *Faith and Reality*, 58–59.

perspective of an eschatologically grounded metaphysics—instances of present order making way for new forms of order. Without the occurrence of contingent events, nature's regularities (the laws of physics and natural selection, for example) would freeze the cosmos into an eternal sameness immured against the future.

In our futurist metaphysics, the world is, in a sense, not yet real and therefore not yet intelligible—at least in a complete way. The existence of the perplexing "contingencies" in evolution, which Gould features so colorfully, is just what one should expect in an unfinished universe whose real character cannot be grasped adequately in the present.[31] Correspondingly, the obsession with clarity and absolute transparency (such as that exhibited in modern scientism) divests the temporal universe of any genuine futurity. The wish for immediate clarity has led to the envisagement of time as mathematically "reversible," so as to render nature completely intelligible and predictable from the point of view of either its past or present.

Both the religious metaphysics of *esse* and the materialist metaphysics of the past are unwilling to wait in hope for an intelligibility not yet visible to us. They insist on present clarity, an obsession that leads inevitably to prematurely closed explanation. They manifest an impatience reminiscent of Gnosticism's unwillingness to let reality unfold at its own pace. A metaphysics of the future, on the other hand, allows for an inevitable uncertainty and ambiguity in every present. Certain events in life's history, whether neutral genetic mutations or occasional asteroid impacts, render the future trajectory of evolution incalculable, humanly speaking. But rather than consigning such contingencies to the realm of sheer "absurdity," for not fitting into what humans understand presently as appropriate order, a metaphysics of hope is willing to wait for a wider intelligibility—even indefinitely. It looks toward a future in which the fuzziness of present chaos may be resolved into meaningful patterning, though perhaps such resolution can occur fully only in the eschatological long run.

If left on its own, natural science, to the extent that it is currently ensconced in a pre-evolutionary materialist metaphysics, can talk about the future only in terms of lines of causation that it determines to have *already* occurred. Inevitably, the orientation of science is going to be influenced by analogies and conclusions pertinent to previous calculations. Whatever predictions science makes about the future are restricted by what it has observed to be the case antecedently. Consequently, if certain events deviate significantly from familiar patterns of physical activity, they are relegated to the status of "accident," and often the inference is made that the whole evolutionary

31. Gould, *Ever Since Darwin*, 13.

process is therefore inherently meaningless. Viewed theologically, however, such events—even the most painful and tragic—may be consistent with the unfinished character of a universe that becomes fully intelligible only when it opens itself completely to the coming of the future.

As pictured by science since the time of Newton, the world *should* be dominated completely by necessity and therefore should be devoid of any inherent uncertainty. It *should* be ruled by linear processes captured easily by mathematical reasoning. Conceived of in this way, nature and its evolution can be imaginatively reduced to an "algorithmic" process, as depicted by Dennett's obsoletely mechanistic ruminations. Thus, when novel, unpredicted events do occur, they are considered absurd or the result of inaccurate measurements and scientific ignorance. Such a universe is so rigid in its obsequiousness to eternal laws that within it nothing could ever happen that cannot be anticipated on the basis of scientific knowledge of the past.

As much as Gould deprecates the ideas of Dawkins and Dennett for being too "fundamentalist," narrow, and rigid, refusing to recognize the role of contingent events in evolution, he shares with them the assumption that "contingency" also implies "meaninglessness." A metaphysics of the future, however, can interpret what is presently perceived as contingency to be an opening to a future coherence whose meaning is yet incalculable. It seems to me that, in a biblical setting, what we translate as "faith" requires an anticipation of such a future resolution.

Obviously, however, nature is stubbornly unpredictable in its actual evolutionary outcomes. The eventual emergence of life and consciousness in evolution, for example, could never have been forecast from even the closest scrutiny of the early phases of cosmic becoming. We need to go beyond the epistemological assumptions of scientism and the metaphysics of materialism and determinism in order to understand why such novel forms of being can emerge in evolution. We need to give an integral place to contingency. Contingency is not a mask for a hidden necessity not yet understood. Rather, it is the way in which the cosmos breaks out of complete subordination to habitual routine and opens itself to the future. Contingent events are an essential part of any world open to evolutionary novelty. They are exactly what we should expect in a world whose ultimate ground and source favors the world's emerging independence as it opens itself to the future.

## Law

What are we to say, then, about the remorseless regularity of laws of nature such as natural selection? Isn't the deterministic invariance that we attribute to the laws of physics or to the inexorable filtering of DNA by natural selection a clear sign of an ultimately impersonal universe, ruled only by blind necessity, and therefore "pointless"—in the same sense as that depicted by the ultra-adaptationist Darwinians? How could such an unforgiving propensity of nature as we find in the "law" of selection, which always protects the strong and eliminates the weak, ever be reconciled with the faith that we live in an ultimately purposeful universe cared for by a compassionate God? Is not natural selection a purely deterministic, "algorithmic," pitiless, and meaningless process, as Dawkins and Dennett have argued? Above all, doesn't the inflexibility of nature's lawful determinism close it off to any truly new future?

For the moment, let us grant that natural selection is just as mindless and impersonal as, say, the law of gravity. Does this element of unbending necessity in natural selection, or, for that matter, any other uniform set of natural occurrences, mean that nature is so driven by mindless determinism that a truly new and unpredictably meaningful future is ruled out? Not at all. Lawfulness at one level of nature's hierarchically emergent structure is essential for the emergence of novelty and indeterminacy at another. Try to imagine a universe devoid of the predictable routines that modern science has uncovered. Such a world would be so utterly bereft of order and identity that no *new* emergence would be possible at all, since there would be nothing definite enough to undergo transformation. Evolutionary novelty cannot become implanted in absolute chaos, for then there would be nothing to distinguish the new from the old. If an aspect of contingency is essential for nature's being open to new creation, it is no less true that some degree of regularity and predictable order, such as we find in the recurring laws of physics or natural selection, is essential for the world's remaining consistent and durable enough even to have a future. A world open to the future without also possessing the reliability of lawful "necessity" would be as unimaginable as one devoid of contingency. Nature's lawfulness and predictability are needed to keep natural processes continuous enough to avoid decaying into utter caprice.[32]

32. See Pannenberg, *Toward a Theology of Nature*, 72–122.

## Time

Finally, the fact of irreversible time, our third essential condition of evolution, can also be given a most satisfying explanation by a theological metaphysics of the future. Ultimately, it is *the arrival of the future* that allows each present to retreat irreversibly into the fixed past so that other new moments may arise in its place. In this sense, the past, out of which science seeks exclusively to explain the present, is itself the "residue" of the openness of nature to a futurity that had formerly come to pass. The past is therefore a gift, whose very stability as fixed facticity is ultimately due to the "fidelity" of an always new future. Without the consistent and faithful coming of the future there would be no pushing of the present into the past and, consequently, no temporal sequence of moments in which evolution could occur; there would be no fixed past that could enter causally into the present.

In summary, then, the synthesis of randomness, regularity, and temporality that makes for biological evolution is actually characteristic of all natural beings. Everything in the universe, including our own existence, participates in contingency, that is, in events that are not inherently necessary; in lawful "necessity," the predictable patterns that organize events into identifiable and intelligible actualities; and in temporality, the succession of moments that allows for continually new kinds of being and for the creative transformation of present forms of order.

When we look for an *ultimate* explanation of evolution, we must account for the cosmic blend of contingency, predictability, and temporality that make evolution possible and that science, limited as it is in its method of inquiry, does not ask about. As such, it has been my contention here that the metaphysics of the future, entailed by the biblical vision of a cosmos sustained by the promise of an Absolute Future, provides a most plausible metaphysical grounding of these three aspects of our world. Without in any way intruding into the specifics of scientific work itself, such a vision of reality provides us with an *ultimate* explanation of evolution.

# Part IV: God, Science & Revelation

# 15: Revelation Theology[1]

RATHER THAN MOVING DIRECTLY into the task of developing a contemporary theology of revelation, it may prove helpful to some readers if we pause here and sketch at least a brief outline of the history of Catholic revelation theology. Such background information may help us to appreciate the extent of the struggle the idea of revelation in Catholic theology has undergone—especially through the work of the Second Vatican Council—to be liberated eventually from association with those theological schemes that tended to narrow its meaning unnecessarily. At the same time, such an outline may help to locate more clearly the distinctive character of the present attempt to develop a theology of revelation.

We noted earlier that Catholic theology of revelation has suffered in the past primarily from a "propositional" and correspondingly impersonal tendency. That is to say, it has understood revelation very much as though it were a set of truths and very little as the unfolding of a dialogical relationship between God and the world. Today, on the other hand, most Catholic theologians, along with an increasing number of Protestants, interpret revelation fundamentally as God's personal self-gift to the world. This is a dramatic departure from the dominantly apologetic treatments of our topic since the time of the Reformation.

The new personalist or dialogical emphasis in revelation theology is not incompatible with a propositional understanding, but it also goes far beyond it. Gerald O'Collins, who certainly agrees with the new accent, observes that the personalist way of looking at revelation as God's self-disclosure does not exclude the possibility of framing its content simultaneously in the form of statements of truth:

> Is there no room left for talk of "revealed truths" and the "content" of revelation? With regard to this question, we should recall that the relationship of the revealing God and the believing man is foremost a living experience which shapes man's personal history. But this experienced reality is not so wholly incommunicable that it remains locked up in inarticulate subjectivity. The faith which arises in encounter with the self-revealing God

1. The following text is an excerpt. Previously published in Haught, *Mystery and Promise*, 29–39. Reprinted with permission.

feels the need to formulate true statements of faith both within
the community of those who share this experience and also for
outsiders.[2]

Still, although traditionally revelation has been understood, in a formal sense, as God's communication of truths to us, materially, in fact, it
has never been reducible to the mere transmission of information. In spite
of the excesses of the propositional approach at the level of theological ar-
ticulation, the lived experience of Christians throughout the ages has been
one in which revelation, even when it is not called by this name, has been
experienced predominantly in a personal, dialogical way. It would be an
exaggeration to say that traditional theology has been mistaken in speaking of revelation in propositional terms, for example, during the period in
which Scholasticism was virtually equated with Catholic theology. But it has
failed, as incidentally all theology has, to an extent, in every age, by speaking
of revelation in a manner that does not adequately thematize what actually goes on in the concrete faith life of Christian believers. The attempt to
reduce revelation to propositional statements of truth may serve the cause
of apologetics, but it leaves out the main substance or content of revelation
as it has in fact been felt and internalized.

Theology has been so preoccupied with what we shall later call "boundary maintenance"—the need to guarantee the integrity of revelation in the
face of skepticism or alternative religious positions—that it has felt the need
to codify its content in the form of creedal and dogmatic propositions. This
attempt at codification is especially understandable, and certainly forgivable, since the content of revelation needs to be guarded in one way or
another. Without conceptually clarified boundaries, any religious tradition
risks being dissolved into culture at large and thereby loses its critical edge
vis-a-vis the social and political environment. The problem, then, is not
with the propositional codification but with the narrow identification of a
set of propositions with the sum and substance of revelation. Such an identification is parallel to the fallacy in science of identifying the world of nature
with the scientific models that we use to organize our understanding of it.
Nature is in fact always much richer and more complex than our imaginative and mathematical models; we unduly shrivel our understanding of the
cosmos if we equate it in a simple way with our scientific schemes. Likewise,
it is of the very essence of faith that we acknowledge the transcendence of
divine mystery over any of our propositional and symbolic representations
of it. Indeed, not to do so is idolatrous. And so, if the ultimate content of

2. O'Collins, *Foundations of Theology*, 27.

revelation is the divine mystery of God, then no set of propositional truths can mediate it to us either. Avery Dulles writes,

> The ineffable experience of the Word holds a certain precedence over its doctrinal statement. In the life of the individual believer and in that of the whole church, as Blondel observed, "it would be true to say that one goes from faith to dogma rather than from dogma to faith."[3]

Few theologians, it turns out, have rigorously equated the marrow of revelation with any particular set of propositional truths. But especially under the pressure of apologetical concerns, they have sometimes caused the theology of revelation to focus so intently on creedal formulations that the life of faith and the intimate relation of God to the world underlying the statements of dogma have often been virtually ignored. The renewal of revelation theology, especially since Vatican II, is trying to redress this imbalance.

We must be careful to avoid caricaturing traditional theology. This is especially the case with the theology formulated along the lines of Thomas Aquinas's great synthesis. Although Thomistic and later scholastic philosophies are rightly criticized for their rationalistic excess, they did not totally obscure the personal dimension of revelation but, in their own way, kept it alive. Aquinas himself did not lock revelation up in a purely logical mold but instead saw it fundamentally as the presence of the Lord in the heart as well as the mind.[4] Religions all have an informational component which requires some sort of propositional formulizing and Christian faith is not exempt from this requirement. But even the most "scholastic" theology of the late Middle Ages did not entirely reduce revelation to a set of sentences. Hidden beneath its rigorous preoccupation with dogmatic clarity, there was still the often inadequately articulated confession of the sense of God's personal presence to the world and to faith. It is this lived faith that revelation theology ideally attempts to clarify.

## Revelation Theology Prior to Vatican II

Whenever the main theological concern is one of defending the faith from the threats of outsiders, it is difficult to undertake the work of a truly constructive theology. The latter occurs more readily in circumstances where religious energy can be focused on the development rather than just the

3. Dulles, *Revelation and the Quest for Unity*, 59.
4. See Aquinas, *Summa Theologiae* Ia.8.3; 2, 3, 5, 6.

protection of doctrine (although sometimes, of course, serious challenges may help to stimulate doctrinal growth rather than retrenchment). Before Vatican II, the Church councils and the Roman magisterium spoke of revelation generally in the context of the condemnation of unorthodoxy.[5] At the Council of Trent, in the sixteenth century, for example, there was no real theological deepening of the notion of revelation because the main concern was with safeguarding the deposit of faith that the council fathers held to have been passed down in Church tradition under the guidance of the Holy Spirit. Although Vatican I did not explicitly dwell on the topic of revelation, its promulgations on infallibility and faith alluded to the "deposit" that comes to us from the apostles and that needs to be protected by Church authority.[6] Vatican I understood revelation as a fixed body of supernatural truths under the protection of papal authority.

Perhaps it is unfair of twentieth-century religious thought to be excessively critical of the rather emaciated views of revelation that came to expression at Trent, later at Vatican I, and in the many manuals that followed. At the same time, however, it is not helpful to imagine that we can find much of a basis for a theology of revelation in these sources. The reason for such a sober conclusion is simply that the apologetic method, almost by definition, leaves too much out. Indeed, while it allegedly defends matters of faith, it typically deals primarily with revelation only from the point of view of what appeals to finite human reason. It rightly allows a place for intelligence and reason within faith, but it simultaneously suppresses much of the very substance of the faith it seeks to defend. Hans Waldenfels observes that, in the standard modern manuals of theology, apologetics does not treat the topic of revelation in so far as it is known through faith, but only in so far as it can be grasped in a purely "natural" way.[7] Such a method is bound to abstract considerably from what lies in the depths of faith experience.

While the topic of revelation appears abundantly in apologetic treatises and manuals after Trent, it is impossible to find a fully developed revelation theology in Catholic circles until the present century. A formal theology of revelation appears neither in the Bible, nor in the Church fathers, nor in medieval scholastic theology. This is not surprising since the fact of revelation was so foundational to Christian faith that it did not need to be reflected upon in the deliberate fashion that apologetics requires. We look in vain for treatises *de revelatione* prior to modern times. Even after the Council of Trent, in the mid-sixteenth century, the theme of revelation entered

5. Dulles, *Revelation and the Quest for Unity*, 82.
6. Moran, *Theology of Revelation*, 27.
7. Waldenfels, *Offenbarung*, 27.

into the realm of theological discussion through the doorway of apologetics rather than as a fully developed theological notion. In their opposition to Protestantism, Tridentine and post-Tridentine theologians sought to defend the revelatory role of tradition and the magisterium over against the *sola Scriptura* (Scripture alone) emphasis of Protestant Christianity. In doing so, they and the many manuals that followed usually understood revelation in a starkly minimal sense as the *locutio Dei*, the speech of God. In order to distinguish the Catholic position from that of the Protestants, they placed enormous weight on tradition and the Church magisterium as vehicles of God's speech. Thus, the Bible as God's Word became a subordinate item in Catholic understanding of divine revelation. In spite of Vatican II's corrections, to this day the Bible is still quite often passed over by many Catholics as they look for the sources of their faith.

In our own century, the famous Dominican theologian Reginald Garrigou-Lagrange, in a massive apologetically oriented two-volume work, *De Revelatione*, gives an elaborate definition of revelation, setting forth its efficient, material, formal, and final causes. According to his definition, revelation is a supernatural action of God made manifest *"per modum locutionis"* (by way of speech).[8] Such manuals as that of Garrigou-Lagrange typically cite Hebrews as a scriptural basis for this understanding: "In many and various ways God *spoke* of old to our fathers by the prophets; but in these last days he *has spoken* to us by a Son" (Heb 1:1). The notion of God's *locutio* is easily assimilable to that of propositional truth which, in turn, best suits the interests of apologetics. It is in this sense that most post-Tridentine Catholic theology prior to Vatican II understood the notion of revelation.

## Vatican II and Beyond

The Second Vatican Council's document on revelation, promulgated November 18, 1965, is entitled *Dei Verbum*, the "Word of God." Perhaps nothing signals more directly the new ecumenical and biblical tone of the council's understanding of revelation. Contemporary theologians, attuned as they now are to the renewal of biblical theology, may find the constitution on revelation quite unremarkable. But when we situate it in the context of previous magisterial statements, it takes on the appearance of a dramatic breakthrough in Catholic teaching. It is helpful to know that this document emerged only after a difficult struggle with those at the council who were simply intent upon restating the ideas of Trent and Vatican I. The first draft of the document was honed in a rigorously unbiblical and unecumenical way.

---

8. Garrigou-Lagrange, OP, *De Revelatione*, 136.

Thanks to the intervention of Pope John XXIII and other bishops, the first draft was rejected. The final, approved text, like many other council documents, gives evidence of the modern Catholic Church's intention to keep the lines of communication open to the world, of its willingness to learn from the experience of non-Catholic churches and theologians, and of a refreshing openness to the results of modern theology and biblical scholarship. It is the spirit of this liberating openness that encourages those of us who are theologians to keep probing ever deeper for the meaning of revelation in terms of our own circumstances almost thirty years later.

By accentuating the theme of God's Word, the final text, known as *Dei Verbum*, clearly signals Catholic theology's exposure to Protestant views of revelation in which the theme of God's Word, rather than Church magisterium and tradition, is given primacy. No longer present is the old temptation to separate tradition or ecclesiastical magisterium from Scripture as autonomous sources of revelation. Instead, the document states, there exists a close connection and communication between sacred tradition and sacred Scripture. For both of them, flowing from the same divine wellspring, in a certain way merge into a unity, tending towards the same end.[9]

In this way, the council avoids any narrow biblicism that would tend to derive all important truths for our lives from the pages of Scripture alone. Fortunately, it declares that the Word of God is not limited to the letter of Scripture: "It is not from sacred Scripture alone that the Church draws her certainty about everything which has been revealed."[10] At the same time, it emphasizes that the teaching office of the Church "is not above the word of God, but serves it."[11] Moreover, the council endorses the methods of modern biblical scholarship which reject literalist and fundamentalist readings of Scripture. It shows an awareness of the need to "search out the intention of the sacred writers" by way of form criticism. It acknowledges our need to become aware of the historical context and different genres of the various books of the Bible. While still conceding points to Trent, Vatican I, and the apologetic orientation of previous Church documents, overall, *Dei Verbum* is an inspiration to those who are concerned with developing and interpreting anew the notion of revelation. Although many of its articles are now commonplace in modern theology, the fact that it sanctions new methods and emphases gives one confidence that the Church's teachers, including its theologians, are commissioned to search for an ever-deeper appreciation of the meaning of revelation.

In addition to the theme of God's Word, the council also reflects the Catholic Church's embrace of twentieth-century theology of history in

9. See Paul VI, "*Dei Verbum*," 9.

10. Paul VI, "*Dei Verbum*," 9.

11. Paul VI, "*Dei Verbum*," 10.

which God's Word is seen as inseparable from events and deeds. By way of revelation, *Dei Verbum* states,

> The invisible God out of the abundance of his love speaks to men as friends and lives among them, so that he may invite and take them into fellowship with himself. This plan of revelation is realized by deeds and words having an inner unity: the deeds wrought by God in the history of salvation manifest and confirm the teaching and realities signified by the words, while the words proclaim the deeds and clarify the mystery contained in them.[12]

Thus, revelation is no longer understood here simply as the communication of knowledge, but as a process, involving events as well as words, by which humans are invited into an ever-deeper relationship with God.[13]

The document on revelation goes on to say that the fullness of God's self-revelation becomes manifest in Christ. It is this personalizing of revelation that we wish to highlight. The notion that revelation is God's *self*-revelation has turned out to be one of the most important developments in all of modern theology. Greatly due to the influence of theologian Karl Rahner, Catholic theology of revelation has now shifted dramatically away from the propositional, impersonal, and apologetic features it carried in the past. In doing so, it has merged in substance with much non-Catholic theology of revelation as well.

## The Present State of Revelation Theology

Although Vatican II's document on revelation has de-emphasized the propositional approach to revelation theology, much work remains to be done in the area of bringing to clarity the unique content and meaning of biblical revelation. This is now a broadly shared ecumenical enterprise. Increasingly since Vatican II, Catholic and non-Catholic theologians have read and appropriated each other's work in this area. The present book will itself reflect how a Catholic theology of revelation can now be animated just as much by the reading of Protestant sources as of Catholic ones. Because of the Second Vatican Council's endorsement of a biblical approach to revelation, with special emphasis on the "Word of God," Catholic theology has been implicitly commissioned to mine the resources of modern Protestant theology of revelation which traditionally has been much more explicitly concerned with the theme of God's word.

The emphasis that both Protestant and Catholic theology must now develop more forcefully (and Vatican II already took implicit steps in this

12. Paul VI, "*Dei Verbum*," 2.
13. Dulles, *Revelation and the Quest for Unity*, 86.

direction) is that God's revelatory word comes in the form of promise. No contemporary theologian has brought out this dimension of revelation more emphatically than Jürgen Moltmann, a Protestant. It is especially in relation to his own bold endeavors that a contemporary, ecumenically viable theology of revelation may be constructed.

Another area of revelation theology needing considerable development today is that of how to interpret the Christocentric character of *Dei Verbum*. The council's constitution on revelation implies that the fullness of the divine self-disclosure occurs only in Christ . . . How literally does this powerful and sweeping claim, supported by several important texts in the New Testament and by centuries of Christian tradition, need to be taken? This question arises for Christian theology today primarily because of our growing awareness of the revelatory claims of other religious traditions. In our conversations with representatives of these alternative visions of reality, what does it mean to say that Christ is the *plenitudo totius revelationis?*

The issue of how to interpret the alleged finality of Christian revelation is receiving considerable attention in theology today. It goes without saying that any efforts we might make with respect to this difficult and controversial matter can only be tentative, not to say clumsy. But it does not seem wise, nor, for that matter, in keeping with the spirit of tolerance and inclusiveness that we associate with Christian faith, simply to ignore it. The question of the meaning of the traditional teaching about the centrality, finality, and unsurpassability of Christ in revelation needs to be raised and discussed over and over. *Dei Verbum* is not as sensitive to this question as we might have hoped, although, in comparison with previous magisterial statements, both its tone and content are significant departures from the apologetically bound past. The decree on revelation, as well as other products of the Second Vatican Council, make initial gestures toward acknowledging the situation of religious pluralism—but we need now to go much further.

Finally, the present condition of revelation theology is one in which the kenotic aspects of God's self-revelation are thankfully being accentuated more forcefully than ever before. *Dei Verbum* implies that God's self-revelation is indeed a self-emptying, but it does not make this point very explicit, nor does it develop it. In the present work, therefore, without in any way claiming adequacy for our treatment, we shall bring to the front the theme of God's self-emptying as central to the theology of revelation. When taken together with the biblical motif of promise, the notion of a divine kenosis may provide for our own situation today a solid and compelling foundation for a fresh theology of revelation.

# 16: Religion and Revelation[1]

THE CONVICTION THAT MYSTERY is revealed to us is not unique to Christianity and biblical religion. Religion, in its entirety, can be viewed generously as the disclosure of a transcendent mystery. In our own cultural context, we call this mystery by the name "God." But peoples of other times and places have also experienced the breaking of mystery into their lives; they have related to it, talked about it, and worshiped it through many different verbal and iconic designations. We cannot appreciate the Christian understanding of revelation unless we keep this wider religious world before us. A Christian understanding of revelation will become distinctive to us only if we view it in the context of other kinds of religious awareness.

Searching for distinctiveness, however, need not imply looking for ways in which Christian revelation might be better than others. Any singularity we may find in Christianity does not necessarily imply "superiority" to other faiths. Such a comparison would be pointless and arrogant. There is, of course, a considerable body of Christian opinion that still insists on a comparative devaluation of other religions. But we are now beyond the time in our global religious evolution when we need constantly to be so exclusivistic. This is not to say that all religions are the same, nor that they can be reduced to some common essence. Such a simplifying perspective would enormously diminish the rich diversity of religious paths that history has bequeathed to us. Religions are not the sort of realities that can easily be comparatively graded. Perhaps aspects of them, such as their ethical implications, may be compared, but as total approaches to mystery, to human existence, and to the world, it makes little sense to say that one is clearly better than another. None of us occupies a neutrally objective perch, above or outside of all traditions, from which we could ever securely make such an assessment.

Fortunately, there is now developing, here and there, a new spirit of mutual openness and respect among influential religious thinkers representing the various faiths. For Catholic theology, the ecumenical movement and the Second Vatican Council have signaled the end of the old "apologetic"

---

1. The following text is an excerpt. Previously published in Haught, *Mystery and Promise*, 61–68. Reprinted with permission.

approach to revelation.[2] In the past, a defensive style of theology (remnants of which, unfortunately, still live on), sought to preserve an often rather narrowly conceived Christian notion of revelation from attack by alternative positions, whether religious or secular. As a result of the self-enclosure of this kind of theology, its treatment of revelation could not receive much nourishment from other traditions. Such isolationism is no longer acceptable in Christian theology.

Still, at this point, it may be useful for us to speculate on why religions are so vigilant in defense of what they perceive to be revealed truth. Such an examination may go some way toward helping us understand why the idea of revelation has been set apart by theology for special treatment in the first place. Why do Christians and members of other faiths stand guard so securely over their respective deposits of faith?[3] The following explanation of religion's preoccupation with apologetics is offered by British theologian John Bowker. It is certainly not intended as an adequate account, but it does offer a rather novel perspective, and it is one that we shall draw on at other points in the present book.[4]

Whatever else they may be (and they are other things besides), Bowker claims that religions are, at the very least, systems for processing information. They are living structures with boundaries built up over the course of sometimes many centuries for the purpose of encoding, storing, retrieving, and transmitting to the next generation a very important kind of information. This information is usually connected explicitly with some notion of revelation. It is a very special kind of information. It may be non-verbal as well as verbal, but it is not trivial. It has to do with salvation, liberation, and fulfillment, the goals that have traditionally mattered most to the majority of the earth's human inhabitants. Religion responds to the deepest and most urgent of all human concerns. It answers questions about the final meaning of life and, in doing so, it shapes the identity of individuals. It responds in a decisive way to the need to be loved or forgiven and to the longing to discover the purpose of the universe.

Religions are so important because they provide information about how to negotiate the most intransigent roadblocks we encounter in life. Whereas other techniques—like those of science and engineering—can remove more mundane obstacles, religions attend to the most irremovable limits on life: fate, guilt, meaninglessness, and death. Since religions deal with such important matters, the information they convey to their followers

2. See the Council's document on revelation, Paul VI, "*Dei Verbum.*"

3. The Greek word for bishop, *episcopos*, literally means "overseer."

4. See Bowker, *Is Anybody Out There?*, 9–18 and 112–43.

is the most valued of all. As such, it needs to be carefully protected—more than any other kind of information. It is no wonder, then, that religions are so defensive and also, for that reason, at times, so dangerous.

Information, Bowker says, does not just float about aimlessly in the universe. It has to be ordered and processed if it is to carry any meaning.[5] For this purpose, it requires a system: an organized channel through which content can flow and be reliably passed on to receivers. Any information system must be allowed to sustain a definite identity throughout the passage of time; it requires some degree of stability. For this very reason, it has to have clear *boundaries*, consisting of sets of constraints. Without such limits, the channeling system would collapse, and any revelatory information would dissolve into the noise of indefiniteness. A cell without a membrane would be too shapeless to carry the information essential for life, and a computer without the constraints of its circuitry or a specific program could not organize and process information. The informational component in a cell, organism, or computer has to be constrained if it is to be informative. Clear boundaries must be imposed upon a system in order to allow for the processing and transmitting of information. Since religions are information systems (or, perhaps more accurately, complexes of informational sub-systems), they are not exempt from the need for definite constraints to protect the information they seek to transmit.

We may now take a step beyond Bowker's illuminating use of the new information-systems model. Information theory also instructs us that religions, like other systems, cannot sustain any vital flow of information if they remain absolutely conservative and defensive. That is to say, information theory requires that there also be an element of *unpredictability* in any truly informative message. In order to be informative, a system not only has to avoid the chaos or "noise" of indefiniteness, which boundary maintenance is designed to assure, but also the monotony of excessive redundancy. Of course, some redundancy or tendency for repetition is a requirement for the flow of information in any system. It is in such redundancy that informational constraints and boundaries are embedded. For example, the constant and repetitive adherence to the rules of grammar is essential for linguistic communication. But if the redundancy is excessive, it will drown out the unpredictability and novelty that the passing on of information also needs.

This holds true for the obvious reason that if information were totally predictable it could not really be informative. If a system were simply an "order"—without any openness to novelty—it would be frozen into a single

5. Bowker, *Is Anybody Out There?*, 114.

identity and would therefore be incapable of anything other than self-duplication. It would be incapable of mediating any genuine revelation. Its absolute rigidity would inhibit the entrance of novel, surprising content. The same material would be repeated over and over again, impeding the flow of real information to present recipients. If I already know the content of the message coming across a telegraph wire, I can hardly call it informative or revelatory when it finally arrives. Absolute predictability inhibits the flow of new information since everything is already fixed irreversibly in a stationary pattern. Only an entropic disassembly of the elements involved in information can allow for a reassembling into truly novel and informative patterns. A leaning toward disorder is necessary if information is to have the surprising character it requires in order to be information. As a system processes information, it needs randomizing moments or trends in order for wider and more intensely informative patterns to emerge.

Thus any kind of information, revelatory or otherwise, has to walk the razor's edge between noise and redundancy, between chaos and monotony, between unintelligibility and repetition. Without a certain amount of redundancy, information would have no intelligible shape. But without a system's capacity for moments of deconstruction, no meaningful or relevant information could be inscribed in it. A periodic veering toward the state of "noise" loosens up a system to receive new life and information. Without such a capacity for randomization, a code would be too "stiff" to carry a message. If religions are information systems, then their revelations must also be in some way continuously open to novelty, precisely in order to sustain their informational character.

The extant religious traditions all began when the boundaries and constraints of their historical predecessors had become too restrictive to mediate the saving information required to interpret new historical circumstances. Buddhism, for example, originated when the Buddha perceived Hindu religious practice to be too confining to bring the fulfillment and release from suffering for which living beings longed; Islam began when Muhammad became sensitive to the dehumanizing implications of the idolatry in popular religious practice; and Christianity started in the fresh experience of the compassion of God by Jesus of Nazareth. Gautama, Muhammad, and Jesus all transgressed the boundaries and constraints that had shaped and channeled the flow of religious information in their respective cultures. It is clear, then, that religion and revelation are more than the passing on of a fixed tradition. The beginnings of influential religious movements are usually tied up with acts of rebellion and revolution. However, adventurous religious movements at some point typically abandon the innovative openness of their originating moments. They circle the wagons, not only to contain their well-winnowed traditions but also in order to seal themselves off from novelty. Too much novelty would lead to chaos—but without some opening toward surprise, a religious system eventually stifles the traditional information it seeks to transmit.

## Christian Attitudes Toward the Religions

As we move forward in our inquiry into the nature and plausibility of revelation, it will be helpful to keep before us the rules by which all systems process information. The transmission of ideas associated with revelation will be especially bounded by protective constraints. But a religion's understandable concern with clear borders may, at times, restrict the very novelty that originally made the ideas seem to be specially revealed. In order, then, for revelation to remain truly alive, it must always be a source of new surprises for each generation of believers.[6] Even though emphasis on doctrinal constraints is an inevitable phase in the formation of a tradition, there comes a time in its unfolding when a purely defensive posture leads to stagnation arising from under-nourishment. At such times, a relaxation of the apologetic approach and a new openness to the foreignness of alternative ways of looking at mystery become essential simply for the sake of the vitality and survival of the tradition's revelatory capacity.

We are now living at such an exciting time for religions. World history is bringing the various traditions together into such mutual proximity that they can no longer ignore one another. Simply thickening their protective membranes—by emphasizing doctrinal constraints or the normative superiority of one deposit of faith over the others—only leads to an obstruction of informational flow. In the final analysis, sheer defensiveness becomes an impediment to the communication of revelation.[7]

Although there is still considerable resistance on the part of many devout Christian believers to the new openness now being extended toward

6. Later we shall see that our conceiving revelation in the form of "promise" allows for just this novelty, whereas a purely antiquarian retrieval of a "deposit of faith" from the past is by itself inadequate as a way of understanding the self-disclosure of God.

7. The openness of authentic Christian faith to the future, to novelty, and to surprise invites it to undergo considerable transformation in its encounter with other traditions. Christianity, following Jesus and Jesus's God, should be expected to be somewhat vulnerable and "defenseless" in any relational encounter with other faiths. If it defends anything vigorously, it should be its own defenselessness and inclusiveness. Informationally speaking, this would entail a willingness to allow its boundaries to shift in response to new information in its encounters. In this way, it preserves its identity instead of losing it. Like persons, a religion must "die" (abandoning any non-relational exclusivism) in order to live.

other religions, there is also a great deal of enthusiasm about it on the part of many others. Religion on our planet is now embarking upon a new and adventurous stage in its history. To an unprecedented extent, members of the various faiths are today in conversation, seeking to learn new things from one another. This occurrence is too threatening for large segments of some traditions or subsystems, so they have retreated into themselves, building thicker walls against the invasion of alternative points of view. But in other respects, these new inter-religious encounters are already changing the religious landscape of our world in a wholesome way, inviting us to rethink our ideas of revelation in terms of inter-religious conversation.

Today, most Christian theologians have rejected, at least in principle, a purely exclusivist approach that would deny the revelatory value of other religions. Where significant controversy now exists, it involves the so-called "pluralists" on the one hand, and the "inclusivists" on the other. Informationally speaking, the pluralist theological option radically relativizes the importance of distinct religious boundaries, proposing that different religious traditions may all be equally valid ways of experiencing the revelation of an ultimate reality, transcending the comprehension of any particular tradition.[8] The inclusivist approach in Christian theology, however, without denying the value of other traditions, is more concerned with boundary maintenance.[9] It is open to dialogue with other traditions, willing to have the Christian faith enriched by ecumenical encounter and exposure to the sacred texts of other traditions, but it is also not willing to sacrifice this teaching, expressed as early as Acts: "There is salvation in no one else [except Jesus Christ], for there is no other name under heaven given among men by which we must be saved" (Acts 4:12).[10]

Whether one takes the pluralist or the inclusivist position, it is generally agreed that any Christian theology of revelation that we construct today has to be sensitive to the new consciousness of religious plurality emerging in our time. Previously, it was especially in the theology of revelation (and also Christology) that Christian theologians argued apologetically for the eminence of the Christian religion. They maintained that

8. See Hick and Knitter, *Myth of Christian Uniqueness.*

9. See D'Costa, *Christian Uniqueness Reconsidered.*

10. We are far from resolving this very important debate. Both the pluralist and the inclusivist positions are making important points. The perspective taken in this book is that of an evolutionary cosmology in which the universe itself is the primary revelation of mystery, and religions and their symbols are seen as expressions of the cosmos (and not just isolated, cosmically homeless human subjects). Religion is something that the universe does through us in its evolutionary journey into mystery. Contemporary theology, including discussions between pluralists and inclusivists, is still hampered by a pre-evolutionary, acosmic understanding of religion.

it has this status by virtue of a privileged access to God given in a special revelation withheld at God's discretion from other religions. Much Christian theology still has overtones of this apologetic approach, but it is being challenged by a more ecumenically minded sensitivity to the revelatory possibilities in all the religions.

The traditional language of Christian religion and theology emphasized the centrality and normativeness of Jesus Christ as the decisive and final revelation of God. For centuries, Christians have been taught that the fullness of God's being becomes manifest *only* in Christ. This teaching seemed to imply that we need not look elsewhere for any further data of revelation, least of all in the other religions. Our theologies of revelation focused almost exclusively on the Christ-event and its biblical environment. The exclusively Christo-centric character of revelation theology made it difficult for us to take seriously the revelatory character of primal religions, of Hinduism, Buddhism, Islam, and other religious ways.

The simple dynamics of human psychology provide some explanation for the tenacity of an exclusivist Christo-centrism. A devotee's concentrated commitment to Christ is not entirely different from one person's loyalty to another in ordinary situations of friendship or romance. Because of the limitations of our existence, it is difficult for us to divide our loves indefinitely. We normally need a central focus of devotion and, in our commitment to one individual, we may sometimes devalue or deny the reality of others. In romantic love, it is sometimes as though virtually nobody else exists outside of the beloved. Even though one may outgrow sheer obsession, to some degree, the normal predilection for a select person or group will still persist. The awesomeness of the world requires that finite beings "partialize" it in order to relate to it at all. We have to bite it off in little chunks, or else risk madness.[11] We simply do not have the capacity to consume it in all its depth and complexity. It would not be surprising, therefore, if this limitation overlays our grasp of any possible revelation of the mystery that encompasses us.

---

11. Ernest Becker, *The Denial of Death*, 244.

# 17: Revelation and the Cosmos[1]

TOWARD THE END OF his life, Albert Einstein is reported to have said that the most important question each of us has to ask is whether the universe we inhabit is friendly or unfriendly. The response we give to this question will, to a large extent, determine the shape of our lives and the degree of satisfaction and joy we find in living. It would seem, then, that if the notion of revelation is to be of any consequence, it must, at the very least, help us formulate some answer to this largest of all puzzles.

In the present chapter, we shall attempt to unfold something of what the universe might look like when interpreted in the light of revelation. We shall propose that, when our consciousness is shaped by faith in the divine promise and a trust in the gift of God's self-limiting love, we will be able to see in the cosmos a depth and breadth otherwise obscured.

We know from modern science that the events of our lives occur within the story of a universe that is much vaster than our earthly history. Even in the Bible, the redemption of Israel and the establishment of the Church fall within the more encompassing chronicle of nature's own creation and liberation.[2] The cosmos itself, having come into being eons before the arrival of human history, is the more encompassing context of God's self-revelation. The divine vision for the world goes far beyond what takes place in the course of our own species' history or of events here on earth. Yet faith allows us to read cosmic events in the light of the revelatory promises of God that occur within our terrestrially bound human history. In the light of Christian faith, we may even say that, billions of years before biblical religion emerged on earth, the universe had already been seeded with promise. The reflections of the present chapter are rooted in the conviction that a faith-enabled consciousness can catch at least a glimpse of this promise in the cosmos.

From revelation's perspective, the world presented to us by science appears to have been shaped by the same longing for future fulfillment

1. The following text is an excerpt. Previously published in Haught, *Mystery and Promise*, 147–66. Reprinted with permission.

2. From one point of view, the doctrine of creation seems to be subordinate to that of salvation history. But it is also possible, as Moltmann in particular has shown, to view salvation within the horizon of creation and cosmology. See Moltmann, *God in Creation*, 1–56.

that came to light consciously, explicitly, and historically in Abraham, the prophets, and Jesus. Science itself does not—nor should it be expected to—discern this promise of fulfillment. It does not concern itself with teleological or "final causal" questions. Yet nothing that faith tells us about the creation or about God's promise contradicts the findings of science. In fact, the perspective of biblical faith actually nourishes and supports the process of pure scientific inquiry.

This faith is rooted in a revelation that comes to us through the medium of human history. But revelation is not simply a plan for God's people, for humanity, or for history, as theology has usually put it. This way of speaking, we are now beginning to see, is too narrowly earth-centered and anthropocentric. It also fails to speak to our current environmental crisis. Revelation must now be interpreted as God's envisagement of the *whole universe's* possibilities and ultimate destiny.[3] Obviously, we ourselves are in no position to grasp what the fullness of this vision entails. From within our human history, God's vision of cosmic destiny can only be grasped through the relatively limited and time-conditioned stories of promise that serve as the foundation of our biblical tradition. And yet faith, aroused by the images associated with revelation, may lead us to look for and see things in the universe that would escape a kind of inquiry not so gifted.

Both the Bible and modern science place the cosmos within a narrative setting. When surveyed from the point of view of current evolutionary models, for example, our universe quite clearly has the character of a story. Like all stories, it is revelatory. From its very beginning, the universe seems to be the unfolding and disclosing of a mysterious secret potential and inexhaustible depth, aspects of which are only now being brought to light by science. The universe itself is, in a sense, an ongoing revelation. In its immensities of time and space, as well as in its love of endless diversity, it sacramentalizes the generosity, extravagance, and unpredictability of the creator known by biblical faith as the God of promise. Let us take a brief look at the cosmic story so that we may eventually explore its relationship to the idea of revelation more closely.

## The Cosmic Story

The outlines of the cosmic story began to appear as early as the seventeenth century, during the period of the birth of modern science. Following the

3. This wider-than-human view of revelation is quite biblical. It is present in the creation story, the Wisdom literature, and the Psalms, not to mention the theology of John and Paul.

triumph of evolutionary theory in the past century, the narrative character of nature's unfolding has become ever more conspicuous (although this is not to deny that, in a subterranean way, the biblical view of time has also prepared for the arrival of evolutionary thinking in the West). Recently, astrophysics has brought us into more intimate proximity to the beginnings of the story. The current scientific consensus informs us that cosmic evolution began in a singular event, known today as the "big bang," occurring fourteen or so billion years ago. After that event, the universe continued to unfold in a series of transformations, none of which could have occurred the way they have unless the cosmic beginnings had already been configured in a very precise way.[4]

After the mysterious big bang, the universe began to expand outward, creating space, time, and the galaxies. For billions of years, its free hydrogen gases labored through various phases, eventually giving rise to stars and constellations. At the heart of immense stellar bodies, lighter elements were compressed and heated to exceedingly high temperatures, to gradually become the heavy chemical elements (carbon, oxygen, nitrogen, phosphorous, etc.) required for life. This process itself took several billion years of "cooking time" before the explosions of supernovae eventually dispersed them throughout space.

Some of these elements eventually began to assemble into planetary bodies like the earth. Chemicals and compounds that had been fashioned in the crucible of some remote burnt-out stars came together five billion years ago and formed our own planet. Then, after another billion years or so, the earth's surface having cooled sufficiently, primitive forms of life began to appear. Biological evolution had begun but, like other cosmic episodes, it was not in a hurry. It was patient, experimental, random, and extravagantly "wasteful." After tossing up and discarding millions of primitive species, it finally gave rise to elaborate arrays of more and more complex organisms, to plants, reptiles, birds, and mammals, most of which are now extinct. And then, perhaps two million years ago, our immediate pre-human ancestors came onto the scene, probably in what we now know as East Africa. Finally, several hundred thousand years ago, our direct human ancestors appeared and began to spread out over the face of the earth.

---

4. This perspective may seem compatible with the ideas now associated with the anthropic principle. According to this principle, at the time of its origins, the physical constants and initial conditions of the universe were fine-tuned so that the cosmos would eventually give birth to life and consciousness. Even if the specific theories of contemporary physicists concerning the anthropic principle turn out to be scientifically unacceptable, a theology of revelation is nonetheless obliged to emphasize that the universe is open—in some way, at least—to such a promise, from its very inception.

We know that the unfolding of cosmic evolution has not always been progressive, but this does not detract from its narrative character. For in all great stories there are numerous dead ends and regressions. In the chronicle of any great struggle, there are long spans of waiting, punctuated by brief but significant episodes of terror, victory, and defeat. Still, over the long haul, the evolutionary story clearly displays a trend toward the emergence of more and more elaborate entities. Matter does not remain lifeless and completely dispersed but rather converges upon itself, gradually evolving in the direction of more complex life and, eventually, consciousness.[5] In spite of what some contemporary scientific skeptics have written about the aimlessness of evolution, it is hard to miss the generic sort of directionality (toward more intensely organized complexity) that the cosmic story has followed thus far.

It is obvious that life and consciousness have come into being out of elementary forms of matter. But after they came onto the cosmic landscape, evolution tended to complicate itself more and more, for reasons that scientists are still trying to unravel. Life was not content to remain stuck at a primitive level but instead advanced toward more sentient, conscious, and eventually self-conscious forms. Having produced the human species, the struggle for further complexity did not suddenly cease. Cultural evolution began to occur. After a long period of hunting and gathering, comprising by far the largest portion of our human history (from at least 100,000 to 10,000 BC), humans invented agriculture, civilization, and other aspects of culture such as art, music, poetry, politics, education, and science. These developments at the level of consciousness are additional evidence that our universe—even as embodied in human life—is still impatient with monotony. It continually seeks more subtle shading, contrast, and novelty. In other words, it has the character not just of a story but of an adventure. The adventure now persists, especially in our religious excursions into mystery.

This cosmic adventure seems to have had a definite temporal beginning, followed by chapter upon chapter of dramatic events. These narrative features make us wonder, as humans always wonder when they attend to a tale, where this immense story might be heading. Toward what sort of destiny does it possibly tend? The expansion of the universe, its experimentation with so many peculiar patterns, and above all its hospitality to the evolution of life and the birth of consciousness, persuade us that it may be a story with great consequence. For this reason, it is more urgent than ever that we connect the story of the cosmos with that of revelation.

5. See Teilhard de Chardin, *Phenomenon of Man*.

We have said that the story is more aptly called an adventure. Adventure may be defined as the search for ever more intense versions of ordered novelty.[6] Adventure is what moves a process beyond triviality and monotony toward more highly nuanced forms of order. Any process that seeks thus to complicate the arrangement of things may be called adventurous. A tendency toward becoming more intensely complex seems to be an intrinsic characteristic of our whole universe, including our own species. The restlessness that impelled matter toward complexity, beginning with the big bang, has not yet been stilled.[7] It continues now in our human inquiry and exploration. The cosmos reveals itself as an adventure of continual experimentation with novel forms of order. Hence, being part of this cosmos already means being a participant in a momentous adventure story.

Is this adventurous evolution of our universe already perhaps an aspect of what we call revelation? Thomas Berry, for one, argues that the universe is indeed not just vaguely revelatory but is instead the "primary revelation."[8] It is the fundamental self-manifestation of mystery. Our religions, then, should be seen as further episodes in a continuous unfolding of the depths of the cosmos itself. Whether or not we wish to understand revelation in such broad terms, it is at least imperative, especially today, that we relate the Christian idea of revelation to the larger story of the evolution of the universe.

It is in God's humility that we discover the foundation of the creation of the universe. The coming into being of the cosmos already involves an act of self-humbling on God's part. Creation may be understood not so much as the consequence of God's self-expansion as of God's self-limitation. God's allowing the world to exist is made possible by a restraining of divine omnipotence. Divine power humbly "contracts" itself, surrendering any urge to manipulate events or persons. This humble retreat is what allows the world to stand forth as distinct from its creative ground. Creation is less the consequence of divine "force" than of God's self-withdrawal.[9] What Wyschogrod says about God's creation of humans can also be adapted to the creation of the cosmos:

6. For more regarding this understanding of adventure, see Whitehead, *Adventures of Ideas*, 252–96.

7. See Young, *Unfinished Universe*.

8. Berry, *Dream of the Earth*, 120.

9. This kenotic view of creation is also found in kabbalistic Judaism. Likewise, it occurs occasionally in the writings of Simone Weil and is described in detail in MacGregor, *He Who Lets Us Be*. It is even more prominent in the later writings of Jürgen Moltmann. See Moltmann, *God in Creation*, 88.

> A world in which the divine light penetrates and fills all is a
> world in which there is nothing but God. In such a world, no
> finitude and therefore no human existence [cosmos] is possible
> . . . The creation of man [the cosmos] involves the necessity for
> God's protection of man [the cosmos] from the power of God's
> being. This protection involves a certain divine withdrawal, the
> *tsimtsum* of the kabbalists, who were also puzzled by how things
> other than God could exist in the light of the absolute being of
> God. To answer this question, they invoked the notion of *tsimt-*
> *sum*, by which they meant that the absolute God, whose being
> fills all being, withdraws from a certain region, which is thus left
> with the divine being thinned out in it, and in this thinned out
> region man [the cosmos] exists[10].

Some such notion seems essential to resolve the theological difficulties, especially regarding human freedom, resulting from the traditional habit of modeling God's creativity on the rather deterministic idea of efficient causation. It is especially in the image of the crucified that Christian faith is given the key to this interpretation of creation. The cross reveals to faith the self-sacrificing of God out of whose limitless generosity the world is called—but never forced—into being.

This kenotic image once again brings a surprising intelligibility to our evolutionary universe. Evolutionary theory has two main features that have made it seemingly irreconcilable with traditional theism. In the first place, it holds that chance or randomness is the raw material of evolution. If chance is real, then it apparently places God's omnipotence and omniscience in serious question. A universe that possesses such a degree of randomness seems to lack intelligibility. God, the alleged divine designer, is apparently not in control. In the second place, evolutionary theory insists that an impersonal and ruthless process known as *natural selection* is the sole and sufficient explanation for the survival of some species and the extinction of others. A process that selects mutant species only on the basis of their accidentally favorable traits seems incompatible with a beneficent and intelligent creator. Evolutionary theory seems to think of the creative process as a prolonged, impersonal lottery rather than the "mighty act" of an omnipotent God.

In the light of revelation, we are provided with a way of addressing these objections. We must begin, though, with a confession that the idea of a designing and controlling deity, whose existence is rightly denied by many skeptics, is also problematic from the point of view of a kenotic theology. If God is all-powerful—in the sense of being able to manipulate things

10. Wyschogrod, *Body of Faith*, 9–10.

at will—then the facts of evolution do indeed cast doubt on the plausibility of theism. However, revelation's image of a self-limiting creator, whose power is made manifest in a kind of defenselessness or vulnerability, is not only congruous with but also possibly explanatory of the world that evolutionary theory presents to us. The randomness, struggle, and seemingly aimless meandering that the theory attributes to the universe is more or less what we should expect if creation is the product of the non-obtrusive love of a self-emptying God. The absence of strict determinism that recent physics has discovered at the most basic levels of matter, the chance mutations that biology finds at the level of life's evolution, and the freedom that comes forth with human existence—all of these are expected features of any world we might claim to be distinct from the being of its creator. In order for the world to be independent of God and possess its own existence, or to undergo a genuine self-transcendence in evolution, its creative ground would, in some way, make itself absent from that world, instead of overwhelming it with divine presence. God would concede to the world its own autonomous principles of operation, such as the "law" of gravity or the "law" of natural selection. A self-limiting God, the humble God of revelation, makes more sense within an evolutionary framework than in any others that have been proposed, so far, by science.[11]

We have been looking at how cosmic evolution may be interpreted in the light of revelation. But how does revelation appear when seen in terms of evolution? We may say that the revelation of God in Christ is the coming to a head of the entire evolutionary process. The intuition that Christ is the fulfillment of a cosmic promise, one that has a breadth that carries revelation beyond the sphere of human existence, is already present in Paul's letter to the Romans: "The creation waits with eager longing for the revealing of the sons of God . . . We know that the whole creation has been groaning in travail together until now" (Rom 8:19–22). When viewed from the perspective of evolution, revelation is the flowering fulfillment of the universe itself.

11. A God who withdraws from the world (in this kenotic sense), however, is nothing like, and should not be confused with, the useless God of deism. Paradoxically, it is out of love of the relationship and dialogical intimacy with the world that God renounces any overwhelming, annihilating "presence" to the world. The retracting of annihilating presence is, as we know even from interhuman experience, the very condition of dialogical presence.

# 18: Revelation and the Self[1]

DOES MY OWN LIFE have any significance? If revelation is to make any difference to *me*, I rightly expect that it will respond to this undying question. In the previous chapters, we portrayed revelation in terms of the universe and history. Here we ask, more explicitly than before, what it may mean for us as individual persons concerned with meaning and, perhaps above all, with freedom. Such preoccupation with individuality would probably not have occurred to Abraham, Moses, and most of the prophets. Their emphasis was on the meaning of God's promises for the family, the tribe, the people, or the nation. They did not formally ask, "what does it all mean for *me*?" Concern for the distinct self in our modern sense had not yet arisen. Perhaps for that reason, even the question of subjective survival beyond death was not a major preoccupation. The Israelites understood God's promise in terms of the survival and status of a whole people. Israel's sense of divine revelation responded primordially to a communal hope in the future rather than to private aspirations.

Up until the time of Jeremiah, Israel's emphasis on collective responsibility and guilt at times obscured any clear apprehension of singular selfhood. But Hebraic thought had long contained the seeds of a sharper sense of individual existence and occasionally showed signs of a quest for personal significance alongside that of the entire people. Even in some of the earliest Psalms, for example, we are presented with prayers that express a deep feeling of aloneness, existential anguish, and an intense preoccupation with Yahweh's significance for the suffering individual. The prophets themselves could not but lament their own personal ostracism. Out of the inevitable loneliness to which rigorous fidelity to the promises of God often leads one, there quite naturally arises the need for clarification of what it means to be a self in relation to God. In the literature of Israel, the book of Job is perhaps the most obvious expression of this demand. This work makes it clear that revelation must respond to our personal suffering as well as to the more global demands of history and the universe.

In the Gospels, the question of human destiny is still largely framed in collective terms. God has visited the *people*, Israel. The Annunciation is

1. The following text is an excerpt. Previously published in Haught, *Mystery and Promise*, 184–98. Reprinted with permission.

understood by Luke as a climactic moment in a long series of divine promises intended not simply for an individual but for the whole people. The meaning of revelation is seldom (if ever) expressed in purely individualistic terms. Even when Jesus is raised up, he is still understood as the firstborn of the *many* who are destined for resurrection. Resurrection is primarily a collective event to which Jesus's personal exaltation provides access for all those devoted to the definitive coming of God's reign. Even in the writings of Paul, who relates revelation more immediately to the individual, it is inappropriate for Christians to think of their redemption in exclusively individualist terms. Fundamentally, the revelation of God is a cosmic and historical occurrence in which the individual is invited to participate. In fact, the individual's consciousness of salvation occurs only in those moments where there is a sense of *belonging* to a larger body composed of others and the entire universe as they are collectively being brought into unity by God. There can be no purely individual salvation.

On the other hand, in the Bible, the promise of deliverance is mediated to a group primarily through the consciousness and responsiveness of exceptional individuals. This is the case from Abraham through Jesus, Paul, and other personal vehicles of the biblical promise. The immediate context for the reception of revelation is the partly incommunicable consciousness of individual persons. Thus, the font of any specifically Christian revelation is, in some sense at least, Jesus's own consciousness.[2] We have previously pondered what seems to have occurred in the privacy of Jesus's own heart as he contemplated the divine promise in the light of his *abba* experience. It is ultimately from this deeply interior and never fully communicable experience of Jesus's relation to God that Christian revelation has its specific origin.

Moreover, it is doubtful that we would be very concerned about revelation apart from its fortifying our own *personal* existence as well. Revelation must speak to our own deepest natural longing to be regarded as intrinsically valuable. That we all crave for such valuation does not need lengthy argumentation. It seems self-evident. Along with common human experience, the behavioral sciences provide much data that can only be explained in terms of the individual's fundamental desire to be valued. Even the pain experienced in our self-rejection stems from the fact that it is so deep in our nature to want to be valued and accepted.

Another way of putting this point is to say that we seek to live without shame. Shame is the feeling that takes us over when we begin to become aware of an aspect of our being that seems unacceptable both to us and to those in our social environment. Shame is a universal human phenomenon,

---

2. This is the conclusion of Moran, *Theology of Revelation*.

and, in a certain sense, it is a necessary response to the facts of social existence. The most intimate aspects of our lives, in particular our sexual and religious feelings, need to be shielded from the objectifying and trivializing gaze of the public. Shame can provide a sort of protective function.[3] But shame may also lead us into self-deception. It may push completely out of consciousness that which we take to be unacceptable in ourselves. Thus we may completely forget essential chapters of our own life stories and repress obvious facets of our personalities for the sake of wanting to fit into some social or even religious habitat. Shame, therefore, holds us back from full self-knowledge, freedom, and the fulfillment of our personal lives.[4]

According to the insights of depth psychology, our denial of any shameful aspect of our character may lead us to project it outside of ourselves onto those in our social surroundings—where it will be interpreted as something alien to ourselves and as deserving of our antipathy. We may easily displace the disowned portions of our self onto others whose existence then becomes interpreted as inimical to our own. The sense of shame may then have disastrous social and political consequences if we decide to harm or destroy those who have become the imagined or real carriers of our own despised features.

Hence, the specter of anything approaching a wholesome life or integral society requires that we eventually learn to live with and accept as part of our own constitution those experiences and those features of our character which at present put us to shame. Revelation, if it is to be of significance to us as persons, and through us to society, must somehow address this nearly universal situation of shame.

The Bible is clearly aware of the human condition of shame. The well-known third chapter of the book of Genesis tells of the embarrassment of nakedness that led the man and woman to hide from God. The aboriginal consequence of sin is shame. The historical books of the Bible, the Prophets, Job, and the Psalms make numerous allusions to the feeling of shame: "All day long my disgrace is before me, and shame has covered my face." (Ps 44:15) Indeed, shame could be said to be one of the dominant themes in the biblical description of the human condition. In Israel's experience, it was considered shameful to be barren, to be sick or menstruating, to be subject to the authority of an alien nation, and to be dying or dead. Such

3. See Frankl, *Unconscious God*.

4. We must distinguish what we are calling shame from the healthier and essential feeling of true guilt or sinfulness, for the latter may itself be concealed beneath shame. The awareness of sin actually becomes most vivid in the experience of grace, an experience in which shame is removed and we are enabled to acknowledge our failings without trying to hide from them

experiences were commonly interpreted as evidence of divine disfavor, of being cut off from healthy relationship to others and the world, and as reasons to hang one's head or to seek refuge from the living God.

Shame still remains as a major facet of our own experience today, thus linking our situation very closely to that of the Bible. This aspect of our existence opens up a common context (a hermeneutical circle), allowing the Bible to speak directly to us in our concrete individual lives. Because of its dominating concern with this common human experience, it is difficult to support the notion that the Bible is too foreign for us to understand it. Shame continues to shade the lives of all of us to some extent, including those who call themselves followers of Jesus. In the case of many individuals, shame is especially crippling. It may not be an exaggeration to say that the anguish of shame is the main problem each human being has to face. The fact of shame also still has enormous social repercussions. How many evils and horrors in our social and historical life can be accounted for simply as the result of attempts by powerful individuals to conquer or cover up their own private disgrace? By overcompensating for some unaccepted weakness in themselves, potentates and tyrants unleash their demand for significance in ways that end up destroying the lives of other people as well as their own subjects.

Erich Neumann, among others, has shown how those who think of themselves as strong and self-sufficient may, at times, project their inner sense of inferiority onto the more vulnerable ethnic, economic, and religious groups in their social environment.[5] This is how he interprets the phenomenon of Nazism. Like the rest of us, the Nazi has a "shadow side," consisting of disowned weakness, cowardice, moral ineptitude, and general vulnerability. When this shadow side is not integrated into self-consciousness, it is easily projected outward, onto others or onto social minorities. This leads to an obsession with eliminating Jews and other groups who seem to embody those features that one hates in oneself. Ideal human development, on the other hand, consists of a conscious and often painful appropriation of this shadow side.

One does not have to be a follower of C. G. Jung, however, to realize that we all have something like a "shadow side"—a complex of feelings and character traits that we have perhaps unconsciously disowned. We usually first encounter this shameful side of ourselves as it is reflected back to us from other people who seem to carry our own despised features. The inability or refusal to acknowledge our own weaknesses then leads us to reject other people who appear to us to embody these traits. It would follow,

5. See Neumann, *Depth Psychology.*

therefore, that whatever propels us toward reintegrating the lost or shameful aspects of ourselves could also facilitate reconciliation between ourselves and other individuals or groups. Does revelation contribute to such integration? And if so, how might we articulate its effectiveness?

## The Humility of God and the Quest for Significance

The portrait of God as self-giving love, capable of sharing in our suffering, can have a very destabilizing effect on society and its history. We may now observe how this same image interrupts the "ordinary" life and self-consciousness of the individual. Those who have truly been conquered by this image have undergone a dramatic, inward transformation. They have found in the image of God's own self-effacement a refuge from the compulsion to persist in a life based on shame. This revelatory image of ultimate reality as self-emptying love liberates them from the anxiety of never having done quite enough to please the other. Let us look more closely at how this may be so.

So powerfully internalized are societal and religious criteria of personal worth that we often cannot conjure up any other images of God than those modeled on significant persons before whom our societal performance is ordinarily executed. Thus, our "God" is likely to be in large measure a projection onto mystery of those very authorities before whom we experience shame whenever our performance is deficient. Hence, by its challenge to our favored images of God, especially those that present God as one whose favor we must win by our religious or ethical performances, the subversive, revelatory image of a God who participates in our own shame pulls the rug out from under a society that seeks by way of religion to legitimate its exclusivism. Simultaneously, it also undermines the individual's compulsion to "perform" in order to prove his or her significance.

In Jesus's teaching about God, our childish projection of a deity who scrutinizes our performance and keeps a record of it as a basis for accepting or rejecting us is shattered. In Christian faith's never fully cherished identification of God with the crucified Christ, the projection is radically dismantled. Death by crucifixion was quite probably the most shameful situation imaginable for an individual at the time of Jesus. And Christian revelation, along with subsequent theological reflection, announces to us that God was fully present in Jesus in this most shameful of conditions. The corresponding image of God as one who embraces this depth of human shame as an aspect of the divine life amounts to nothing less than a metaphysical abolition of all the alternative ideas of God, most of which lend sanction to our exclusivist heroics. By identifying with the outcast Jesus, the man slain through the most shameful form of execution, God is disclosed as one who includes all that we normally exclude. This means not only others that we may have rejected. It also includes our own weakness and shame.

Devotion to the kenotic God can be altogether disruptive of our "normal" social arrangements, all of which have some degree of exclusivism. The possibility of such suspension of normality helps us understand why so few societies and religions (including most forms of Christianity and Christian theology) have taken this image seriously. On the whole, they have been much more comfortable with the dictatorial image of God, an image that legitimates and preserves the status quo with all the built-in exclusivity that this implies. They have eschewed the defenseless deity revealed on the cross and have preferred instead one whose central function is to keep a record of our ethical and religious achievement. This works-oriented deity legitimates the comfortable, informational boundaries that keep us segregated from one another in our social and religious worlds, as well as from the suppressed dimensions of our own selves.

Any revolution at the social level cannot be effective in a lasting way apart from a radical change in our personal self-understanding. It is doubtful whether social transformations that might open us to the otherness within society could really become actual unless individual persons within that society simultaneously learn to accept the "shameful" otherness within themselves.[6] The individual's own partialized sense of selfhood is inseparable from and reflective of the exclusivist social situations in which we learn how not to be whole. A society that avoids the alien elements within itself teaches us as individuals to accept only those aspects of our own private existence that correspond favorably to the system of heroics that shapes our performance. For that reason, someone whose personal character becomes clearly manifest in its willingness to accept compassionately the excluded and forgotten, those whose lives are burdened with shame, will be exceptionally disruptive both to society and the individuals within that society.

By virtue of our personal avoidance of the shameful side of ourselves, we become accomplices of society's neglect of those elements that do not fit into its requirements of worth. Our self-definition in terms of a society's

6. See Neumann, *Depth Psychology.* At the same time, as we have been arguing, the revolution within the self cannot take place independently of a social revolution which dismantles those external, informational boundaries that we internalize in such a way as to cause shame. It is not a question of the priority of self-transformation over systemic societal change. Rather, both can occur only in an ecology that involves an ongoing dynamic reciprocity between individual and society.

restrictive standards, as existentialist philosophers have taught us, is rooted in our own free decisions. We choose freely to shape our private lives by making concrete selections from the list of criteria of self-worth already available in society's inventory of values. Of course, for the most part, we have not made these choices consciously, but it is important nevertheless to acknowledge our responsibility for them. Otherwise, we will become paralyzed by the illusion that we can do nothing to help change things in a fundamental way.

In summary, how, then, does revelation confront this situation? By our faith in the God who identifies with Jesus, the God who is inseparable from the man forsaken and abandoned on the cross, we announce not only a revolution in our fundamental image of mystery but also a drastic revision of our self-understanding. This inner revolution involves the conquering of shame and of the need for self-deception. It opens access to the otherness within ourselves even while it embraces the others without.

# 19: Reason and Revelation[1]

EVEN THOUGH IT PRESUPPOSES the idea of revelation, the Bible does not make it an explicit topic of discussion. There is no self-conscious theology of revelation in the Scriptures, and the topic receives little formal attention even in the history of doctrine up until about the time of the Enlightenment. But we need not be surprised at this apparent neglect. Precisely because everything in the Bible presupposes something like what we are calling "revelation," it did not need to be an independently justified theme during most of the Christian centuries. The pervasive notion of God's word is already, in substance, equivalent to what we have been calling revelation. The tendency to establish, on rational grounds, the plausibility of revelation, or even to set it apart as a distinct subject of theological discussion, did not arise very explicitly until the birth of modern skepticism. The highly critical consciousness of modernity began to question the existence of God and therefore also the possibility of revelation. And so, the formal concept of revelation became a major preoccupation of fundamental theology only in modern times.[2] The problem of revelation coincides (though it is not coextensive) with what might be called the "God-question." Deliberate theological defense of revelation occurs only in an age that has come to doubt the reality of any divine transcendence at all.

The modern situation of skepticism, however, has led to an overburdening of the notion of revelation in much contemporary theology. Since mystery often fails to show up palpably in ordinary experience or in the investigations of science and academic life, many Christian theologians have argued that it is the task of special divine revelation to give us our first awareness of the dimension of transcendence essential to religious experience.[3] Mystery, they imply, touches our lives only in our contact with the

---

1. The following text is an excerpt. Previously published in Haught, *Mystery and Promise*, 199–214. Reprinted with permission.

2. See Weber, *Foundations of Dogmatics*, 172.

3. This is implicit, for example, in Thiemann, *Revelation and Theology*. It is also the approach taken by Karl Barth and many other (mostly Protestant) theologians. Pannenberg rightly states: "It is not true that the revelation, the self-disclosure of God, falls from heaven ready-made. Nor must it be the starting point of all knowledge of God, as if one could not otherwise know anything about him." See Pannenberg, "Revelation of God," 118.

Christian Gospel. Evangelically inclined theologians, for example, generally insist that a special Christian revelation is our only authentic access to the sacred. Thus, for them, mystagogy no longer precedes a theology of revelation, but it is a consequence thereof. Revelation provides the answer not only to the question about what God is like or who God is but also to *whether* there is any divine mystery at all.

This approach, which makes the event of revelation also do the work of fundamental theology, is not always helpful for Christian faith's encounter with the modern world. First, it displays an unwarranted distrust of human nature and of the created order inasmuch as it denies our native capacity to know something of sacred mystery apart from our being specifically Christianized. Second, it undermines the possibility of our learning anything about God from an encounter with other religions. Third, it ignores the legitimate demands by sincere critics that a theology of revelation, though it cannot be derived from reason and science, must at least show itself to be consonant with them.

A theology of revelation that ignores these three objections collapses into an esotericism, releasing Christians from their obligation to participate in the realm of public discourse. Thereby, it renders their faith of little consequence to communal human life and, at times, also allows it to retreat into political and social irrelevance. Earlier, we supported the first objection by arguing that a theology of revelation must be prefaced with a mystagogical opening to the silent dimension of mystery from which any revelatory word or vision might come forth to us and thus be experienced as disclosed or "unconcealed." The very notion of revelation cannot make sense without some pre-apprehension of mystery. We articulated the second objection by insisting that a Christian theology of revelation must not be isolated from the revelation of mystery as it occurs in the sacramental, mystical, silent, and active features of other religions as well.

Having already addressed these first two issues, the present chapter shall focus on the questions raised by modern critics about the consonance of rational and scientific discourse with the idea of revelation. Though it is not possible to establish that revelation is a fact on rational or scientific grounds alone, can we at least show that our trust in revelation bears the mark of truthfulness, especially in the face of so much contemporary skepticism rooted in the enlightenment and the scientific revolution? Is trust in revelation a "truthful" posture for human consciousness to assume?

## Truth as Disclosure

Traditionally, truth means the *correspondence* of the mind with reality. In this sense, truth is formally an aspect of propositions or judgments. But there are other ways in which the word "truth" can be understood. One of these is the *pragmatic* model of truth, according to which the truth of something is assessed in terms of its functional value or its usefulness. Another is the *disclosure* model of truth, according to which truth is that which manifests or "unconceals" itself. For example, a great work of art or literature can have such a profound effect on us that we are immediately certain that a new depth of reality, previously unknown, has now been revealed to us. This experience of truth as disclosure is most naturally congenial to the idea of religious revelation, though in a limited sense the correspondence and pragmatic models may also be used in our assessment of its truth status.

If there is truth in religion or in revelation it would fall, primarily at least, in the category of "manifestation" or "disclosure." In this case, it would be inappropriate to employ the notion of truth as correspondence of mind and reality since, by definition, the content of revelation far surpasses the adequacy of our own minds. As in art, music, and poetry, the truth of revelation is not something that we might arrive at in the same way as scientific or logical truth. It is, instead, a truth that grasps us by its disclosive power. We could hardly subject it to our verificational control, but would instead be required to surrender ourselves to it in order to encounter its content.

Still, after acknowledging this obvious fact, we are nonetheless obliged to determine whether there is a positive relationship between revelation and a scientifically enlightened reason which employs the correspondence notion of truth. If these are in conflict, as indeed they seem to many critics to be, then the notion of revelation will not be taken seriously by intelligent people. We must, at the very least, establish that revelation does not contradict science and reason. If we go beyond this assertion, to demonstrate that a trust in revelation actually *supports* the work of science and reason, we will have taken a step further in responding to the skeptics.

Skepticism approaches the question of revelation's truth-status by asking whether its content can be independently verified by science or reason. However, it seems that the very character of revelation places it beyond the scope of any procedure that might demonstrate, here and now, its congeniality to rational or scientific inquiry. For, as we have been emphasizing, revelation comes to us in the form of promise. If this is the case, then it would seem that, in the present, we are simply not in a position to verify it. We can do so only if and when the promise comes to fulfillment. As

Ronald Thiemann argues, any justification of truth-claims about revelation "has an inevitable eschatological or prospective dimension. The justifiability of one's trust in the truthfulness of a promise is never fully confirmed (or disconfirmed) until the promiser actually fulfills (or fails to fulfill) his/her promise." He adds: "Until the time of fulfillment, the promise must justify trust on the basis of a judgment concerning the character of the promiser."[4] It is only in relation to what we can discern from our faith story about the character of God that we can make any defense of revelation in the face of critical objections to its validity.

How such discernment itself takes place, though, is itself not entirely clear. It would seem that, once again, we have to resort to something like Niebuhr's distinction between internal and external history—at least as a point of departure. It is not unreasonable to insist that an adequate discernment of God's character as "faithful to promise" could take place only from within the framework of our involvement in a faith community built up around the narration of *previous* instances of God's fidelity. To attempt a justification of revelation from a foundational standpoint completely detached from an involvement with the stories about God would be futile. Such an approach would amount to something like an attempt to prove logically or scientifically that someone has fallen in love with you, even though you have never met that person or experienced his or her love. The experience of revelation occurs only in the concrete context of attending to the accounts of God's fidelity as they are told to us (or in some alternative way brought home to us) by others who have actually, according to their own testimony at least, been touched by God's fidelity in their own lives. It is especially in our experience of the ways these others themselves sacramentally embody and live out the character of God's faithfulness in their own lives that we become convinced of the fact of a transcendent fidelity. The justification of revelation requires that we ourselves first risk involvement in a community that promotes a life of promise-keeping.[5] It seems fruitless to attempt any adequate justification of Christian revelatory truth claims if, at the same time, we make the requirement of belonging to a sacramental community only optional.

Nevertheless, it is not entirely without value for theology to attempt, at the same time, in a subordinate and supportive manner, some kind of

4. Thiemann, *Revelation and Theology*, 94.

5. It is especially for this reason that the lifetime marriage commitment is such a powerful sacrament of God's own character as promise-keeper. Without sacraments of promise, we might wonder how we could ever be led to the belief that the fidelity to promise is also the nature of ultimate reality. Such sacraments (and not necessarily in the formal sense) are our most powerful media of revelation.

rational "justification" of the central claims of revelation. Such an effort is a necessary component of any sort of engagement of theology with those who live outside the context of the faith community. If we fail to make such an effort, we risk isolating Christian faith from cultural and academic life. It might even be arrogant (and "gnostic") for us to refrain altogether from such a dialogical enterprise. The recent trend of much Christian theology toward a so-called non-foundational approach runs the risk of such esotericism. Its a priori ruling out of the possibility that there are shared cognitional characteristics between the members of the Christian tradition on the one hand and the kind of critical thinking that goes on outside of it on the other is defeating to both faith and thought. Only a joint faith in the possibility of finding some common ground can bring about genuine conversation between believers and non-believers, or between and among representatives of various faith traditions.

Chastened by our new awareness of the historicity, relativity, and linguistic constraints that shape all modes of human experience and consciousness, we may nonetheless attempt here to demonstrate that there already exists, even in the consciousness of skeptics and critics of revelation, a natural and ineradicable experience of the fact that reality, at its core, has the character of consistency and "fidelity" that emerges explicitly in the self-revelation of a promising God. It is possible to argue that without an implicit conviction that reality is, in its depths, faithful and not capricious, even doubt and criticism are inconceivable. The reflective discovery (by what is called transcendental inquiry) that reality is grounded in that most faithful bedrock, namely, "truth itself," is not incidental to a justification of Christian revelation's central truth-claim that reality, at its core, is forever faithful. While such assurance only emerges in an adequate way in the sacramentality of religious existence, it can also be argued that it is even implicit in criticism, doubting, and suspicion.

We have been looking into the question of the rational justifiability of faith's trusting in God's self-humbling love. But the other aspect of revelation that we have been highlighting throughout this book is its promissory character. In the biblical experience of revelation, mystery has the character of promise. Ontologically speaking, revelation is the self-gift of God, but historically and linguistically speaking, this gift takes the shape of a promissory utterance. Apparently, within our finite temporal context, the infinite mystery we call God can be received only indirectly as promise, rather than directly as knowledge.[6] Finite reality, in any case, could not assimilate the fullness of infinity in any single receptive moment. Hence, God's revelatory

---

6. See Thiemann, *Revelation and Theology*, 151–56.

self-gift could hardly become fully manifest in any particular present. In its superabundance, it conceals itself, according to the nature of promise and hope, in the mysterious and inexhaustible realm of the future.

For this reason, Wolfhart Pannenberg rightly refers to revelation as the "arrival of the future."[7] The divine futurity only reveals itself to us in our present history in the mode of promise. The God of the Bible constantly goes "before" us and speaks to us out of an always new future. In order to receive this revelation, the addressees of promise must in turn assume a posture of radical openness to the future. This is the posture known as *hope*.

Once again, we must emphasize that what we are calling critical consciousness is shaped primarily by what it can clearly determine to have happened in the past. Scientific method relies on present data deposited by the past. For example, evolutionary theory needs the present fossil record, left over by past cosmic happenings, in order to arrive at appropriate judgments about the emergence of the various forms of life. The situation is quite different, though, when it comes to revelation. Here, the data from which the hypothesis of revelation is construed by faith have their proper origin in the domain of the promised future. It is from out of the future that the divine reality discloses itself. And since the future lies beyond what can be made empirically available, there is a sense in which we must conclude that it is impossible for us to justify revelation according to critical methods. If we had complete access to or possession of revelation, moreover, it would no longer hold out any promise to us. Hope would fade in the face of the total presence of what had been concealed but now has become perfectly clear. Life would lose its depth and there would be no more future to look forward to.[8]

Our thesis, then, is that revelation (as we have understood its substance throughout this book), though not verifiable by science, is fully supportive and nurturing of the faith assumptions that undergird science as well as reason. In the context of a university, for example, revelational knowledge does not conflict with but rather can be properly understood as assisting the autonomous search for truth undertaken by the various disciplines. We may recall how our limit-questions place all the disciplines in

7. According to Pannenberg, it is especially in Jesus's resurrection that we are met by our ultimate future: "By contemplating Jesus's resurrection, we perceive our own ultimate future." He adds: "The incomprehensibility of God, precisely in his revelation, means that, for the Christian, the future is still open and full of possibilities." Pannenberg, *Faith and Reality*, 58-59.

8. It is questionable, therefore, whether even an eschatological fulfillment for finite beings could be one in which the divine presence completely obliterates the futurity (mystery) of God.

question and demand a justification that lies outside the boundaries of the disciplines themselves. Why bother with science? Why be concerned about the ethical life? Why seek beauty? What started out in this chapter as a question concerning the rational and scientific justifiability of revelation has, at this point, turned into a question about the justifiability of the enormous amount of trust that underlies the critical scientific enterprise itself. That there is such trust beneath reason and science now seems undeniable. And this trust is no less in need of justification than faith in the word of promise that we find at the heart of revelation.

It seems, therefore, that critical consciousness itself cannot find a point outside of or devoid of trust, whereby it could settle the issue of the justifiability of the trust that motivates science and reason. Trust is a condition that makes critical consciousness possible in the first place; it would also be a factor in all critical efforts we might undertake to justify any beliefs. The validity of trust in truth, goodness, and beauty, therefore, is incapable of being scientifically grounded, for it would have to be already present in every such grounding activity. Hence, faith in revelation's word about the ultimately trustworthy character of reality is no less rational than is the trust in truth, goodness, and beauty that makes all academic pursuits possible. It is a companion to, and not an opponent of, the trust without which there simply can be no rational and scientific inquiry. Hence, it seems inappropriate for criticism to demand a scientific justification of faith in revelation when it cannot do the same with respect to the very trust in which it is itself rooted. In the case of both faith and criticism, human consciousness seems to be related, at some level, to what we can only call trustworthiness or—in terms of revelation—fidelity.

We started out by asking whether the claims of revelation are in conflict with the desire to know. The fundamental test of the truthfulness of any content of consciousness is whether our holding onto it promotes the interests of our desire to know. We have argued that faith in the promise of divine fidelity given through revelation liberates our desire to know from the self-deception that stands between it and reality. By allowing our lives to be informed by trust in God's fidelity, our desire to know can flow more freely toward its objective than could a life in which such trust is absent. Therefore, reason, science, and criticism are not in conflict with, but are actually supported by, the trust evoked by the promises of revelation.

# 20: Science and Revelation[1]

CHRISTIANITY IS A RELIGION whose teachings are said to come from a special *revelation*. But what is revelation? Is revelation not a set of events that interrupts and contradicts the natural manner in which things take place? Is Einstein perhaps correct in his assertion that revelation is incompatible with science? Revelation, like miracles, seems to breach the tightly closed continuum of causes and effects that make up the natural world, at least as science sees it. Consequently, many scientists and philosophers—especially those I have been referring to as scientific naturalists—find Christianity, as well as other revealed religions, unbelievable.

This book, as the reader will already have noted, is a theological conversation not only with believers, scientists, and other inquisitive people but also with scientific naturalists: the main contemporary representatives of what Friedrich Schleiermacher called the cultured despisers of religion.[2] As I have already pointed out, it is not science as such, but the modern belief-system of scientific naturalism that rejects the possibility of any special revelation. It is important that contemporary theological reflections on nature remain aware of the naturalistic belief system and its claims that theology has no business commenting on nature at all. According to scientific naturalists, reliable understanding must be publicly accessible and subject to empirical testing. Since revelation does not submit to such criteria, naturalists dismiss Christianity as illusory.

Christians understand their faith as a response to the divine mystery that presents itself in the person, life, words, actions, death, and resurrection of Jesus. But I think we can say that this revelation is an eruption, not an interruption, of nature. Accordingly, revelation is not a violation of nature's inviolable routines, but an expression—in symbolic terms—of a deep and momentous drama always going on in the depths of the universe and human history. The reality and power of this drama are inaccessible to science and can only become part of the worldview of people of faith who have allowed themselves to be swept up into it. Revelation, like science, is about what is *really* going on in the universe, but it discloses to faith a dimension of reality

---

1. The following text is an excerpt. Previously published in Haught, *Christianity and Science*, 34–50. Reprinted with permission.

2. See Schleiermacher, *On Religion*.

that necessarily goes unnoticed by scientific inquiry. It does not contradict science, but it does call for acknowledging the limitations of science.

Theology must respect the integrity and autonomy of science but, at the same time, it may question whether science alone can capture everything that is going on in the universe. A theology of nature does not deny that science can put the human mind in touch with nature or that science can reveal previously unknown things about the universe. Yet, without taking anything away from science, it proposes that there are levels of depth in nature that science simply cannot reach. A theology based on revelation does not compete with science or conflict with it in any way. It is complementary to it, in the sense that it contributes something to the larger picture of reality that science cannot. A theology of nature construes the universe in such a way as to support the work of science while refusing to confuse science with scientism and scientific naturalism.

Like science, revelation implies that there is always much more to the world than what *seems* to be the case.[3] Good scientists are willing to abandon or revise their theories and hypotheses whenever they sense that there is deeper intelligibility beneath their all too simple models and mathematical calculations. Hearers of a divine revelatory word, for their part, are also at times obliged to reach for fresh symbols, or perhaps lapse into complete silence, in the presence of the incomprehensible mystery that grounds, sustains, and fulfills the universe.

The God of Christian faith is encountered in and through the observable world. Revelation unveils the divine mystery by way of symbols derived from our experience of nature and social existence. Revelation occurs not only in words but also in sacraments derived from nature. That is, natural phenomena, and not just events in human history, participate in and thus point us toward the mystery of God. Water, light, food, soil, fertility, life, and human personality are indispensable to the experience of revelation. God is known not apart from nature but in and through it. By virtue of the Incarnation, the entire drama of nature, unfolding across billions of years, is also the revelation of God.


## The Gift of an Image

In the Christian context, however, revelation is fundamentally the gift of the infinite mystery of God's own being *to* the finite world. The primary sacrament or symbol of God's self-gift is the person of Christ, but scientific awareness, today more than ever, allows us to assume that the entire universe, by virtue

3. Smith, *Forgotten Truth*, 97.

of the incarnation, is tied inseparably into the revelation of God in Christ.[4] Contemporary astrophysics compels us to acknowledge that the emergence of human life—with its capacity for thought, morality, hope, and worship— is seamlessly connected to the birth and development of an entire universe. Over the last half-century, we have learned more and more about the cosmic conditions, starting at the first instant of cosmogenesis, that had to be in place if life and thought were ever to exist at all. The cosmos and consciousness can no longer be dualistically split off from each other. Theologically, the new scientific awareness means that the appearance in our midst of the person of Christ, therefore, is not just a historical but also a terrestrial and cosmic event. From now on, when we tell the story of Jesus, we need to include not only its biblical setting, but its natural prelude as well.

Theology, until recently, has not had the opportunity to tie all the ages of the cosmos so tightly to God's revelation in Christ . . . Revelation is much more, therefore, than the *locutio Dei*, the "speech of God." It is more than what Saint Augustine called the divine "illumination" of our souls. Revelation's first meaning is not the passing on to us of propositional truths from God. It is not simply "the communication of those truths which are necessary and profitable for human salvation . . . in the form of ideas."[5] Nor is revelation reducible to "direct discourse and instruction on the part of God." It means much more than "an act by which God exhibits to the created mind his judgments in their formal expression, in internal or external words." Revelation, before everything else, is the gift of God's own being and selfhood to and through the entire *universe*.

Theologian Karl Rahner writes that the "primary phenomenon given by faith is precisely the self-emptying of God."[6] A theology of nature, therefore, will ask whether this shocking theological proposal can help people of faith make sense of what science is now finding out about the physical universe. Contemporary theology, both Catholic and Protestant, increasingly interprets revelation to mean the gift of God's own self to the world. This is an idea that flickered feebly even at the First Vatican Council: "It has pleased God to reveal himself and the eternal decrees of his will to the human race."[7] But up until not too long ago, Christian theology usually featured an excessively intellectualized and propositional understanding of revelation. Today, as the result of a closer reading of the Bible and other traditional theological sources—and thanks especially to the Second Vatican Council—theology

4. See Schillebeeckx, *Christ*.

5. Bulst, *Revelation*, 18.

6. Rahner, *Foundations of Christian Faith*, 222.

7. Neuner and Dupuis, *Christian Faith*, 43.

has been moving toward the view that the actual content of revelation is the infinite mystery of God's own being.

This content, however, comes to faith in the first place not in theological formulas, but in startling images. As the theologian H. Richard Niebuhr puts it, revelation is "the gift of an image."[8] It is "that special occasion which provides us with an image by means of which all occasions of personal and common life become intelligible."[9] A truly revelatory image must be able to render meaningful what might otherwise seem meaningless. Niebuhr goes on to say that the revelatory image offers a "pattern of dramatic unity . . . with the aid of which the heart can understand what has happened, is happening, and will happen to selves and their community." A theology of nature will add, however, that a truly revelatory image illuminates not only human history and social existence but also the entire universe.

Perhaps the reception of revelation is analogous to what happens in science when a new insight suddenly flashes into our awareness, shedding light on previously unsolved problems in a most surprising way. For example, when Copernicus and Galileo redrafted the cosmological map, construing the heavens as heliocentric rather than geocentric, numerous difficulties associated with the older Ptolemaic system suddenly went away, and more intelligible models of the heavens abruptly took their place. Imaginative breakthroughs in science have the effect of bringing to light previously hidden aspects of nature. Theories associated with Newton, Darwin, and Einstein, along with the more recent ideas in physics and geology, have all brought a surprisingly fresh coherence to our understanding of nature. These new models have also had the effect of leading to further fruitful research. Today, scientists are looking for an elegant formula that will tie together the four main physical forces in nature.[10] When and if such a theory comes along, we can safely predict that it will lead not to the end of science, as some fear. Rather, it will come as a gift that opens up surprising new areas for ongoing research and discovery.

In order to be of interest to us, revelation must, at the very least, have a similarly startling, illuminating, and fertile effect. Its content must shake our understanding of reality, including our understanding of the natural world, but in such a way as to make it more, not less, intelligible. Revelation will not compete with scientific understanding, but, in order to qualify as a momentous event of disclosure, it must help us not only

8. Niebuhr, *Meaning of Revelation*, 80.
9. Niebuhr, *Meaning of Revelation*, 80.
10. Hawking, *Brief History of Time*, 155–69.

make sense of our personal lives and human history but also of the general features of the cosmos itself.

Revelation has no answer to specific scientific questions such as how life evolves or what the mechanisms of evolutionary change might be. Revelation responds to limit-questions—not unsolved scientific problems. For example, when we ask why we should bother to do science at all, revelation may at least be able to help us understand in more depth why truth is worth seeking. Perhaps it may also be able to shed light on why nature and life are subject to evolution at all, why intelligent life appeared in the universe, why the universe is such as to allow new things to happen, and why it is such an exquisite blend of accidents, laws, and deep time as to unfold in the narrative way that allows it to be the bearer of meaning.

The "gift of an image" that Niebuhr associates with revelation will not provide any information that adds to the mound of scientific ideas, nor will it compete with science in any way. Yet revelation may still provide an enlivening sense of the *meaning* of the universe that science is now setting before us. What would be the point of our making so much of "revelation," after all, unless it has the power to make things—including the discoveries of science—even more intelligible than before?[11] Once again, revelation must be able to shed new light not only on human selfhood and human history but also on the universe.

## Christianity's Revelatory Image

But where, more specifically, can we encounter a revelatory image that would justify such an ambitious expectation? A Christian theology of nature may find its starting point in the image of a self-giving, promising God, as made manifest in Jesus of Nazareth. On the one hand, Christian faith presents the image of an infinitely loving God in Jesus, who bends humbly toward the creation in order to relate to it with unsurpassable, incarnate intimacy. On the other hand, the Scriptures, canonized by Christian tradition in narratives ranging from those about Abraham to those about Jesus's resurrection, give us the picture of a God who makes promises and, in doing so, opens up the whole of created being—not just human history—to an always new future.

Reflecting on the natural world as science understands it today, we may find that the two related themes of the "descent of God" and the "futurity of God" are most instructive. The revelatory disclosure in Christ of God's humble self-emptying may help us understand aspects of

11. See Niebuhr, *Meaning of Revelation*, 69.

nature—not least its very creation, its processive character, and the evolutionary way in which life develops—that would otherwise ultimately
remain unintelligible, no matter how far science goes in disclosing the
details of natural occurrences. At the same time, the biblical image of a
God who makes promises and remains faithful to them can help our theology of nature make new sense of the whole suite of scientific discoveries
associated with the idea of *emergence*.

The image of a self-emptying and hence intimately *relational* God,
the absolute outpouring of goodness and love, is the very essence of the
Christian experience of revelation. Reflection on the universe in light of this
image, therefore, is not optional to a theology of nature. The self-giving of
God is what the doctrines about creation, Christ, redemption, eschatology,
and the Trinity are really all about.[12] Theology more than occasionally loses
contact with the "irrational" revelatory notion that the ground of all being
is endless, unbounded, and self-giving love. But apart from the descent of
God, all the complex, systematic theological tracts, whose alleged purpose
is to clarify revelation, fall flat. They fail to illuminate what is going on not
only in our own lives but also in the depths of nature. Hence theology, especially in its dialogue with science, must keep the mystery of a dwindling,
humble, self-emptying God at the very center of its reflections. If it does so,
it may discover, to its surprise, that the recent scientific discoveries about
the universe, especially about cosmic origins, evolution, and emergence, are
not nearly so problematic theologically as they are when God is presented
as an omnipotence without love, an intelligence without compassion, an
absoluteness without relationality, an eternity purified of temporality, or an
immutability sterilized of inner drama.

## The Task of a Theology of Nature

A theology of nature should address these and similar questions that scientifically informed people are asking. Not all of them can be given full cov-
erage in the present book, of course, but my point is that they should not
remain off-limits to theological reflection on the meaning of revelation. The
universe attracts a great deal of attention today, but theological reflection
seems, at times, to take pains to avoid it. I suspect that behind this indifference, theology still harbors a residual dualism, an otherworldliness, or a kind
of cosmic pessimism of its own. Throughout the modern period, theologians
have been content, for the most part, to hand over to science the task of understanding nature while they have retreated into preoccupation with issues

12. See Jüngel, *Doctrine of the Trinity*.

of personal and social concern. The latter are worthy issues too, of course, but if theology fails to respond to the largest of human questions—those having to do with the meaning of the universe—it will seem increasingly irrelevant to those who appreciate the vistas of scientific discovery.

As Galileo insisted several centuries ago, religion and theology have no business dishing out information that human intelligence can find on its own. Nevertheless, theology's business *is* that of addressing the larger questions that arise when enlightened inquirers find themselves wondering about the meaning of what science has observed. Always respecting the autonomy of science, a theology of nature may still ask whether the emergent universe of contemporary science can be fruitfully situated within the wide circle of meaning evoked by the revelatory images of God's descent and promise. A theology of nature must never give the impression of intruding into the work of scientific investigation, but it lies within theology's proper sphere of concern to connect the substance of scientific understanding of nature to faith's sense of a self-giving mystery opening up the world to an ever-new future. Situating scientific results within a revelatory worldview can even have the effect of liberating science from the materialist quagmire into which naturalists continue to dump the data of scientific research.

A theology of nature is not indifferent to the individual's personal search for meaning. Revelation must speak to each of us in our solitude and our social existence as well. Here, however, my efforts will be directed toward connecting the revelatory image of Christian faith with the universe of the natural sciences. This perspective will allow us to de-privatize revelation and reach even beyond its socio-political meaning. Of course, an awareness of God's self-revelation first occurs in Jesus's intimate *personal* experience of God as *abba*, but a full examination of the meaning of revelation eventually carries our concern for its application outward, into the wider universe. Jesus and his work of redemption cannot be isolated from the web of natural relationships that tie him and us into the cosmos and its history. Our being is essentially cosmic as well as communal; even in our aloneness, each of us is tied to the universal. A theology of nature will keep in mind the four infinites—the immense, the infinitesimal, the complex, and the future—of nature. It will speak especially to those questions that have to do with this mystery-encompassed universe from which we are inseparable.

Among such questions today, those raised by our global environmental situation are paramount. For many people, it is proximately the current global ecological predicament that leads to the most theologically momentous limit-questions about the universe: What is the universe all about? Why should we bother to care for our little corner of it? If nature seems finally indifferent to life, why should we be worried about conservation? What are our obligations to the universe that bears us along?

Can the revelatory image of God's descent and futurity shed any light on these and similar issues? A theology that focuses exclusively on personal and social issues is ill-equipped to do so. The acosmic leaning of traditional theology deserves the accusation that "revealed" religions are responsible for promoting a noxious idea of cosmic homelessness that sets humans spiritually adrift in the universe, leading us to be indifferent toward nature. A theology of nature will take into account and respond to such criticism. Here, again, theology cannot dictate specific environmental policies any more than it can lay out definitive social or economic programs. Nevertheless, it may attempt to answer the limit-question that asks why we should bother to take care of our natural environment at all. The revelatory image of a self-humbling and promising God may help shape a vision of reality that will help us address this urgent concern.[13]

13. I do not have the space to address the question of revelation and ecology in the present book. I have attempted to do so, however, in Haught, *Promise of Nature.*

# Part V: God, Science & Purpose

# 21: Does the Universe Have a Purpose?[1]

IN ARISTOTELIAN SCIENCE, THERE can be no comprehensive understanding without knowledge of final causes . . . Prior to the modern scientific revolution, Western "science" consisted mainly of exploring all four causes, but especially the last. Cosmology itself was a search for the four causes of the universe, and both philosophy and theology simply assumed that the cosmos as a whole had a final cause: God. God was not only the ground but also the end of all things. Prescientific consciousness, shaped by philosophy and religion, nestled snugly in the impression that we live in a purposeful cosmos and that our individual lives need only conform obediently to the designs of God if we are to find ultimate happiness. It was within the framework of a teleological cosmology that theism received its classical expressions.

Modern science, however, has challenged all of this, renouncing teleological or final causal explanations as unworthy of science. Already in the sixteenth century, Francis Bacon had said that experimental observation of efficient and material causes, not "sterile" speculation about final causes, is the way to genuine knowledge. Ever since its formal debut in the seventeenth century, science has concerned itself almost exclusively with efficient and material causes—with the question of "how" things work and what they are made of. It wants nothing to do with final causes, or with "why" things are the way they are.

At the present time, there are signs that science is once again flirting with formal and final causes. It shows a fresh interest in the patterns and questions about why the world is arranged the way it is. For the most part, however, scientific thought still avoids any suggestion that questions about the purpose of things can lead us to true or useful knowledge.

Does science, therefore, completely rule out the idea of cosmic purpose as a completely obsolete kind of fiction? What follows is a summary of the ways in which each of our four "combatants" might interpret science's apparent expulsion of teleological explanation. [To understand the four sections below, first read chapter 8 above (pp 75–86)].

1. The following text is an excerpt. Previously published in Haught, *Science & Religion*, 162–82. Reprinted with permission.

## Conflict

It was only when scientists dropped the Aristotelian and theological concern about "why" objects fall and started investigating the laws that determine "how" they fall that physics was finally emancipated from its suffocating conflation with religion. By breaking free of the religious obsession with purpose, physics could at last become a truly illuminating science. Only after biology dropped its formerly mystical habits and turned its attention to the chemistry of life did it experience a truly scientific birth in the present century. As long as vitalism ruled the day, leading us on the futile search for some mysterious or supernatural "life-force," biology made no progress. Only after the life sciences began to base themselves on the mechanistic explanations of the hard science of chemistry did their practitioners become rigorously scientific.

We realize that some physicists, even of the stature of John Wheeler and Freeman Dyson, are now suggesting—on the basis of the anthropic principle—that the universe does have a kind of point to it after all. However, we [proponents of the "conflict" position] do not think there is sufficient evidence to confirm such a quasi-religious hypothesis. Cosmic pessimism seems to be the most realistic position to take, even if it sometimes hurts to do so.

The Cornell professor of natural history, William Provine, has recently written a clear summary of the stance of scientific skepticism vis-a-vis the question of cosmic purpose. His words aptly depict our position:

> [Modern evolutionary biology] tells us (and I would argue that the same message flows in from physics, chemistry, molecular biology, astrophysics, and indeed from all modern science) that there is, in nature, no detectable purposive force of any kind. Everything proceeds purely by materialistic and mechanistic processes of causation or through purely stochastic processes . . . All that science reveals to us is chance and necessity . . . modern science directly implies that the world is organized strictly in accordance with mechanistic principles. There are no purposive principles whatsoever in nature. There are no gods and no designing forces that are rationally detectable. The frequently made assertion that modern biology and the assumptions of the Judeo-Christian tradition are fully compatible is false.[2]

2. Provine, "Evolution and the Foundation of Ethics," 261.

## Contrast

The idea that the universe is "just a physical system" (as Margaret Geller states) or that it "proceeds purely by materialistic and mechanistic processes" (Provine) is not the consequence of science but of the beliefs we have been calling scientism, materialism, and reductionism.[3] It is these—and not science itself—that conflict with teleology. Cosmic pessimism is the comprehensive viewpoint of modern scientific skepticism, arising as the logical consequence of the three other components of the skeptic's belief system (scientism, materialism, and reductionism). At the deepest level, beneath cosmic pessimism there is the *belief* that the only evidence that counts is scientific evidence (scientism); then, there is the naturalist *belief* that matter is all there is to reality (materialism); and finally, there is the *belief* that only physical analysis can give us a satisfactory understanding of matter (reductionism).

Once again, we must emphasize that these are faith statements and not knowledge gained from scientific experience. They are unfalsifiable, quasi-religious assumptions. Cosmic pessimism is no less rooted in belief than is religious teleology. It is the result of conflating science with suppositions that have nothing to do with science itself. If one believes that the universe is "just a physical system," then obviously one will also have to believe that there is no point or purpose to it either. These are beliefs *about* some of the results of science, arising from outside of science, and not an inevitable consequence of scientific observation itself.

## Contact

It would be most convenient if the relationship of science to religion were as crisp and clean as the contrasters see it. However, in the real-world, things are not that uncomplicated. So here, once again, we are compelled to point out that the particular discoveries of science cannot help but have a bearing on the question of cosmic purpose. In an age of evolutionary biology and big bang physics, we cannot help asking how *this* particular universe could be said to have any point to it. We cannot protect a simplistic religious faith in cosmic purpose from facing the new challenges that come from science. Unlike the contrasters, we have no desire to divert the questions about cosmic purpose that arise out of new scientific ideas.

We agree that cosmic pessimism is a fabric woven out of a few tantalizing scientific threads mixed up with a lot of unfounded stoical, rationalistic,

3. Lightman and Brawer, *Origins*, 377.

and other sorts of belief. But we also think that, even in its purest formulations, science still poses questions about cosmic purpose that theology must address. Fortunately, where it has undertaken to do so, theology has not only met the challenges but has also undergone considerable growth in the process. It is very much to the advantage of theology that it engage in vigorous dialogue with scientific discoveries rather than incarcerate them in separate quarters where they can do no mischief. At the same time, it is entirely appropriate for cosmologists to point out to us the serious religious questions they think arise with their new findings about the universe.

But what about the issue of cosmic purpose? What contribution to its general vision of things can theology glean from conversations with physics, evolutionary biology, geology, astronomy, chaos theory, etc.? At the very least, we would answer, science has already helped us widen our teleological outlook. In its moving us away from narrow concepts of the cosmos, it has implicitly forced us to abandon unduly cramped concepts of God's designs. It has caused us, in the process, to change, in significant ways, our very understanding of the divine. The pre-Copernican pictures of God, for example, are clearly too cosmically provincial for us today. As the world-picture of science has expanded, theology has been challenged to move away from its formerly naive and generally anthropocentric articulations of nature's possible purpose.

Looking back, for example, at nature's birth and evolution with a sensibility shaped by participation in the story of our common father Abraham, we cannot help but see it all as part of one long story of promise. From the first moments of the cosmic dawn, for example, matter—though there was no known physical necessity that it do so—already arranged itself within the almost unimaginably narrow spectrum of numerical possibilities that would allow it to become hydrogen atoms, galactic clusters, supernovas, carbon, life, and eventually minds. Science itself now confesses that it could never have predicted such outcomes at the time of cosmic beginnings. It could, at that point, have had no mathematical certitude that matter would end up in all the various forms of life, of immeasurable biodiversity, or of a complexity that would lead to consciousness. The various episodes in this amazing story all came about in ways that could not have been anticipated, even in principle.

Nature, as it turns out, then, has always been pregnant with promise. Who knows what else it may have in store for the billions of years of evolution that probably lie ahead of it? Recent scientific innovations (such as those of quantum physics and chaos theory) have alerted us in totally unexpected ways to nature's continual openness to indeterminate outcomes. We realize now that cosmic pessimism was believable only because it was based on the non-narrative, abstract oversimplifications of a purely linear science. The simplistic formulas of modern science, mostly innocent of the narrative depth of the natural world, made the cosmos seem absolutely determined by the dead necessity of the past, utterly closed off to unpredictable modes of patterning. All the morose, modern ruminations about the remorselessness of the second law of thermodynamics and final cosmic doom were plausible only so long as science had fixated on emaciated abstractions that ignored the contingent openness of nature's *de facto* historicity.

Today, however, science is beginning to realize that its linear over-simplifications had indeed left out of the picture altogether the inherently unpredictable, chaotic, and open character of most natural processes. Even entropy, the notion that had formerly led to so much despair, is now being given a new reading. Instead of signaling only the heat death of the universe, entropy is now embraced as an essential condition for matter to realize new possibilities. Without a cosmic tendency toward disassembling or fragmentation, the most primitive forms of order would have dominated indefinitely, stuck in their inflexible sameness from age to age; there would have been no room for emergent complexity, since the cosmos would have solidified into triviality.

Without entropy there can be no information and, therefore, no possibility of the cosmos carrying a meaning. Entropy is what allowed the universe to cool, primordial physical symmetries to be broken, atoms to emerge out of the plasma, and acid bases in DNA to be jumbled. Without the breakdown of trivial instances of order, there could be no reconfiguration into newer forms of emergent complexity. Entropy guarantees that the cosmic story will avoid repeating forever the same old refrains and permits it to wend its way toward an always open and often surprising experimentation with novelty.

It is such openness to an indeterminate future that the new scientific accounts of the universe are now generously setting before us. A theology that makes contact with this cosmic openness will be immeasurably enriched. Materialist reductionism, on the other hand, still tries—almost in defiance of the inner logic of current scientific discovery—to suppress the obvious fact of nature's inherent openness. In its obsession with "explaining" emergent new phenomena (such as living and thinking beings) in terms of already mastered principles of chemistry and physics, reductionism damps out any appreciation of the world's future indeterminacy. Apparent novelty is interpreted simply as a reshuffling of the same old stuff that has been there forever. Matter is forced to be eternal or necessary so that the cosmos cannot open itself up to a truly new and creative future.

The new sciences of chaos and complexity (along with other developments in contemporary physics) have put an end to the idea of a necessary, closed universe. They have set before us the horizon of an unpredictable cosmic future. No longer, therefore, is there any scientifically compelling reason for a doctrinaire and pessimistic exclusion of future cosmic outcomes that might correspond to the shape of our religious hopes. There is no longer any solid reason to force the world's future trajectory into the narrow tunnel of a despair based on an obsolete scientific materialism.

Cosmic pessimism, in fact, no longer seems nearly as "realistic" as it used to in the old days when science ignored anything that could not be expressed in the form of linear mathematics. Scientific honesty now compels us to acknowledge that we can know the natural world in its actual concreteness only by watching and waiting to see how things turn out. The modern pretense of scientifically predictive power over the future has been effectively deflated. The cosmic future seems more open today than it has at any time since the birth of modern science. Our conviction, then, is that, in such a universe, there is room for surprise, promise, and hope. There is at least the *possibility* that the nature of things runs more along the contours of promise than of fate.

This opening to possibility, we are convinced, means that, once again, there is at least some room in a scientific age for religious faith. We are not suggesting, of course, that we can base the certitude of faith on any particular scientific hypotheses, but, at the same time, we cannot ignore the general demise in science of those exclusively mechanistic and deterministic notions that made modernity so suspicious of all religious aspiration. Thus, as far as we are concerned, it is a rather dramatic development that science can no longer legitimately claim, through the voice of scientism and mechanism, that the future is indifferent to our hopes.

In our faith-and-hope perspective, the "point" of the universe is closely tied up with a cosmic openness to the implantation of new forms of order. Another way of putting this is to say that the cosmic story seeks to express itself in diverse forms of beauty. By beauty we mean "the ordering of novelty" and, since beauty is a high "value" (having the same status as other transcendental values such as goodness and truth), we can say that its orientation toward beauty is what gives the cosmos a "directional" character. Although the aim toward ever new forms of beauty is not necessarily realized in a progressive fashion, it is not difficult for our new scientific-historical reading of the cosmos to detect in it a disposition to unfold in novel forms of order.

The aim toward beauty harmonizes nicely with our faith's sense that a God of promise and fidelity is the ground and artisan of the elaborate cosmic story. As we have noted before, this creative God is not coercive but persuasive. If God is love, the world will not be forced to fit into some preconceived plan; it will be gently lured toward such beauty as we see in atoms, cells, brains, and societies. This process does not need to be directional in any rigid sense. If we speak of the cosmos as purposeful, we do not mean that it is compelled toward a specific pre-established goal. For the cosmos to have a "point" to it, it is sufficient that it be open to future outcomes that take the shape of unanticipated beauty. We are convinced that the universe science is now laying out so richly before us is truly open to this kind of teleological interpretation.

## Confirmation

Without taking anything away from honest attempts to articulate the "point" of the cosmos, we prefer to highlight our faith's own reluctance, and even aversion, to saying very much about such a colossal matter. Along with the contrast position, we agree that it is not the business of science to say anything about the point of the universe. However, we wonder if it is religion's business to do so either. It's not that we suspect that there may be no point to the universe. Rather we are skeptical of any human attempts—whether scientific *or* religious—to say anything that would come close to capturing just what cosmic purpose might be. Such matters are best left shrouded in mystery.

The difference between our hesitancy and the contrasters' is that we suspect that even religion cannot say much about cosmic purpose. A radically theocentric perspective not only confirms the modesty of scientific method and its refusal to get involved with final causes. It also compels us to ask whether even our religions and theologies can make it their business to give "answers" to the question of cosmic purpose.

The contrast position correctly allows science to bracket out questions of final cause. This avoidance of teleology is not a defect but rather a strength of science. Any transgressions of the imperative to avoid discussions of purpose are not to be laid at the feet of science itself but at those of us frail human beings who have a tendency to bite off more than we are capable of theologically chewing. Both cosmic pessimists and theologians are inclined toward pretensions of omniscience. Cosmic pessimists tell us that their judgments about the indifference of the world come directly from science, even though science itself is not equipped to give us any information of this kind. However, our own position—and here is where we differ from the contrasters—is that even theologians are not able to articulate the "point" of things with anything approaching substance and clarity.

Genuine religion, after all, always has an "apophatic" aspect, that is, an inclination to silence. Silence in religion is essential in order to betoken the inadequacy of all our responses to the large questions of life. The silence of religion cautions us against trying to state in a clear and distinct way what the "point" of the universe might be. In this sense, then, religion "confirms" the reluctance of science to talk about purpose. The scientific refusal to enter into the issue of teleology is also consistent with the religious inclination to keep still about matters that are simply too big for us. In this sense, science joins with the deepest elements of religion in keeping us firmly tied to our own proper sphere, restraining our flights into things we can know nothing about.

This sharing of silence could well be one of the reasons why some deeply religious women and men have entered quite naturally and enthusiastically into scientific work. There is a humility about authentic scientific research that corresponds very well with a religious perspective on the limits of human knowing. By entrusting the answers to all of the big questions to God's mysterious providence and love, religion liberates the finite human mind so that it can concentrate, day by day, on issues more proportionate to its finite capacities. Science is one way in which the human mind finds its proper groove, so it thrives best under the umbrella of a theocentric vision of things.

A theocentric faith allows us to relax into scientific pursuits because it instructs us that the big issues—such as cosmic purpose—need not become our own worry. Therefore, we have a great deal of respect for those scientists who, in their role as scientists, refuse to get side-tracked into answering questions about the "point" of the universe. Their reticence is not always a sign of cosmic pessimism. Perhaps, just as often, it is an implicit protection of the mystery they implicitly sense at the heart of the universe. Theological attempts to articulate the point of the universe inevitably sound flat and inconsequential, so it is sometimes refreshing to see scientists diverting the issue with humorous or irreverent remarks.

Teleological discourse, then, is not something we should casually enter into. The wisdom of our religious traditions almost unanimously instructs us that it is not necessarily our business to know the purpose of the universe.

# 22: Do We Belong Here?[1]

Do HUMAN BEINGS REALLY belong in this universe? Were we "meant" to be here? We usually think of ourselves as special, mostly because of our capacity for reflective thought: we are beings endowed not only with life but also with a high degree of "mind." But doesn't the fact of mind—in a universe that seems largely mindless—somehow estrange us from that very universe? How do beings endowed with consciousness and self-awareness fit into the general picture of nature that science has given us? Or do we fit in at all?

One prominent form this kind of "explanation" is taking today is the *anthropic principle*.[2] Derived from the Greek word "anthropos" which means "human being," the anthropic principle maintains that the cosmos, from its very opening moment, was set up in such a way that allows for the eventual existence of persons endowed with mind. This would sound hopelessly obvious except that there is, as of yet, no known scientific reason why it might not have been "set up" in a different way. There is a "remarkable" congruity between the physics of the early universe and the eventual appearance of mind in cosmic evolution. Doesn't the eventual existence of mind, then, have something to do with the force of gravity, the rate of cosmic expansion, the critical density of the cosmos, and the relative values affixed to the primordial particles and forces?

This truly "astonishing hypothesis" is receiving an enormous amount of press today. Some scientists consider it outrageously unscientific, while others find it intriguing and even compelling. Though it is extremely controversial, talk about an anthropic principle, whatever its merits, at least demonstrates how difficult it now is for science to situate the observing human mind outside of the observed world. Even though it could formerly get by with this expulsion, science itself now implies that our minds cannot help casting their subjective shadow over all that we observe, perhaps even the physics of the early universe.

It seems that our subjectivity is mixed in with everything we try to set forth in purely objective daylight. Mind is at least dimly present even in the earliest phases of cosmic evolution—at a time when we were not

1. The following text is an excerpt. Previously published in Haught, *Science & Religion*, 120–41. Reprinted with permission.

2. See Barrow and Tipler, *Anthropic Cosmological Principle*.

supposed to have been present in any way. Along with relativity and quantum theory, discussions surrounding the anthropic principle seem to suggest that the fundamental features of the physical universe might not be completely separable from the existence of observers. Some physicists are now even proposing that the anthropic principle requires the existence of a transcendent, ordering providence. In other words, we are getting perilously close to a new version of natural theology's old design argument for the existence of God.

It is important to point out, though, that the anthropic principle has both weak and strong versions. In its "weak" formulation, it sets forth no more than the obvious, namely, that we can see in the cosmos only what the conditions that produced us allow us to see. The Weak Anthropic Principle (WAP) maintains that the early universe looks the way it does to physics because, were it otherwise, we wouldn't be here to observe it. We are only able to understand a universe that could produce minds capable of understanding it. In this weak version, the principle has no explanatory value and therefore hardly deserves the name of "principle." Nor does it seem to evoke much in the way of theological interest.

The Strong Anthropic Principle (SAP) goes much further. It holds that the physical character of the universe is the way it is *because* of mind. It is the natural world's impetus toward evolving into beings with minds that has shaped the fundamental features of the universe from the beginning. An acorn's tendency to grow into an oak tree is the best explanation for the seed's properties. Likewise, the propensity of the universe to ripen in the direction of conscious beings is the best explanation for why the seedling universe was the way it was.

The eventual production of conscious beings is the simplest and most elegant explanation of why the universe began to expand at the rate that it did, why gravity has the force that it does, and why the ratio of electron mass to proton mass was fixed exactly the way it is. Its bent toward producing persons with minds best explains why the universe has so many stars and why it is so vast and old. A younger or smaller universe could never have produced mind.

Even if Earth is the only place where mind concretely exists, the universe as a whole would still have to be as old and as big as it is for this to happen in just one place. Moreover, a universe with an actual density that was different from its critical density by as little as a trillionth could probably not have produced us. If the total mass of the universe were not exactly the right amount to keep it from expanding too fast, mind could never have appeared. The existence of mind, therefore, is "exquisitely sensitive" to the initial conditions and fundamental constants that were fixed during the first second of the universe's existence.

The cosmic inclination or *nisus* toward mind explains why the force of gravity, for example, balances so delicately with the rate of cosmic expansion. If gravity had been only slightly stronger, it would have put the brakes on the universe's expansion long before sufficient time had transpired to cook up the carbon and other heavy elements that go into the evolution of brains—a process that requires several billion years of baking time. If gravity had been only infinitesimally weaker, cosmic expansion would have been too rapid, the force of attraction between clouds of hydrogen gas too slight, to allow for the formation of the kind of stars that could produce the heavier chemicals needed for making living and thinking beings.

If there was ever to be anything like mind, an incredibly delicate balancing act between gravity and cosmic expansion was required *at the very beginning* of the universe. Thus the simplest way to explain all the physical properties of the early universe, all the "fine-tuning" of initial cosmic conditions and fundamental constants, is that they are oriented toward mind. No other explanation is more direct and economical. A Copernicus, Darwin, or Einstein could hardly have provided a simpler and more satisfying solution to so many scientific puzzles.

The SAP implies, therefore, that, since the cosmos has always had an inclination to evolve into mind, it can no longer be said to be indifferent to the eventual appearance of human beings capable of thought. The SAP affirms that we do indeed belong here. This, at any rate, is the argument of those scientists who embrace the Strong Anthropic Principle. But is the SAP really a valid scientific explanation? Or is it just one more instance of the conflation of science with a belief system—in this case, the belief that human beings are the central reality in this vast universe?

Before we examine the possible answers, it is only fair to point out that many of its proponents now agree that "anthropic principle" is not a felicitous label for what we are talking about here. Making the cosmic process center so much on *human* mentality smacks of arrogance. What if there are other intelligent beings in the universe? Or what if our own minds are simply the initial sparks of an eventually wider and deeper kind of mentality (or information processing) that will continue to grow in new and grander ways in the future evolution of the cosmos? Would it not be more appropriate to speak somewhat less immodestly of a "mind-bearing" principle, or perhaps of a "life-and-mind-bearing" principle? This would allow for life and intelligence in other parts of the universe and eliminate criticism that the principle is too provincial and human-centered to be taken seriously.

Let us grant this necessary qualification. Is the central idea behind the Strong Anthropic Principle still worth discussing, namely, that mind is an inherent part of nature and not just an evolutionary accident? A good number of scientists and theologians now think the SAP is indeed at least worthy of close examination. Cannot the existence of mind account for all the main physical features of the material universe? Or is it more likely that the idea of a completely mindless evolution of matter, blindly following the laws of natural selection, still contains the best explanation for the apparent fit mind has to nature? Let us look now at how our four approaches might react to the SAP as an issue in science and religion.

## Conflict

Those of us who have any esteem at all for authentic science will immediately detect something very dubious about the SAP. We smell the aroma of metaphysics and final causes, features that have no place in our discipline. If it were not for the fact that the SAP is being put forth by respected scientists themselves, we would not pay any attention to it at all. It clearly runs against the grain of scientific method by attempting to explain a chronologically earlier set of occurrences (the initial cosmological conditions and fundamental constants) in terms of results (life and mind) that don't appear until much later in time—indeed billions of years later! How can you call that "explanation" in any genuine sense of the term? To science, only those events that chronologically precede or lead up to other events may be called explanatory. The SAP is simply another unscientific instance of teleological speculation, so it merits no further consideration by self-respecting scientists.

As we have been saying throughout this book, the existence of living and thinking beings can be adequately accounted for by chemistry and physics, along with, of course, the immense spans of time by which life and mind have had the opportunity to come about accidentally. Through a combination of physical necessity and chance combinations of mindless particles, life and mind will eventually issue forth, if given enough time, and there has been time aplenty. There is no sound reason to fancy that all fifteen billion years of evolution happened *in order* to produce humans with minds or any other kind of "mental" realities that might exist. The SAP is really nothing more than a rationalization of anthropocentric hubris. It is just another attempt to make our existence seem special and privileged in the face of the universe's unfeeling immensity.

It is not surprising, of course, that the structure of the universe conforms to our existence. Obviously, the material circumstances have to be just right for life and mind to come about. So we readily accept the Weak Anthropic Principle (WAP), according to which we can understand only those physical conditions that have allowed our minds to evolve. But this weak version has no explanatory value and is scientifically useless, although it is not wrong. It explains nothing that we did not already know. It is not remarkable that we can become aware only of those physical parameters that have allowed us to exist.

The SAP, on the other hand, is completely repugnant to us. Perhaps it would have more allure if we could be certain that the present universe were the *only* one that has ever existed. For it is undeniable that the physical constants and initial conditions of *this* universe are indeed suited with great precision to the evolution of living and conscious beings. We must admit that if these conditions had been different we would certainly not be here. We accept all of this.

But the real question at issue here is whether the emergence of mind is "remarkable" enough to call forth a theistic explanation. A few of our number would suggest that no other universe is physically possible than this mind-bearing one, in which case the existence of mind is not anything to wonder about. For all we know, the universe just *had* to be this way, by virtue of an impersonal necessity that we do not yet fully understand. But most of us are willing to concede now, in the light of big bang cosmology, that the physical properties of this universe are not necessary and that they well could have been other than the mind-bearing variety.[3] As far as we know, most other sets of cosmic conditions and constants would not have permitted life and mind to evolve. But contemporary physics allows for a multiplicity of worlds, perhaps even an infinite number of them. Most of these worlds would probably be stillborn and mindless. If, as we think may well be the case, there are an infinite number of universes, most of which are not fit for mind, then it is not so arresting that at least one of them would, just by accident, favor the evolution of beings like ourselves.

3. Perhaps the inflationary hypothesis that came out of the early 1980's eliminates the need to pack so much into the initial cosmic conditions. Many of the remarkable coincidences that the SAP attributes to initial conditions may have also come about by physical necessity during an "inflationary epoch," only small fractions of a second after the big bang. See Smoot, *Wrinkles in Time*, 190–91.

## Contrast

We are not enthusiastic about the SAP either. Unfortunately, well-intentioned but theologically naive scientists and believers are likely to seize
upon it and use it as a "proof" of God's existence. They will argue in the
fashion of natural theology's dubious design argument that only God could
have arranged the world in so delicate and harmonious a fashion that matter
would lead eventually to mind. They will seek in the SAP scientific support
for their religious faith, a faith which loses its intensity and depth as soon as
it begins to rely upon any such rational or scientific props.

It is primarily on religious and theological grounds that we distance
ourselves from the SAP. We have previously shown how "unreligious" such
attempts at scientific validation of God really are. Even if scientists concluded that some intelligent being had tinkered with the initial conditions
and cosmological constants, pointing them in the direction of life and mind,
this "being" would still be an abstraction, not the living God of religion.
It would be a great empty plugger of gaps, and not the personal God of
Abraham, Moses, Jesus, and Muhammad. The SAP is no more capable of
confirming or deepening our religious life than are the old arguments for
God's existence. The realms of science and religion are radically distinct.
Once again, then, in the interest of maintaining the integrity of both religion
and science, we refuse to derive any theological consequences or religious
comfort from this spuriously "scientific" theory.

Finally, it would not be such bad news to us even if science concluded
that mind does not fit very comfortably into the cosmos. At the core of our
being, faith tells us, we don't really belong to this world anyway. Our home
is elsewhere. Look at all the religious texts that instruct us to accept our
situation as only pilgrims in a foreign land. We are no more than "strangers
and exiles on the earth" as the Christian author of the Epistle to the Hebrews
puts it (Heb 11:13), so we are not impressed by a cosmological thinking
that makes mind and personality too much a part of the "natural" order.
This only trivializes humanity, absorbing us into the material dimension
and loosening the eternal connection that our mind or soul has with the
transcendent world. For these reasons, we are not interested in pursuing any
possible religious implications in the SAP.

At the same time, we are not impressed by the implicit materialism
that lies behind much scientific debunking of the SAP. This usually takes
the form of imaginatively multiplying worlds, as Gribbin does, so that the
present, mind-bearing universe would be only one of perhaps an infinite

number of worlds, most of which remain mindless.[4] The idea here is that if there are countless possible universes to choose from, the fact of mind existing in this one would not be quite so "remarkable" as advocates of the SAP maintain. Given an infinite number of "attempts" at shuffling and dealing in the cosmic poker game, it would not be surprising that one of the hands dealt would eventually be a royal flush.

## Contact

The contrast position is partially valid, but it always plays it too safe. It fails to take advantage of the exciting theological opportunities provided by new developments in scientific cosmology. Discussions surrounding the SAP are, we think, of interest to theology. Of course, we do not want to make too much of the principle either and we have no investment in defending its allegedly scientific status. But to ignore it altogether, out of fear that the science underlying it might be wrong, or that it is theologically innocuous, is not fruitful either. As is our habit, we would like to probe it, at least tentatively, to see if there might not be some substantive way in which the SAP can contribute to our theological vision of the universe.

Why do the conflict and contrast approaches simply dismiss the SAP out of hand? Is it for purely scientific reasons in the first case and for purely theological reasons in the second? We suspect that more is involved in each instance. Scientific skeptics throw it out not only because the SAP's flirtation with teleology is unscientific but also because it doesn't fit materialist and reductionist ideas of what the universe *should* be like. If there were anything to the SAP's thesis that mind somehow causally shapes the evolution of matter so as to bring conscious beings into existence, this would shatter the reductionist claim that emergent mind is fully explainable in terms of lower and earlier levels of physical reality. What is at stake in skepticism's dismissal of the principle, then, is not just the integrity of science, but the validity of materialist and reductionist ideology.

At the same time, the contrast approach dismisses the SAP not only because it threatens to confuse science with theology but also because to embrace it would mean that the whole cosmos is somehow inseparable from mind. This would be offensive to the dualism so characteristic of contrast theology. You will note that, throughout this book, the contrast approach has been consistent in segregating physical nature from conscious personality. It maintains the same divorce between consciousness and cosmos that we find implicit in scientism. It allows for divine influence

4. See Gribbin, *In the Beginning*.

in the arena of private freedom and personality (and also in human history), but it wants little to do with the possibility that God is intimately related to the whole of nature or that humans are inextricably connected to the universe—for if we insert humanity too deeply into the cosmos, we might forget that we also transcend nature.

The SAP is one of a number of recent cosmological developments that hint at the inseparability of the human subject from the natural world. This is an intimacy that has little appeal to the contrast theologians. If the cosmos and humanity are as mutually interwoven as the SAP implies, then contrast theology, which seems so logically clean, precise, and acosmic, would no longer be appropriate to the real complexity of the universe. The SAP clearly puts mind back into the physical universe, and we think that both science and theology need to take this connection more seriously. The SAP is obviously a threat not only to the materialist interpretation of science but also to the dualistic leanings of traditional theology.[5]

We are willing to concede that the SAP is not conventionally acceptable science and that scientists have every reason for being suspicious of its teleological nature. But we cannot simply brush it aside, as though it has nothing to offer. We see it, at the very least, as a protest against a reductionism that pretends to explain the more (mind) in terms of the less (matter). Although the SAP may not be purely scientific, it may, nonetheless, still be explanatory. Of course, in order to accept the possibility of there being non-scientific ways of explaining phenomena, one would have to give up the scientistic belief system that rules out all other ways of arriving at knowledge.

If there is any over-arching significance to the universe, it would be too elusive for science to grasp all by itself. Even if the anthropic principle were an accepted scientific idea, it could still not be sufficient to place us in touch with God. To this extent, we can agree with both the conflict and contrast positions. However, if we approach the universe with the eyes of a faith that instructs us to see promise in all things, it comes as no surprise to us that science now discerns the prospect of life and mind in the finely tuned early universe.

Without rooting our faith directly in science, we are yet heartened by the emerging sense in biology and cosmology that the universe is not the enemy of mind, but that, from the beginning, it has actively cooperated in its creation. We are also grateful that theology is now making contact with those new developments in astrophysics that correspond so well with

---

5. Moreover, in the final chapter of this book, we shall point out how the SAP's connecting our existence so closely to the physical cosmos also has a bearing on ecology.

our conviction that the universe is and always has been the embodiment of a promise.

## Confirmation

The confirmation approach looks not only for ways in which religion may cohere with scientific ideas but also for how it may support the scientific adventure. We have been arguing that, in many respects, religion and theology nourish rather than inhibit scientific knowing.

We are somewhat disturbed about the rather abrupt way in which some of our fellow theologians have dismissed the "multiple-worlds" hypothesis that is now favored by an increasing number of physicists. Although we concede that, so far, there is no scientific evidence to support it, we shall make the case here that it is entirely plausible on theological grounds. In addition, we shall propose that a wholesome theology confirms the overwhelming scientific suspicion that the SAP is too anthropocentric.

First of all, then, from a theological point of view, the idea that there might be a plurality of "worlds" is quite compatible with the idea of God. Given the extravagant graciousness that religion attributes to the Creator, God could quite conceivably bring about a great abundance of worlds. The God of prophetic religions is anything but miserly. We are instructed by faith to expect that the Creator's works far surpass any cosmic immensity that we humans can imagine. Consequently, contemporary scientists' luxuriant speculation about a plurality of worlds is not at all inconsistent with a healthy religious openness to the overflowing abundance of an infinite love. Religion, after all, invites us to keep our imagination of the divine munificence fully alive and never to allow the cosmos to close in upon us. And while it may be simpler to think both scientifically and theologically in terms of only one world, it is certainly also appropriate, from a religious point of view, to be suspicious of any unnecessary narrowing in our cosmologies.

Hence when scientists express their sense of the possibility of many worlds or world-epochs, speculation on such a grand scale—at times approaching infinity—is not as opposed to religious sensitivity as some theologians and skeptics maintain. Even though the multiple-worlds hypothesis is, at times, the product of a materialist longing to make the origin of life and mind seem purely natural, as "unplanned" accidents, the extravagance of cosmic creativity is also a thoroughly religious motif. It has its roots in the long religious quest for limitless horizons. Although the physical universe is finite, its unimaginable magnitude—and the possible plurality of its epochs—remains a vital religious metaphor of the divine infinity. In any case, it is ironic that some kinds of theology, whose purpose is to open our minds to the infinite, would gratuitously exclude the possibility that there is an enormous expanse of worlds.

In the second place, a theocentric (God-centered) perspective may also confirm the suspicion many scientists have that the anthropic principle is too narrowly focused on human existence. We would agree that talk about an "anthropic" principle, or any principle that focuses only on "mind" in the sense of *human* consciousness, lacks sufficient cosmic breadth. The anthropic principle is indeed too anthropocentric if taken in this limited sense.

Our theocentric perspective, on the other hand, requires that we considerably broaden the anthropic principle, to give it a wider cosmic scope. We find intriguing, therefore, a proposal made by eminent physicist Freeman Dyson. In his somewhat sympathetic discussion of the anthropic principle, Dyson argues that we might speak more magnanimously about a "principle of maximum diversity."[6] The physics of the early universe may or may not have been biased toward the evolution of consciousness, but, what does seem obvious—and scientifically irrefutable—is that the cosmos has always somehow been intent upon diversifying into as many experiments with form as possible, one of which (fortunately, for us) turns out to be human consciousness. We do indeed belong here, but so does much else of great interest in addition to us as well.

Another way of putting this is to say that the universe, no matter how many worlds or cosmic epochs it includes, seems to be influenced by what might be called an "aesthetic" cosmological principle. We do not need to think narrowly of a cosmic *nisus* toward life and mind. It is remarkable enough that the universe is bent upon expanding and intensifying beauty. Therefore, we would include the evolution of life and mind within a more encompassing cosmic adventure toward an ever-greater breadth of beauty.

The God of our religion is, in fact, best understood as one who wills the maximization of cosmic beauty.[7] As science and theology continue to make sense of our vast universe, only small parts of which have yet been opened up to us, they will find that a God who wills adventure, beauty, and diversity corresponds more closely to the nature of things than one whose only concern is with humankind. As Job reminds us, we humans may be important, but the universe is much, much broader than anything our own finite minds can conjure or comprehend.

6. Dyson, *Infinite in All Directions*, 298.

7. I have developed this Whiteheadian theme at length in Haught, *Cosmic Adventure*.

# 23: What's Going on in the Universe?[1]

"Thou hast made thy promise wide as the heavens."

—PSALMS 138:2

IN CHRIST, THE ULTIMATE mystery that encompasses all created being is revealed not only as self-giving love but also as saving future. What, then, should we expect the universe to look like in light of the promise that enfolds it? Over the past century and a half, science has demonstrated that the universe is an ongoing process, unfathomably vaster and older than we had ever imagined before. The cosmos came into being billions of years before the arrival of human history, Israel, and the Church. Apparently, God's creative vision for the world stretches far beyond what transpires in terrestrial and ecclesiastical precincts. Nevertheless, a Christian theology of nature has to wager that the promissory perspective of biblical faith that first came to light—in a tiny nation, on a very small planet, and not very long ago (in cosmic time)—is applicable to cosmic reality in all its enormous breadth and depth. The promise of God is "wide as the heavens," and, if the heavens seem immensely wider today than ever before, so should our sense of the reach of God's promise as well.

Thus, the long cosmic epochs that preceded the emergence of humanity, Israel and Christianity must also be interpreted by faith as having always been touched by the futurity of God. In the Bible, there is no separation of nature from the history of promise. With eyes of hope inherited from the faith of Abraham, Christians are encouraged to look for signs of a salvific future opening up amidst all the ambiguities of natural, and not just human, history. Today, this may prove to be less difficult than ever before since the latest developments in natural science now show that the universe has always had an emergent or *anticipatory* character. Even in the midst of the perpetual perishing that is the lot of all created

1. The following text is an excerpt. Previously published in Haught, *Christianity and Science*, 51–64. Reprinted with permission.

being, the universe, it seems, has never been closed off to surprising future outcomes. From its beginning, fourteen billion years ago, it has continually made room for new and unprecedented achievements. It still does, especially through one of its most enthralling evolutionary inventions, the restless hearts and minds of human beings.

Once the phenomenon of mind had burst onto the terrestrial scene, the world's posture of straining toward the future began to take the form of religious aspiration everywhere. In the world of Israel, this longing broke through in a new surge of hope for the future, a disposition that shaped the religious awareness of Abraham, the prophets, Jesus, and the earliest Christian communities. This habit of hope is not just human imagining. From a cosmological point of view, it is the way in which the universe, of which we are fully a part, opens itself to new creation up ahead. Through our own expectant posture, the cosmos still continues to scan the horizon for the dawning of a mysterious and elusive new future. It is from this future that we still look for the coming of God and new creation.

And yet, these days, many people still wonder how Christian hope for cosmic redemption could ever be reconciled with what science has to say about nature. A scientific perspective understands the universe to be hidebound by deterministic laws. No room seems to be available for a truly new future ever to occur. Natural science, because of its method of understanding present phenomena in terms of earlier and simpler lines of causation, can know nothing of any promise of fulfillment, nor is it supposed to. When science makes predictions it does so only on the basis of what it already knows. Its pictures of the future are extrapolations from the invariant routines known as physical laws.

Take, for example, the Second Law of Thermodynamics. It holds that the most probable future state of the universe is one in which the available energy to produce and sustain such remarkable emergent phenomena as life will become irreversibly lost. The universe is subject to entropy. Like a clock spring winding down over the course of time, it keeps losing the power to do work, including, most notably, the building up of organic complexity. And science knows of nothing that will wind it up again. At some point far away in the future, the universe that still holds an enormous reserve of energy will expire completely. On the basis of what scientists are aware of at present, it will eventually arrive at a state of energetic paralysis. This ending will cause life, consciousness, and every other significant outcome of natural and historical processes to disappear forever from the smoldering remains of the cosmos.

## Theology and Cosmic Pessimism

What response can theology make, then, to this placid certainty that the cosmos will indeed eventually perish—and, along with it, all traces of life and culture? At present, one must admit, there is no scientific reason to expect that the universe can avoid an eventual death by entropy. But to theology, this should be no surprise. Is it not true that every finite reality, including the expansive and long-enduring set of things we call the universe, is still limited in space and time? Theology has generally thought this to be the case. To be finite, after all, is to be subject to the threat of nonbeing. The physical universe cannot be an exception.[2] Only a new creation can save the universe. It is for this, not the indefinite prolongation of the present cosmos, that Christianity hopes.

Nevertheless, it is toward a new creation of *this* universe, and not its replacement by another, that Christians look. If there is a reason for our hope, there cannot be a complete discontinuity between what is going on in the cosmos right now and any final, redeemed state of things. In a very deep sense, the present, perishable world must matter eternally to providence, so it is proper to look for signals, here and now, perhaps very subtle ones, that this may be so. Theology, it seems, is obliged to show how a perishable cosmos need not be a meaningless one.

However, to do so, theology would first have to assume that there is a sense in which perishing is not absolute. Theologically speaking, nothing finite could be purposeful unless it partakes of the eternal—even in the midst of its perishing. Christians are encouraged to hope, therefore, that everything that has ever happened or will happen in the universe is taken into the compassionate care of God. In an ever intensifying relationship to God, all things that perish, including the whole course of events we call the universe, can be transformed into a beauty beyond imagining. "We hope to enjoy forever the vision of Your glory."

But isn't such hope too much of a stretch, especially in an age of science? Once again, science itself, because of its orientation toward earlier and simpler lines of causation that can establish only what is "probable" in the future, cannot promise any such fulfillment, nor should we expect it to. If science were our only way to true and complete understanding, we would have to conclude that sheer nothingness awaits the cosmos. However, science by definition sketches only a limited picture of what is really going on in the universe. It follows Occam's razor, the axiom that one should not resort to multiple or complex explanations when a single

---

2. Tillich, *Courage to Be*, 23–39 and Tillich, *Systematic Theology*, 1:209.

or simpler one is available. Scientists are instructed to explain presently visible phenomena on the basis of fixed laws, in terms of what has already happened in the causal past and in the currency of elemental units such as atoms, molecules, cells, or genes.

Scientifically speaking, this way of looking at nature is unobjectionable—as long as scientists acknowledge the inherent limitations of their method. A reductive method, one that employs simplifying mathematical models to represent complex entities, is essential to scientific understanding. Reductive generality has proven to be insightful as well as technologically fruitful. Scientific method, however, is not equipped to reach into the ultimate depths of nature or the world's open future. It cannot predict with full precision the genuine novelty that will arise today, let alone what will happen in the cosmic future. When science sees something new and remarkable in nature, its habit of mind is to show that, at bottom, it is really an instance of what is old and unremarkable. Every apparently new occurrence is at bottom an expression of unbending physical laws that apply everywhere and always. Life, for example, is an instance of chemical processes already functioning in nonliving stuff. To a reductive method, there is nothing really new about living organisms since the entire realm of living beings is simply an interesting application of invariant physical and chemical laws operative in cosmic history long before the first living cells emerged. If it can be shown that biology is ultimately reducible to chemistry and physics, as Francis Crick and many others have claimed, then what appears newly emergent in life will be exposed as a mask behind which there exists only a humdrum physical simplicity. All the living extravagance and versatility brought into being by the twists and turns of evolution, according to the Oxford physical chemist Peter Atkins, are mere simplicity masquerading as complexity.[3]

Of course, since they are human persons like the rest of us, scientists are tacitly captivated by the puzzling fact of emergent new phenomena in cosmic history. But no sooner do they observe that life, mind, and other emergents are "interesting" or "remarkable," than they try to suppress their surprise by explaining the later-and-more in terms of the earlier-and-simpler. The dimension of futurity is ignored. Thus, everything that occurs in nature's evolution is taken to be a kind of façade, behind which one will eventually discover the unchanging laws of physics and chemistry that have been running on in the same way unceasingly. In all the wide array of novel cosmic creations, the underlying constants of nature go on functioning as always. Novelty, therefore, must be an illusion.

3. Atkins, *2nd Law*, 200.

However, this denial of novelty and, along with it, the subversion of hope, is not a conclusion that science itself can legitimately reach. Rather, it is a core doctrine of the beliefs known as scientism and scientific naturalism. Truly thoughtful scientists willingly acknowledge the self-limiting methods of their various disciplines. They realize that every distinct scientific field can make progress only by leaving out, or abstracting from, what other disciplines cover. But to the scientific naturalist, there is nothing real that cannot be reached and fully explained by science. This belief entails a suppression of what I have called the fourth infinite—that of the always open future—which, in a Christian worldview, provides the space for faith, hope, and cosmic emergence yet to come.

Theological reflection rightly opposes naturalistic pessimism. It concurs with the more thoughtful scientists who are fully aware that their method of inquiry inevitably leaves out a lot. Science does not have any access, for example, to the realm of *subjectivity*. Scientific method, which idealizes publicly accessible understanding, cannot get inside the sentient phenomena in nature. It has no direct access to those centers of experience that allow certain beings to feel or become conscious of their environments. Science cannot even say what it means for each atom, molecule, cell, or organism to be itself. All real individuality dissolves in the acids of scientific generality. Scientific hypotheses, theories, and laws inevitably abstract from the uniqueness of every entity or event. Faith, on the other hand, sets before us a God concerned with the "thisness" of everything.

Is the perishable universe bringing about anything of lasting value? Theological responses to this question cannot ignore the prospect of an eventual physical death of the entire universe, as well as the troubling features in evolution . . . But for now, I want only to reflect on two items in the current store of scientific information that make it at least conceivable that something of great significance is going on beneath the surface of nature. These are features that can easily be mapped onto the revelatory theme of divine futurity and promise. The first is that the physical universe is still in the process of coming into being. The second is that what has come into being already includes such an intensity of beauty that nature may be read as a great promise of more being and value up ahead. If the first fact reminds us to be realistic, not to expect too much here and now from an unfinished universe, a taste of the second allows us to hope in a power of renewal that can eventually bring new birth to the whole universe. Let us look at each of these two aspects of nature more closely:

1. *The universe is still coming into being.* Evolutionary biology, geology, and cosmology have now established as fact that the cosmos is still

emerging and that it remains incomplete. It is a work in progress, a book still being written. The incontestable fact of an emergent, unfinished universe may not seem to be much of a footing on which to erect a sense of cosmic meaning or find a good reason for hope, but at least it invites us to keep on reading. If a wondrous plot is still unfolding beneath our feet and over our heads, we cannot expect its inner meaning to be fully manifest yet. Any purpose the universe may have will be at least partially hidden from our view—at least for now.

Hope is still possible in such a universe. As with any book in progress, we cannot yet read the universe all the way down to its ultimate depths, whether we are looking at it through science or theology. Its vistas are too large to permit such a grasp. However, we may still feel ourselves being swept up in the story in such a way as to experience the emerging cosmos with a spirit of expectation. The cumulative impression one gets from recent scientific discoveries is that the unfinished universe is continually greeted by an inexhaustible reservoir of freshness, which, as the poet Gerard Manley Hopkins puts it, lives "deep down things."[4] The universe, both in its monumental temporal and spatial scale as well as in its extravagant diversity, bursts with creative novelty. Nature can seem, at times, indifferent to individual organisms striving to adapt and survive. But even as it relies on a monotonous substrate of physical and chemical invariance, it is still open to being taken up into a fascinating and unpredictable tale of suspense. It is the universe's narrative character that will allow us, as we move through the chapters ahead, to connect science more and more intimately to the revelatory themes of divine descent and promise.

2. *The universe is the story of an unimaginably wide display of beauty.* By beauty I mean the harmony of contrasts, the ordering of complexity, the fragile combining of what is new with what is stable, and of fresh nuance with persistent pattern.[5] The still developing cosmos, we now know, has gradually made its way from primordial radiation, through the emergence of atoms, galaxies, stars, planets, and life, to the bursting forth of sentience, mentality, self-consciousness, language, ethics, art, religion, and now science. Such emergence has not been without setbacks, but, by any objective standard of measurement, it is gratuitous to deny that something momentous has been going on in the

---

4. See Hopkins, *"God's Grandeur."*

5. See Whitehead, *Adventures of Ideas*, 252–96; Whitehead, *Process and Reality*, 62, 183–85; and Whitehead, *Modes of Thought*, 57–63. See also Hartshorne, *Man's Vision of God*, 212–29.

universe. The cosmos has, at the very least, busied itself with becoming *more* than what it was. What has emerged, so far, is not just a masquerade concealing an underlying physical simplicity. For all we know, the universe of today may itself be an early chapter in a deeply meaningful story that is still far from having been fully told.

So how are we to read a cosmic narrative that is still being written? Toward what ending can we see the story heading? These are appropriate questions for a theology of nature. Although they admit no easy answer, they will stay with us throughout the pages ahead. Even at this point, we may find it remarkable that the universe eventually abandoned the relative simplicity of its earliest moments and flowered, over the course of billions of years, into an astounding array of emergent complexity and diversity, including human consciousness—with its moral and religious aspirations. There is plenty of room for wonder here. Something other than just the mere reshuffling of atoms has been going on in cosmic history. And while the journey from primordial cosmic monotony to the intense beauty of life, mind, and culture is no hard proof of an intentional cosmic director, this itinerary is at least open to the kind of "ultimate" explanation that a theology of nature rightly seeks to articulate. The universe, in any case, has had an overarching inclination to make its way from trivial toward more intense versions of beauty.[6] Purpose, as I understand it, means the working out or actualizing of something of self-evident value, and beauty certainly qualifies as such. Cosmic purpose consists, at the very least, of an overall aim—not always successful, but nonetheless persistent—toward the heightening of beauty.

But what about the dark side of things—the loss of life, the struggle and pain in evolution, and the moral evil pertaining to human existence? What sense can we make of the dismal scenarios that cosmologists are now entertaining about the eventual, although certainly far off, demise of the universe? How do we know that all things will not finally trail off into lifeless and mindless oblivion? Organisms all die and great civilizations, sooner of later, decay. Hence, if there is any purpose to the universe, perishing must be redeemable—not only our own, but *all* perishing. There has to be a permanence in the depths of the world-process that redresses the fact that nothing lasts. Beneath the transient flux of immediate things, there must be something that endures everlastingly and in whose embrace all actualities attain a kind of immortality. Only a kind of cosmic redemption could finally justify our hope.

6. This aesthetic directionality was enough finally to convince the great philosopher Alfred North Whitehead, after a long period of agnosticism, that there must indeed be a profound point to the universe; see Whitehead, *Adventures of Ideas*, 252–96.

It is this hope that religions seek to express—in many different ways. Although religions are imprecise and inconsistent, their visions may be able to penetrate deeper into the essence of the universe than the lucid abstractions of science. Science may be able to deal with the surface of nature, but the Christian intuition has always been that we shall find beneath the temporal flux of finite being an everlasting redemption, a "tender care that nothing be lost."[7] In God's experience, the entire sweep of events that we call the universe is endowed with permanence along with purpose.[8] Even the final dissolution of our own expanding universe does not necessitate the meaninglessness to which cosmic pessimists consign it. If its history, down to the last detail, can be forever internalized in the life of God, the universe will not be pointless after all.

Today, a theology of nature needs to extend faith's trust in God's care far beyond the terrestrial and human spheres to the totality of cosmic being. The God of revelation, therefore, is not only the promise-maker who summons the world to exist and arrive at ever more intense beauty; not only the humble and compassionate co-struggling and co-suffering companion as revealed in Christ; and not only the tender care that preserves everlastingly all the transient value that emerges during the becoming of nature; but also the one who, through the Spirit of life, continually renews the face of creation.

In the context of contemporary science, as I shall continue to emphasize, any distinctively Christian theology must think of God as having the breadth and depth of feeling to take into the divine life the entire cosmic story, including its episodes of tragedy and its final expiration. Within the embrace of a self-humbling God, the whole universe and its finite history can be transformed into an everlasting beauty. Meanwhile, the ever-expanding divine beauty becomes the ultimate context for the ongoing becoming of the world. Out of the infinite divine resourcefulness new definition is continually added to what has already been. In the divine futurity, the entire world becomes forever new, even if many of its temporal epochs are now over.

But is such a proposal believable? Certainty, of course, is impossible here. Yet, as Teilhard de Chardin observes, such uncertainty is itself completely consistent with the fact that we (and our religions) are also part of an unfinished universe. We cannot reasonably expect a theology of nature to answer with climactic clarity the truly big questions humans ask, at least as long as the universe itself is *in via*—and we along with it. Faith

---

7. Whitehead, *Process and Reality*, 346.

8. God "saves the world as it passes into the immediacy of his own experience" (Whitehead, *Process and Reality*, 346).

reads the universe now only "through a glass darkly"; the darkness and risk that go with faith are somehow inseparable from the fact that the cosmos is still incomplete. However, the incompleteness of the cosmos, my first point, is inseparable from the second: out of nothingness, a world rich in beauty and consciousness has already begun to awaken. If the cosmos is an unfinished story, it is also a story that, at least up until now, has been open to interesting and surprising outcomes. For fourteen billion years, the universe has shown itself to possess a fathomless reserve of creativity. It has not only been winning the war against nothingness but, in its emergent beauty and its capacity for feeling, thought, and love, perhaps it has also already begun to taste victory. If the uncertainty in our faith has something to do with the fact that we live in an unfinished universe, then the creative resourcefulness embedded in the same universe cannot fail to give us, even now, "a reason for our hope" (1 Pet 3:15).

# 24: Purpose[1]

*I sing the goodness of the Lord*
*That filled the earth with food;*
*He formed the creatures with his word*
*And then pronounced them good.*

—ISAAC WATTS, 1715

*Is it the goodness of the Lord*
*That fills the earth with food?*
*Selection has the final word*
*And what survives is good.*

—KENNETH E. BOULDING, 1975[2]

IN CONTEMPORARY CONVERSATIONS ABOUT the relationship of religion to science, two questions stand out: Is nature all there is? And does the universe have a purpose? The two issues are inseparable. For if nature is all there is, there could be no overall purpose to the universe. That is, there could be no goal beyond nature toward which the long cosmic journey would be winding its way. But if the logic here is correct, then the detection of an overarching purpose in nature would imply that nature is not all there is. In the broadest sense, purpose means "directed toward a goal or *telos*." The question before us, then, is whether the cosmos, as a whole, is *teleological*—that is, goal-directed. Is there perhaps a transcendent goodness

---

1. The following text is an excerpt. Previously published in Haught, *Is Nature Enough?*, 98–116. Reprinted with permission.

2. Boulding, "Toward an Evolutionary Theology," 112–13.

luring it toward more intense modes of being and, ultimately, toward an unimaginable fulfillment? How can we find out?

If cosmic purpose were to manifest itself palpably anywhere in nature, would it not be in the life-world? Yet contemporary biology finds there only an *apparent* purpose. Scientists, for the most part, seem to agree that there is indeed a kind of purposiveness, or teleonomy, in living phenomena.[3] The heart has the purpose of pumping blood, eyes of seeing, brains of thinking, and so on. Purposiveness, in this sense, is an indisputable fact of nature. However, the orientation toward specific goals in the life of organisms is not enough to demonstrate that there is an across-the-board purpose to the universe itself. Darwin's impersonal recipe for evolution now seems to be enough to account for what scientists used to think were signs in living organisms of a divine intelligence that orders all events toward a meaning-ful end. The adaptive complexity that gave earlier generations of biologists reason to believe in an intelligent deity now only *seems* to have been pur-posefully intended.[4] Blind evolutionary mechanisms are the ultimate expla-nation of purposive design.

In a recent interview, the famous evolutionist Richard Dawkins states: "I believe, but I cannot prove, that all life, all intelligence, all creativity, and all 'design,' anywhere in the universe, is the direct or indirect prod-uct of Darwinian natural selection. It follows that design comes late in the universe, after a period of Darwinian evolution. Design cannot precede evolution and therefore cannot underlie the universe."[5] So purpose, at least in the guise of design, has apparently been fully naturalized by evolution-ary science. Natural phenomena that formerly seemed to bear the direct imprint of divine intelligence are now exposed as outcomes of a completely mindless process. The adaptive design of organisms gives only the illusion of being deliberately intended. Purpose, at least in any theologically signifi-cant sense of the term, simply does not exist.

Dawkins is willing to grant that we humans have "purpose on the brain," and many other naturalists allow that we need a sense of purpose to live happy lives, but this does not mean that life at large or the universe as a whole is in fact purposeful.[6] Viewed from the perspective of evolutionary biology, the old human habit of looking for meaning in nature may be adap-tive, but it is illusory. Nature itself has no goals in mind and the purposive-ness of organisms is no signal of an eternal divine plan. It is natural—even

3. See Monod, *Chance and Necessity.*
4. See Ruse, *Darwin and Design,* 324–28.
5. Brockman, "God (or Not)."
6. Dawkins, *River Out of Eden,* 96.

for naturalists—to seek purpose, but whatever purpose people seem to find in nature as a whole is, in fact, a purely human construct and not a reflection of the world as it exists "out there."

Biologically speaking, evolutionary naturalists emphasize, there is no significant difference between our own brains and those of our ancestors who sought purpose through religion. Our brains and nervous systems are built to look for meaning in things, but, in an age of science, the personal search for purpose can no longer presume the backing of the universe in the way that religions did in the past. After Darwin, the ancient spiritual assumption that purpose is inherent in the natural world has been exposed as nothing more than an evolutionary adaptation.[7] Maybe the illusion of purpose was invented by our genes as a way to get themselves passed on to subsequent generations. Or, if not directly rooted in our genes, the human passion for purpose is a freeloading complex, parasitic on our brains, fashioned by natural selection ages ago for more mundane tasks.[8] By either account, the penchant for purpose is *ultimately* explainable in a purely naturalistic way. All human yearning for lasting purpose, whether in the universe or in our personal lives, is groundless. At best, religious myths about purpose are noble lies, perhaps convincing enough to help humans adapt, but too imaginative to be taken seriously in an age of science.[9] There is not the slightest evidence that the whole scheme of things makes any sense ultimately.

## Can Purpose Be Fully Naturalized?

However, it is necessary to make two points here. First, it is not evolutionary biology, but *evolutionary naturalism* that rules out purpose. Dawkins himself, as we have just seen, admits that he *believes*—but cannot scientifically demonstrate—that evolution undermines any theological sense of purpose. Science as such, even the naturalist must agree, has nothing to say one way or the other about any overarching purpose in nature. Science, strictly speaking, is not preoccupied with questions about values, meanings, or goals. Teleology is not its concern. My second point is that evolutionary naturalists, along with some religious believers, tend to confuse purpose with "divine intelligent design." Since Darwinism can explain local organic "design" naturalistically, they claim that there is no longer any need to look for purpose in the universe as a whole. To the pure Darwinian, organisms may seem to be designed, but divine intelligence is not the ultimate cause of

7. See Wilson, *Consilience*, 262 and Burkert, *Creation of the Sacred*, 20.

8. See Atran, *In Gods We Trust*, 78–79 and Boyer, *Religion Explained*, 145.

9. See Rue, *By the Grace of Guile*, 261–306.

their "apparently" purposive features.[10] Design is the outcome of an evolutionary recipe consisting of three *unintelligent* ingredients: random genetic mutations along with other accidents in nature, aimless natural selection, and eons of cosmic duration. This simple formula has apparently banished purpose once and for all from the cosmos.

However, the idea of purpose is not reducible to intelligent design. Design is too frail a notion to convey all that religions and theologies mean when they speak of purpose in the universe. Purpose does not have to mean design in the adaptive Darwinian sense at all. Rather, purpose simply means *the actualizing of value*. What makes any series of events purposive is that it is either aiming toward or actually bringing about something that is undeniably *good*. Is it possible that the actualizing of value is what is *really* going on in the universe? And isn't critical intelligence, with its capacity to know truth, direct evidence of it?

## The Self-Contradiction of Evolutionary Naturalism

Evolutionary naturalists, as a rule, do not seem to notice the logical inconsistency between their Darwinian accounts of value, truth, and meaning on the one hand and their minds' actual performance on the other. They instinctively glorify the value of truth—especially scientific truth—as something to which the mind must bend. But their ultimately evolutionary explanations, as both Darwin and Rorty rightly point out, should also lead them to doubt their minds' capacity to put them in touch with truth after all.[11] Assuming that their minds are a product of evolution, there is nothing in the Darwinian recipe alone that would justify their trust that these same minds can reliably lead them to the truth rather than a state of deception. That is to say, if they took Darwinian naturalism as the ultimate explanation, they would have every reason to doubt that they have the capacity to know truth at all.

Even the late Harvard paleontologist Stephen Jay Gould, who was not a strict adaptationist, could not overcome the naturalistic inconsistency. For Gould, no less than for Flanagan, Dennett, E. O. Wilson, and Dawkins, the ultimate explanation of every living phenomenon, including our capacity for truth, is evolution. Life's diversity and versatility is based on three general features of nature: accidents (undirected events), the law of selection (along with the laws of physics and chemistry), and lots of time. Gould gives more explanatory weight to contingency (especially accidents of natural history) than Dawkins and Dennett do, but the ultimate explanation of organic

10. See Dawkins, *River Out of Eden* and Ruse, *Darwin and Design*, 268–70 and 325.

11. Richard Rorty, "Untruth and Consequences," 32–36.

phenomena, including the brain, is still a combination of blind chance, impersonal necessity, and deep time. As far as our inquiry into the deepest ground of intelligence is concerned, it matters little what proportion is given to each ingredient. The point is that Gould's evolutionary naturalism views the ultimate explanation of mind—and this would have to include its tendency to value truth—as itself mindless and valueless.[12]

According to naturalism, there is nothing beyond nature that could conceivably give any value to the world, so it is left to our own human creativity to give value to things. Does this mean that it is also entirely up to us to decide that truth is a value? According to Gould, values and meaning have no objective status, either in nature or God. The ultimate ground of value is not nature, evolution or God but our own "moral consciousness." Since there are no values "out there" in the real world, their existence can only be the result of human creativity, solidified by cultural consensus. To be consistent, Gould would also have to claim that the value that naturalists accord to truth is dictated not by nature or God, since nature is valueless and God (probably) does not exist. And yet, Gould's own life and work give evidence of a mind that *in fact* takes truth to be an intrinsic good. In his actual cognitional performance, both truth and his valuing of truth are irreducible to evolutionary or human creations. The unconditional value Gould finds in pursuing truth cannot be fully explained naturalistically or culturally without rendering that pursuit groundless.

Product of modernity that he was, Gould would probably respond that the naturalist's sense of human inventiveness allows us to recapture some of the self-esteem that our ancestors gave away to the gods. We can now take back what humans had forfeited during all those millennia when they naively assumed, in keeping with religions, that nature is intrinsically purposeful and that truth, value, and purpose are not our own inventions. For Gould, the modern impression of a teleological void is an opportunity to fill the cosmos with our own values and meanings. Once again, however, if we were fully convinced that the value we attach to truthfulness were no more than our own, apparently groundless, creation, then devotion to truth could no longer function as the source of meaning for our lives. Truth would be subordinate to the discretion of our own inventiveness rather than a torch that guides our minds more deeply into the marrow of the real. If evolutionary naturalists took their own doctrines seriously, this would only have a corrosive effect on the trust they place instinctively in their own minds' imperatives to be open, intelligent, and critical.

---

12. See Gould, *Ever Since Darwin.*

As a way of driving home this point, I will ask you, the reader, to suppose once again that you subscribe to the tenets of *evolutionary* naturalism. Then I shall ask you whether the facts associated with the actual performance of your own mind are logically compatible with this naturalistic view of reality.

If you are an evolutionary naturalist, you will quite likely account for living phenomena, including *your own mind*, ultimately in terms of the mindless Darwinian recipe for life. As an evolutionary naturalist, you will also agree that the *ultimate* explanation of your various organs—your nose, mouth, eyes, ears, and everything else functionally adaptive about you—is Darwinian natural selection.[13] And, to be completely consistent, you will be compelled to admit that your critical intelligence, which to the pure Darwinian is not a blank slate but has been molded to think the way it does by natural selection, can be explained ultimately in terms of Darwin's recipe as well.[14] If you follow Gould, you may also appeal to the role of accidents in natural history—and not solely to selective adaptation—in explaining why you have a mind and why it works the way it does. But if you follow ultra-adaptationists such as Dawkins, then the ultimate explanation of your mind and all its features is the (mindless) natural selection of adaptive populations of related genes.

In either case, whether by Darwinian adaptation or by sheer accident (or a combination of the two), the *ultimate* explanation of your capacity to think is itself a set of mindless and unintelligent factors. But if this is right, then on what basis can you trust your critical intelligence, the outcome of an unintelligent process, to lead you to right understanding and knowledge of the truth at this instant? Darwin himself, as we have seen earlier, raised this troublingly subversive question, but he did not follow it up carefully. Evolution produced intelligence, declares Owen Flanagan, but evolution does not require intelligence to produce intelligence: "Evolution *demonstrates* how intelligence arose from totally insensate origins."[15] How, then, do you and Flanagan justify the confidence you *now* place in your mental functioning, especially if the ultimate ground of your intelligence is not only unintelligent, but even insensate? If not by magic, then how did your dazzling intellectual prowess and the trust you place in it ever pop into this universe from a state of unutterable cosmic dumbness? It would appear, to me at least, that something momentous in the way of explanation has been left out here. A simplistic appeal to deep time and gradualism alone cannot bridge this

13. Cziko, *Without Miracles*, 121.

14. See Pinker, *The Blank Slate*.

15. Flanagan, *The Problem of the Soul*, 11 (emphasis added).

explanatory gap since the passage of time itself does nothing to cure the fundamental blindness of the process.

If either aimless evolutionary selection or sheer contingency is the *deepest* possible explanation of your own mental endowment, then why should I pay any attention to you? How do I know—if I follow your own premises—that your mind is not just taking part in one more adaptive (and possibly fictitious) exercise, rather than leading you and me to the truth? In company with Dawkins, Gould, Flanagan, and others, you are telling me that a mindless evolutionary process (along with physical and chemical laws) is the *ultimate* explanation of your mind and its properties. Darwinism, you say, is true. I can agree with you, scientifically speaking, but what I need to find out is how your mind's capacity for truth-telling slipped into the fundamentally unintelligent Darwinian universe that you started with. Although evolutionary explanation is essential, any attempt to answer this question in Darwinian terms alone will be circular and magical. In order to justify the assumption that your own mind is of such stature as to be able to understand and know the truth, you will need to look for a kind of explanation that evolutionary science, at least by itself, cannot provide.

If you resort only to the idea of adaptation, this will not work, since mindless adaptations, as you know well, can be illusory and deceptive. Perhaps, then, you will tell me that your highly prized human capacity for truth-telling is an incidental, unplanned byproduct of evolution. Perhaps it is something like what Stephen Jay Gould calls a "spandrel." That is, maybe your cognitional talent is analogous to the arched surfaces (spandrels) that appear *incidentally* around the tops of columns, whose main function is to hold up the roofs of cathedrals, like San Marco in Venice. Such features are not the main architectural objective but instead they simply appear, unintended in themselves, as the basilica is being erected. The spandrels, though unintended as such, may be taken as opportunities for great artists to cover them with frescoes or mosaics. It may be the spandrels and the works of art, rather than the columns, that attract our focal interest as we enter the building.[16] Maybe, in a similar way, your mind's capacity for truth-telling is a spandrel that just happened to show up as a contingent side-effect of the adaptive (and otherwise often deceptive and deluded) human brain.

Or, again, perhaps your critical intelligence is essentially the consequence of cultural conditioning that has little to do with natural selection. In any case, whether you interpret your capacity for truth-telling as a Darwinian adaptation, a spandrel, an accident of nature, or the consequence of enculturation, you will still have failed to justify the *trust* you are now

16. Gould and Lewontin, "Spandrels of San Marco," 581–98.

placing—at this very moment—in your own intellectual activity. Both naturalistic and culturally relativistic explanations of mind provide too shallow a soil to ground the inevitable confidence that underlies your actual cognitional performance. Consequently, if, up to this point, you have professed official allegiance to evolutionary naturalism, you must now roam outside the circle of that creed in order to find a more solid reason for why your mind can be trusted to know and communicate the truth.

If you are a Darwinian naturalist, you will be given to making claims such as this one by biologist David Sloan Wilson: "Rationality is not the gold standard against which all other forms of thought are to be judged. Adaptation is the gold standard against which rationality must be judged, along with all other forms of thought."[17] I wonder, however, if Wilson is even remotely aware of how thoroughly his subordination of rationality to evolutionary adaptation logically undermines not only his claim but also the confidence with which his own mind makes such a claim. Assuming that the statement just quoted is one that comes from Wilson's own brain and assuming that his brain is also the outcome of an adaptive evolutionary process, on what grounds can Wilson justify his assumption that readers should take his claim to be rational and true rather than simply an attempt to adapt? If a proposition contrary to Wilson's assertion had been the one to survive adaptively, then would it not have to be judged rational and true, according to Wilson's proposal? If so, truth would have no stable meaning whatsoever and pursuit of it could scarcely function to give purpose to one's life.

Are Darwinian selection, sheer contingency, and the vicissitudes of enculturation, therefore, the best we can come up with by way of an ultimate account of intelligence? In particular, can evolutionary science, in any of its expressions, be the ultimate explanation of the spontaneous trust that all of us place in our rational faculties? Or isn't Darwinism, at best, just one of several levels of explanation needed to understand critical intelligence? If the critical (truth-seeking) aspect of our cognitional life could ultimately be explained in Darwinian terms, on what grounds can we trust it? We do not have to deny that physics, chemistry, and evolutionary biology are all essential layers in the explanation of mind, but, in order to account *fully* for the mind's natural longing for truth, we have to move beyond naturalistic explanation.

17. Wilson, *Darwin's Cathedral*, 228.

# 25: Astrobiology and Cosmic Purpose[1]

FOR MANY YEARS, MY main academic and theological interest has been the relationship of science to religion.[2] I have come to the conclusion that, when we get down to the bottom of the many specific questions that surround this conversation, there are two big issues. First, is nature all there is? And second, is there any purpose to the universe? My objective in this chapter will be to ask whether the discovery of life elsewhere in the universe—including intelligent life—can make any difference as to how we would answer these two questions.

## 1. Is nature all there is?

I suppose that almost anybody who has ever been impressed by the robust explanatory power of science may have wondered, at one time or another, whether there is need for any kinds of explanations other than those that science has to offer. A lot of smart people would say absolutely not. In the intellectual world today, there is a powerful temptation to settle for purely naturalistic explanations of everything, so I must begin by talking about *naturalism*: the belief that the world available to ordinary experience and scientific inquiry is all that exists. Naturalism claims that there is no room for the existence of anything other than the natural world. Nature, in this definition, includes us humans and all of our creations. The world, according to naturalism, is Godless, and theology—as far as explaining the origin of life, mind, or, for that matter, anything else—is made superfluous.

There are different ways of understanding naturalism, but I intend to use the term the way many philosophers, scientists, and theologians use it, namely, to designate the belief that nature, as it is available to common experience and scientific method, is literally *all* there is. The fundamental tenets of scientific naturalism are as follows:

1. Only the world of nature is real.

---

1. This essay was previously unpublished.

2. Parts of this text are loosely adapted from Haught, *Purpose, Evolution, and the Mystery of Life.*

2. Since nature is all there is, nature must be self-originating. After all, there is nothing outside of nature that could cause it to exist.

3. Since there is nothing beyond nature, there is no goal that it could be striving toward, that is, nothing in the order of teleology.

4. Hence, all causes must be natural causes and there is no room for the miraculous. Every natural event is itself the product of other natural events.

5. Finally, according to naturalists, the existence of life is unplanned and unintended. Nature is *really* all there is.[3]

Until not too long ago, naturalistic explanations seemed inadequate, even in the sciences. This was partly because vitalistic assumptions were widely accepted. "Vitalism," from the Latin word *vita* (life), claims that in order for life to exist at all, a non-material force must intervene in lifeless matter and elevate it to the status of life. According to vitalists, there is something supernatural about life that science cannot touch. Until recently, not only life but also human intelligence, morality, and religious aspiration were considered off-limits to naturalistic explanation. Scientists did not dare stray into any regions of reality that bordered on the spiritual. Today, however, scientific naturalists see no reason to be so reverential.

## 2. Is there Purpose in the Universe?

Before going any further, it may be useful to ask why anyone would be concerned about cosmic purpose at all. One very good reason is that modern science—biology, evolution, cosmology, and physics—has now shown how intricately each of us is tied into the whole universe. We are inseparable from it. If the whole universe is pointless, then each individual's identity and destiny shares in that general state of things. Another reason is given by Vaclav Havel, the former president of the Czech Republic. He declares that the crisis of global responsibility is due to the fact that we've lost the sense that the universe has a purpose.[4] The religions of the world would mostly agree that it is important, especially for the sake of sustaining moral aspiration from generation to generation, that people believe that the universe is here for a reason.

However, we live in an age of science and many people, especially in the intellectual world, doubt that belief in cosmic purpose is compatible

3. See Hardwick, *Events of Grace.*
4. See Rupnik, "Vaclav Havel," 44.

with what the natural sciences are saying. Steven Weinberg has stated that "the more [scientifically] comprehensible the universe has become, the more pointless it also seems," and Richard Feynman, another widely respected twentieth-century physicist, writes that "the great accumulation of understanding as to how the physical world behaves only convinces one that this behavior has a kind of meaninglessness about it."[5] Many other scientists agree.

Compare such sentiments, however, to the beliefs of the wisdom traditions that operate according to the "hierarchical principle." This principle holds that a higher level can encompass or comprehend a lower level, but a lower level cannot comprehend or encompass a higher. What this means is that achieving cognitional competency at the lower levels of the cosmic hierarchy does not render you competent to understand the higher levels.[6] In order to attain that competence, you have to undergo a personal transformation, usually not without a long and adventurous struggle. The wisdom traditions prescribe religious exercises, regimes of discipline or apprenticeship to spiritual masters, as well as immersion in sacred texts as a condition for understanding the higher dimensions of reality. One must achieve *adaequatio* (competency) in order to be in a position to comment authoritatively on what's *really* going on in the universe. A personal transformation is necessary before one can be grasped by the most important dimensions of being. The more valuable something is, the more elusive it is to ordinary human consciousness. And so, if there is an *ultimate* purpose to the universe, it would lie far beyond the comprehension of mundane consciousness, including scientific method. If there is an ultimate purpose to things, it might comprehend us, but we could not comprehend it.[7]

Does this mean, therefore, that ultimate reality is unknowable in every sense? Not necessarily. Those who are properly disposed can have *an awareness of being grasped* by ultimate meaning, but they can never attain a grasping or comprehending understanding of it. Absolute clarity would actually diminish their sense of the ultimate. So if there is any purpose to the universe, it can be referred to only by way of symbols, metaphors, and analogies.

Two twentieth-century religious and scientific thinkers comfortable with cosmic extravagance are Alfred North Whitehead and Pierre Teilhard de Chardin. Both provide fruitful frameworks for thinking about

---

5. Weinberg, *First Three Minutes*, 144 and Feynman, *Meaning of It All*, 32.

6. Instead of speaking of *levels* of being, I prefer—after Paul Tillich—to speak of *dimensions*. I only use the term *level* here for the sake of simplicity.

7 See Schumacher, *Guide for the Perplexed*, 18.

astrobiology, many universes, and cosmic purpose. Before looking into what they have to say, however, I should pause at this point and define what I mean by purpose. Purpose quite simply means the realizing of a value. Any process that seems to be bringing about what is self-evidently *good* may be called purposive. We know from personal experience, for example, that what ties together the moments of our own lives, insofar as we think of our lives as having a purpose, is the sense that somehow we are actualizing or helping to bring about something worthwhile. Both Whitehead and Teilhard saw something undeniably *important* coming to birth not just in our own lives but also in the universe as seen by science. Let us look at each of their perspectives briefly and then connect their thoughts to astrobiology.

## Whitehead and Cosmic Purpose

Whitehead was a widely read, deeply learned intellectual who taught mathematics at Cambridge University and then later in London. When he was on the brink of retiring from a lifetime of teaching, Harvard University invited him to come to Cambridge in the United States. He accepted the invitation, took up the post of University Professor and eventually became one of America's great philosophers. After coming to the United States, he increasingly talked about science and religion, stating that the future of civilization hangs on their getting along with each other.[8]

In his book *Adventures of Ideas*, Whitehead speaks explicitly about what he considers to be the fundamental aim or purpose of the universe. The purpose of the universe, as he sees it, is simply to bring about more and more intense versions of *beauty* and the capacity to enjoy it. He takes beauty to be a self-evident value. We find great beauty irresistible and allow ourselves to be carried away by it. So much do we value it that we cannot help being taken captive by it. Keeping in mind the definition of purpose I just gave—the actualizing of value—any process that is in the business of bringing about more and more intense versions of beauty, which, for Whitehead, is the greatest of values, could be called, at least in a loose sense, teleological or purposive. The universe is, at bottom, precisely such a process.[9] For Whitehead, beauty is not just in the eye of the beholder, it is inherent in nature, and not merely something that we humans arbitrarily invent.

8. Whitehead, *Science and the Modern World*, 181–82.

9. See Whitehead, *Adventures of Ideas*, 252–96; Whitehead, *Process and Reality*, 62, 183–85, and 255; and Whitehead, *Modes of Thought*, 8–104. See also Hartshorne, *Man's Vision of God*, 212–29.

What Whitehead means by beauty is the synthesis of novelty on the one hand with order on the other. Beauty is the combining of contrast with harmony.[10] If there is too much novelty, and not enough order, there will be chaos. But too much order and not enough novelty, or too much harmony without abundant contrast, results in monotony.

The universe, therefore, needs contingency, extravagance, and "waste" in order to attain intense beauty—otherwise, monotony prevails. The cosmic aim toward beauty is always risky. At times, there can be too much novelty or too much order. Too much chaos or too much monotony is the basis for *evil*. They call out for redemption by an ever wider and deeper intensification of beauty. Whitehead calls the cosmos an "adventure" because the risk of evil is always present. Indeed, anything purposive has great peril attached to it.[11] As we've learned from the sciences, we live in a restless, extravagant universe. Thus religious thought, Whitehead insists, must come to grips with that fact. Whitehead himself wants to know why the universe is so restless, so interested in producing the kind of living diversity that astrobiology anticipates. His thought is also comfortable with the idea that there may be many worlds or "cosmic epochs" of which ours is but simply one.

However, all the restlessness and diversity of nature requires an *ultimate* explanation. If God is the ultimate source of order, then God must be the ultimate source of novelty, diversity, and extravagance as well. Divine extravagance is the ultimate reason why the universe doesn't just stand still, staying stuck in monotony. God is not just the upholder of the status quo but also its disturber. God is not only interested in order but also in more intense versions of order. God, in other words, is concerned that there be evolution, diversity in life, intense instances of beauty—and perhaps many worlds as well.

A universe in the process of being created requires that there be a reservoir of novel possibilities available to it. These possibilities have to be waiting somewhere; they do not simply come into the cosmos from nowhere. God, in that understanding, means that the possibility of becoming new is present to the cosmic process at each moment of of its passage through time. God is the source of the novel possibilities that allow the universe to be a great adventure rather than a stagnant monotony. But God does not forcefully stamp new possibilities onto the cosmos. Rather, as befits the character of love (and here, Whitehead takes seriously the religious notion that God is love), God acts persuasively rather than coercively. Love does not force, love is not dictatorial, and love lets the other be. Insofar as love acts persuasively rather than

10. Whitehead, *Adventures of Ideas*, 265.

11. Whitehead, *Adventures of Ideas*, 252–96.

coercively, God allows for a universe in which there is room for abundant experimentation, disorder, accidents, chaos, extravagance—and freedom. I would like to add that only such a universe can allow for the kind of meandering and experimentation that we find in Darwinian evolution.

You can gather from this brief sketch that both biological evolution and the astrobiological distribution of life can dwell rather comfortably within a Whiteheadian vision of things. If God's will or God's purpose for the universe is the maximizing of beauty, then the pervasiveness of life in the cosmos fits easily within such a wide worldview. The intensifying of cosmic beauty is what God wants. This also means that the universe, or multiverse, since it is not forcefully managed by an engineering deity, is likely to be one in which there is a great risk of evil and what we would call waste. However, in Whitehead's view, there is also the possibility of redemption. Whitehead's God experiences everything that goes on in the universe, taking everything that happens in the world into the divine life ultimately.[12] In ways that science itself cannot articulate, God patterns the totality of things into a wider and increasingly more intense beauty.

I like to view Whitehead's cosmos, therefore, as configured primordially by an *aesthetic cosmological principle* as distinct from the narrower *anthropic* cosmological principle. It seems to me that, in the light of science, we can speak theologically about a universe that is ordered not so much by an initial design or plan but rather by the *promise* of more and more intense versions of beauty.

Whitehead, I should add, also thinks of God not as standing aloof from the suffering of life but rather as taking the world's suffering into the divine. God is a "fellow sufferer" who embraces the world's entire evolution. In the beauty of God's own experience, the universe finds its everlasting redemption, even though it will eventually experience some sort of physical "death" itself. Thus, a universe that is oriented, even if not always successfully, toward bringing about more and more intense versions of beauty deserves to be called purposeful. Finally, in this Whiteheadian framework, the meaning of our own lives would consist, in part at least, of our own creative participation in the ongoing process of intensifying the beauty—and that means, especially, the diversity—of life in the universe.

12. For this and many other features of Whitehead's religious vision, see Cobb and Griffin, *Process Theology*, 123–24.

# Teilhard de Chardin, Cosmic Purpose, and SETI

Another notable scientist and religious thinker who has sought a wider-than-human understanding of life was the geologist and Jesuit priest Pierre Teilhard de Chardin (1881–1955). If the universe is to have a purpose, Teilhard argued, it has to have at least a loose kind of directionality to it. In other words, it has to be doing more than just aimlessly wandering around. It is not hard to make out, at least dimly, an axis of directionality running through the history of nature as we know it. This directionality is measurable since it consists of the gradual increase in organized physical complexity during the course of cosmic history. As atoms become molecules, molecules become cells, and cells become organisms, the universe grows increasingly more complex in its organization. Then, in the emergence of vertebrates, primates, and finally humans, nervous systems and brains become almost unimaginably more complex in their organization.[1]

Furthermore, there is no invincible reason to suspect that evolution has now come anywhere near the end of its journey. If you look under your feet, behind your back, and over your head, you will see a new type of organized physical complexity now taking shape around you. Teilhard calls this latest evolutionary level of being the "noosphere," from the Greek word *nous*, which means "mind." The thinking layer of terrestrial evolution is now weaving itself in a complex way around our planet, taking advantage of politics, economics, education, scientific developments, and especially communication technology. Teilhard, incidentally, is sometimes called the "prophet of the Internet" because he predicted that, through technological complexification, the earth would continue to clothe itself in something like a brain.

This layer of thought and its planetary growth is the noosphere. It is all so new that science still doesn't yet know quite what to make of it. In evolution, after all, things take millions and millions of years, yet the formation of the noosphere so far is only a matter of thousands. So we should not assume that the universe's aim toward more and more complex physical developments is anywhere near its end. Perhaps, for all we know, evolutionary creation is still at the cosmic dawn.[2]

In general, physical complexification in evolution is interesting to Teilhard primarily because, in direct proportion to the gradual increase in organized physical complexity, there is a corresponding increase in *consciousness*. Teilhard refers here to the "law of complexity-consciousness,"

1. For a fuller picture of this notion, there is no substitute for reading Teilhard de Chardin, *Human Phenomenon*.

2. Teilhard de Chardin, *Prayer of the Universe*, 120–21.

which maintains that consciousness increases in direct proportion to the degree of increase in physical complexity. What's going on in the universe, at the very least, is a gradual increase in the intensity of consciousness. This is enough to fill the cosmos with purpose, a notion that I defined earlier as the "realization or actualization of a value." It is impossible to deny consistently that consciousness is a self-evident value, for, if you find yourself denying it, this can only be because you value your consciousness enough to make such a judgment. Since consciousness is clearly a value, a universe that is in the business of bringing about more and more intense versions of consciousness is a pretty interesting universe. It would not be rash to call it purposeful.

But now let us take these reflections further and ponder the possibility of both life and intelligent life elsewhere in the universe. I think that if he were here today Teilhard would probably pay even more attention to this topic than in the few scattered allusions he did make to it. I believe that Teilhard's thought could be extended in an age of SETI (the "Search for Extraterrestrial Intelligence") in the following way.[3]

Let us start with what is undeniable scientifically. We now know that, throughout the universe, there has occurred a gradual increase in organized physical complexity, starting with pre-atomic matter, then moving on to atoms, molecules, and what Christian de Duve, the Belgian biologist, has called "vital dust"—referring to the carbon compounds that make up as much as 40% of interstellar dust. We are certain today that the complexification process has advanced at least this far extraterrestrially as well as here on earth. We also know that on earth, at least, the process of complexifying matter has gone even further. Out of the vital dust have emerged cells, organisms, vertebrates, primates, and humans. And now the noosphere is beginning to take on an even more complex shape on a planetary scale. Who knows what else might emerge beyond that?

According to Teilhard, we also know that, in direct proportion to the increase in organized physical complexity, on our planet at least, there has arisen a corresponding increase in consciousness.

So don't we have here a framework of inquiry in terms of which we could make cosmic and theological sense of extraterrestrial intelligent life if we were ever to encounter it? Teilhard was experimenting only gingerly with such ideas during his lifetime, but, on the basis of his general understanding of evolution, isn't it possible that, if extraterrestrial life and intelligence turn out to be plentiful, something like extraterrestrial noospheres are also in the process of being created? If this turns out to be the case, then these

3. Teilhard de Chardin, *Activation of Energy*, 126–27.

individual noospheres would become the cells, the atoms, the fundamental units, of an unimaginable cosmic extension of consciousness. We don't yet know how such a network would be possible, since the noospheres would have to communicate with one another if a new phase of convergence is to occur. No doubt, such speculations will sound too wild for most people, but we should have learned enough from science by now not to underestimate the universe's creative potential. Nor should we be so narrow as to confine our sense of the Creator's vision of cosmic possibilities to the dimensions of our own minds and imaginings. In any case, Teilhard provides an intelligible framework for thinking on a grander scale about cosmic possibilities—and in the context of a purposeful unfolding—than either our science or religion has typically done.

So let me go back now to the question I asked earlier: can cosmic purpose be an intelligible idea in an age of science? Human religious sensibilities were first shaped in terms of a prescientific, vertical hierarchy of being. Even to this day the spiritual lives and ethical ideals of most of us, including scientists, have been molded by traditions that arose long before we had any sense of an evolving universe—although we must acknowledge that even the ancients saw life as existing elsewhere. How, then, can we map the vertical hierarchy of the Wisdom Traditions onto our thirty-volume, horizontal unfolding of life, mind, and meaning from a state of lifeless and mindless matter?

Teilhard's answer to that question is not terribly complicated. First of all, think of God as "up ahead" and not so much as "up above." In fact, this is a very biblical way of thinking about God. The God of the Bible is the God who comes from the future and encourages the people of Israel to move toward a fulfillment that lies only in the future. The God of Abraham, the God of promise, draws the world toward unity from up ahead. Second, think of the cosmic hierarchy not as a vertical but an *emergent* one, in which matter historically prepares the way for the appearance of life, life for mind, and mind for spirit. It is not so difficult, after all, as Teilhard himself proposed, to connect what I have been calling the Wisdom Traditions with the evolutionary world view. Just rearrange the religious furniture in your mind a little. Think of the world not so much as leaning on the past as on the future, a future which, for Teilhard, is ultimately nothing other than God. God is the world's Future and it is as future that God is the world's ultimate support.[4] In this reconfiguration, it is not inconceivable that the vine of religious meaning that traditionally twined itself around the vertical hierarchical lattice-work can

4. Teilhard, *Activation of Energy*, 239.

now be rewound around the horizontal-evolutionary picture of a still unfinished creation in which the adventure of life is only just beginning.

Finally, if a multiverse is the widest context of life, then the matrix of life is the totality of worlds. Even if we view the many universes only as a statistical background, they are still complicit in the emergence of life anywhere. Even if most worlds are locally devoid of living and thinking beings, life is still somehow everywhere and everywhen. The multiverse theory does not necessitate an ontology of death. No matter how many universes there are, ontologically speaking, they still enjoy a togetherness inasmuch as they all participate in being. To all those people—most of us being instinctively panvitalists—who cannot separate being in its more intense versions from "being alive," the universe, or multiverse, could never, at any time or place, have been essentially dead. Theologically, the fact that that all worlds participate in being is enough to allow us to affirm that all creation is one. The existence of life anywhere in the immensity of creation is the existence of life everywhere.

# Part V: God, Suffering & Death

# 26: Suffering[1]

ONE OF THE MAIN reasons religion and theology are so appealing to their followers is that they provide answers to the problem of suffering. Today, however, the traditional answers do not always seem believable, and suffering, no less than death, seems to be just one more fact of nature. Especially after Darwin, all aspects of life, including suffering, can apparently be understood in natural terms. To the strict naturalist this means that, as far as life's suffering is concerned, there is no need to fall back on obsolete religious interpretations, nor is there any good reason any longer for invoking the idea of a redeeming God. Humans, with the aid of science, can understand and respond to the fact of suffering all by themselves.

From Darwinian biology's point of view, suffering (which, in this chapter, I shall take to be inclusive of the sensation of pain by all sentient life) is simply an adaptation that enhances the probability of survival and reproductive success in complex organisms.[2] How, then, could theology plausibly add anything of explanatory substance to the Darwinian naturalist's account? Darwin himself observed that suffering is "well adapted to make a creature guard against any great or sudden evil."[3] Suffering, he surmised, is life's warning system and if, at times, the torture it brings seems exorbitant, the excess is still consistent with a purely naturalist understanding of life.[4] A follower of Stephen Jay Gould and Richard Lewontin might even suggest that the surplus of suffering is a byproduct of adaptation rather than an adaptation itself.[5] In any case, when compared to Darwin's understanding, religious and theological views of suffering may seem to have little if any explanatory value.

---

1. The following text is an excerpt. Previously published in Haught, *Is Nature Enough?* 167–190. Reprinted with permission.

2. Although some writers do not attribute "suffering" to nonhuman forms of life, reserving for them only the term "pain," I consider the distinction somewhat arbitrary, unnecessarily anthropocentric, and fundamentally Cartesian, as the following reflections will try to make clear.

3. Darwin, *Autobiography*, 88–89.

4. However, deadly viruses can also invade organisms painlessly, so the warning system, like other evolutionary adaptations, is not perfect. See Hick, *Evil and the God of Love*, 333–38.

5. See Gould and Lewontin, "Spandrels of San Marco," 581–98.

Nowadays, of course, some evolutionists go beyond classical Darwinism by accounting for the suffering of sentient life in terms of genes striving
to make their way into subsequent generations. Genes somehow sense that
they will not get passed on to the next generation unless they fashion for
themselves organic vehicles endowed with sensory feedback equipment that
can alert living beings when their survival is in jeopardy. Their own good
genes have to take it upon themselves to engineer delicate nervous systems
that will secure their immortality. Such machinations may seem intelligent
and even ingenious to those who are unaware of how evolution works, but
to Darwinian naturalists there is nothing intelligent about it at all. The process is, at bottom, blind and impersonal.

Still, it seems to be nothing short of remarkable that the life-process,
however one explains it, has gradually woven into organisms more and
more delicate and pain-sensitive nervous systems. It is impossible not to
remark at how an allegedly unintelligent evolutionary process, no matter
how much time it takes and how gradually it all unfolds, could turn out to
be so ingenious. And yet, Darwinians endowed with a sense of deep time
have no difficulty at all conceiving of a purely natural, *because very gradual*,
emergence of sensitive organisms. Furthermore, at least for some people,
the haphazard way in which pain is distributed in the organic world is a
most disturbing challenge to religious interpretations of life.

Even if there is a fascinating ingenuity to such phenomena, it seems
silly to attribute it to a beneficent divine designer. Darwin himself was led
to reject the idea of divine design, at least in the biological world, after
learning about such indecencies as ichneumon wasps laying their eggs
inside living caterpillars (so that their larvae will have fresh meat rather
than decaying flesh upon which to nourish themselves). Those of us who
take the idea of a good and powerful creator seriously must also wonder
if there is anything in such performances that theology could possibly illuminate. What holy message can we wrest from the book of nature as we
read about fluke worms and ichneumon wasps?

For centuries, religions and theologies have been explaining suffering
without the benefit of Darwinian expertise. They have been persuasive to
most people not only because their sacred stories seem to account quite
satisfactorily for the origin of suffering, but even more because they offer
hope of release from it. Religious salvation, although it means much more
than a final release from suffering, means at least that much. Religions generally encourage people to trust that, in the end, all tears will be wiped away
and pain and death will be no more. But now that evolutionary biology has
graced us with an elegant "naturalistic" answer to the question of why suffering occurs in sentient life, what are we to do with all the convoluted but

apparently healing and adaptive perspectives of our religions? After Darwin, can religious myths about the origin and end of suffering have either explanatory power or salvific efficacy?

Any plausible theological response to suffering cannot simply overlook ichneumon wasps, fluke worms, and countless other instances of nature's indifference to suffering. Clearly, the natural world has *never* been a paradise, contrary to what a literal reading of Genesis may suggest. The emergence and evolution of life have been rather messy. As we now realize, suffering, death, and mass extinctions have been constitutive of—and not just accidental to—the ongoing creation of life on earth. Religious belief encourages people to hope that "alas far off" all tears will be wiped away and death will be no more.[6] For people of faith, it should not be a terribly uncomfortable doctrinal stretch to extend such extravagant hopes, as Buddhism does, to the release of *all* life from suffering. But our theologies, with only a few exceptions, generally avoid the issue of why God's universe would be the theater of so much evolutionary struggle, travail, and death in the first place. Theology still needs to consider in depth what biology tells us about God, sin, evil, redemption, and especially the meaning of suffering. It needs to ask more sincerely than ever whether a purely naturalist—and that means evolutionary—understanding is not the best answer to the question of why life brings so much suffering.

The question "why suffering?" is irrepressible, and, along with the prospect of death, it has been the main stimulus to the countless stories about the origin and end of evil that humans have been telling one another for thousands of years. Myths about how suffering came about have provided reassurance that life is not absurd. Religious conjectures about how suffering can be redeemed have carved out the spiritual space in which most peoples have lived, hoped, and aspired to ethical goodness. Is it wise, then, to ignore these venerable accounts, as naturalism would propose? Or can we repossess them, even after Darwin, as a great treasury of wisdom deserving of ever deeper exploration? Whatever answer one gives, it is at least necessary to admit that none of the ancient myths of evil and suffering said anything about evolution. That they did not do so is entirely forgivable, of course, but it is no mark of theological courage that, even today, so many religious thinkers still touch only lightly on Darwin's science—if they mention it at all.

I shall propose in this chapter, then, that it is entirely appropriate to keep telling the old stories about the origin and end of suffering, but that our religions and theologies should no longer recite them as though Darwin

6. See Tennyson, "In Memoriam."

never lived and evolution never happened. Evolutionary biology clearly requires the widening of theological reflection so as to take into account the enormous breadth and depth of nonhuman pain and the unfinished character of the universe. Even if theology is a reasonable alternative to naturalism, it must not be seen as an alternative to good science.

## Evolutionary Naturalism and the Suffering of Sentient Life

To the evolutionary naturalist, religious stories about suffering lack the explanatory economy of evolutionary science, so they will be of little interest to the intellectually enlightened. Any supernormal accounts of human suffering—indeed, the whole panoply of religious mythology and doctrine—appear to the naturalist to be, at best, nothing more than an empty, though perhaps occasionally heartwarming, illusion. This impression applies especially to "theodicy." Broadly speaking, any attempt to understand or explain suffering may be called a theodicy. In theistic contexts, theodicy is the theoretical attempt to "justify" the existence of God, given the facts of evil and suffering. If God is all-good and all-powerful, then God must also be able and willing to prevent life's suffering. But suffering exists. Why? Theodicy is the branch of theology that tries to answer this question. Many theodicies are highly philosophical and their rarefied speculation does little or nothing to remove actual suffering. For that reason, today, the whole business of theodicy often seems useless—even to the devout. Yet finding an answer to the question of suffering is an irrepressible concern of most people, so *any* intelligible explanation of suffering can be a kind of theodicy.[7] Even Darwinism itself now functions, at least for scientific naturalists, as an ultimate answer to the ancient question of how to locate and understand the fact of suffering.

Evolutionary theory, in fact, is satisfying to so many people today because it proposes in effect to have found a "theodicy" that surpasses all previous ones in clarity and simplicity. For many thoughtful people, Darwinism, employed as a kind of Occam's razor, has made the ideas of God, sin, punishment, demons—and perhaps even human guilt—worthless, as far as the understanding of suffering is concerned. Nobody pretends that Darwinism can wipe away all tears and do away with death. To those who find evolutionary accounts of suffering sufficient, the universe still remains pointless and hope for redemption an idle dream. But the price of surrendering religious hope seems well worth the intellectual luminosity that Darwinism brings to an issue that has befuddled humanity for so many centuries.

7. Following the broad usage of the term in Berger, *Sacred Canopy*, 53.

Nevertheless, religious theodicies still persist and Darwinism is having a tough time dislodging the venerable sources of comfort.[8] Is this persistence of religion simply due to recalcitrant human irrationality and poor science education? Or to an all too human refusal to grow up and face reality? Whatever the answer, Darwinian naturalism, with its promise to provide a complete explanation of life, is now obliged to account not only for suffering but also for the tenacity with which most people still adhere to allegedly obsolete religious and theological myths about suffering.[9] If the Darwinian answer to the question of suffering is so easy to understand, then why do religious myths and theodicies still captivate the minds of most people, including many who are scientifically educated and fully up to date with evolutionary biology?

A simplistic Darwinism might reply that religious myths of suffering still have an adaptive function.[10] Religions trick people into *believing* that their lives are worthwhile. Religion promotes gene-survival—that is why God won't go away for good. Religion, according to at least some Darwinian naturalists, is, in fact, a "noble lie," but it is still adaptive. Its illusory projections help keep individuals and communities together so as to allow their genes to get into future generations. Recognizing the evolutionary effectiveness of religion, some disciples of Darwin even propose that we should never let the deceptions of religion die out completely, lest our species perish from having abandoned one of its most adaptive inventions.[11]

However, a more chastened Darwinism now admits that religious theodicies may not necessarily be adaptive *per se*. Rather, religious ideas and aspirations are only "parasitic" upon cerebral modules (which themselves can be accounted for in terms of evolutionary adaptation) originally meant for other purposes than that of providing religious consolation. This hypothesis modifies earlier and cruder Darwinian interpretations of religion's persistence. It concedes that humans will always have a propensity for religion as long as they continue to carry around the same kind of brains that our ancestors acquired during the Pleistocene period. Pascal Boyer and Scott Atran, for example, find the roots of our "counterfactual" religious ideation not so much in culture as in the kinds of hominid brains that became adept at "agent detection," starting several million years ago.[12]

8. See Hinde, *Why Gods Persist*; Burkert, *Creation of the Sacred*; and Boyer, *Religion Explained*.

9. For an extended discussion of this question, see Haught, *Deeper Than Darwin*.

10. See Wilson, *Consilience*.

11. See Rue, *By the Grace of Guile*, 82–107.

12. See Boyer, *Religion Explained* and Atran, *In Gods We Trust*.

Ideas about invisible supernatural beings, Atran claims, "are, in part, by-products of a naturally selected cognitive mechanism for detecting agents—such as predators, protectors, and prey—and for dealing rapidly and economically with stimulus situations involving people and animals."[13] Such mechanisms are ready-made for the religious enterprise of looking for unseen deities to sooth our suffering.

In response to this Darwinian debunking of religion and theodicy, I believe theology would be well advised to make two moves. First, it must undertake a thorough critique of the naturalist conviction that Darwinism provides an exhaustive and adequate explanation of the suffering of sentient life. The Darwinian naturalist's virtual claim to complete and final understanding of suffering in evolutionary terms, after all, is an exceptionally audacious one. If justifiable, it would bring down the entire classical edifice of ethics, religion, and theology. However, just as the Darwinian naturalist's claim to be able to explain critical intelligence and moral responsibility fully in evolutionary terms has proven to be inflated and even self-subverting, so also the belief that Darwinism can at last make suffering *fully* intelligible will also prove to be groundless. It is groundless, as I will show, because of its failure to understand fully the intimate connection between suffering and the more mysterious fact of subjectivity that is required to register both pain and pleasure.

The second theological move, however, is to attend carefully to the evolutionary accounts of the suffering involved in pre-human and non-human forms of sentient life. Without embracing scientific naturalism, theologians can still accept the discoveries of evolutionary science, one of which is that suffering occurs much more extensively in nonhuman life than religions had previously noticed. My proposal is that, by looking closely at evolution, theology may be aroused to find fresh and profound meaning in many of the classical religious myths and teachings about suffering.

## Summary and Conclusion

It is not natural selection alone but, even more fundamentally, the universe and life's anticipation of a fullness of being up ahead that allows suffering to show up wherever and whenever perfection still remains out of reach. Suffering is the dark side of any universe that remains unfinished and in which anticipation remains alive. The thread of anticipation that our richer empiricism has located as the dynamic core of critical intelligence, life, emergence, evolution, cosmic process, and moral aspiration

13. Atran, *In Gods We Trust*, 15.

is inseparable from the occurrence of life's suffering as well. For wherever there is anticipation there will also be frustration. And although a Darwinian look at life will be able to see suffering as adaptation, at another layer of understanding, suffering is information about the unfinished status of an anticipatory universe.

At the end of this chapter's reflections, however, a big question still remains. No doubt, the scientific naturalist has been raising it all along. The question is this: why is it that the universe, if it is indeed grounded in something other than itself, remains unfinished? Why does the universe have an anticipatory bearing at all? What sort of creator would have failed to round nature off into final perfection in the beginning (or, at least, by this time in cosmic history)? Why not create the universe fully and finally in the beginning, so as to avoid all suffering, struggle, and even striving? Why all this fooling around for fourteen billion years—and the trillions that may lie ahead?

The only answer that makes sense to me is that any notion of an originally completed cosmos would be theologically incoherent. As Teilhard and others have already suggested, there is no plausible alternative, theologically speaking, to an unfinished initial creation. An originally perfect creation—an idea that seemed tenable before we became aware of the unfolding, unfinished character of the universe—is theologically inconceivable. Why? Because if a creator, in the beginning, made a perfectly finished, fully completed world, such a world would not be distinct from its maker. It would not be *other* than God. If the world were created perfectly in the beginning, then this world would be nothing more than an extension of God's own being, an appendage to a dictatorial deity. It would not be a world at all.

Not just Christianity, but Islam and Judaism as well, have always emphasized that God is not the world. They have persistently rejected pantheism along with materialist monism. This means that, theologically speaking, the world must, in some sense, be radically other than God. But for the world to be truly other than God, it has to be given the opportunity to *become* itself. In other words, it has to be given permission to experiment, often unsuccessfully perhaps, with new possibilities of being. This experimental self-actualizing may take a long time—deep time.[14]

Try to imagine the alternatives: an originally perfect world might be a world without suffering, but it would also be a world without a future because everything would have been fixed in place, once and for all. It would also be a world without freedom, since all events, including human actions,

14. For a much more extensive development of this perspective, see Haught, *God After Darwin.*

would be determined, from the very start, to be just what they are. There would be no indeterminacy or contingency, essential ingredients in any world open to the newness of the future; it could anticipate nothing. An originally perfect world would be one without life. Theologically speaking, there can be no reasonable alternative to an unfinished initial creation.[15] For that reason, theology should be completely comfortable with an evolutionary understanding of nature as essentially anticipatory.

15. These thoughts are based on my reading of the many works of Pierre Teilhard de Chardin, but especially his essays in Teilhard de Chardin, *Christianity and Evolution*.

# 27: Suffering: From Expiation
to Expectation[1]

CATHOLIC THOUGHT STILL STRUGGLES to make sense of the four billion years of life's evolution. Our theologians renounce scriptural literalism, of course, but Catholic religious instruction generally reflects a prescientific understanding of cosmic and human origins. Teachers and homilists continue, at least unconsciously, to imagine the universe as having been made perfect by an almighty Creator in the beginning. They may accept, in principle, the traditional doctrine of ongoing creation (*creatio continua*), but they usually fail to reflect on the opportunities for theological renewal resident in Darwin's revolutionary understanding of life.

Moreover, our theological anthropology has failed to ponder the gradualness of *human* evolution.[2] Even though Catholic theologians do not turn away from the undeniable trail of evidence for human evolution (as do creationists and other opponents of Darwin), our understanding of sin, suffering, evil, and redemption still generally ignores scientific accounts of how modern humans came to be on earth during the last 200,000 years. Even though paleontological evidence of the slow and ragged arrival of anatomically modern humans out of a primate and hominid ancestry is now abundant, theologians and catechists habitually speak about the creation of human beings as though it occurred instantaneously, at some definite moment in the remote past. The *Catechism of the Catholic Church* reflects this literalism.[3]

Although a plain recital of the biblical narrative may have pedagogical suitability for the young, educated Catholics require a more sophisticated understanding of those texts that deal with origins. In the religious formation of adults, Catholic teaching generally turns a blind eye to scientific

1. The following text is an excerpt. Previously published in Haught, *Resting on the Future*, 85–100. Reprinted with permission.

2. For a theologically informed study of this evidence, see Huyssteen, *Alone in the World?*

3 See Catholic Church, "Original Sin," 396–421; Acker, "Creation and Catholicism"; and Domning, "Evolution." As mentioned earlier, the *Catechism* does (in principle) allow for an evolutionary understanding of *cosmic* creation overall: "Creation . . . did not spring forth complete from the hands of the Creator" (Catholic Church, "God Carries Out His Plan," 302). However, it does not seriously consider the meaning of the gradualness of human evolution.

information essential to an educated vision of the natural world. Secular thinkers assume, therefore, and not always without reason, that Catholic faith requires of scientifically educated people a stultifying sacrifice of intellect. This is a scandal, both theologically and pastorally. Departments of theology routinely fail to deal with evolution and other scientific discoveries head-on, and science education is seldom part of the training of priests and religious educators. In my own experience, the closest most Catholic pastors come to paying attention to Darwinian science is in their granting permission to lay adult religious educators to hold lectures or sponsor study programs on topics related to science and faith. Having offered numerous lectures and workshops on evolution and theology in American Catholic settings over the past several decades, I now recall only a handful of occasions where local clergy participated. Furthermore, the theological mindset of most Catholic bishops remains largely untouched by science except for those issues relating to human fertility, technological advances, and (occasionally) environmental abuse.[4] Even though Catholic history includes periods of expansive openness to lively intellectual discussion, substantive ecclesiastical conversations about evolutionary science are uncommon today.[5] Consequently, many scientifically educated Catholics now struggle intellectually to hold onto their faith.

As long as theology, preaching, religious education, and official church documents fail to connect the promises of Jesus or the Church's sacramental vision to the fascinating new portraits of an unfinished universe, Catholicism cannot be an inviting spiritual home for many educated seekers. The timidity with which official Catholic thought typically engages evolutionary science shows up, for example, in Pope Benedict XVI's 2007 encyclical, "Spe Salvi." Commenting on a text from Saint Gregory Nazianzen, the Pope writes:

> at the very moment when the Magi, guided by the star, adored Christ the new king, astrology came to an end, because the stars were now moving in the orbit determined by Christ. This scene,

4. See O'Leary, *Roman Catholicism and Modern Science*. A notable exception among Catholic bishops is the late Polish philosopher, Józef Życiński, author of *God and Evolution*.

5. The "Science and Human Values" committee of the American Conference of Catholic Bishops sponsored several discussions about evolution, involving scientists and theologians (1984–2003). This committee, however, no longer exists. The Vatican itself has also sponsored occasional conferences that deal with biological evolution. The proceedings of the best of these meetings are to be found in Russell, et al., *Evolutionary and Molecular Biology*. In general, however, the Church has done little, in my opinion, to promote the thoroughgoing reformation of Catholic thought that science now requires.

in fact, overturns the world-view of that time, which in a different way has become fashionable once again today. It is not
the elemental spirits of the universe, the laws of matter, which
ultimately govern the world and mankind, but a personal God
governs the stars, that is, the universe; it is not the laws of matter
and of evolution that have the final say, but reason, will, love—a
Person.[6]

Inspiring as his profession of faith may be, Benedict does not address here,
or anywhere else that I am aware of, the questions educated readers will ask
about how divine "governance" overrules "the laws of matter and evolution."
Unintentionally, Benedict even seems to place theology into a competitive relationship with science. It is not essential that an encyclical engage in extended
theological argument, of course, but scientific readers will certainly wonder
how it is that the laws of matter don't have "the final say." Even if Benedict
personally sees no conflict of science with faith, the fact is that countless scientists, philosophers, and other educated people do. After Darwin, the idea of
a personal God who providentially "governs the stars" seems less believable to
them than ever. Even though Albert Einstein and other physicists may have
dimly discerned an "intelligence" behind the laws of physics, it is not easy for
secular thinkers to discern any religious meaning at all in the fog of evolutionary accidents, waste, and wild experiments.

   One thoughtful evolutionary philosopher who has commented explicitly on Pope Benedict's theology of nature is Philip Kitcher. Kitcher speaks
for many philosophers and biologists today, claiming that "a history of life
dominated by natural selection is extremely hard to understand in provi-
dentialist terms."[7] Puzzled by the long and painful evolutionary struggle of
life on earth, Kitcher concludes that "there is nothing kindly or providential
about any of this and it seems breathtakingly wasteful and inefficient. Indeed, if we imagine a human observer presiding over a miniaturized version
of the whole show, peering down on his 'creation,' it is extremely hard to
equip the face with a kindly expression."[8]

   The question of evolution's compatibility with divine providence
has been central to conversations in theology and science ever since Darwin's day, but Catholic theologians have only occasionally dealt with it
directly and systematically. They have been content to comment vaguely
that science does not contradict the teachings of the Church, but they
have undertaken little sustained investigation of the relationship between

6. Benedict XVI, "Spe Salvi," 5.

7. Kitcher, Living With Darwin, 124.

8. Kitcher, Living With Darwin, 124.

theology and evolutionary biology. Even Pope John Paul II's 1996 endorsement of evolutionary biology refrained from addressing the difficulty scientists and philosophers have in reconciling the randomness and contingency of evolution with trust in divine providence.[9] A 2004 International Theological Commission, working under the supervision of Cardinal Joseph Ratzinger—who later became Pope Benedict XVI—took up the issue of contingency and divine governance, but it also assumed that classical Catholic philosophy and theology, especially that of Saint Thomas Aquinas, is intellectually resourceful enough to make good sense of the accidents in evolution. It failed to consider the possibility that Darwin's science requires a much more sweeping overhaul of theological understanding than a prescientific metaphysics allows.

"According to the Catholic understanding of divine causality," the Commission summarily remarked, "true contingency in the created order is not incompatible with a purposeful divine providence."[10] And yet, no attempt was made to address the sort of difficulties that Kitcher and many other scientists and philosophers have flagged. The document simply asserts that accidents in nature fall "within God's providential plan for creation."[11] It appeals for support to Aquinas, citing the *Summa Theologiae*: "The effect of divine providence is not only that things should happen somehow, but that they should happen either by necessity or by contingency. Therefore, whatsoever divine providence ordains to happen infallibly and of necessity happens infallibly and of necessity; and that happens from contingency, which the divine providence conceives to happen from contingency."[12] The Commission went on to say that "neo-Darwinians who adduce random genetic variation and natural selection as evidence that the process of evolution is absolutely unguided are straying beyond what can be demonstrated by science. Divine causality can be active in a process that is both contingent and guided."[13] Finally, the Commission stated that "an unguided evolutionary process–one that falls outside the bounds of divine providence–simply cannot exist because . . . [according to Aquinas] 'all things, inasmuch as they participate in existence, must likewise be subject to divine providence.'"[14]

9. See John Paul II, "Magisterium." Other important papal statements on science include John Paul II, "Address to the Pontifical Academy of Sciences," 391; John Paul II, "Letter to the Reverend George V. Coyne, SJ," 377; and Poupard, "Galileo," 375.

10. International Theological Commission, "Science."
11. International Theological Commission, "Science."
12. International Theological Commission, "Science."
13. International Theological Commission, "Science."
14. International Theological Commission, "Science."

Here the theological question of *how* to reconcile contingency in the world with divine providence is left hanging. The document rightly admits that true accidents exist in nature, but from the point of view of critics such as Kitcher, the real issue still remains: what does it say about God that the randomness in evolution and the undeserved suffering of sentient life fall under divine providential governance? Kitcher, along with most other contemporary scientific skeptics, cannot imagine how the idea of providential "guidance" makes any sense at all in view of natural evolutionary processes. He even quotes Saint Basil the Great: "Some . . . deceived by the atheism they bore within them, imagined that the universe lacked guidance and order, as if it were at the mercy of chance."[15] But as far as Kitcher and many other critics of theology are concerned, Darwinian science has simply restored to respectability what Pope Benedict considers to be the pre-Christian, pagan, fatalistic view that nature and life are indeed at "the mercy of chance."[16] After Darwin, countless other honest people also find it hard to embrace the Christian exhortation to trust in a providential God.

As "faith seeking understanding," Catholic theology must try harder to understand how natural processes can be both contingent and "governed" (to use Pope Benedict's term) or "guided" as the International Theological Commission states. Are "governed" and "guided" the most appropriate terms in which to speak of how providence relates to the meandering, experimental, and ungainly, not to say cruel, ways of evolution? Reference to providential governance and guidance in a world riddled with misery seems to exacerbate the problem of theodicy—that is, the persistent question of how God's capacity to order events could also be consistent with an infinite love. Moreover, if governance and guidance entail a "plan" or "design," critics of theology rightly wonder how such terms protect the Creator from the accusation of complicity in the excessive suffering of sentient life. Designations such as governance, guidance, design, order, or plan, when associated with divine providence, raise serious questions about the adequacy of traditional Catholic metaphysics to deal with the undeniable degree of accident and indifference in Darwinian process.

It seems to me, moreover, that, when associated with the idea of divine providence, terms such as "guidance" and "order" are too closely tied to the perfectionist metaphysics of the eternal present to frame a contemporary

15. Kitcher, *Living With Darwin*, 73.

16. See Kitcher, *Living With Darwin*, 73–116. Kitcher, like Richard Dawkins and other evolutionary materialists, apparently thinks that divine providence means intelligent design. This is just one more example of an evolutionary naturalist playing the role of the theologian by privileging creationist and ID notions of deity as the only ones worth debating.

Catholic theology of evolution. For this reason, I am arguing that a shift from the metaphor of divine governance toward that of God as goal—in accordance with a metaphysics of the future—is more appropriate to a theology for an unfinished universe.[17] Accordingly, the place for theology to engage with evolution is not on the question of the origin of design but on that of the meaning of life's drama. In the present chapter, I argue that an exclusive theological reliance on the metaphors of design, guidance, and order in our depictions of divine action also lends too much weight to theologies that interpret suffering primarily as *expiation*.

## Order and Expiation

Our new awareness of an unfinished universe—one whose internal arrangement has never been fixed or finalized—raises serious questions about the meaning and value of expiatory theologies of suffering and redemption. There is a close connection, after all, between the idealization of order or design on the one hand and the demand for expiation on the other. Biology and cosmology, however, now render both the metaphysics of the eternal present and the ancient expiatory understanding of suffering theologically questionable. Although he did not develop the point in systematic detail, Teilhard was rightly sensitive to the tie-in between expiatory theology and the theological assumption of a perfectly ordered initial state of creation.

An expiatory understanding of suffering survives and thrives in the shadows of an idealized cosmic order. It presupposes a metaphysics in which change means the defilement of an initial integrity and in which development often appears to be a violation of order that may need to be compensated by suffering. At times, the theme of reparation by paying a penalty in pain can lead to hopelessness and self-hatred, yet it still lives on in contemporary Catholic religious education and popular piety. The controversial film *The Passion of the Christ*, produced by actor Mel Gibson, represents an approach to the problem of evil and suffering that many Catholics still find redemptive: the more serious the moral offense, the more intense the suffering needed to expiate it. By portraying in the most graphic images the stripes of Jesus, the innocent victim, the film's message is that the faithful can now be assured of full atonement for their sins. Order has been restored through suffering.

Expiation, it needs to be said, is not the only way in which Catholic theology has understood what God is doing in the incarnation, crucifixion, and resurrection of Jesus. Citing the writings of Saint Irenaeus and

17. See Chapter 2 above.

Duns Scotus, theologians have also connected Christ's significance to the doctrine of creation—and not solely to that of redemption.[18] Today, Roman Catholic theologians are also paying closer attention to Eastern Christianity's theme of divinization as more central to the work of Christ than satisfaction, reparation, or expiation.[19] Nevertheless, the idea that an originally perfect order was disturbed by a sinful human act of rebellion against God *in the beginning*—and that expiation is required to make things right again—continues to provide much of the dramatic backdrop of Catholic intuitions about Jesus's significance.

The order/expiation theological formula, when taken alone, implies that the work of Christ is essentially atonement for an initial transgression. Here, the Cross is a necessary condition for repairing a state of divine and cosmic order that was soured by human sin in the beginning. When it is taken literally, the expiatory vision of suffering turns human moral effort into a project of restoration. Virtue, along with suffering, then has the meaning of repairing a lost perfection—instead of contributing to the growth of the world or the emergence of something truly new.[20] It follows that wherever expiation has been theology's main way of addressing the question of suffering, nostalgia for a state of initial cosmic perfection easily becomes a substitute for genuine hope. The supplanting of hope by nostalgia then gains support liturgically wherever eucharistic theology interprets the Mass as *mainly* a reenactment of Christ's expiatory sacrifice rather than as a foretaste of new creation and future communion of humanity and the whole cosmos with God.

If, as I have just supposed, expiatory theology is inseparable from the perfectionism that accompanies a theological metaphysics of the eternal present, it is not surprising that adherents to this ancient worldview usually ignore evolution or, at least, play down its significance to faith. Evolutionary biology, if correct, excludes the possibility that the biblical story of the Garden of Eden and the sin and punishment of Adam and Eve can ever again be taken literally. Proponents of an expiatory theology of atonement, however, fear that if Darwin is right, the redemptive significance of Jesus—insofar as it is taken to be expiation for the sin of our first parents—will be diminished or lost. Their ongoing infatuation with a theology of expiation helps explain why biblical literalists are the most vocal anti-Darwinians today.

18. See Flynn and Thomas, *Living Faith*, 246–56.

19. On "divinization" and its meaning for Christians, both East and West, see Finlan and Kharlamov, *Theiosis*.

20. Teilhard de Chardin, *How I Believe*, 42.

Even Catholics who say they accept evolution have yet to abandon all traces of such literalism, so they fail to think out consistently what the new scientific setting implies for Christology and soteriology. Catholic theodicies, moreover, have concentrated almost exclusively on human misery and have typically construed our own suffering as the penalty for our sin. However, biological and paleontological awareness of the millions of years of life's innocent suffering prior to the recent evolutionary emergence of humans clearly challenges both the traditional emphasis on expiation and the metaphysical assumptions that underlie it. Since there is suffering in all of life, and not just among sinful humans, Catholic theology now needs to bring the pre-human epochs of innocent suffering, death, predation, disease, and extinction formally into its reflections on the problem of evil and its understanding of the meaning and scope of redemption. Insofar as it is still tied to a tacitly Edenic literalism—as well as to a metaphysics of the eternal present—expiatory theology is usually too narrow, sometimes to the point of denying that a larger than human arena of innocent suffering even exists. What, then, would Catholic theology look like if it considered more straightforwardly the evolutionary fact that the universe is still an unfinished creation and that most of life's suffering is completely innocent? [This question is addressed in the following chapters and elsewhere in this Reader.]

# 28: Drama[1]

Evolution means that life has not only the character of design, diversity, and descent but also of *drama*. What makes the *Origin of Species* a compelling read is that beneath all its elaborate and often tedious scientific detail, it tells the story of a long struggle accompanied by risk, adventure, tragedy, and by what Darwin called "grandeur." A Christian theology of evolution locates this drama within the very heart of God. The becoming of the universe, including the emergence and evolution of life, are woven everlastingly into the kingdom of heaven. Within the ultimate environment that Christians call the Trinity, beneath the emblem of suffering that we call the cross, and in the radiance of Christ's resurrection—the evolution of life merges with the great epic of grace, promise, and liberation narrated in the Bible and codified by the doctrines of creation, incarnation, and redemption. Understood theologically, what is *really* going on in evolution is that the whole of creation, as anticipated by the incarnation and resurrection of Christ, is being transformed into the bodily abode of God. It is not in the design, diversity, and descent, but in the transformative drama of life, that theology finally makes its deepest contact with Darwin's science.

Ordinarily, science does not formally focus on this dramatic level of evolution, but nothing in the scientific picture of life and the universe contradicts a theological sensitivity to the dramatic character of evolution. It is actually because of scientific discoveries that theology now realizes more clearly than ever that nature is not a fixed set of things suspended indefinitely in space but rather a narrative unfolding in time. Although Darwin's scientific intent is to provide a superabundant amount of observational data in support of his theory of natural selection, the *Origin of Species* is also distinctive for laying out a majestic story. Distracted by the recording of minutiae that was Darwin's greatest talent, readers may fail to notice the narrative thread that weaves together the book's pages and chapters. However, if they look carefully beneath Darwin's account of life's design, diversity, and descent, they will find that they are being drawn into the subtext of a compelling drama of creativity, loss, suffering, and promise that is especially congenial to theological comment.

1. The following text is an excerpt. Previously published in Haught, *Making Sense of Evolution*, 53–66. Reprinted with permission.

This deeper drama—and not the themes of design, diversity, and descent taken alone—needs to be the *main* focus of a theology of evolution. I propose that most of the religiously distressing issues associated with natural selection can achieve a theologically satisfying resolution once we recognize them as essential to the dramatic character of life and the cosmos as a whole.

Theologically speaking, the central point of interest is whether the Darwinian drama should be read as tragedy or comedy. Do all the countless moments of the life-story add up to absurdity and nothingness in the end? Or is there a direction to the story, perhaps even a redemptive climax yet to come, an outcome that might give a lasting meaning to it all?

## The Struggle for Existence

The story told by the *Origin of Species* is one in which organisms constantly face enormous odds against their surviving and flourishing. Darwin often speaks of living beings *struggling* to exist. Making an effort to exist seems to be an essential trait of all life. One way to distinguish between life and nonlife is to examine whether a being is capable, even minimally, of self-exertion. The nature of living beings is to strive and often to struggle. Whether it is a bacterium motoring toward a food supply or a human being reading books in search of meaning and truth, all of life *endeavors* in one way or another. In more technical language, life is "conative" (from the Latin verb "to try"). To try means to move from what is toward what might be. Life lies along the pathway between present actuality and future possibility. Even as it bears within it the causal past, life feeds on what is yet to come; when life becomes human, it does so especially by putting on the raiment of hope. Hope is essential to human life, and our vitality weakens in proportion to the ebbing of our capacity for expectation. But even before our appearance in evolution, life always had an anticipatory quality, a reaching toward new possibilities, a feeling its way forward that has now reached a critical juncture in the human capacity for hope or despair.

Since life and hope are both modes of striving, they are risky ventures. They have the quality of wager. For wherever there is striving, there is the possibility of failure as well as success. As the scientist and philosopher Michael Polanyi puts it, since life always strives, it operates according to the "logic of achievement."[2] Living organisms have a capacity to achieve goals, but they can also fail to achieve them. No wonder the study of life is so

---

2. On the "striving" of living beings and the "logic of achievement" that differentiates life from nonlife, see Polanyi, *Personal Knowledge*, especially 327–380.

interesting. Since living beings can fail, they are susceptible to tragedy as well as triumph. Unlike purely chemical processes that unfold unfeelingly and have nothing at stake, living entities risk the possibility of *not* realizing the goals they seek, however rudimentary these may be.

In the preceding chapters, I have limited my discussion to separate theological inquiries into life's design, diversity, and descent, following the outline of most contemporary discussions of evolution. Up to this point, I have left out what is most theologically tantalizing about life: the enveloping drama in which design, diversity, and descent are embedded. In this chapter, therefore, I begin probing deeper into the dramatic character of life as revealed by Darwin and subsequent science. Theologically speaking, I want to ask eventually, what is the drama all about?

## Theology and the Drama of Life

As it turns out, the three components of Darwin's recipe for evolution—accidents, natural selection, and time—are instances of the elements essential to *any* dramatic story. Recall your own witnessing of a drama, whether a soap opera or Shakespeare's *Macbeth*. To hold your attention, it has to have (1) an openness to novelty or surprise, (2) a continuity or coherence that ties the stream of events together, and (3) a passage of time sufficient for the drama to unfold. A series of occurrences adds up to a drama only if it fuses unpredictability with some degree of predictability and a span of time ample enough for the relevant events to happen. This triplet of components is also the medium in which religions, myths, and theologies seek to make the world intelligible. All three elements—contingency, continuity, and time—are essential to any story, and they cannot be isolated from one another without splintering the narrative into disconnected droplets.

Christians who find evolution contrary to faith usually do so because they are focusing abstractly on design, diversity, or descent rather than the drama going on beneath the surface. The typically design-obsessed frame of mind with which so many devout Christians as well as staunch atheists have usually dealt with the question of God and evolution is a dead end. For theology, however, focusing on evolution as a still-unfinished drama rather than a factory of designs is crucial.

Unfortunately, contemporary evolutionary materialists have seized Darwin's rich story of life and bled the drama right out of it. Their mechanistic treatments separate the element of contingency in the life-story from that of predictability, destroying both suspense and coherence. Simultaneously, they turn life's temporal depth into a rambling series of meaningless moments leading to a final abyss. They typically refer to contingency as "chance" and to nature's lawful reliability as "necessity," both terms signaling for them the ultimate meaninglessness of evolution. Deep time becomes a battlefield on which chance and necessity fight a long and pointless war. Viewed in this fashion, evolution remains forever resistant to theological interpretation.

## A Deeper Coherence

Chet Raymo is a religiously inquisitive evolutionary naturalist who now doubts the existence of a personal God. When he speaks of "intelligent design," he is far from endorsing the views advocated by Michael Behe, William Dembski, and other ID defenders. Instead, he is drawing attention to what I am calling the dramatic makeup of evolution, and he seems to suggest that the drama is not devoid of a deeper coherence than the idea of design usually suggests. The dramatic character of life, he seems to realize, is not immediately transparent to minds preoccupied with design. Life's drama, in turn, invites the open-minded evolutionist to *wait* before making a final judgment about whether an overall meaning may be coming to expression in our still-emerging universe.[3]

A theology of evolution, in any case, takes drama to be a much more exciting road to the discovery of God after Darwin than are analyses of fleeting and always imperfect instances of adaptive design. It allows that there is more than one way to bring coherence to events. Design is satisfying to those who think statically, spatially, and nonhistorically, but to those who welcome time's long reach and narrative nuance, design considered apart from drama is trivial. Contemporary ID proponents can take no comfort in Raymo's reference to a deeper kind of "intelligent design." Unlike ID proponents, Raymo embraces a fully Darwinian account of life. Nevertheless, the evolutionary theologian will be intrigued by Raymo's search for a deeper coherence in the evolutionary narrative than most other Darwinians are interested in excavating.

Can theology penetrate to a dimension of nature that lies deeper than design? Can it arrive at a region of being beneath the surface of life where religious faith and Darwinian biology may coexist comfortably? Ever since Darwin, in ways that most scientists have scarcely noticed, adventurous religious thinkers have sought a "deeper coherence" of faith and evolution beneath the "shallow coherence" of ID and other design-obsessed versions of theism. In the spirit of this generally ignored theological quest, I am

3. See Raymo, "Intelligent Design."

proposing that a scientifically informed theology will focus less on patently visible instances of design in nature than on the following question: why is the natural world endowed with the exquisite blend of indeterminacy, lawfulness, and temporality giving it the dramatic substructure that allows an evolutionary story to occur at all?

Digging beneath contemporary controversies carried on by evolutionary naturalists and their ID opponents, theology may seek contact with Darwin's science at a deeper level than either of the two opposing sides has reached. Scientists and philosophers who insist that Darwin has disposed of theology altogether have usually done so by embracing the same engineering and architectural ideal of design as their ID opponents. Clearly, if God is the author of life, they argue, nature should be more elegantly and skillfully designed than it is. Don't the adaptive imperfections and the general inefficiency of evolutionary outcomes prove that life was not intelligently designed after all? Far from opposing ID advocates on this point, Dawkins and other evolutionary naturalists agree with them that an intelligent deity would have to do a better job than human designers when it comes to manufacturing ears, eyes, and digestive systems. But since attempts at design in nature have been botched, God cannot possibly exist.

The science writer David Barash typifies this design-obsessed mindset of most evolutionary atheists. Like Dawkins and Coyne, he begins with the assumption that theology stands or falls on the question of design. If God is the author of living design, he reasons, the design has to be *perfectly* engineered. All religious believers, he assumes, must attribute the intricate design in life directly to an intelligent designer, since in their view "only a designer could generate such complex, perfect wonders."[4] Next, Barash goes on to point out that "in fact, the living world is shot through with imperfection." From there he reaches his conclusion: "Unless one wants to attribute either incompetence or sheer malevolence to such a designer [God], this imperfection—the manifold design flaws of life—points incontrovertibly to a natural, *rather than* [my emphasis] a divine process, one in which living things were not created *de novo*, but evolved." It follows that Darwin's science has decisively destroyed any basis for theology. We find in Barash, once again, an evolutionary naturalist trying to put religious ideas behind for good and who, in doing so, holds himself forth as an authority on the question of what is permitted to pass as acceptable theology.

However, Raymo's suggestions, as I implied above, point beyond Barash, Dawkins, Coyne, and ID—in a third direction. Raymo also wants to avoid theology, but unlike Barash, at least he is not fixated on the engineering

4. Barash, "Does God Have Back Problems Too?"

ideal of "design." In principle, he allows for a deeper coherence or intelligibility in natural processes, a kind of narrative arrangement of life that
transcends the triviality of engineering elegance or industrial efficiency. His
reflections seem open to my proposal that the wild experiments of evolution, the inevitable imperfection of adaptations, and the crazy convolutions
of eyes, ears, and digestive tracts are not necessarily incompatible with a
deeper kind of (dramatic) wisdom at work in nature.

Neither Raymo nor Darwin would go as far as I am going here, but my
point is that their ideas are—at least logically—open to theological understanding. A theology of evolution need not ignore the fact that life on earth,
in all its waste and wildness, has actually brought about a far more interesting, inventive, and beautiful set of outcomes than ever could have occurred
if nature had been put together from the beginning with no "design flaws,"
as Barash's stringent theological criteria require. Instead of a universe instantaneously ordered to fit Barash's and ID's stiff architectural standards,
Darwin has laid open a world in which adaptive imperfections turn out to
have been necessary portals to future creative results that flawless engineering could never have allowed to occur.

Darwin, in other words, has portrayed the life-story as a true adventure. Evolution is a risk-taking and extravagantly inventive drama. Alongside its lush creativity, there always exists the possibility of tragic outcomes,
including abundant suffering and perpetual perishing. To Christians, there
is something "cruciform" about the whole drama of life.[5] Sensitive people
may not like this, but before sneering at the crudity of evolutionary "design,"
it may be wise to look carefully at the preposterous theological alternative
tacitly espoused by Barash and ID theists. The flawlessly engineered world
they prefer would be dead on delivery. Since it would already be perfect, it
would also be finished; if finished, it would have no future.

In other words, there could be no dramatic *transformation* going on in
the kind of universe they idealize. Determined by a hypothetical intelligent
designer to correspond impeccably in every detail to an eternally fixed master plan, such a world would be devoid of the contingency, indeterminacy,
freedom, and futurity that give a truly dramatic character—and possibly a
meaning—to evolution and the larger world process.

If you are the kind of theist or atheist who demands here and now a
world with no design flaws, you are asking for an anemic idea of deity and
a divine creation devoid of a deeper, dramatic coherence. If a fixed and
frozen universe is what you want, then you may insist on perfect design—
as envisaged by ID and most contemporary evolutionary atheism. But if

5. See Rolston, *Science and Religion*, 144–46.

you prefer a truly surprising and richly creative universe, then you may be religiously open to evolution. Isn't it conceivable that Darwin's three-part recipe for evolution wells up from a hidden dramatic depth of nature wherein there resides an inaccessible wisdom that those obsessed with perfect design simply cannot fathom?

Christian belief, at any rate, does not depend for its credibility on the existence of a world without design flaws. Among notable Christian thinkers, Cardinal John Henry Newman (1801–1890) expressed an exceptionally strong distaste for any theology that supports itself by leaning on the vapid criterion of design. Even before Darwin published the *Origin of Species*, Newman had written in 1852 that William Paley's design-oriented natural theology could "not tell us one word about Christianity proper," and that it "cannot be Christian, in any true sense, at all."[6] Paley's brand of theology, Newman goes on, "tends, if it occupies the mind, to dispose it against Christianity." For Newman, in other words, it is not the task of theology to discover a divine designer lurking immediately beneath or behind the data of biology or physics.

Furthermore, if you explore the Bible carefully, you will not find an elegant engineer there either. God's intimate relation to the world is before all else one of *liberation* and *promise* rather than the imposition of design. Consequently, any respectable theology after Darwin will not insist that the Creator is so petty as to function like an engineer tinkering mechanically with life. Theologians in the biblical tradition normatively understand divine creativity, providence, compassion, and wisdom as inseparable from the more basic motifs of liberation and promise, notions that do not correspond easily with that of engineering. Israel's idea of God is shaped above all else by its experience of the exodus from Egypt and Christianity's God is inconceivable except in terms of the experience of being delivered from the most profound forms of enslavement, sin, and death. The God of Abraham and Jesus is a promising God, a God who seeks the transformation of all things, who dreams of renewal beyond the deep freeze of design, and who opens up the future even where it seems to mortals that there are dead ends everywhere.

It follows, therefore, that whenever the idea of God is separated from the conjugate themes of freedom and futurity, it is an idolatrous distortion, at least by biblical standards. This is why the engineer-God seems so remote from any genuinely biblical sense of the divine. At times, biblical metaphors, adapting to the popular imagination, may portray the Creator as an artisan, potter, builder, or planner. Such images serve to fortify believers' trust that

6. Newman, *Idea of a University*, 411.

their lives are not pointless and that goodness will prevail in the end. Yet only an extreme literalism can segregate these images from the dominant motifs of liberation and promise that frame the whole body of Hebrew and Christian reflection on God.

A properly biblical theology of nature will view divine wisdom, providence, and compassion less as a guarantee of the world's safety—as the idea of design encourages—than as an unbounded self-emptying graciousness that grants the world an open space and generous amount of time to become *more*, giving it ample opportunity to participate in its own creative self-transformation. A God of freedom and promise does not compel but rather invites the creation to experiment with many possible ways of being, allowing it to make "mistakes" in the process. This is the God of evolution—one who honors and respects the indeterminacy and narrative openness of creation and, in this way, ennobles it.

The God of evolution is a humble, self-donating liberality that avoids any unmediated manipulation of things. Contrary to what Barash states, in the creation of life's diversity, it is not a matter of natural processes *rather than* God doing all the work, but instead one of God creating through a drama of nature. The universe is not "designed" to immediate perfection, but seeded with promise and potential for indeterminate outcomes, including the eventual emergence of human freedom. Theology's proper engagement with Darwinian science, therefore, need not be limited to a defense of suffocating notions of design. Theology after Darwin is much more interested in the drama that is still working itself out in nature.

# 29: Death[1]

It has always appeared to me more satisfactory to look at the
immense amount of pain & suffering in this world, as the inevitable result of the natural sequence of events, i.e., general
laws, rather than from the direct intervention of God.

—CHARLES DARWIN, LETTER TO MARY BOOLE, 1866[2]

The last enemy to be destroyed is death.

—THE APOSTLE PAUL, IN 1 CORINTHIANS 15:26

Promise the earth a hundred million more years of continued growth. If, at the end of that period, it is evident that
the whole of consciousness must revert to zero, *without
its secret essence being garnered anywhere at all*, then,
I insist, we shall lay down our arms—and mankind will be
on strike. The prospect of a *total death* (and that is a word
to which we should devote much thought if we are to gauge
its destructive effect on our souls) will, I warn you, when it
has become part of our consciousness, immediately dry up
in us the springs from which our efforts are drawn.

—PIERRE TEILHARD DE CHARDIN[3]

---

1. The following text is an excerpt. Previously published in Haught, *Making Sense of
Evolution*, 99–108. Reprinted with permission.
2. Darwin, "Letter to Mary Boole."
3. Teilhard de Chardin, *How I Believe*, 43–44.

EVOLUTION HAS PRODUCED A stupendous display of diversity, innumerable species of life, multiple modes of sentience, and, most recently, the human capacity for self-awareness. However, the drama of life on earth has also featured at least five massive extinctions; on a smaller scale the evolutionary story is one in which every living, sentient, and conscious organism eventually dies. From all appearances, if evolution is a drama, it is a tragic one. Every organic actor in the production called "life" eventually perishes and becomes interred in the irretrievable past. All living beings are eventually lost and forgotten. In the long run, nothing in the universe is forever, and physics informs us that the universe as a whole will not last indefinitely either.

The fragility of life is especially troubling. Living organisms flourish for a season at best and then vanish. New birth is inseparable from the mortality that opens up a space for it. In the meantime, however, the life-story keeps going on in a continuous and unbroken way. Individual organisms disappear, but every one of them contributes to a trail of events that, as we can see clearly after Darwin, accumulates into a most intriguing set of outcomes—not the least of which is the human species. Without the death of individual living beings in each new generation, the story of life would never have gone far and would have even come to a dead end. If they were immortal, organisms would pile up on one another and the countless variations needed by natural selection to fashion new species would be limited by lack of space. Evolution relies on variation and selection if it is to make any advances in complexity and diversity. Variation, as Darwin came to realize, needs to be abundant if it is to produce even a few accidentally adaptive forms. Thus, it also requires an enormous spread of *time*. With ample time, it stipulates the death of every present generation of living beings; without death, evolution could not be truly inventive. If a sufficient supply of variations is to become available for selection, death is a necessity, not a riddle to fret over.

So even though death is an agonizing puzzle to most human beings and their religious faiths, a purely naturalistic method of inquiry after Darwin can find an intelligible place for it in the total scheme of life. Just as suffering makes natural sense as an evolutionary adaptation in sentient beings (helping them survive by warning them of impending harm or fatality), so death seems to make sense as part of the overall evolution of living diversity. Death and suffering are both essential to the survival of populations of genes as they flow from one generation to the next. Why bother, then, to look for a theological meaning to suffering or death? Hasn't Darwin's science in company with the field of genetics taken us as far into the depth of life, suffering, and death as the human mind can possibly reach?

To evolutionary naturalists, death seems to make good sense scientifically, even though it is no less personally agonizing to them than to anyone else. It is essential to Christianity, however, *not* to tolerate any intelligible place for death and suffering—at least in the larger setting of being. Christianity is about the eventual wiping away of all tears by God, the final release from suffering, and the ultimate defeat of death through the resurrection of Christ. So what sense can Christian theology make of the riddle of evolutionary extinction and the demise of every organism? How can Christians pronounce life to be good, as God does in Genesis, if death, along with so much struggle and pain in sentient beings, is so integral to the creative process? To Darwin, evolution seemed increasingly godless the deeper he saw into the enormity of suffering, struggle, and death that are part of it. Yes, something grand had come into existence as a result of births, deaths, variation, natural selection, and deep time; but can one plausibly connect nature to the purposes of a beneficent deity after looking directly at how evolution relies so heavily on death?

Along with Darwin, many evolutionists today deny that there can be a persuasive theological answer to this question. However, unlike scientific naturalism, it is the task of Christian theology to make it clear that death has no intelligible place in the total—and dramatically speaking, that means the "final"—scheme things. It is theologically inappropriate to look for a rationally acceptable place for death in God's creation. Doing so would give death a legitimacy that might lead us to tolerate and even justify it here and now, rather than taking it as an evil to be fought against and overcome. It is not the job of theology to justify death by situating it solely within the context of a purely naturalistic understanding of the universe. Instead, theology asks whether the naturalistic point of view as such is intelligible.

It is not. Evolutionary naturalism has no reasonable answer to the question of why there is anything at all rather than nothing, or why the universe is intelligible at all, or why the universe is the blend of contingency, law, and time, which gives it a narrative character that in turn allows life to evolve in the dramatic way it does. Evolutionary naturalism has no answer to these questions other than to say, "This is just the way things happen to be." Theologically speaking, this naturalistic answer is unacceptable; it amounts to saying that our search for intelligibility will ultimately be met with final absurdity. This is hardly a prediction that can sustain an endless, ongoing search for understanding. Scientists themselves should take no comfort in a vision of reality that perches the natural world on the pedestal of final unintelligibility. Theology, on the other hand, because of its insistence that nature must be ultimately rooted in a transcendent ground of intelligibility, goodness, beauty, and truth, turns out to be a much better friend and supporter of scientific inquiry than evolutionary naturalism could ever be.

Theology is critical of evolutionary naturalism most of all, however, because the latter makes such an easy settlement with death. Even though death may be intelligible to science as part of nature, nature itself remains unintelligible to theology when considered apart from its eternal ground and depth. Consequently, the present chapter makes no attempt to make sense of death by staying within the cramped confines of a naturalistic worldview. Instead, it looks for a way to understand the Christian hope for redemption from and final victory over death in a post-Darwinian age. To do so, however, it does not in any way challenge evolutionary science, only evolutionary naturalism.

## A Wider Vision

To Christian theologians, the challenge after Darwin is to think of the universe as a place of promise and purpose *in spite of* the fact that everything in the life-story—and eventually the universe itself—fades into oblivion. Life, it is clear, is not an unmixed good, especially since it is all subject to death. Is it possible, then, to arrive at a plausible theological understanding of death that does not contradict evolutionary science, but that takes us deeper into the drama of life and the universe than science alone can?

I believe our theological conversation with Darwin may be considerably broadened and enriched at this point by considering several ideas of the philosopher and religious thinker Alfred North Whitehead (1861–1947). I shall not give a full account of Whitehead's thought or defend every aspect of it here. Instead, I shall focus on what he has to say about the general fact of nature's *perishability*, of which the death of living organisms is the most troubling kind.

Whitehead observes that the fact of evil in the natural world comes down, in the end, to the plain and simple fact that things perish. The naked fact of perishing is the fundamental issue that religions, philosophies, and theologies have always had to address. Organic death is the major instance of a larger enigma: why does anything in nature perish at all? Perishing as such is the problem, but what bothers us in a special way about the death of every sentient being is that a center of experience—in other words, a *subject*—apparently disappears for good. Nowhere is this dissolution more agonizing than when the mind of a loved one disintegrates or a formerly healthy person suddenly lapses into a vegetative state and then finally into death. However, theology must connect even these most disquieting examples of decomposition to the more general fact that *nothing* in nature lasts forever.

As each new moment arrives in the flow of time, the present moment is thrust into the past. There it eventually is lost, at least to human memory. It is this fading of every present pulse of actuality into the forgotten past that constitutes the "ultimate evil in the temporal world." "The world," as Whitehead puts it, "is haunted by terror at the loss of the past, with its familiarities and its loved ones. It seeks escape from time in its character of 'perpetually perishing.'"[4] When things perish, it is the loss of immediacy that evokes the kind of anguished concern to which religions have tried, in diverse ways, to apply some measure of consolation. Theology, therefore, needs to situate our uneasiness about the perpetual dying that goes on in evolution within the wider fact that all finite things perish.

Theologian Paul Tillich, whom we met in a previous chapter, conjectures that beneath our human anxiety about death lies a more fundamental concern, that of being forgotten forever. As the present is being pushed into the past and then becomes lost to human memory, we worry that we, too, shall eventually be forgotten. The anxiety of having to die and, indirectly, our sensitivity to the fact that every organism is mortal, is the "anxiety of being eternally forgotten."[5] This is why people of all times and places have sought, through a variety of ways, to ensure that they will be remembered.

If Tillich and Whitehead are correct, unless there exists, beneath the abyss of death, a ground of permanence that can redeem *all* perishing, we would have to conclude that evil is finally victorious. If the evolutionary drama is to make *final* sense, then somehow the dissolution of even the most trivial instances of life cannot be absolute. If redemption is a realistic possibility, the series of events that make up the life-story and the larger universe must flow into the bosom of an everlasting compassion that saves it all from final nothingness and rescues it from eventual incoherence. Deeper than evolution, if evolution is to escape final absurdity, there must be something that gathers up and holds, in eternal memory, the stream of events that make up the drama of life and the cosmic process as a whole.

## The Limits of Science

Needless to say, any sort of scientific proof of this theological proposal is out of the question. For the Christian, everything I have proposed here is a matter of hope, not scientific certainty. The power of God to redeem all of life from

4. Whitehead, *Process and Reality*, 340.
5. Tillich, *Eternal Now*, 33–34.

death cannot be justified by intellectual effort, but only by trust in the love and fidelity of God as made manifest in Jesus Christ. But if, as Jesus promised, the hairs of our head are numbered, and if, as the psalmist earlier proclaimed, all our tears flow into God's flask (Ps 56:8), then somehow every perishing life and every past event is preserved eternally in God.

Whitehead would add that, in God's experience, the cumulative series of cosmic events and experiences never fades. Each instance of life that perishes in the context of our own limited experience or that goes extinct during an epoch of evolution, dwells forever in God, without loss. God is the underlying permanence that fully preserves everything that occurs in the entire cosmic process. From our own transient perspective, each momentary event eventually drifts into the past, where it is eventually forgotten—but it still remains in the divine memory with lasting intensity.

Again, we cannot prove any of this scientifically, nor should we even want to do so, given the limitations of the scientific method. Nevertheless, science has stretched our awareness of the extent of perishing that occurs in evolution, so it demands a corresponding enlargement of our sense of God and divine compassion. Consequently, Christian hope after Darwin assumes the reality of a God large and generous enough to embrace the entire drama of life and the cosmos, into which the evolution of life is intricately woven.

Whitehead's understanding of religion in the age of evolution necessitates such an expansiveness in our understanding of God. In this philosopher's understanding, God is that which stands beyond, behind, and within, the passing flux of immediate things, rescuing whatever may seem from our own vantage point to be "utter final wreck and tragedy."[6] God "saves the world as it passes into the immediacy of his own experience." In a world conceived of as a temporal process, each experience adds something new, by way of contrast, to the divine experience. Every perishing event and every death of every organism is eternally redeemed by its "relation to the completed whole." Taken into the endless breadth of the ever-intensifying beauty that we may call God, evolution and the universe from which life emerges are endowed with imperishable value and meaning.

Each life is invited to participate in and contribute itself to this wider beauty. For human beings, this self-contribution is symbolized especially in acts of worship. In a most intimate way, my entire existence, vitality, and subjectivity are, in the act of worship, made available to be synthesized into the transformative world process and, ultimately, into the life of God. My personal existence is still continuous with cosmic beginnings and is

6. Whitehead, *Process and Reality*, 345–51.

everlastingly so. For even after the cosmos eventually dissolves, the story of its having been will still be true—preserved forever in God's saving memory. Accordingly, the question of who I am, how I came to emerge from the universe, and whether I can be redeemed from absolute perishing—all of this is inescapably bound up with the universe and its final destiny. In a communal setting, religious worship symbolizes my grateful consent to contribute my life and efforts to this everlastingly significant cosmic drama.

The idea that the *whole* scheme of perishing things can be saved in God's transforming love may be easier to grasp if we learn to think, along with Whitehead, that, at its most elemental level, the universe is made up not of spatially measurable bits of matter but of temporal events, occasions, or happenings. The problem with thinking of the elemental cosmic components simply as physical units, as materialists usually do, is that these spatialized bits of stuff eventually dissolve and disappear. Events, on the other hand, have the quality of being able to keep adding up into a continuous series in which what goes before is never completely lost. Material entities disintegrate, but events accumulate. Whitehead and Hartshorne emphasize that the cosmos is a cumulative temporal series of events, not just a collection of things hanging around in space. Modern scientific materialism, on the contrary—especially in its mechanistic portraits of nature—has unfortunately rigidified nature by trying to fit it fully into spatially measurable models. But in their most concrete actuality, both the evolution of life and the larger cosmic process—as a more up-to-date physics also allows—consist of narrative happenings, not bits of matter. The totality of events in nature gathers itself into an unbroken drama, one that theology may think of as being taken forever into the life of God.

## The Hiddenness of God

Still, along with the Darwinian skeptics, we can only wonder why the God who promises deliverance of all beings from absolute perishing remains so hidden and seemingly far off as deaths keep mounting up in evolution. Why does what Whitehead call "the final good" and "the ultimate ideal" remain beyond all reach? Why does "that which gives meaning to all that passes" always elude present apprehension?[7] By itself, science can make no sense of what lies hidden "beyond, behind, and within" the flux of natural and historical events. It insists on clarity here and now since it can base its predictions only on what is presently available to empirical inquiry. Can theology make better sense of it all?

7. Whitehead, *Science and the Modern World*, 191–92.

Theology may at least point out that the hiddenness of God to conscious beings here and now is consistent with the fact that the universe is still coming into being. Religious expectation or hope, though quite distinct from science, is logically compatible with the fact that we humans are part of an immense cosmos still in the making. An undeniable implication of science today is that we live in a still-unfinished universe. If our universe were completely finalized here and now, we could justifiably insist on absolute clarity. However, as long as the world is still being created and as long as the drama of life has yet to be concluded, we cannot reasonably expect, here and now, to make out clearly what it is all about, or what lies beyond, behind, and within it. We have to wait.

For this reason, it is not unexpected that what Whitehead calls the greatest of present facts—in other words, God—must remain beyond our grasp. An unfinished universe is one in which awareness of God comes only in the mode of promise rather than conclusive comprehension. The religious intuition of a divine permanence beyond, behind, within—or beneath—the passing flux of immediate things can take hold of us only if we are willing to sacrifice our longing for present clarity and allow our hearts and minds to be suffused with patient and long-suffering hope.

# 30: Death, Resurrection, and the Unfinished Universe[1]

"God did not make death, nor does he rejoice in
the destruction of the *living*."

—WISDOM 1:13

IF THE NEWS OF Jesus's resurrection from the dead was hard for his disciples and the first Christians to embrace, it seems all the more so for those of us who live in the age of science. The earliest Christian witnesses experienced the resurrection as a completely surprising event, so rising from the dead would be even more startling to sensibilities shaped primarily by modern science and its inductive methods of knowing. Science cannot make sense of unique events of any sort, let alone those so bereft of antecedents as the resurrection. Even if it connects powerfully with the hope that persists in human hearts, Jesus's resurrection would appear—scientifically—to transcend all "realistic" expectations. The origin of the Big Bang universe is also a singularity that eludes complete scientific comprehension. Science, as we have often observed, is most at home with generalizations based on the observation of large numbers of similar events obeying invariant physical laws. It squirms anxiously in the presence of what is completely unprecedented, and it looks for ways to reduce what seems exceptional to what is already known. It is the nature of science to suppress the truly unique by fitting it into the universal. Indeed, such an approach to understanding is a defining characteristic of modern intellectual culture. The difficulties that scientifically educated people have with the notion of resurrection stems, in large measure, from the nearly unshakeable assumption that nature and history are simply not open to anything so impossibly new as Christ's victory over death.

It is important to add, however, that it is not science as such that renders Jesus's resurrection, along with the prospect of our sharing in his

---

1. The following text is an excerpt. Previously published in Haught, *Christianity and Science*, 153–165. Reprinted with permission.

destiny, incredible. Science would simply pass over such an event without even noticing it. On the other hand, there can be no doubt that scientific naturalism stands in opposition to resurrection—whether that of Jesus or ourselves (and in this chapter I am referring to both). According to scientific naturalism, all causes are natural causes, so there are no events that cannot be explained exhaustively by the scientific method. For that reason, the origin of life would have to be a purely natural event, fully explainable in chemical and physical terms. The emergence of mind, ethics, and religion can also be fully accounted for naturalistically, as unplanned outcomes of blind evolutionary mechanisms. Of course, there can be no resurrection to new life beyond death.

According to the outspoken naturalist philosopher Owen Flanagan of Duke University, "most philosophers and scientists in the twenty-first century see their job as making the world safe for a fully naturalistic view of things."[2] In this chapter, I shall refer on several occasions to this eminent scholar's opinions since they also represent so accurately and clearly the thinking of many other prominent intellectuals. One of naturalism's chief claims is that ideas about God and ideas about life after death, "stand in the way of understanding our nature truthfully and locating what makes life meaningful in a nonillusory way."[3] However, as Flanagan comments, once we have resigned ourselves to the gravity of naturalism, life does not have to be sad. The universe is pointless and death final, he declares, but human life can be meaningful and happy anyway. When we die, our personalities disappear forever, but, in the meantime, we can still live satisfying lives. Flanagan's is an interesting claim for many reasons, but here I want only to flag his assertion that belief in life after death, however one conceives of it, is "irrational." By this stern marker, he means to emphasize that there is no scientific evidence that could conceivably support the expectation of resurrection or the subjective survival of death; reasonable people cannot take the idea of the existence of the soul, immortality, or bodily resurrection seriously.

In the world of religious ideas, nothing, including belief in God, stands out as a violation of naturalistic assumptions more starkly than the expectation that the dead will rise again. It is simply not in the nature of things, naturalists claim, that resurrection could ever happen. On top of this, science has shown, quite clearly, that the direction of all physical processes—and that of the universe as a whole—is toward final and irreversible disintegration. The entirety of life, of which human history is only a

2. Flanagan, *Problem of the Soul*, 167–68.
3. Flanagan, *Problem of the Soul*, 167–68.

recent and precarious chapter, departs from the entropic cosmic decline only temporarily. Blank deadness will have the final word. Now that physics has linked human existence more tightly than ever to the natural world, the dreary outcome that awaits the whole of our universe seems to swallow up any hope that individual persons can escape it either.

What response can a Christian theology of nature make to this gloomy prognostication? At first, it may be tempted to revert to the traditional idea of the soul's immortality as the simplest way out of the stated predicament. That is, it might assume that there is an immaterial part of us which, upon our dying, can eventually be severed decisively from the cosmic plunge toward death by entropy. The second law of thermodynamics, with its dour news of a dying cosmos, may simply be ignored as theologically inconsequential. If the immortal human soul can break out of its material prison, the demise of the physical universe should have no bearing whatsoever on our hope for immortality.

## How Can We Understand "Resurrection"?

Owen Flanagan, as cited above, admits that most people still believe the human soul or self will live on after death. To him, such obsolete beliefs are an annoying impediment to the spread of naturalism, a dominant strain of contemporary thought. There are different kinds of naturalism, but Flanagan's is uncompromisingly materialistic. Ever since the seventeenth century, some of the most influential scientific materialists have sponsored the belief that matter is all that is real. Consciousness itself, according to the materialists, is so completely dependent on physical brains that no personal selfhood could be rescued from the organic disintegration that comes with death. The modern commitment to materialism logically excludes any possibility of conscious survival beyond the grave. More than this, it also logically excludes the possibility that all the human centuries of effort and creativity can have any permanent significance either. Disturbed by such a prospect, the great American psychologist and philosopher William James provides a candid summation of what materialist naturalism logically entails—as far as natural and human achievements are concerned:

> That is the sting of it, that in the vast driftings of the cosmic weather, though many a jewelled shore appears, and many an enchanted cloud-bank floats away, long lingering ere it be dissolved—even as our world now lingers for our joy—yet when these transient products are gone, nothing, absolutely nothing remains, to represent those particular qualities, those elements

of preciousness which they may have enshrined. Dead and gone
are they, gone utterly from the very sphere and room of being.
Without an echo; without a memory; without an influence on
aught that may come after, to make it care for similar ideals.
This utter final wreck and tragedy is of the essence of scientific
materialism as at present understood.[4]

The vast majority of the earth's inhabitants today still share the sentiments of James rather than Flanagan. They would consider the final ex-
tinguishing of minds and persons—as well as the utter obliteration of all
the impressive ethical and aesthetic achievements of humanity—to be the
greatest of evils. They deny, either explicitly or implicitly, that everything
ends up in absolute nothingness. Of course, their instinctive revulsion is
no proof that they are right, but it still seems appropriate to ask whether
they are all as deluded and "irrational" as Flanagan and most other scientific naturalists suspect. The highly respected sociologist Peter Berger
has argued that our everyday (prototypical) gestures of laughing, playing,
and hoping—the very activities that keep us sane—could never occur if
we were completely convinced, deep down, that death is the final word.[5]
Once again, this is no proof that hope is realistic. In fact, naturalists today
often explain hope away as a deceptive survival mechanism, a Darwinian adaptation out of touch with reality. But scientific naturalists very
seldom think through to the end—in the way that James does in the above
quote—what would be the full consequences of their confident claim that
absolute death and nothingness await everything real.

Very few scientific materialists can embrace, with full consistency, the
sober logic of, for instance, the eminent physicist Stephen Weinberg, who
says that if there is no God and no life beyond death, the most we can rescue
from our absurd situation is a sense of honor in accepting this fate without
flinching. In the end, even Weinberg finds his life meaningful, for there can
be no doubt that he implicitly believes that truth is worth seeking. Indeed,
one can assume that the latter pursuit gives him a kind of joy, rescuing his
life from utter meaninglessness.

Even the most pessimistic naturalists value truth, and their devotion
to it energizes their lives at least tacitly. There seems to be great inconsistency here, but it is necessary to ask how thoroughly one can value anything
that is taken to be destined for nothingness in the end. There must be something everlasting about truth or else we would all, sooner or later, get tired
of seeking it. Furthermore, without at least a vague sense that our lives are

4. James, *Pragmatism*, 76.

5. See Berger, *Rumor of Angels*.

intertwined with the eternal, as Teilhard declares, we could hardly sustain any real "zest for living" for long. It is not enough to settle for tragic heroism or a sense of honor in undertaking an aimless struggle, as sober naturalists such as Weinberg prescribe, nor is it enough to understand action simply as a way of purifying our intentions in order to be right with God, as religious moralists have often taught. Instead, what is needed is a sense that our actions, however insignificant, have an indelible impact on the universe and that something about this same universe lasts forever. As Teilhard has written, only a "passion for being finally and permanently more" can lead to a substantively ethical life.[6] This passion is empty if our efforts are going to be felt as making no real difference in the end.

Alfred North Whitehead, no less ardently than James and Teilhard, ponders what it might mean if the universe as a whole were unable to attain some kind of immortality. Like Teilhard, he thinks that a consistent expectation of absolute death for the universe would trivialize and eventually paralyze human ethical aspiration. A persistent stimulus to the forming of Whitehead's own religious cosmology was his personal revulsion at the proposal by modern materialists that everything eventually comes to naught. The most coherent philosophy, he believed, is one that makes explicit room for the reality of something everlasting, something that might rescue all cosmic events—and not only individual human lives—from perishing absolutely. This is why we shall always have to take religions seriously, in spite of their obvious defects. For at least religions give expression to our need for the eternal. Here is Whitehead's famous depiction:

> Religion is the vision of something which stands beyond, behind, and within, the passing flux of immediate things; something which is real and yet waiting to be realized; something which is a remote possibility and yet the greatest of present facts; something that gives meaning to all that passes and yet eludes apprehension; something whose possession is the final good and yet is beyond all reach; something which is the ultimate ideal and the hopeless quest.[7]

In stubborn opposition to scientific materialism, Whitehead argues that nothing actual can ever lapse *completely* into absolute oblivion. Even though it may perish individually, everything worthwhile that happens is received into God's own unfading experience, endowed with a permanent significance. Our own efforts, too, no matter how futile they may seem at times to us, are not wasted. The cosmic past, though perhaps lost to our

6. See Teilhard, *Activation of Energy.*

7. Whitehead, *Science and the Modern World*, 191–92.

own memory, is forever preserved in the eternal immediacy of the divine experience—so nothing that ever happens can be *lost absolutely*. Everything has at least an objective immortality, as it is received into the compassionate feelings of God (what Whitehead calls the "Consequent Nature of God").[8] Even though Whitehead is unsuccessful in stating how subjective immortality might be possible (a topic that I shall look into below), he is able to address, at least partially, the materialist claim that the universe will dissolve into absolute nothingness.

In order to understand how such a proposal can avoid being labeled irrational, one must take seriously the recent revolutions in cosmology, physics, and biology that have shown the universe to be a process rather than a static mass of irreducible material particles. A processive universe, by definition, is made up not of material bits but of transient events. These events or happenings can be related to each other in a temporal rather than a simply spatial way. Every occurrence persists enduringly as an ingredient in those that follow. This means that everything that has happened in the past still has some impact on the present. In other words, the series of perished occasions still "matter" to all events that follow. It is in this temporally ordered, rather than spatially frozen, way that the universe hangs together. The past, though faded and fixed, still adheres to the present and it will also be part of the future. Passing events accumulate rather than vanish entirely. In a processive universe, things keep adding up, as it were, so significant events that happened in the remote past, such as the Big Bang or the origin of life, can still be "felt," either faintly or forcefully, in present experience. The same is true of every past event in our personal lives. Each present moment in any process is a "subject" that synthesizes the series of preceding events into itself in one way or other. In doing so, it rescues the past from absolute perishing and makes it available for what is yet to come. Think of God, therefore, as the supreme subject that "stands beyond, behind, and within the passing flux of immediate things." God is real, but at the same time "waiting to be realized." That is, in a most vulnerable way, God is always being moved and even "changed" by what happens in the created world. This is not a denial of God's immutability, at least in any theologically relevant sense, for God's love and fidelity still abide forever, unshaken. It is precisely God's immovable love, expressed for Christians in the doctrine of the Trinity, that paradoxically allows God to be moved by what happens in the world. God feels and thus saves the world by giving "meaning to all that passes," even while this divine graciousness "eludes apprehension."

8. Whitehead, *Science and the Modern World*, 194.

## Can God Change?

The eternal God's vulnerability to what happens in the world, including both creative and tragic episodes, is consistent with our revelatory image of the divine descent. God becomes small in order to establish the most intimate relation to the world and to feel it and be moved by it in its tiniest details. This is the responsive God of biblical faith. Moreover, the theme of divine futurity is also implicit in Whitehead's depiction of religion, inasmuch as God is "something whose possession is the final good, and yet is beyond all reach; something which is the ultimate ideal, and the hopeless quest."[9] God, from the depths of endless resourcefulness, continually offers the procession becoming, becoming universe relevant possibilities for actualizing itself anew in each moment. God faithfully opens up the future to creation by greeting the universe and the perishable lives within it with a wealth of possibilities for becoming new. God's Divine power consists, in part at least, of providing the possibility (*potentia*) for new being. Thus God, in self-effacing humility and fidelity, acts powerfully and effectively in the world without violating the laws of nature. Such is the God, we may add, who can also raise the dead to new life. God is thus not only the inspiration to novelty but also the savior of all the events that make up the cosmic drama. What happens in the world matters eternally to the self-giving love that we call God. In this sense, God can be changed by what happens in the world. The Christian teachings about the dynamism of the Trinity are a way of expressing this intuition. As the Father, God's generative love first arouses the universe to new being; as the Son, God gives the divine fullness to the world irreversibly and forever; and then, in the Spirit, God assimilates into the divine life all the transience in the cosmos that would otherwise mean eternal loss. Incarnation, redemption, and eschatological hope, in all of their cosmic ramifications, also imply that God is forever affected by events in the physical world.

Theology in an age of science cannot do justice to faith's claims about God's kenotic love unless it allows that the divine Mystery can undergo change—and even, paradoxically, suffering—precisely because God remains immutably faithful to the covenantal promise. Even Teilhard, though less explicitly than Whitehead, allows that God is truly changed by what happens in the world and, in such a way, as not to diminish the divine perfection whatsoever. God, he says, is in a sense self-sufficient "and yet the universe contributes something that is vitally necessary to him."[10] If God truly loves the world enough to take on its materiality in the incarnation, how could it be other-

---

9. Whitehead, *Science and the Modern World*, 191–92.

10. Teilhard de Chardin, *Writings in Times of War*, 167.

wise? What happens in the world must matter forever to a God of limitless love: "My wanderings you have counted; He has put all our tears in his flask; are they not recorded in your book?" (Ps 56:9). We may trust that even our smallest efforts and experiences can have cosmic significance. Along with all the world's occurrences, including the entire evolution of life, they, too, are taken everlastingly into the immediacy of God's subjective experience. Here, a resurrection faith allows us to hope that even tragic and evil occurrences in natural and human history will never be forgotten, but can instead be given a redemptive meaning by assimilation to the redemptive cross of Christ and the Trinitarian drama of salvation.

# Part VII: God, Hope & Atheism

# 31: Science and Christian Hope[1]

"Shatter, my God, through the daring of your revelation
the childishly timid outlook that can conceive of nothing
greater or more vital in the world than the pitiable perfection of our human organism."

—PIERRE TEILHARD DE CHARDIN[2]

CHRISTIAN FAITH IS ESSENTIALLY about the future—not simply a future
beyond the world but also the future *of* the world. Of course, it is also concerned with the meaning of the present and the past, but what this meaning
is can be fully revealed only in the future. Christian faith is, above all, a quest
for the ultimately new; it hopes for the radical renewal of "the whole of reality," and not just human history.[3] Christians are called upon to extend their
religious expectations outward, beyond human preoccupations, toward the
entire universe and its future. Science can help them do so.

Science, as I noted in the introduction, has exposed the three infinites—the immense, the infinitesimal, and the complex. But Christian faith
has already opened up a fourth, the infinite horizon of the future. It is the
Future beyond all futures that Christian hope seeks. The heavens may entrance us, but, even in their staggering expansiveness, we cannot find all
that our hearts are longing for. The human spirit's quest for final liberation
leads beyond all present times and past all perishing, beyond this universe
and any others, toward the absolutely new—in other words, to God, the
one whose promises open up all of life and all universes to an endless and
unimaginable future. "Christian hope," says theologian Jürgen Moltmann,
"is directed towards . . . a new creation of all things by the God of the resurrection of Jesus Christ."[4] At the very heart of Christianity lies a trust that

1. The following text is an excerpt. Previously published in Haught, *Christianity and
Science*, 1–18. Reprinted with permission.

2. Teilhard de Chardin, "Mass on the World," 150.

3. Moltmann, *Theology of Hope*, 34.

4. Moltmann, *Theology of Hope*, 33.

the world remains forever open to a new future. The name of this future is "God." God, however, is not just any future that we dream up. The futures we conjure up and plan for ourselves are inevitably inadequate to what we really need. Rather, as Karl Rahner has put it, God is the *Absolute Future*, deeper and more surprising than anything we could possibly wish for ourselves: *Deus semper maior*.[5]

God is the "power of the future"[6] that rises up to greet the universe anew at the place where each present moment passes away. Although we cannot grasp this elusive Future, we can allow ourselves to be grasped by it. "The coming order is always coming, shaking this order, fighting with it, conquering it and conquered by it. The coming order is always at hand. But one can never say: 'It is here! It is there!' One can never grasp it. But one can be grasped by it."[7]

Perhaps "future" is not the first idea that people today, including Christians, associate with the word "God." For centuries, the essential "futurity" of God that shaped the biblical experience has hidden behind a fogbank that is, only now, very slowly, beginning to dissipate. As the mists that had enshrouded the future begin to fade, we may still prefer not to expose ourselves to the wide vista that opens up ahead. The future that Israel, Jesus, and the early Church felt to be dawning so dramatically, the "coming of God" that gave their lives a sense of adventure and unparalleled excitement, many of us would still prefer to hold at bay. The restlessness that accompanies exposure to the future is easily suppressed, especially if we are comfortable with the way things are right now.

And yet, even in the best of circumstances, at some level of our being we still long for a new future, even as we cling to what is past or present. A sense of the coming (*adventus*) of God stirs us up, makes us yearn for deeper freedom, for a more wide-open space in which to live. Yet, like idlers standing by in the market place, our lives remain tied to what is or what has been rather than to what will be. It is the destitute, those who now have nothing to fall back on, who are most open to the promise of a radically new world. It is their ears that the fire of the Gospel first singes with the unsettling news of God's coming.

But how are we to connect the thought-world of the natural sciences to the Christian revelation of a God who is coming and seeks to renew the world? If we are receptive to the Gospel and serious about making sense of Christian faith today, we need to tie what science is telling us about the

5. Rahner, *Theological Investigations*, 59–68.

6. Pannenberg, *Faith and Reality*, 58–59.

7. Tillich, *Shaking of the Foundations*, 27.

universe to Jesus's own infectious excitement about the coming of God's reign. The fervor of expectation aroused by Jesus in his followers and the news of his resurrection must be the framework of any truly Christian reflection on the meaning of the entire universe as it is being laid open to us by the natural sciences today. A Christianity that avoids reflecting on scientific understanding of what is going on in the universe is less than realistic. Christian faith needs to be not only consistent with what the sciences are saying but also eager to render more intelligible than ever the world that science has been setting before us. It is the purpose of this book to suggest ways in which science can influence and challenge Christian faith as well as how the light of faith can illuminate what we are learning from science about nature.

## A New Day for the Universe

The new day that Christianity expects, however, is not exclusively one of personal, political, and social liberation. It is also a new day for the entire universe, the heavens and the earth, for what is visible and invisible. It is just this cosmic expectation, on the part of Christianity, that I shall emphasize in these pages. For Christian theology, Moltmann continues, there is essentially "only one problem: the problem of the future."[8] But the future will comprise not only those episodes of the human story that are yet to unfold but also the ongoing story of a still unfinished universe. If we fail to keep our sights trained on the distant cosmic future, and instead focus myopically only on human destiny, we shall shrink even our human hopes to the point where they no longer energize our lives and works. Consequently, this book's focus must be primarily on how the Christian hope for a new creation of the *cosmos* can frame the picture of the world that the natural sciences are now laying out before us.

Creeds that profess to be based on the biblical experience claim, in effect, that *everything* can be made new. In the modern period, however, there has emerged—not for the first time in human history—a pessimistic picture of the universe that denies that any *real* renewal of its being is possible. What seems new to us, this belief-system maintains, is in fact always old and unchanging. There is really nothing new under the sun. Therefore, the truly lucid consciousness, Albert Camus writes, must be cleansed of hope.[9] Bertrand Russell echoes this sentiment: "Only on the firm foundation of unyielding despair can the soul's habitation henceforth

8. Moltmann, *Theology of Hope*, 16.
9. See Camus, *Myth of Sisyphus*.

be safely built."[10] Further still, the Nobel prizewinning physicist Steven
Weinberg declares, "it would be wonderful to find in the laws of nature a
plan prepared by a concerned creator in which human beings played some
special role. I find sadness in doubting that we will."[11]

There can be no doubt that the birth of modern science, exciting as
its discoveries have been, has simultaneously ushered in a fierce strain
of pessimism about the future. Once again, this is partly because science looks essentially into the past, into the timeless laws of physics, for
a "fundamental" understanding of how things will eventually turn out.
Explanation, as far as natural science is concerned, means tracing a line of
causation back into a series of events that have already happened. If you
want to understand how snow rabbits came to be white, for example, you
have to imagine a process of natural selection whereby predators *in the
past* devoured all the dark or spotted rabbits who could not camouflage
themselves against the snowy backdrop of a northern climate. If you want
to understand the expansion rate of the universe you have to go back fourteen billion years to the Big Bang itself.

Habituated to science's method of looking back, modern intellectual
life has adopted a picture of reality that stands in tension with Christian
hope and its expectation of future transformation. The practice of looking
into a past inertial chain of causes to acquire present understanding has
swept over the whole world. It has found a comfortable home in academic
thought and, from there, it has oozed out into modern and postmodern
culture. It has shaped dominant views of economics, politics, and personality. It continues to influence social thought and the practice of medicine. It
has even infiltrated the world of religious reflection. But its primary place of
residence is the impressive edifice of the natural sciences.

This scientific abode has not only functioned as a forum in which
to celebrate great discoveries and intellectual achievements but it has also
served as a kind of customs house where all who enter into the world of
"true" knowledge must check much of their cognitional apparel at the door.
In exchange for a ticket to see what science has uncovered, visitors must
agree not to ask questions about the meaning or value of things. They must
look at the objects on display through lenses that filter out any shade of inherent importance or purpose. Furthermore, they must focus not so much
on wholes but instead on component parts, processes, and mechanisms that
cause things to function in a specific way.

10. Russell, *Mysticism and Logic*, 48.
11. Weinberg, *Dreams of a Final Theory*, 256.

For much of the modern period, the search for explanation in the domain of what is earlier-and-simpler has meant endorsing the point of view known as "scientific materialism."[12] Materialism is the belief that reality consists ultimately of mindless and lifeless bits of "matter." This belief still provides the backdrop of much research. Today, many philosophers call it "physicalism" rather than materialism in order to signify their awareness that, during the past century, matter has increasingly shown itself to be much more subtle and slippery than we used to think. But physicalism no less than materialism takes the natural world, as made accessible to us by science, to be all there is. The most fundamentally explanatory science, therefore, is physics.

Materialism—or physicalism—implies a Godless world, whatever finer distinctions one might make. Here I wish only to indicate that in the intellectual world, it is materialist belief, and not science itself, that still constitutes the main challenge to religion and Christianity.

Any worldview that excludes the divine is also known more generally as "naturalism."[13] Naturalism is a broader notion than either materialism or physicalism and it comes in many flavors. Its followers include not only the harder materialists and the softer physicalists but also those who are impressed by what seems to them to be the infinite resourcefulness and expansiveness of nature. Some naturalists are pantheists, others are "ecstatic naturalists," and still others are materialists. Some think the universe is for us, others against us. But at least as I shall be using the term, naturalism is best defined as "the belief that nature is all there is."[14]

Naturalism arose historically—and understandably—as a reaction to a one-sided, world-despising supernaturalism, the kind of religiosity that finds in the transient, natural world little to inspire hope and so looks for salvation only up above, in another world apart from this one.[15] In its extreme forms, supernaturalism blunts the sense of a future for the world, persistently translating the invigorating sense of the "up ahead" into a stagnating "up above"—an interpretation that, in turn, can lead to a religious hatred of nature. This perspective, it goes without saying, has little to do with the incarnational and eschatological perspective of biblical Christianity.

Naturalism is a powerful protest against extreme supernaturalism, and this protest comes in different forms. For example, there are both sunny and

12. For a profound analysis and critique of scientific materialism, see Whitehead, *Science and the Modern World*, 51–59.

13. Tillich, *Systematic Theology*, 2:5–10.

14. "The universe is all that is, all there ever was and all there ever will be" (Sagan, *Cosmos*, 1). See also Hardwick, *Events of Grace*.

15. Tillich, *Systematic Theology*, 2:5–10.

shady naturalists. Sunny naturalists insist that nature is enough to satisfy all of our spiritual needs. To them, there is no need for traditional kinds of worship since the universe itself is large enough to fulfill our hearts' deepest longings. To the sunny naturalist, Christianity is misguided in focusing on a God distinct from nature. According to this species of naturalism, the idea of God is not only scientifically unnecessary but also religiously and morally superfluous. Nature is enough. Shady naturalists, on the other hand, claim that since nature is the source of suffering and death (and not just of life and beauty), it would be silly to make any religious covenant with it. Shady naturalists are sad that the world seems so Godless. It would be comforting, they admit, to know that a beneficent providence governs the world, but scientific honesty requires that we now abandon such naïve trust. The world is headed toward final oblivion, so the best we can do is acquire a sense of honor for not having denied the fact of nature's tragic destiny.[16]

As far as the present study is concerned, I shall use the term "naturalism" to designate the broadly shared conviction, whether sunny or shady, that nature, as made available to ordinary experience and scientific discovery, is literally "all there is." And when I use the term "religion," I am referring henceforth to any the belief that nature is *not* all there is. Christianity is a religion in this sense, but it is also one whose core teachings emphasize the goodness and what I shall call the *promise* of nature. In spite of the well-known historical difficulties associated with Galileo and Darwin, Christianity has no quarrel with science, as Pope John Paul II recently emphasized.[17] But Christianity is inalterably opposed to naturalism. This book will take the position that it is not science, but a kind of materialist naturalism often mistaken for science, that stands in conflict with the beliefs of Christianity and other faiths. When Christian faith comes face to face with science itself, it finds a friend with whom it can converse, whatever blunders and misunderstanding there may have been in the past. With naturalism, however, there can be no such fruitful coalition.[18]

Science, as Alfred North Whitehead acknowledged in the early twentieth century, has often metamorphosed into the defense of materialist naturalism, much to its own detriment.[19] In doing so, it has implicitly abandoned the idea that anything in the universe can truly be new. It is this

---

16. Weinberg, *Dreams of a Final Theory*, 255, 260.

17. See John Paul II, "Address to the Pontifical Academy of Sciences"; John Paul II, "Letter to the Reverend George V. Coyne, SJ," 377; and Poupard, "Galileo," 375

18. This is not to say that Christians cannot form fruitful alliances with *naturalists* as distinct from naturalism. Indeed, on many ethical issues, such as the ecological predicament, cooperation is both warm and fertile.

19. Whitehead, *Science and the Modern World*, 51–59.

dogma, and not science itself, that stands in opposition to the essential biblical belief in God. In a materialist venue, every scientific finding is just one
more monotonous unearthing of what we already knew about the inner essence of things. Life, for example, is really "just chemistry." Mind is nothing
more than matter parading itself under peculiar organic conditions. And
the world deep down is really nothing more than a set of timeless physical
routines *masquerading* as matter, life, mind, and spirit.[20]

Christianity, on the other hand, believes in an eternal freshness of being. Its God is one "who makes all things new" (Rev 23:5). Its expectation
is that a new world is already being created. So Christian faith, though not
irreconcilable with science, *is* irreconcilable with the modern materialist
naturalism which logically rules out any such novelty. The really important
disagreement therefore lies between naturalist physicalism on the one hand
and a belief that the world can be made anew on the other.

## The Promise of Nature

In Christ, the ultimate mystery that encompasses all created being is revealed as self-giving love and saving future. What, then, should we expect
the universe to look like in light of the divine humility and promise that
enfolds it? My proposal is that a faith shaped by a Christian sense of God's
self-limiting love, a love that lays open the future to new creation, should
already have prepared our minds and hearts for the kind of universe that
science is now spreading out in front of us.

Over the past century and a half, science has demonstrated that the
universe is a still unfolding process, unfathomably vaster and older than
we had ever imagined before. The cosmos came into being long before the
arrival of human history, Israel, and the Church. Apparently, God's creative
vision for the world extends far beyond terrestrial precincts and ecclesiastical preoccupations. Nevertheless, a Christian theology of nature ema-
nates from and tries to remain faithful to the teachings of the community
of hope known as the Church. Inspired by the "cloud of witnesses" (Heb
12:1) that has kept hope alive since Abraham, it wagers that the promissory
perspective of biblical faith which enlivens people of faith is also applicable
to cosmic reality, in all of its enormous breadth and depth. "Thou has made
thy promise wide as the heavens," the psalmist exclaims (Ps 138:2). From
the perspective of biblical faith, all those billions of years that preceded the
emergence of Israel and Christianity were already seeded with promise.

---

20. See Atkins, *2nd Law*, especially 200.

With the eyes of hope, one may still apprehend a vein of promise in this ambiguous cosmos. Genuine hope does not lead to escapist illusions but instead opens a space in which the scientific mind can breathe more freely than in the stagnant atmosphere of modern materialism. Hope will allow us to see that the world given to us by contemporary science has always possessed an *anticipatory* character. It has always been open to future surprise, though naturalistic pessimism has failed to notice. From the beginning, the universe has extended itself toward the actualizing of new and unprecedented possibilities. It is still doing so, especially through one of its most recent evolutionary inventions, human consciousness. Through our own forays of hope, the universe now continues to seek out its future, a future whose ultimate depth we may call God.

After the phenomenon of mind had burst onto the terrestrial scene, the world's emergent straining toward the future took the form of religious aspiration everywhere. In the West, it broke through in the hope we associate with Abraham, the prophets, and Jesus. Science itself, because of its orientation toward earlier and simpler lines of causation, knows nothing of any promise in nature, nor should we expect it to. Nevertheless, even though science cannot accurately predict the actual shape of the real novelty that will emerge in the future, this is no reason to assume that future cosmic happenings will somehow contradict the laws of physics, chemistry, and biology. The predictable habits of nature will go on functioning as before, but they will be taken up into an indefinite array of novel configurations.

# 32: The Congregation of Hope[1]

JESUS'S LIFE AND DEATH had a profoundly transformative effect on his followers. So moved were they by their encounter with him that they interpreted their subsequent existence together as a whole new "way "(the Greek word is *hodos*). Originally, they did not conceive of themselves as starting or belonging to a new religion, since this was not even a formal concept in their self-understanding, but as followers of the *hodos*. But while this "way" was, in some sense, a new departure, it still emanated from the context of Israel's ancient hope in God's promises. Out of the experience of renewed trust aroused by Jesus's life, death, and resurrection was born what has come to be known as the *ecclesia*. Literally, this word means the community of those who have been "called out." The *ecclesia* is the new congregation of hope.[2] This community of those who have been called to follow the new way toward the future is referred to as the "Church."

The Church may be defined as the community through which God's revelatory promise in Christ is received, celebrated, and communicated to the world. In word, sacrament, and mission, the Christian Church mediates to the world, of which it is a part, the promise received in Christ. Because of its promissory mission, the Church is continuous with "the people of God," first shaped into a community by events in the lives of Moses, the kings, and the prophets of Israel. The Church's distinctiveness within this tradition lies simply in the fact that it bears witness to the eternal promise especially (but certainly not exclusively) by reference to the life, death, and resurrection of Jesus. In essence, therefore, its mission is to convey Jesus's own proclamation of an inclusive reign of God and to rehearse, for each age, the reasons we have for a sustained hope in God's encompassing vision of fulfillment for the entire world. By our belonging to such a community of hope and vision, we remain within the horizon of the paradigmatic biblical Stories of promise and liberation that begin with Abraham and culminate in the resurrection of Jesus from the dead.

Although there is no evidence that Jesus self-consciously contemplated the institution of a new *ecclesia*, we may legitimately maintain that

---

1. The following text is an excerpt. Previously published in Haught, *Mystery and Promise*, 126–146. Reprinted with permission.

2. Moltmann, *Experiment Hope*, 58

the Christian way, with its incipient ecclesial character, was founded by
the revelatory promise that came to expression in him and his proclamation of the reign of God. In that sense, he is the Church's foundation.
The Church's existence, then, remains essential to revelation as the sign or
"sacrament" of God's fidelity to the promise first given to Abraham and
ratified in Jesus's being raised up to new life. And our participation in
the life of the Church provides a special (though not exclusive) access to
revelation. Through participation in the life of the Church, its liturgy, sacraments, teachings, and praxis, we are enabled to situate ourselves within
the revelatory vision of Christ with its promise for the liberation of the
whole of history and creation.

Human nature is such that we exist and come to understand ourselves,
our identities, and our destinies only in community with others. Existence
alongside others who share our sense of life's meaning is not accidental but
rather essential to our being human. Through participation in the rituals,
actions, and stories of a common tradition, a people is molded into a fel-
lowship of shared destiny. Every community with a tradition understands
its existence and identity in terms of the narratives that recount the process
of how it came into being and that tell where it is going. It is questionable
whether any of us can live meaningfully without relation to such stories.

It is primarily through participation in shared stories about Jesus and
the effects of what the New Testament and later Trinitarian theology call
the "Spirit"—felt by Jesus's contemporaries and poured out at Pentecost
upon the early Christian community—that we experience the promise offered anew in his life even today. Therefore, our reception of a specifically
Christian revelation ordinarily requires that we abide within a communal
context, guided by the Spirit and given expression through the Christian
story in word and rite. Living inside this community of faith gives us intimate access to revelation that we could not have if we remained outside,
as disinterested and uncommitted observers. Sharing membership with
a body of fellow believers allows the content of God's promise to insinu-
ate itself into our lives with a depth of penetration that an external or
detached standpoint would not allow.[3]

In his important book, *The Meaning of Revelation*, H. Richard Niebuhr
writes that our knowledge of revelation is transmitted to the Church not
so much through impersonal, external, and historical reporting as through

---

3. In ways that we cannot examine here, it could be said that all of us, whether
churched or unchurched, indwell—to some degree—the Christian story, a story that,
despite how Western culture has become deeply secularized, has remained so determinative. For even the contours of modern secularism were subtly molded by biblical
motifs.

a feeling-laden involvement with the community's internal memory of its founding events.[4] These events will probably have little more than academic interest to non-believers, and the latter will often cast doubt on the objective historicity of certain occurrences (such as the Exodus or the resurrection of Christ). But to the believer, only an affectionate, faithful involvement in the saving character of the events mediated to us through the inner history of the Church can put us deeply in touch with the reality of revelation.

Niebuhr provides a helpful analogy, illustrating how relation to a community's "internal history" can connect contemporary believers with the saving events that are often of little interest to those outside of the Christian faith tradition.[5] Consider, he says, the case of a man who has recovered his sight through a medical operation. As this former patient gives his enthusiastic and grateful account of the event of his recovery of sight, the quality or tone of his account will differ considerably from a purely clinical digest of the same event. The doctor who performed the operation will use a scientifically detached, personally uninvolved kind of discourse in order to describe what has happened, and the physician's words are taken to be objectively true. But is the physician's report any more true to the reality of the event than the recovered patient's own emotionally involved account? Does the fact that the latter talks with such feeling and enthusiasm about his recovery constitute an obstacle to the truthfulness or objectivity of his report? Or is it not possible to say that the one who has been healed can give a no less truthful report of what happened than the clinician?

Clearly, we may view the two accounts as complementary rather than as inevitably conflicting. Likewise, what we are here calling internal and external history may be seen as mutually supportive ways of knowing events. It is not impossible that a faith community's enthusiastic, internal story of its own recovery of vision has the capacity to retrieve aspects of salvific occurrences that a more scientific account would leave out. Even in science, Michael Polanyi notes, the range of data that is visible to inquirers is determined in large measure by what is interesting to scientists as persons in a community endowed with passions and feelings.[6] This element of interest will cause certain items to show up and others to remain in obscurity. Likewise, the specific focus of faith will highlight certain events of history and read them as interesting, whereas an inquiry devoid of this focus may scarcely notice them at all. The Church is a community held together in part by its shared internal interest in a specific set of events out

4. See Niebuhr, *Meaning of Revelation*, 44–54.
5. Niebuhr, *Meaning of Revelation*, 44.
6. Polanyi, *Personal Knowledge*, 135.

of which it reads a special promise. This interest is an essential part of a community's search for truth.

Of course there is always a need to be critical about accounts of events given by internal history, for sometimes they are distorted by the sheer force of enthusiasm. Even so, what appears as exaggeration from the point of view of external history is itself a way of calling attention to aspects of events that might otherwise pass us by. At times, our internal memories are subjective to the point of being unrelated to reality, so they need the correction of a more clinical examination. But this does not mean that every place we find enthusiastic, emotionally tinged descriptions of events we should conclude that they lack objectivity or that they bear no relation to the real. For it may be that the interlocking of our lives with momentous events, especially salvific ones, can occur in depth only by our sharing with others a life and language that evokes in us a certain *feeling* of involvement. We may need to look at the world through the eyes of the shared expectations of a tradition and community of faith and hope if we are to be grasped by the substance of revelation. It is equally possible that the exclusive use of a completely external, scientifically historical method would leave us still stranded at a distance from the reality of saving events.

Thus, the Church's language is primarily confessional, enthusiastic, and involved, rather than scientifically detached. But this does not mean that we need to be a priori suspicious of its authenticity. At the same time, however, it is important for us to add that a scientifically historical study of the tradition is an important and necessary corrective to the possible excesses of a more passionate approach. In recent years, for example, the Church has learned much from a detached, scientific study of the Bible and its traditional teachings. Niebuhr says, "There is no continuous movement from an objective inquiry into the life of Jesus to a knowledge of him as the Christ who is our Lord."[7] Only a decision of faith can make this jump. But recent developments in biblical research, using various kinds of scientific methods, have added helpful corrections to our pictures of Jesus and other events that faith perceives as revelatory.

The heavy reliance on its own internal historical memory may seem to imply that Christianity is just another esoteric religion, accessible only to a group of insiders. There is, of course, a certain insider's perspective in any faith tradition, but it would be contrary to the inclusive character of Christianity to interpret our belonging to a Church community as though it were a position of privilege that separates us from those not so gifted. In the past, some forms of Christian faith have not escaped the tendency to close

---

7. Niebuhr, *Meaning of Revelation*, 61.

all doors to outsiders. It is clear that a one-sided reliance on what insiders think to be normative to faith can at times lead to an elitist gnosticism. If the content of a faith is not checked by some externally objective evaluations, it can easily become too esoteric. In recent years, the work of scientific historians, philosophers, sociologists, and psychologists of religion has built up an impressive roadblock to the evils of esotericism. The dangers of enthusiasm are present in all religions, but given the proviso just noted, the passion and joy that bond members of the Church to its founder and his message of hope need not necessarily be taken as interfering with the truthfulness and openness of faith in that promise. For without the feeling of excitement which belonging to a community of shared hope provides, it may be difficult for us to be grasped deeply by the reality of the mystery revealed in Jesus.

After emphasizing the advantages of such belonging, though, we should not push too far the necessity of formal membership in the Church as a condition for the reception of revelation. People who are unchurched may be touched deeply by the power of God's promise and even more specifically by Jesus's personality. In the latter case, this may happen by reading books about him, by immersing themselves in the history of Christian art and architecture, or by living alongside those who are explicitly members of its Churches. Portraits of Jesus abound in various media, and the individual can derive much hope and inspiration from them without necessarily having formal association with a church. Today, for various reasons that we cannot explore here, many individuals have lost confidence in all formal ecclesiastical institutions, but they have not necessarily lost faith in Jesus and his teachings. They find access to his personality—and even to his saving presence—through art, novels, films, academic studies of Christology, or private reading of the Gospels. The commanding authority of the figure of Jesus overflows the boundaries of purely ecclesiastical vigilance.

Still, in its fullest flowering, following in the footsteps of Christ requires, in some sense or other, the sharing of his promise and praxis with others. Christian faith pushes us beyond a purely private piety. A sense of promise can only be felt fully when it leads to a *shared* hope and common action. Christian faith is essentially, and not just accidentally, ecclesial. This does not mean that the prevalent Church structures and practices of any particular age are inevitably ideal vehicles for the conveying of the substance of revelation's promise to the world or even its own members. *Ecclesia semper reformanda*: the Church is itself ever in need of conversion. However, it is normally through shared life, prayer, and ritual activity with others, through common reception of the Word, that we are brought into an encounter with the Christ of promise. It is the function of the Church to facilitate this encounter. Where it fails to do so, it is to that extent unfaithful to revelation and in need of self-revision in order to execute its sacramentally representative mission.

According to the teaching of Jesus, what is asked of those who belong to his circle is a complete trust in God's love and fidelity to the covenantal promise, now renewed in the coming reign of God. However, the breadth and inclusiveness of God's promise and reign present an enormous challenge to us. They invite us to put into practice the acceptance and promotion of others that Jesus's God manifests toward us. Those officially enrolled in the Churches often show anything but this latitude, so it is possible for us to remain, in some sense, outside the faith—even in the midst of our membership in the Church that proclaims the bold and inclusive message of God's reign. Moreover, many of those who have no formal membership in the Church are actually more inside the real circle of the tolerant faith that Jesus spoke of than those of us who have been baptized and participate bodily in the worship of the Church.

## Revelation, Past and Present

An essential condition for the Church's communication of revelation is that it have a deposit of faith that remains fixed or finished, in order to remain a continually reliable source to draw on in new circumstances. But revelation is not fundamentally the normative deposit of accounts of saving events in the past. If revelation is to be real to us, it must be something that is occurring now in the concrete events, trivial and important, of our everyday lives. To encounter revelation is not primarily to look back or to dig into a sacred book or a traditional set of teachings. These monuments of faith, of course, all carry with them essential constraints, shaping the relevant information, but experiencing the self-revealing God is not simply a matter of looking at the scriptural and doctrinal boundaries laboriously established by the Church and its traditions. Such limits *do* give definiteness to the content of faith, but encountering revelation means, above all, being confronted by the inviting and challenging futurity of divine mystery in the immediate context of our own concrete situations. The content of revelation is a promise which, because it has never yet been completely fulfilled, can never be fixed or finished but rather remains incalculable and, to some extent, mysteriously incomprehensible. The reception of this revelation means that we experience a gracious, extravagant, and surprising future dawning at the frontiers of our own lives, here and now. The Church's teaching tradition exists primarily to make it possible for us to look forward to God's promises in a new way every day. We make an idol of this tradition if we read it in any other way.

The content and substance of revelation is always mystery and, for biblical faith, this elusive but endlessly fulfilling mystery comes to us in the shape of an unfathomable future which promises complete liberation. Our being inserted into a community of fellow believers who have been gathered together on the basis of historical events in their past is an indispensable dimension of our encounter with this future. We indwell these past historical events not to make them absolutes but rather in order to look *with* them into the mystery they anticipate. Living within a tradition is not so much a matter of looking *at* the past but rather *with* it, toward a still unfulfilled promise latent within it. Tradition invites us not to make an absolute of its constraints, but to focus our gaze toward the future in accordance with the coordinates it bequeaths to us. We continually recount our common past and seek to incorporate it ever more coherently within our memory, but we experience revelation concretely only by looking *forward*, along with this past, to the fulfillment of God's promise. To live within the horizon of Easter is not simply to look at an event that took place long ago but, even more, to look forward to the fulfillment that it promises for our future and that of the whole world.

If we do look back to the record of God's mighty deeds accomplished in the past, as indeed we must, it is not in order to restore something that is no longer but instead to find the basis there for hope here and now. We dwell within our tradition in order to be more sensitive to the promise and futurity of God that are still on the way. Too often, theology and religious education have left us with the impression that everything important has already happened and therefore faith's main posture is one of restoring the past. We are often instructed to look back into Israel's history or into the time of the New Testament in order to find the fullest appearance of God's revelation. But this is a way of "abolishing time" that finds no authority in the Bible. The Bible constantly invites us to look ahead, into the future, for the fullness of revelation. Repristinating the past, even if it is a glorious past, is asking for the impossible. It contradicts the very nature of human existence with its essential orientation to the future.[8] The fact is, people are not looking only for a "salvation history" somewhere in the traces of historical events. Rather, they are fundamentally in search of the meaning, purpose, and renewal of their own lives as they exist in the here and now.

We look to the past, then, not in order to absolutize or romanticize a lost age but rather to find some ways of orienting ourselves toward our future. If the idea of revelation is to have any relevance, it must be essentially a *present* experience of God's coming to us—from the future—and not simply

8. Pannenberg, *What Is Man?*, 41–53.

a set of stories dragged out of the past. The deposit of revelation is said to be finished or fixed, but this can only be a salvific teaching if it means that there is sufficient evidence in our past history to convince us that we live within the present horizon of a promise which, by its nature, always looks to the future for fulfillment. Revelation fundamentally means the arrival of this future—and not a retrieval of the past.

Still, the ancient stories are obviously indispensable, for it is in their continual retelling that we find the informational constraints that give appropriate shape to our hope. The Church community, its normative writings, and its traditions are repositories and mediators of those stories of hope that we stand within as we reach toward the future. Ideally, the Church is a community in which hope is kept alive by the retelling of the mighty acts of God. In a sense, revelation is simply the unfolding of a great story of which we ourselves are a part, but which has its fulfillment only in the future. We need, then, to know the earlier chapters in order to have at least a dim sense of the story's more complete unfolding. We cannot look toward the ending of a story unless we know where we have been. In recounting the past acts of God, we are placed within the horizon of the hope awakened by those events.

In conclusion, we may say that biblical inspiration is the effect of God's promise on those individuals writing within the context of a community of faith brought into existence and sustained by a vision of promise emanating from the Spirit of hope.

# 33: How New Is the New Atheism?[1]

"When the Son of Man comes, will he
find faith on earth?"

—LUKE 18:8

THE DAY AFTER THE World Trade Center's twin towers came down in
September 2001, my wife and I attended a special service at Holy Trinity
Catholic Church near Georgetown University where I had been teaching
for many years. Bill Byron, the Jesuit pastor and former president of The
Catholic University of America, celebrated Mass and delivered a prayerful
homily. If you want peace, he said, practice justice. People of faith should
never give up their hope for improving the quality of life all over the world.
We need to avoid simplistic solutions and blanket condemnation of religions. We must all work for a more just world, no matter how long it takes,
without the use of violence. Amidst the enormous shock and grief in the
aftermath of 9/11, a similar encouragement to practice tolerance, love, and
justice pealed through places of worship all over the world.

Around the same time these services were going on, a young Stanford
University philosopher and student of neuroscience named Sam Harris was
devising another much more radical solution to the escalating problem of
world-wide terrorism. Tolerance and compassion simply will not work, he
thought. Indeed, tolerance of faith is a major cause of the problem. Harris's
proposal, as presented in his best-selling books *The End of Faith* and *Letter
to a Christian Nation*, is crystal clear.[2] We can rid the world of faith not by
violence but by reason and the spread of science. Envisioning himself as a
Buddha of sorts, Harris resolved to share with his readers—and with the
whole world—something like a new version of the ancient Buddha's Four
Noble Truths. Both Richard Dawkins and Christopher Hitchens essentially
make the same set of claims.

1. The following text is an excerpt. Previously published in Haught, *God and the
New Atheism*, 1–14. Reprinted with permission.

2. See Harris, *End of Faith*; Harris, *Letter to a Christian Nation*; and Harris, "Atheist
Manifesto."

## The First Evident Truth

Many people in the world are living needlessly miserable lives, Harris notes, faintly echoing the Buddha's First Noble Truth that "all life is suffering." Harris's background assumption is that the purpose of human life is to find happiness. The philosopher Immanuel Kant, as well as other wise thinkers and spiritual masters, taught that happiness can come only as a byproduct of the search for something eternal. Aiming for happiness directly is a sure way not to find it. However, if God does not exist and the universe is purposeless, the best we can do is strive for a world in which happiness, "a form of well-being that supercedes all others," is ensured for the greatest number of individuals.[3] Harris does not define happiness, nor does he distinguish it from other kinds of gratification. He simply assumes that we all know intuitively what happiness is and that we should make it the goal of all ethical existence.[4]

## The Second Evident Truth

The cause of so much unnecessary distress, Harris declares, is faith, particularly in the form of belief in God. Faith is "belief without evidence," and, as it is for Hitchens, this is what "poisons everything."[5] Dawkins also agrees, and all three authors try to convince their readers that the monotheistic faiths—Judaism, Christianity, and Islam—underlie a sizable portion of the evils human beings have afflicted on one another throughout the last three millennia. But it is not just the horrifying ideas of God that those such as al-Qaeda and other fanatics promulgate that causes so much unnecessary pain. It is faith itself, pure and simple.[6]

This claim is not quite the same as the Buddha's Second Noble Truth, which states that the cause of suffering is greedy desire (*tanha*). But there is a resemblance, since faith, too, seems to be an inexhaustible craving to satisfy the seemingly bottomless appetite so many humans have for delusions.[7] In a formula almost as compact as the Buddha's—the cause of suffering is faith—our new atheists want to focus our attention on exactly what needs to be eradicated if true happiness is to be realized.

---

3. Harris, *End of Faith*, 205.
4. Harris, *End of Faith*, 170–71.
5. Harris, *End of Faith*, 58–73 and 85.
6. See Hitchens, *God Is Not Great* and Dawkins, *God Delusion*.
7. See Harris, *End of Faith*, 23, 26–27, 38–39, and 58–73.

The idea of God fabricated by faith is "intrinsically dangerous" and morally evil, no matter what form it takes in our imaginations.[8] Why so? Because there is no evidence for it—in fact, "no evidence is even conceivable."[9] Basing knowledge on evidence is not only cognitionally necessary but morally essential as well. By failing the test of evidence that makes science reliable, "religious faith represents so uncompromising a misuse of the power of our minds that it forms a kind of perverse, cultural singularity—a vanishing point beyond which rational discourse proves impossible. When foisted upon each generation anew, it renders us incapable of realizing just how much of our world has been unnecessarily ceded to a dark and barbarous past."[10]

## The Third Evident Truth

The way to avoid unnecessary human suffering today is to abolish *faith* from the face of the earth. The Buddha's Third Noble Truth states that the way to overcome suffering is to find release from clinging desire. The new atheists, especially Harris (who favors a very highly edited version of Buddhism), believe that release from bondage to faith can help rid the world of unnecessary suffering. Here "faith" is the bottomless cave in consciousness that gives domicile to everything from belief in UFOs, to witches, souls, angels, devils, paradise, and God. Most of these beliefs seem harmless enough, but if we allow people to get away with even the most innocuous instances of faith, what is to prevent a Muslim radical from believing that God's will is the destruction of Israel and the United States, or a Zionist from believing that God wants us to murder innocent Palestinians, or a Christian from believing that it is God's will to bomb abortion clinics? Once God's will is fancied to favor such acts of violence, then anything is possible—including the most unthinkable horrors.

Understandably, then, the new atheists ask how we can bring about a world where indiscriminate killing and maiming in the name of God becomes truly unthinkable. Since such a world does not yet exist, a radical solution is required: we must get rid of faith altogether. Everyone needs to just stop believing in any assertion that cannot be backed up by "evidence." This applies not just to *Harry Potter* but also to all the books that religious people have held holy for ages. Since the allegedly inspired literature of the God-religions is a product of faith, there is no reason to take it seriously.

8. Harris, *End of Faith*, 44.

9. Harris, *End of Faith*, 23.

10. Harris, *End of Faith*, 25.

Aside from an aesthetically appealing passage here and there, the scriptures of all religions are worthless. Furthermore, whatever seems morally right or aesthetically charming in our allegedly sacred books and traditions could also have been arrived at by reason operating independently of faith.

Rather than embracing the ancient Buddha's milder Third Noble Truth as the way to end suffering, the new atheists seek to initiate us into a radically different—and, by their thinking, more effective—kind of asceticism, namely, cleansing our minds of faith. This new discipline of purification, if executed according to the new atheists' severe standards, will lead to the suppression of all childish inclinations to believe without evidence. The idea of God must therefore be erased from human awareness forever, but this cannot take place apart from the "end of faith." Cleansing the world of the likes of Osama bin Laden and al-Qaeda by force is not going to do the job. What needs eliminating is faith, pure and simple, and our new atheists all think of themselves as pioneering this unprecedented purge.

At this point, our debunkers might seem to be finished, but they are just getting started. Here they begin offering something startlingly new, at least outside the reach of atheistic dictatorships. It is not just faith, they say, but our polite and civil *tolerance* of faith that must be uprooted if progress toward true happiness is to be made. Harris is most explicit on this point. It is religious moderates and their defense of the right to faith, he fumes, that are, "in large part, responsible for the religious conflict in our world."[11]

Tolerance of faith remains an unquestioned part of democratic societies, but the evil illusions that this forbearance allows will continue to cause untold misery. If we indulge any kind of faith at all, we set ourselves up for victimization by true believers of all sorts. Indiscriminate respect for faith is enough to make each tolerant soul among us a *de facto* accomplice in evil.

Instead of compromising with religious faith in the genteel way that secular and religious moderates have done in the past, the new atheists want us to abandon any such respect for freedom of faith and religious thought altogether. Nothing impedes a clear-sighted grasp of the world's most urgent problem today—religiously-inspired terrorism—more thoughtlessly than moderate theology and liberal secular tolerance of faith. We must realize at last that our theological, secular, leftist, postmodern, and simply good-mannered tolerance of faith has become intolerable. Religious moderates, Harris writes, "imagine that the path to peace will be paved once each of us has learned to respect the unjustified beliefs of others," but the "very idea of religious tolerance—born of the notion that every human being should be free to believe whatever he wants about God—is one of the principal forces

11. Harris, *End of Faith*, 45.

driving us toward the abyss."[12] Abjuring any concern for political correct-
ness, Harris seems deadly serious in his proclamation that we can no longer
tolerate the liberal tolerance of faith.

   I should emphasize that Dawkins and Hitchens fully support Harris's
edict for an intolerance of tolerance. Here, we finally meet something truly
new in the writings of the new atheists. The closest facsimile I can think of in
the recent historical past is the kind of ideology that has led to atheistic dictatorships. I doubt that the new atheists would endorse a coercive implementa-
tion of their proposed solution since violence is not part of their program.
Still, it seems appropriate to ask—in the interest of balance—how their own
radical proposal to rid the world of faith and theological tolerance of faith can
avoid the accusation that it, too, is inherently tolerant of those horrific outcomes that we have witnessed over the last century. Harris notes that intolerance is "intrinsic to every creed" and apparently his own creedal commitment
to radical secularism and scientific naturalism is no exception.[13]

   Also new in Dawkins, Harris, and Hitchens is an intolerance not only
of theology but also of the soft, "Neville Chamberlain" accommodation that
most of their fellow atheists and scientific naturalists have made toward the
existence of faith.[14] In many years of studying and conversing with scientific naturalists, I have yet to encounter such a sweeping intolerance of tolerance. Intolerance of tolerance seems to be a truly novel feature of the new
atheists' solution to the problem of human misery. Nearly everything else
that Dawkins, Harris, and Hitchens (and their philosophical mentor Dennett) have to say about religion, faith, and theology has been said before.
Certainly, their blanket rejection of religious faith's cognitional standing is
not new, nor is their moral indictment of religion. Scientific naturalism, in
whose tenets our new atheists have been methodically schooled, has long
held that nature is all there is and that science is the privileged road to
understanding the world. However, most devotees of scientific naturalism
in the modern period have recognized that they are fortunate to live in cultures and countries where a plurality of faiths is accepted. They have been
grateful for this leniency, since otherwise scientific naturalism may never
have been allowed to exist alongside belief-systems that are ideologically
opposed to it. In fact, if it were up to a vote in the United States today, as
the new atheists would surely agree, scientific naturalism would be voted
off the map by a majority of citizens.

   12. Harris, *End of Faith*, 14–15.
   13. Harris, *End of Faith*, 13.
   14. Dawkins, *God Delusion*, 66–69.

The new atheists are right in pointing out how so many other belief-systems than their own are often intolerant and barbaric. But surely they must realize that their own belief system, scientific naturalism, would never have established itself in the modern world were it not for the tolerance extended to "freethinkers" by the same religious cultures that gave rise to science. Their reply is that religious cultures themselves never had any real moral or rational justification for existing in the first place. Faith, since it is intrinsically evil, should ideally never have been tendered any right to exist at all. Furthermore, when human intelligence first emerged in evolution it should never have allowed itself to be taken captive by faith, no matter how biologically adaptive this alliance of mind with unreason happened to be.

Harris thinks he can get by with this extreme intolerance since, as far as he is concerned, it is based on reason rather than faith. However, Harris's and Dawkins's own scientism, the epistemic component of their scientific naturalism, is a belief for which there can be no "sufficient" scientific or empirical "evidence" either. There is no way, without circular thinking, to set up a scientific experiment to demonstrate that every true proposition must be based in empirical evidence rather than faith. The censuring of every instance of faith, in the narrow, new atheist sense of the term, would have to include the suppression of scientism as well. The truly thoughtful scientific naturalists—Einstein is a good example—have been honest enough to admit that faith, especially faith that the universe is comprehensible at all, is essential to ground the work of science itself. Moreover, the claim that truth can only be attained by reason and science functioning independently of any faith is itself also a faith claim. Complete consistency would require that the new atheists' world of thought be cleansed of scientism and scientific naturalism as well.

## The Fourth Evident Truth

The way to eliminate faith and, as such, to get rid of suffering, is to follow the hallowed path of the scientific method. Issued by Harris and endorsed by the other new atheists, this difficult but indispensable avenue to true enlightenment is the new atheists' version of the Eight-fold Path as prescribed by the Buddha's Fourth Noble Truth. Following the path of science will give people a new kind of "right association," namely, with those who have caught the spirit of science, and "right understanding," an empirical method that will take our minds far beyond the fantasies and banalities of religious faith. We can find true enlightenment only if we apprentice ourselves to those masters—Harris, Dawkins, Dennett, and Hitchens among them—who have reached enlightenment by way of scientific reason.

This solution is matched in its shallowness only by the religious fundamentalism it mirrors even while opposing it. In a messy and uncertain world, the appeal of a single, simple solution can be irresistible. When things turn sour, it is tempting to demonize and rip out one of the countless strands in the complex web of human life, blaming everything on it alone. For example, some devout American Christians today locate the single main cause of all the ills of modernity in "Darwinism." Get rid of Darwinism, as they call it, and everything will get better. Charles Darwin, the modest naturalist from Downe, is now often identified by many Christians as the main cause of our social and ethical misery. Darwin's novel ideas are held to be the ultimate source of atheism, Nazism, Communism, and the breakdown of religion and family values. Intelligent design proponent Philip Johnson's solution to these ills is to get Darwinism out of the minds of people, and the way to do that is to begin by presenting alternatives to evolutionary theory in the public schools.[15]

Faith, for the new atheist, is the equivalent of what Darwinism is to the creationist. Get rid of faith and everything will get better. For Dawkins, Harris, and Hitchens, the banishing of faith from our minds and public life is the panacea that will bring an end to suffering and evil, at least so far as nature allows it. The best way to dispose of faith, then, is not by violence or even political action, but by filling minds with science and reason. Our atheist friends firmly *believe* in the effectiveness of this program—so maybe there will still be at least one instance of faith left on the earth when the Son of Man returns.

## The Meaning of Faith

If it is not yet clear to the reader, the understanding of "faith" that the new atheists take for granted bears very little resemblance to that of theology. The main difference is that the new atheists think of faith as an *intellectually* erroneous attempt at something like scientific understanding, whereas theology thinks of faith as a state of self-surrender in which one's whole being, and not just the intellect, is experienced as being carried away into a dimension of reality that is much deeper and more real than anything that could be grasped by science and reason. This is why faith is so often accompanied by ritual. But the definition of faith that Dawkins, Dennett, Harris, and Hitchens all embrace is "belief without evidence." They think

15. See Johnson, *Darwin on Trial*.

of faith as a set of hypotheses—such as the God-hypothesis or the soul-hypothesis—that lack sufficient scientific or empirical evidence for reasonable people to accept. They allow that, if the right kind of empirical evidence ever turns up, then reasonable people will be permitted to give assent to the God-hypothesis or the soul-hypothesis, but by then there will no longer be any need for faith. Knowledge will have replaced it.

For theology, however, the goal is to deepen faith, not eliminate it: "I believe; help my unbelief" (Mark 9:24). In theistic traditions, the essence of the ideal life, even the heroic life, is being willing to wait in faith, trust, and hope for ultimate fulfillment and final liberation. Consequently, when Harris and the others invite people to give up their faith and live only by reason, they have no idea what they are asking. The invitation to join them in a world without faith will sound to most people like a petition to shrink our world to the point where we can all be suffocated. For even if the universe contains three-hundred billion galaxies, and the multiverse, if it exists, billions more, educated people know that the world is still finite and perishable. By anybody's mathematics, an infinite divine mystery is still more impressive than any finite spatial and temporal magnitude at science's command. Advising people to give up what they take to be—whether rightly or wrongly—their lifeline to the infinite greatness of a divine mystery, inviting them to squeeze their lives, minds, and hearts into the comparatively miniscule world of scientific objectification, is not going to be met with enthusiasm all around. There is nothing wrong with science, of course, but, if we may be permitted to adapt Edwin Abbot's timeless imagery, Harris, Dennett, Hitchens, and Dawkins seem like the inhabitants of a two-dimensional world. Having mastered that sphere of being, they are now busy inviting those who occupy the admittedly more disorienting world of many dimensions to please come down and live with them in Flatland.

# 34: How Atheistic Is
# the New Atheism?[1]

"If anyone has written a book more critical of religious
faith than I have, I'm not aware of it."

—SAM HARRIS[2]

FOR MANY YEARS, I taught an introductory theology course entitled "The Problem of God" to Georgetown University undergraduates. It was always a challenge to make a suitable reading list for this important academic experience, but my fellow instructors and I were convinced that our students should be exposed to the most erudite of unbelievers. Our rationale was that any mature commitment intelligent young people might make to a religious faith, if they so chose, should be critically tested by the very best opponents. The course was, at times, troubling to some students, especially to the rare youngsters who came from creationist backgrounds or whose previous religious education had not dealt frankly with the natural sciences. But it was also an eye-opening course for students from non-religious and atheistic backgrounds. They had to go through the process of learning that religion is infinitely more nuanced than they had ever imagined. Additionally, they would be exposed to theologies that would be much more devastating in their criticism of the demonic and barbaric aspects of human religiosity than any of the new atheists are.

I cannot speak for other college professors today but, in my own classes, the new books by Dawkins, Harris, and Hitchens would never have made the list of required readings. These tirades would simply reinforce students' ignorance not only of religion but, ironically, of atheism as well. At best, the new atheistic expositions would have been useful material for outside reading, group projects, or class presentations. The point of these peripheral exercises would not have been to provide anything in the way of an increase

---

1. The following text is an excerpt. Previously published in Haught, *God and the New Atheism*, 15–27. Reprinted with permission.

2. Harris, "Rational Mysticism."

of wisdom and knowledge. Rather it would have been to see how well the relatively light fare the new atheists serve up compares with the gravity of an older and much more thoughtful generation of religious critics.

The most original "new" insight in Hitchens's book, for example, is that "religion is man-made."[3] This refrain rattles through the pages of his critique with all the force of a startling new revelation. My students would have found it interesting, to say the least, that such a hackneyed insight would be the organizing center of a best-selling new book. After coping with the science-inspired atheism of Sigmund Freud or Bertrand Russell and the humanistic idealism of Ludwig Feuerbach and Karl Marx, the new atheism would have appeared rather haggard since it provides little in the way of a new understanding of why religions can be so dangerous.

Why self-contradictory? Because scientism tells us to take nothing on faith, and yet, faith is required to accept scientism. What is remarkable is that none of the new atheists seems remotely prepared to admit that his scientism is a self-sabotaging confession of faith: "If one must have faith in order to believe in something, then the likelihood of that something having any truth or value is considerably diminished."[4] But this statement invalidates itself since it, too, arises out of faith in things unseen. There is no set of tangible experiments or visible demonstrations that could ever scientifically prove the statement to be true. In order to issue the just-quoted pronouncement with such confidence, Hitchens already has to have subscribed to the creed of a faith-community for which scientism and scientific naturalism provide the dogmatic substance. Hitchens must know that most people do not subscribe to that creed—perhaps because there is no "evidence" for it.

"Our god is *logos*," Freud exclaims proudly in *The Future of an Illusion*, candidly signifying the creedal character of the central dogma enshrined by the whole community of scientific rationalists.[5] The declaration makes for good class discussion, but whenever I asked my classes to evaluate Freud's claim that science is the only reliable road to truth, it did not take them long to recognize that the claim itself is logically self-defeating; it could never be justified by any conceivable scientific experiment. Most of my students would have had no difficulty realizing that scientism is also the self-subverting creed that provides the spongy cognitive foundation of the entire project we are dignifying with the label "new atheism."

---

3. See Hitchens, *God is Not Great*, 8, 10, 17, 52, 54, 99–100, 115, 130, 151, 156, 167–68, 181, 202, 229, and 240.

4. See Hitchens, *God is Not Great*, 71.

5. Freud, *Future of an Illusion*, 69.

Unlike the sheltered circumstances that the socially conservative new atheism seeks to save, the classical atheists, whose writings my students were required to read, generally demanded a much more radical transformation of human culture and consciousness. This became most evident when we moved on from Freud, Feuerbach, and Marx to the much more severe Godlessness in works by Friedrich Nietzsche, Albert Camus, and Jean-Paul Sartre. These were the really hardcore atheists. To them, atheism, if one is really serious about it, should make all the difference in the world—indeed, it would take a superhuman effort to embrace it. Nietzsche, Camus, and Sartre realized that most people will be too weak to accept the terrifying consequences of the death of God. However, anything less would be escapism, cowardice, and bad faith.

Not that the new atheism, once implemented, will make no difference at all, but it will be a cosmetic correction in comparison with the seismic redefinition of human existence demanded by the truly serious atheists. The two most significant changes the new atheists want to make are, first, that science, rather than faith, will become the foundation of the new world culture (as Freud and Russell had already anticipated) and, second, that morality will be completely rooted in reason. Science, they hope, will become emancipated from superstition and the ethical instincts that natural selection has been sculpting in our species for over two million years will finally be liberated from their crippling bondage to religion. People will continue to cultivate essentially the same values as before, including altruism, but will get along quite well without inspired books and divine commandments. Educators will be able to teach science without creationist intrusion and students will learn that evolution, rather than divine creativity, is the ultimate explanation of why we are the kind of organisms we are. Only propositions based on "evidence" will be tolerated, but the satisfaction of knowing the truth about nature by way of science will compensate for any ethical constraints we shall still have to put on our animal instincts.

This, of course, is precisely the kind of atheism that nauseated Nietzsche and made Camus and Sartre cringe in their Left Bank cafés. Atheism at the least possible expense to the mediocrity of Western culture is not atheism at all. It is nothing more than the persistence of life-numbing religiosity in a new guise. Please note that I am not promoting Camus's absurdist philosophy or a Nietzschean and Sartrean nihilism either. But these more muscular critics of religion were at least smart enough to realize that a full acceptance of the death of God would require an asceticism completely missing in the new atheistic formulas. Atheism, as my students' acquaintance with Nietzsche, Camus, and Sartre would have clarified, must be thought out to its final, logical conclusion. In this respect, the new atheism, when measured against the stringent demands of a truly thoroughgoing unbelief, would be exposed as differing only superficially from the traditional theism it wants to replace. The blandness of the new softcore atheism lies ironically in its willingness to compromise with the insipid kind of theism it pretends to be ousting. Such a pale brand of atheism uncritically permits the same old values and meanings to hang around, only now they can become sanctified by an ethically and politically conservative Darwinian orthodoxy. If the new atheists' wishes are ever fulfilled, we need anticipate little in the way of cultural reform aside from turning our places of worship into museums, discos, and coffee shops.

In this respect, the new atheism is very much like the old secular humanism rebuked by the hardcore atheists for its mousiness in facing up to what the absence of God should really mean. If you're going to be an atheist, the most rugged version of Godlessness demands complete consistency. Go all the way and think the business of atheism through to the bitter end. This means that, before you get too comfortable with the Godless world you long for, you will be required by the logic of any consistent skepticism to pass through the disorienting wilderness of nihilism. Do you have the courage to do that? You will have to adopt the tragic heroism of a Sisyphus or realize that true freedom in the absence of God means that *you* are the creator of the values you live by. Don't you realize that this will be an intolerable burden from which most people will seek an escape? Are you ready to allow simple logic to lead you to the real truth about the death of God? Before settling into a truly atheistic worldview, you will have to experience the Nietzschean Madman's sensation of straying through "infinite nothingness."[6] You will be required to summon up an unprecedented degree of courage if you plan to wipe away the whole horizon of transcendence. Are you willing to risk madness? If not, then you are not really an atheist.

Predictably, nothing so shaking shows up in the thoughts of Dawkins, Harris, and Hitchens. Apart from its intolerance of tolerance, which we noted earlier, and the heavy dose of Darwinism that grounds many of its declarations, softcore atheism differs scarcely at all from the older secular humanism that the hardcore atheists roundly chastised for its laxity. The new softcore atheists assume that, by dint of Darwinism, we can just drop God like Santa Claus, without having to witness the complete collapse of Western culture—including our sense of what is rational and moral. At least the hardcore atheists understood that if we are truly sincere in our atheism, the whole web of meanings and values that had clustered around the idea of God in Western culture has to go down the drain, along with its organizing center.

6. Nietzsche, *Gay Science*, 181–82.

Nietzsche, Camus, and Sartre, as well as perhaps several of their postmodern descendants, would have nothing to do with the country-bumpkin skepticism that fails to think atheism through with perfect consistency.

"If anyone has written a book more critical of religious faith than I have, I'm not aware of it," declares Sam Harris.[7] My students might not be so sure of that. Has Harris really thought about what would happen if people adopted the hardcore atheist's belief that there is no a priori basis for our moral valuations? What if people will have the sense to ask whether Darwinian naturalism can provide a solid and enduring foundation for our truth-claims and value-judgments? Will a good education in the sciences make everyone simply decide to be good if the universe is inherently valueless and purposeless? At least the hardcore atheists tried to prepare their readers for the pointless world they would encounter if the death of God were ever taken seriously. They did not form a project to kill God—they assumed that deicide had already taken place at the hands of scientism and secularism—but rather, they wanted people to face up *honestly* to the logical, ethical, and cultural implications of a Godless world.

It is hardly relevant to point out that Nietzsche, Camus, and Sartre also failed to embody the tragic heroism they thought should be the logical outcome of atheism. They turned out to be very much like the rest of us. Still, their failure actually fortifies the conclusion that at least some of my students arrived at in the "Problem of God" course: a truly consistent atheism is impossible to pull off. If hardcore atheism cannot succeed, it is doubtful that the softcore variety will make it either. After reading Nietzsche's fevered discourses about the creation of new values that would need to take place once people realize that the God-idea is fiction, the actual ethical prescriptions he endorsed end up sounding, at best, like a juiced up version of the old. He thought that, once we realize there is no Creator, our own, newly liberated creativity would be able to impregnate the infinite emptiness left behind with wholly new meanings and values. After we have drunk up the sea of transcendence, there should be endless room for a whole new set of ethical imperatives. Yet one can only be disappointed with what Nietzsche came up with. His new set of rules for life sound, at one extreme, suspiciously like monkish asceticism and, at the other, like run of the mill secular humanism: "Be creative," "Don't live lives of mediocrity!" "Don't listen to those who speak of otherworldly hopes!" "Remain faithful to the earth."[8] Nietzsche in no way leaves behind what he first heard from the Bible. His call to a fresh "innocence

7. Harris, "Rational Mysticism."
8. See Nietzsche, *Gay Science.*

of becoming" and "newness of life" is a faint echo of the biblical prophets and Saint Paul—only without the virtues of love and hope.[9]

Similarly, Camus made a curious transition (without telling us exactly why) from the absurdism of his early writings, *The Stranger* and *The Myth of Sisyphus*, to the moving humanism of *The Plague* and the rather traditionalist preoccupation with moral guilt in *The Fall*. He must have come to realize that the utter hopelessness of his early nihilistic atheism could not provide a space within which people can actually live their lives. Meanwhile, Sartre, once he had assured us that there are no God-given commandments, ended up sounding almost religious in issuing his "new" imperative, namely, "accept your freedom!" For the early Sartre, it was always wrong ("bad faith") to deny our freedom and that of others, but, despite as much as he wanted all of this to sound radically new, in order to make his atheism palatable, he inevitably had to argue that his "existentialism" is really a form of "humanism" after all.[10] If even the hardcore atheists fail to carry out their program of erasing every trace of transcendent values from their moral universe, then how much less can our softcore atheists expect, logically speaking, to accomplish such a goal?[11]

## Rightness

The hardcore atheists set very exacting standards about who will be allowed into the society of genuine unbelief. They insisted that every serious atheist must think out fully what atheism logically entails, even if they did not succeed in doing so themselves. The new softcore atheists don't even try. They agree with their hardcore cousins that God does not exist, but where logical rigor would require that they also acknowledge that there is no timeless heaven to determine what is good and what is not, their ideas go limp instead. Our new atheists remain as committed unconditionally to traditional values as the rest of us. They do so most openly in every claim they make that religious faith is bad and that, for the sake of true values, moral people must rid themselves of it as soon as they can!

All three of our softcore atheists are absolutely certain that the creeds, ideals, and practices of religion are essentially evil. In fact, a distinguishing mark of the new atheism is that it leaves no room for a sense of moral ambiguity in anything that smacks of faith. There is no allowance that religion might have at least one or two redeeming features. No such waffling is permitted. Their hatred of religious faith is so palpable that the pages of their

9. Nietzsche, *Gay Science*, 181–82.

10. See Sartre, *Existentialism is a Humanism*.

11. See Ogden, *Reality of God*.

books fairly quiver in our hands. Such outrage, however, can arise only from a sense of being deeply grounded in an unmovable realm of "rightness." The fervor in the new atheists' outrage against faith, and especially belief in God, is as resolute as any evangelist could marshal. To know with such certitude that religion is evil, one must first have already surrendered one's heart and mind to what is unconditionally good.

The books by Dawkins, Harris, and Hitchens are not mild treatises like those that trickle tentatively, and often unreadably, from departments of philosophy. They are works of passion and I suspect that most philosophers would be embarrassed by their intemperate style of presentation. I do not expect that philosophers would recommend these writings to their own students, either, although the books might usefully serve as case studies for classes in critical thinking. At their most tender point, justifying the values that lie behind their moral evaluation of religion, logical coherence abandons each of the new atheists.

With the hardcore atheists, one has to ask this newer breed: what is the basis of your moral rectitude? How, in other words, if there is no eternal ground of values, can your own strict standards be anything other than arbitrary, conventional, and historically limited human concoctions? If you are a Darwinian, how can your moral values *ultimately* be anything more than blind contrivances of evolutionary selection? And yet, in your condemnation of the evils of religion, you assume a standard of goodness so timeless, binding, and absolute that it must be God-given. Of course, no one objects to your making moral judgments. But if you, your tribe, or mindless mother nature are the ultimate ground of values, why does your sense of rightness function with such assuredness in your moral indictment of all people of faith? Can your own frail lives and easily impressionable minds—since you are human, just like the rest of us—be the source of something so adamantine as your own sense of rightness? "Excuse us for being so direct," my students would ask, "but if you are going to fall back now on evolutionary biology, how can random events and blind natural selection account for the *absoluteness* that you in fact attribute to the values that justify your intolerance of faith? Or, if you do not want Darwin to give the whole answer, can the historically varying winds of human culture fully account for the rock-like solidity of your righteousness?"

Dawkins declares that the biblical God is a monster, Harris that God is evil, and Hitchens that God is not great. But without some fixed sense of rightness, how can one distinguish what is monstrous, evil, or "not great" from its opposite? In order to make such value judgments, one must assume, as the hardcore atheists are honest enough to acknowledge, that there exists somewhere, in some mode of being, a realm of rightness that does not owe its existence completely to human invention, Darwinian selection, or social construction. To allow the hardcore atheists into our discussion, we can draw this conclusion: if absolute values exist, then God exists. If God does not exist, then neither do absolute values—and one should not issue moral judgments as though they do.

Belief in God or the practice of religion . . . is not necessary in order for people to be highly moral beings. We can agree with our softcore atheists on this point. But the real question, which comes not from me but from the hardcore atheists, is: can you rationally justify your unconditional adherence to timeless values without implicitly invoking the existence of God? The hardcore atheists say "no," but we shall have to return to this question in a later chapter.

# 35: Christian Theology and
the New Atheism[1]

> "The history of Christianity is principally a story of man-
> kind's misery and ignorance rather than of its requited
> love of God."
>
> —Sam Harris[2]

> "How extraordinarily stupid it is to defend Christianity
> ... To defend something is always to discredit it."
>
> —Søren Kierkegaard[3]

THE POINT OF CHRISTIAN theology, the late Pope John Paul II wrote in his encyclical, "*Fides et Ratio*," is to explore the mystery of God's self-emptying love: "The prime commitment of theology is the understanding of God's *kenosis* [self-emptying], a grand and mysterious truth for the human mind, which finds it inconceivable that suffering and death can express a love which gives itself and seeks nothing in return."[4] No theological radical himself, John Paul expressed here what countless other Christian thinkers now agree is the radical message of Christian faith. The God who, for Christians, became manifest in Jesus of Nazareth is vulnerable, defenseless love. It is this same love that Christians confess to be the ultimate environment, ground, and destiny of all being.

Following the advice of Kierkegaard, however, in this final chapter, I shall not try to defend Christianity's understanding of God against the

---

1. The following text is an excerpt. Previously published in Haught, *God and the New Atheism*, 92–108. Reprinted with permission.

2. Harris, *End of Faith*, 106.

3. Kierkegaard, *Sickness Unto Death*, 218.

4 John Paul II, "*Fides et Ratio*," 93.

assaults of the new atheists. It needs no defense since it never comes up in their polemic. Moreover, the many abuses committed in the name of the self-centered potentate—Dawkins might say "monster"—that has often been substituted for Christianity's God do not deserve to be defended anyway. As far as the existence of the self-giving love that Christians call God is concerned, there is nothing in the books by Dawkins, Harris, and Hitchens that could be called a serious theological provocation. Sadly, the deepening of theology that has occurred in previous conversations between serious atheists and Christian thinkers has little chance of happening here. As examples of more fruitful conversations, I am thinking of how the theology of Paul Tillich was deepened by his encounter with the writings of Friedrich Nietzsche and atheistic existentialism; of Karl Barth with Ludwig Feuerbach; of Karl Rahner and Rudolf Bultmann with Martin Heidegger; of Jürgen Moltmann with Ernst Bloch; of Gustavo Guttierez with Karl Marx; and of many contemporary theologians with Jacques Derrida, Jacques Lacan, and Jürgen Habermas. At least the atheists on this list had enough understanding of theology to make the conversation interesting and productive. In marked contrast, the level of theological discernment by the new atheists is too shallow and inaccurate even to begin such a conversation.

What might be worthy of theological attention, however, is the moral perfectionism that energizes the new atheism, making it so appealing to some of its disciples. Sam Harris's heartfelt indignation against Christianity, as expressed in the citation above, is typical of the new atheists' arraignment of theistic faiths for their failure to actualize their own ethical ideals. It is certainly not hard for any impartial reader to agree that devotees of the theistic faiths have often failed miserably to practice what they preach. In the enormous sins of omission—as well as commission—by their members, the Abrahamic religions have undeniably deserved the justifiable wrath of the righteous. And there is no lack of righteousness on the part of the holy trinity we have been listening to in the preceding chapters.

The scolding of religious abuse and mediocrity, however, was already a major motif in the prophetic voices that pestered the consciences of the citizens of ancient Israel and Judah. It would be hard to find in all the annals of atheism any more *substantive* denunciation of religious abuse than those memorialized in the words of Amos, Hosea, Isaiah, Jeremiah, Ezekiel, Micah, and their ilk throughout the ages. With enormous force, the prophets among us have repeatedly risen up in self-endangering revolt against the sanctimonious fat-cat religiosity of their own times. Without any attempt to prettify their outrage, they have roundly condemned their fellow believers, especially for failing to practice justice. It was in the prophetic tradition of those who thirst after justice that Jesus of Nazareth was to discover his own identity and mission.

## Puritanism

Concern with issues such as social justice and environmental responsibility are not important in the new atheists' critique of Christianity, as they have been for other atheists. Nevertheless, it is still in the name of morality that our three Godless perfectionists send down their most energized bolts of lightning. In fact, from a Christian theological point of view, what stands out above everything else in the new atheism is its cognitional and ethical puritanism. Its proponents are so confident of having unimpeded access to truth and ethical rightness that they can now make a complete break from the intellectual and moral impurity of faith-crippled human beings up to this point. They claim, in effect, to have finally delivered our native rationality and capacity for moral discernment from centuries of thralldom to the ancient literature and Iron Age lunacy of Abrahamic religions. Intellectually, the new atheistic puritanism takes the form of an uncompromising scientism that sanitizes our minds by scrubbing off all the griminess of faith. Ethically, the same puritanical obsession manifests itself in a promise to ground morality henceforth in a rationality cleansed by science of all its ties to religiosity.

Ironically, the promoters of this neo-puritanism seem to have no awareness that their own perfectionistic program has hardly purified itself of ancient, dualistic, and mythic accretions that go back centuries before Christianity. The new atheists are not the first cognoscenti to have promised salvation by pure knowledge. The absence of any sense of paradox, irony, tolerance, and ambiguity in their teachings is symptomatic of a persistent human temptation to become obsessed with cognitional and ethical purity at the expense of nuance and complexity.

This obsession itself stems from a sense of disembodiment promulgated by the dualistic—some would say "Gnostic"—mythology that has never been fully expurgated from Western thought. I would suggest, therefore, that the cultural roots of the new atheistic disgust with biblical faith lie not only in an uncritical academic strain of scientism but also in the same ancient, dualistic trends that still live on unconsciously in the puritanical vision of reality.[5] As the great philosopher Paul Ricoeur has shown, this puritanical vision goes back to ancient myths that sepa-

---

5. Scientism is also an offshoot of dualistic mythology, but I cannot develop this point further here.

rated the soul (and later "mind") completely from matter and bodiliness, a vision that Christianity has denounced from the beginning, but so far, obviously, without complete success.[6]

Most scandalous to the puritanical mindset of the new atheistic exegetes is that the God of the Bible seems so erratic, jealous, angry, violent, legalistic, and judgmental.[7] It is disgusting, especially to Dawkins and Hitchens, that biblical faith is so anthropomorphic. Measured by their puritanical standards, the Almighty should be above all such compromising associations with human characteristics. Moreover, if the Bible is supposed to be "written by God," as Harris puts it, why can't its Author come across as intellectually, scientifically, morally, and emotionally more respectable?[8] Hitchens is so appalled that the Bible fails to live up to his perfectionistic portrait of the ideal divinity that he is forced to conclude that, alas, religion is something human beings "manufactured."[9] The main reason for his writing *God Is Not Great* appears to be that of letting the rest of us in on his discovery.

## Incarnation

The very idea of a *personal* God, regardless of specific characteristics, is problematic to the new atheists—as it is to almost all scientific naturalists. However, it is hard to imagine how the reality of a divine mystery, if it exists at all, would capture the attention and allegiance of personal human beings if it presented itself as anything less than personal. The fact that an ancient tribe of warriors would portray its deity anthropomorphically as, of all things, a warrior-God should be surprising only to a kind of Gnosticism that insists on the complete disassociation of faith from history and of God from being involved in specific times, places, and events. To an incarnational faith, however, divine perfection does not mean God's apartness from the world, but God's absolute relatedness to it.[10] This relatedness cannot be brought home to religious persons by way of impersonal imagery.

If God is absolute self-giving love, as Christian faith proclaims, it would not be surprising that this love would humbly and hiddenly disclose itself to members of our species in the modest raiment of human personality.

6. Support for my suggestion comes especially from Ricoeur, *Symbolism of Evil.*

7. It goes unmentioned that, in other moods, Yahweh is slow to anger, lenient, loving, caring, and forgiving.

8. Harris, *Letter to a Christian Nation*, 60.

9. See Hitchens, *God Is Not Great.*

10. See Hartshorne, *Divine Relativity* and Ogden, *Reality of God.*

The Christian belief that God is fully present in Jesus the Christ means, at the very least, that God's perfection consists not of a self-purification from ambiguity in nature's evolution or from sinfulness in human history but rather an unequaled intimacy with the world in all of its struggles and iniquity. The goal of this intimacy is the lifting up or "divinization" of the world, but the point of departure for this adventure is a very unfinished and imperfect universe. Christian theology is not at all embarrassed that anthropomorphic imagery would be essential to the gradual self-revelation of God. To hold, with Hitchens, that religion is therefore "man-made" is only half the story. The other half is that it is God's intimacy with the world that evokes the "manufacture" by human persons of a truly revelatory personal imagery in the first place.

Theologically interpreted, not only biblical faith but also the long religious journey of our whole species is a series of responses to an invitation to intimacy by the inexhaustible mystery of God. Since no particular imagery can ever capture the fullness and depth of this elusive infinite mystery, humanity's religious search, including that of Christians, is never conclusive. Hence, the many births and deaths of gods and goddesses throughout the ages is logically consistent with the quiet but constant presence and invitation of the infinite. The divine invitation grasps us more than we grasp it, so we cannot subject it to our intellectual control. We can talk about it only in the vague but rich language of culturally conditioned symbols, analogies, and metaphors. Perhaps it is intellectual control that we want, but, if so, in our frustration that the divine mystery eludes scientific comprehension, we are likely to interpret the absence of God as an infinite emptiness. The confusion of infinite fullness with endless emptiness is one of the essential marks of atheism.

The fact that religious icons come and go, or that early biblical symbolism of God is not to our tastes, is not enough to prove that the world's ultimate environment and final destiny is infinite nothingness. In fact, our perpetual religious discontent, and even our sincere frustration with religion as such, can occur only if our consciousness is already in the grasp of something deeper. If it were not, then there would be no basis for our iconoclastic protests. Sensitive souls, in every period of religious history, can grow weary of the unsatisfactory ways in which contemporary religions represent their ideal. Sometimes serious atheists might grow so weary of representations of the sacred that they denounce all religion as crude and vulgar. But even well-intentioned protest against "God" or images of God can have no teeth unless its executors are already standing in deeper ground themselves. A good name for this deeper ground is God.

## The Tolerance of Ambiguity

In effect, therefore, the new atheists are demanding that religions either provide *perfect* representations of God (suitable to their tastes) or abandon these images altogether. But Christianity tolerates ambiguity and imperfection in the Bible's struggle to imagine God. Why? Because the alternative is much worse—namely, an Absolute that remains eternally above the world's struggles in splendid isolation from the hopes, tragedies, sorrows, and struggles of weak human beings and the larger story of cosmic and biological evolution. Such a detached God would be an accurate reflection of the new atheists' moral ideal, but this would not be the God of Christian faith. In fact, from the point of view of the Bible's prophetic tradition, the puritanical God of splendid isolation would be the truly immoral "role model" for humans.

The new atheists' job-description for the ideal deity calls for a perfection purified not only of the vulgarity of tribal existence but also of contamination by human existence as such. The Christian God does not qualify. Christianity's intuition is that God is incarnate, that the Creator fully embraces the world in all of its imperfections, even to the point of becoming a child, eating with sinners, and experiencing death on a cross. Christian theology's advice to readers of those chapters in the Bible where God does not seem quite up to snuff morally is always to interpret everything in the Bible in light of its dominant themes of hope, liberation, incarnation, and God's self-emptying love. As soon as we let these main motifs out of sight, we end up reading passages in literalist isolation, as Dawkins does when he comes up with his portrait of the monster-God of the "Old Testament." Reading certain passages in the Bible, including the Christian Scriptures, can be a dangerous and bewildering experience if one has not first gained some sense of the Bible's fundamental themes. Perhaps the most important of these is that of freedom, which, along with the topic of God's promise and fidelity, binds most of the Bible's books into a coherence unnoticed by the new atheists. It was in their own deliverance from slavery and genocide that the Hebrew people found the experiential basis of their symbolizing of God as Liberator. And yet, the close association of God with liberation, a defining feature of the Abrahamic traditions, is nowhere mentioned, let alone seriously discussed in the books we have been examining.

## Evolution and Christian Theology

The same puritanical premise that leads Dawkins to reject Christianity on moral grounds also underlies his belief that the Christian God must be rejected on scientific grounds as well. Darwin's picture of life, according to Dawkins, decisively demolishes the God of the Bible.[11] How so? Evolutionary science shows that nature exhibits no sign of intelligent design. Dawkins wants a universe that fits his idea of engineering elegance and perfect design, just as he wants a God who corresponds to his notion of moral perfection. He gets neither. Therefore, for Dawkins, God simply cannot exist. A perfectly good God would never have made a world in which so much evolutionary struggle, waste, suffering, and death take place. If God were a perfect engineer, there would be no room for the imperfections biologists find in the organic world.

Here, then, the puritanical view of morality characteristic of the new atheism finds its parallel in a perfectionistic model of divine creation in which God *should* have created the world in a finished and finalized state, once and for all, in the beginning. Either the God of the Bible must be a *perfect* moral role model and a *perfect* engineer, or else this God is not permitted by Dawkins to exist at all.

To Christian faith, Dawkins's species of perfectionism, both moral and cosmic, is a dead end. If the universe were finished instantaneously, where could it go from there? Maybe, then, there is a good theological reason why a God who wants the universe to have an open future would put up with imperfection and ambiguity. If you don't like a world in which either suicide bombers or evolutionary monstrosities are permitted to exist, a good mental experiment is to imagine what it would be like to exist in the perfectly designed universe idealized by the new atheists and their creationist forbears. In keeping with their biblical literalism, the universe they want would have to have been finished to perfection on the first day of creation. An instantaneously completed initial act of divine prestidigitation would guarantee that there would be no suffering, no evil, and no need for the creation to evolve into something different over immensely long periods of time. In their instructions as to how a decent God should act, the new atheists demand that either the world be finished once and for all in the beginning, or else there is no role for God to play at all. A morally acceptable God would have gotten things completely right in the beginning; the universe would be an unblemished, unchanging reflection of its divine engineer. There would be no growing pains, no death, no terrorists. There would be no theodicy problem, either, since there would be no evil to reconcile with the existence of God.

Neither, of course, would there be any life, any freedom, any future, any adventure, any grand cosmic story, or any opening to infinite horizons

11. See Dawkins, *Blind Watchmaker* and *River Out of Eden*.

up ahead. Nor would there be the opportunity for each of us to develop character and practice virtue. The problem with the new atheists' magical ideal of creation—one that they seem to have borrowed, yet again, from creationists and ID theists—is that creation would have nowhere to go. Locked eternally into splendid perfection, the universe would allow no room for indeterminacy, accidents, or freedom. Every last detail would be frozen into its destined position from the beginning. And human beings, if one can imagine them existing at all, would be puppets and statues.

The shadow side of any unfinished—and, as such, imperfect—universe is ambiguity and evil, including the poison in our religions. Understandably, we long for a world without evil, so it is appropriate to hope for the eventual fulfillment of our lives and the whole universe. The Christian hope is for a universe in which evil will be conquered and all tears will be wiped away. Such a hope, by setting forth the possibility of a new future, is a great incentive to moral action. But we need to be very careful about what we ask for as far as the past and present state of the universe is concerned. An initially perfect design, which is what Dawkins asks for—otherwise he would not be so cynical about God's failure as an engineer—would mean the end of evolution before it even began, and perfectionism, both moral and scientific, would mean the end of hope. Perfectionism is a sure way to close off the future and prevent the world and our lives from ever becoming new.

# Bibliography

Acker, H. M. "Creation and Catholicism." *America* 183 (2000) 6–8.

Angier, Natalie. "My God Problem—and Theirs." *The American Scholar 72* (2004) 131–34.

Appleyard, Brian. *Understanding the Present: Science and the Soul of Modern Man*. New York: Doubleday, 1993.

Atkins, Peter W. *Creation Revisited*. New York: Freeman, 1992.

———. *The 2nd Law: Energy, Chaos, and Form*. New York: Scientific American, 1994.

Atran, Scott. *In Gods We Trust: The Evolutionary Landscape of Religion*. New York: Oxford University Press, 2002.

Ayala, Francisco J. "Darwin's Revolution." In *Creative Evolution?!*, edited by John H. Campbell and J. William Schopf, 110–34. Boston: Jones & Bartlett, 1994.

Bacik, James J. *Apologetics and the Eclipse of Mystery: Mystagogy According to Karl Rahner*. Notre Dame: University of Notre Dame Press, 1980.

Baltazar, Eulalio R. *God Within Process*. Mahwah, NJ: Paulist, 1970.

Barash, David. "Does God Have Back Problems Too?" *Los Angeles Times*, 27 June 2005.

Barbour, Ian G. *Religion in an Age of Science*. New York: HarperCollins, 1990.

Barrow, John D., and Frank J. Tipler. *The Anthropic Cosmological Principle*. New York: Oxford University Press, 1986.

Becker, Ernest. *The Denial of Death*. New York: Free Press, 1973.

Beer, Gavin de. "Evolution." In *New Encyclopedia Britannica*, 15:101–109. London: Encyclopedia Britannica, 1974.

Behe, Michael J. *Darwin's Black Box: The Biochemical Challenge to Evolution*. New York: Free Press, 1996.

Benedict XVI. "*Spe Salvi*." http://www.vatican.va/holy_father/benedict_xvi/encyclicals/documents/hf_ben-xvi_enc_20071130_spe-salvi_en.html.

Benz, Ernst. *Evolution and Christian Hope*. Garden City, NJ: Doubleday, 1966.

Berger, Peter. *The Sacred Canopy*. Garden City, NJ: Anchor, 1990.

Bergson, Henri. *Creative Evolution*. Translated by Arthur Mitchell. Lanham, MD: University Press of America, 1983.

Berry, Thomas. *The Dream of the Earth*. San Francisco: Sierra Club, 1988.

Bloch, Ernst. *The Principle of Hope*. Translated by Neville Plaice, et al. 3 vols. Oxford: Basil Blackwell, 1986.

Bonhoeffer, Dietrich. *Letters and Papers from Prison*. New York: MacMillan, 1967.

Boulding, Kenneth. "Toward an Evolutionary Theology." In *The Spirit of the Earth: A Teilhard Centennial Celebration*, edited by Jerome Perlinski, 112–26. New York: Seabury, 1981.

Bowker, John. *Is Anybody Out There: Religions and Belief in God in the Contemporary World*. New York: Christian Classics, 1988.

———. *The Sense of God: Sociological, Anthropological, and Psychological Approaches to the Origin of the Sense of God*. London: Oneworld, 1995.

Bowler, Peter. *Reconciling Science and Religion: The Debate in Early Twentieth-Century Britain*. Chicago: University of Chicago Press, 2001.

Boyer, Pascal. *Religion Explained: The Evolutionary Origins of Religious Thought*. New York: Basic, 2001.

Braaten, Carl E., and Philip Clayton. *The Theology of Wolfhart Pannenberg*. Minneapolis: Augsburg, 1988.

Brockman, John. "God (or Not), Physics, and, of Course, Love: Scientists Take a Leap." *New York Times*, 5 January 2005. https://www.nytimes.com/2005/01/04/science/god-or-not-physics-and-of-course-love-scientists-take-a-leap.html.

———. "Introduction: The Emerging Third Culture." In *The Third Culture*, edited by John Brockman, 17–37. New York: Touchstone, 1996.

Burkert, Walter. *Creation of the Sacred: Tracks of Biology in Early Religions*. Cambridge, MA: Harvard University Press, 1996.

Camus, Albert. *The Myth of Sisyphus and Other Essays*. New York: Vintage, 1955.

———. *The Stranger*. New York: Vintage, 1946.

Catholic Church. "God Carries Out His Plan: Divine Providence." In *Catechism of the Catholic Church* 302. http://www.catholicdoors.com/catechis.

———. "Original Sin." In *Catechism of the Catholic Church*, 396–421. http://www.catholicdoors.com/catechis.

———. "Warning Considering the Writings of Father Teilhard de Chardin." 30 June 1962. https://www.ewtn.com/library/CURIA/CDFTEILH.HTM.

Chang, Chung-yuan. *Tao: A New Way of Thinking*. Philadelphia: Singing Dragon, 2014.

Cobb, John B., and David Ray Griffin. *Process Theology: An Introductory Exposition*. Philadelphia: Westminster, 1976.

Conway Morris, Simon. *Life's Solution: Inevitable Humans in a Lonely Universe*. Cambridge, MA: Cambridge University Press, 2003.

Cziko, Gary. *Without Miracles: Universal Selection Theory and the Second Darwinian Revolution*. Cambridge, MA: MIT Press, 1995.

D'Costa, Gavin, ed. *Christian Uniqueness Reconsidered*. Maryknoll, NY: Orbis, 1990.

Davies, Paul. *The Mind of God: The Scientific Basis for a Rational World*. New York: Simon & Schuster, 1992.

Dawe, Donald G. *The Form of a Servant*. Philadelphia: Westminster, 1963.

Darwin, Charles. *The Autobiography of Charles Darwin*. Edited by Nora Barlow. New York: Harcourt, 1958.

———. *The Correspondence of Charles Darwin*. Edited by James A. Secord. New York: Cambridge University Press, 1993.

———. *The Origin of Species*. New York: Random House, 1993.

Dawkins, Richard. *The Blind Watchmaker: Why the Evidence of Evolution Reveals a Universe Without Design*. New York: Norton, 1995.

———. *Climbing Mount Improbable*. New York: Norton, 1996.

———. *The God Delusion*. New York: Houghton Mifflin, 2006.

———. *River Out of Eden*. New York: Basic Books, 1995.

———. *The Selfish Gene*. Oxford: Oxford University Press, 2016.

Delio, Ilia, OSF. "The Humility of God in a Scientific World." *New Theology Review* 11 (1998) 36–50.

Dembski, William A. *Intelligent Design: The Bridge Between Science and Theology*. Downers Grove, IL: InterVarsity, 1999.

Dennett, Daniel C. *Breaking the Spell: Religion as a Natural Phenomenon*. New York: Viking, 2006.

———. *Darwin's Dangerous Idea: Evolution and the Meaning of Life*. New York: Simon & Schuster, 1995.

———. "Intuition Pumps." In *The Third Culture*, edited by John Brockman, 181–197. New York: Touchstone, 1996.

Domning, Daryl. "Evolution, Evil, and Original Sin." *America* 185 (2001). https://www.americamagazine.org/content/article.cfm?article_id=1205.

Donne, John. "An Anatomy of the World." *Poetry Foundation*. https://www.poetryfoundation.org/poems/44092/an-anatomy-of-the-world.

Dulles, Avery. *Revelation and the Quest for Unity*. Washington, DC: Corpus, 1968.

Dupre, Louis K. *The Other Dimension: A Search for the Meaning of Religious Attitudes*. New York: Doubleday, 1972.

Dyson, Freeman. *Infinite in All Directions*. New York: Harper & Row, 1988.

Eldredge, Niles. *The Monkey Business: A Scientist Looks at Creationism*. New York: Washington Square, 1982.

Feynman, Richard. *The Meaning of It All: Thoughts of a Citizen Scientist*. New York: Perseus, 1999.

Finlan, Stephen, and Vladimir Kharlamov, eds. *Theosis, Deification in Christian Theology*. Eugene: Pickwick, 2006.

Flanagan, Owen. *The Problem of the Soul: Two Visions of Mind and How to Reconcile Them*. New York: Basic, 2002.

Flynn, Eileen, and Gloria Thomas. *Living Faith: An Introduction to Theology*. 2nd ed. New York: Rowman and Littlefield, 1989.

Francis. "*Laudato Si.*" 24 May 2015. http://w2.vatican.va/content/francesco/en/encyclicals/documents/papa-francesco_20150524_enciclica-laudato-si.html.

Frankl, Victor. *The Unconscious God*. New York: Simon & Schuster, 1975.

Freud, Sigmund. *Civilization and Its Discontents*. New York: Norton, 1962.

———. *The Future of an Illusion*. Translated by James Strachey. New York: Norton, 1961.

Garrigou-Lagrange, Reginald, OP. *De Revelatione*. Rome: F. Ferrari, 1945.

Gillispie, Charles Coulston. *Genesis and Geology: A Study in the Relations of Scientific Thought, Natural Theology, and Social Opinion in Great Britain, 1790–1850*. Cambridge, MA: Harvard University Press, 1996.

Goebel, Bernardin. *Katholische Apologetik*. Freiburg: Verlag Herder, 1930.

Gould, Stephen Jay. *Ever Since Darwin*. New York: Norton, 1977

———. "The Piltdown conspiracy." *Natural History* 89 (1980) 8–28.

———. "Piltdown in letters." *Natural History* 90 (1981) 12–30.

———. "Piltdown revisited." *Natural History* 88 (1979) 86–97.

Gould, Stephen Jay, and Richard C. Lewontin. "The Spandrels of San Marco and the Panglossian Paradigm: A Critique Of The Adaptationist Programme." *Proceedings of the Royal Society of London* 205 (1979) 581–598.

Greene, John C. *Darwin and the Modern World View*. Baton Rouge, LA: Louisiana State University Press, 1973.

Gribbin, John. *In the Beginning: After COBE and before the Big Bang*. Boston: Little, Brown, 1993.

Hardwick, Charley. *Events of Grace: Naturalism, Existentialism, and Theology*. New York: Cambridge University Press, 1996.

Harris, Sam. "An Atheist Manifesto." *Truthdig*, 7 December 2005. http://www.truthdig.com/dig/item/200512_an_atheist_manifesto.

―――. *The End of Faith: Religion, Terror, and the Future of Reason*. New York: Norton, 2004.

―――. *Letter to a Christian Nation*. New York: Knopf, 2007.

―――. "Rational Mysticism." *Free Inquiry* 25 (2005). http://www.secularhumanism.org/index.php?section=library&page=harris_25_6.

Hartshorne, Charles. *The Divine Relativity*. New Haven, CT: Yale University Press, 1948.

―――. *Man's Vision of God*. Chicago: Willett Clark, 1941.

Hitchens, Christopher. *God is Not Great: How Religion Poisons Everything*. New York: Hachette, 2007.

Haught, John F. *Christianity and Science*. Maryknoll: Orbis, 2007.

―――. *The Cosmic Adventure: Science, Religion, and the Quest for Purpose*. New York: Paulist, 1984.

―――. *Deeper Than Darwin: The Prospect for Religion in the Age of Evolution*. Boulder: Westview, 2003.

―――. *God After Darwin: A Theology of Evolution*. Boulder: Westview, 2007.

―――. *God and the New Atheism: A Critical Response to Dawkins, Harris, and Hitchens*. Louisville: Westminster John Knox, 2008.

―――. *Is Nature Enough: Meaning and Truth in the Age of Science*. Cambridge: Cambridge University Press, 2006.

―――. *Making Sense of Evolution: Darwin, God, and The Drama of Life*. Louisville: Westminster John Knox, 2010.

―――. *Mystery and Promise: A Theology of Revelation*. Collegeville, MN: Liturgical, 1993.

―――. *Nature and Purpose*. Lanham, MD: University Press of America, 1980.

―――. *The New Cosmic Story: Inside Our Awakening Universe*. New Haven, CT: Yale University Press, 2017.

―――. *Purpose, Evolution, and the Meaning of Life*. Ontario: Pandora, 2004.

―――. *The Promise of Nature: Ecology and Cosmic Purpose*. New York: Paulist, 1993.

―――. *Religion and Self-Acceptance*. New York: Paulist, 1976.

―――. *Responses to 101 Questions on God and Evolution*. New York: Paulist, 2001.

―――. *Resting on the Future: Catholic Theology for an Unfinished Universe*. London: Bloomsbury, 2015.

―――. *The Revelation of God in History*. Wilmington: Michael Glazier, 1988.

―――. *Science and Faith: A New Introduction*. New York: Paulist, 2013.

―――. *Science and Religion: From Conflict to Conversation*. New York: Paulist, 1995.

―――, ed. *Science and Religion in Search of Cosmic Purpose*. Washington: Georgetown University Press, 2000.

―――. *What Is God?* New York: Paulist, 1986.

―――. *What Is Religion?* New York: Paulist, 1990.

Hawking, Stephen. *A Brief History of Time: From the Big Bang to Black Holes*. New York: Bantam, 1990.

Hick, John, and Paul Knitter, eds., *The Myth of Christian Uniqueness*. Maryknoll, NY: Orbis, 1987.

Hinde, Robert. *Why Gods Persist: A Scientific Approach to Religions*. New York: Routledge, 1999.

Gerard Manley Hopkins. *"God's Grandeur" and Other Poems*. New York: Dover, 1995.

Horgan, John. *The End of Science.* Reading, MA: Addison-Wesley, 1996.

Huyssteen, Wentzel van. *Alone in the World? Human Uniqueness in Science and Theology.* Grand Rapids, MI: Eerdmans, 2006.

Innes, J. B. "1 December 1878." *Darwin Correspondence Project.* https://www.darwinproject.ac.uk/letter/DCP-LETT-11768.xml.

International Theological Commission. "Science and the Stewardship of Knowledge." In *Communion and Stewardship: Human Persons Created in the Image of God.* https://www.catholicculture.org/culture/library/view.cfm?id=6664.

James, William. *Pragmatism.* Cleveland: Meridian, 1964.

John Paul II. "Address to the Pontifical Academy of Sciences." *Origins* 9 (1979) 391.

———. "*Fides et Ratio.*" http://w2.vatican.va/content/john-paul-ii/en/encyclicals/documents/hf_jp-ii_enc_14091998_fides-et-ratio.html.

———. "Letter to the Reverend George V. Coyne, SJ, Director of the Vatican Observatory." *Origins* 18 (1988) 377.

———. "Magisterium Is Concerned with Question of Evolution for It Involves Conception of Man." http://www.catholicculture.org/culture/library/view.cfm?id=80.

Johnson, Phillip E. *The Wedge of Truth: Splitting the Foundations of Naturalism.* Downers Grove, IL: InterVarsity, 2000.

Jonas, Hans. *The Phenomenon of Life.* New York: Harper & Row, 1966.

Jüngel, Eberhard. *The Doctrine of the Trinity: God's Being is in Becoming.* Translated by Scottish Academic Press. Edinburgh: Scottish Academic, 1976.

Kierkegaard, Søren. *Fear and Trembling and The Sickness Unto Death.* Translated by Walter Lowrie. Garden City, NJ: Doubleday Anchor, 1984.

———. *The Sickness Unto Death: A Christian Psychological Exposition For Upbuilding And Awakening.* Princeton: Princeton University Press, 1983.

King, Thomas SJ. "Teilhard and Piltdown." In *Teilhard and the Unity of Knowledge,* edited by Thomas King et al., 159–169. New York: Paulist, 1983.

Kitcher, Philip. *Living with Darwin: Evolution, Design, and the Future of Faith.* New York: Oxford University Press, 2006.

Kohlberg, Lawrence. *The Philosophy of Moral Development: Moral Stages and the Idea of Justice.* Essays on Moral Development 1. New York: Harper & Row, 1981.

Küng, Hans. *Does God Exist?* Translated by Edward Quinn. New York: Doubleday, 1980.

———. *Eternal Life.* Translated by Edward Quinn. Garden City, NJ: Doubleday, 1984.

Lightman, Alan, and Roberta Brawer. *Origins: The Lives and Worlds of Modern Cosmologists.* Cambridge: Harvard University Press, 1990.

Lonergan, Bernard, SJ. "Cognitional Structure." In *Collection,* edited by F. E. Crowe, SJ. New York: Herder and Herder, 1967.

———. *Insight: A Study of Human Understanding.* Toronto: University of Toronto Press, 1992.

Lovejoy, Arthur O. *The Great Chain of Being: A Study of the History of an Idea.* New York: Harper & Row, 1965.

Lynch, William. *Images of Hope.* Notre Dame: University of Notre Dame Press, 1974.

MacGregor, Geddes. *He Who Lets Us Be: A Theology of Love.* New York: The Seabury Press, 1975.

Macquarrie, John. *The Humility of God.* Philadelphia: Westminster, 1978.

Marcel, Gabriel. *Being and Having: An Existentialist Diary.* New York: Harper & Row, 1965.

Mattill, A. J., Jr., *The Seven Mighty Blows to Traditional Beliefs.* 2d ed. Gordo, AL: Flatwoods, 1995.

Mayr, Ernst. "Evolution." *Scientific American* 239 (1978) 50.

McGrath, Alister. "A Blast from the Past? The Boyle Lectures and Natural Theology." *Science and Christian Belief* 17 (2005) 25–33.

Miller, Kenneth R. *Finding Darwin's God: A Scientist's Search for Common Ground Between God and Evolution.* New York: Cliff Street, 1999.

Moltmann, Jürgen. *The Coming of God.* Translated by Margaret Kohl. Minneapolis: Fortress, 1996.

———. *The Experiment Hope.* Edited and Translated by M. Douglas Meeks. Philadelphia: Fortress, 1975.

———. *God in Creation.* Translated by Margaret Kohl. San Francisco: Harper & Row, 1985.

———. *Theology of Hope: On the Ground and the Implications of a Christian Eschatology.* Minneapolis: Fortress, 1967.

Monod, Jacques. *Chance and Necessity.* Translated by Austryn Wainhouse. New York: Vintage, 1972.

Mooney, Christopher F. *Theology and Scientific Knowledge.* Notre Dame: University of Notre Dame Press, 1996.

Moran, Gabriel. *Theology of Revelation.* New York: Herder & Herder, 1966.

Morowitz, Harold J. *The Kindly Dr. Guillotin: And Other Essays on Science and Life.* Washington, DC: Counterpoint, 1997.

Nasr, Seyyed Hossein. *Religion and the Order of Nature.* New York: Oxford University Press, 1996.

Neumann, Erich. *Depth Psychology and a New Ethic.* Translated by Eugene Rolfe. New York: Harper Torchbooks. 1973.

Neuner, Josef, and Jacques Dupuis, eds. *The Christian Faith.* Staten Island, NY: Alba House, 2001.

Newman, John Henry. *The Idea of a University.* Garden City, NJ: Image, 1959.

Niebuhr, H. Richard. *The Meaning of Revelation.* New York: Macmillan, 1960.

Nietzsche, Friedrich. *The Gay Science.* Edited by Walter Kaufmann. New York: Vintage, 1974.

O'Collins, Gerald. *Foundations of Theology.* Chicago: Loyola University Press, 1970.

O'Donnell, John J. *Hans Urs Von Balthasar.* Collegeville, MN: Liturgical, 1992.

O'Leary, Don. *Roman Catholicism and Modern Science.* New York: Continuum, 2006.

Ogden, Schubert M. *The Reality of God and Other Essays.* Dallas: Southern Methodist University, 1992.

Otto, Rudolf. *The Idea of the Holy.* Translated by John W. Harvey. New York: Oxford University Press, 1950.

Paley, William. *Natural Theology.* Edited by Matthew D. Eddy and David Knight. New York: Oxford University Press, 2006.

Pannenberg, Wolfhart. *Faith and Reality.* Translated by John Maxwell. Philadelphia: Westminster, 1977.

———. "Human Life: Creation Versus Evolution?" In *Science and Theology,* edited by Ted Peters, 122–139. Boulder: Westview, 1998.

————. "The Revelation of God in History." In *Theology as History*, edited by James M. Robinson and John B. Cobb Jr. New York: Harper & Row, 1967.

————. *Systematic Theology: Volume 2.* Translated by Geoffrey W. Bromiley. Grand Rapids: Eerdmans, 1994.

————. *Toward a Theology of Nature.* Edited by Ted Peters. Louisville: Westminster John Knox, 1993.

————. *What Is Man?* Translated by Duane A. Priebe. Philadelphia: Fortress, 1970.

Paul VI. "*Gaudium et Spes.*" 7 December 1965. http://www.vatican.va/archive/hist_councils/ii_vatican_council/documents/vat-ii_cons_19651207_gaudium-et-spes_en.html.

————. "The Second Vatican Council's Dogmatic Constitution on Divine Revelation: *Dei Verbum.*" http://www.vatican.va/archive/hist_councils/ii_vatican_council/documents/vat-ii_const_19651118_dei-verbum_en.html.

Peacocke, Arthur. *Intimations of Reality.* Notre Dame: University of Notre Dame Press, 1984.

Peters, Ted, ed. *Cosmos as Creation: Theology and Science in Consonance.* Nashville: Abingdon, 1989.

————. *God—The World's Future: Systematic Theology for a New Era.* 2nd ed. Minneapolis: Fortress, 1993.

Pinker, Steven. *The Blank Slate: The Modern Denial of Human Nature.* New York: Penguin, 2002.

Polanyi, Michael. *Personal Knowledge: Towards a Post-Critical Philosophy.* Evanston, IL: Harper Torchbooks, 1958.

————. *The Tacit Dimension.* Garden City, NJ: Doubleday Anchor, 1967.

Polkinghorne, John. *The Faith of a Physicist.* Princeton: Princeton University Press, 1994.

Popper, Karl. *Conjectures and Refutations.* 2nd ed. London: Routledge, 1965.

Poupard, Paul. "Galileo: Report on Papal Commission Findings." *Origins* 22 (1992) 375.

Provine, William. "Evolution and the Foundation of Ethics." In *Science, Technology, and Social Progress*, edited by Steven L. Goldman, 253–67. Bethlehem, PA: Lehigh University Press, 1989.

Rahner, Karl, SJ. *Foundations of Christian Faith.* Translated by William Dych. New York: Crossroad, 1984.

————. *Hominization.* Translated by W. J. O'Hara. New York: Herder & Herder, 1965.

————. *Theological Investigations.* Translated by Karl and Boniface Kruger. Baltimore: Helicon, 1969.

Raschke, Carl A. *The Interruption of Eternity: Modern Gnosticism and the Origins of the New Religious Consciousness.* Lanham: Rowman & Littlefield, 1979.

Raymo, Chet. "Intelligent Design Happens Naturally." *Boston Globe*, 14 May 2002.

Ricoeur, Paul. *The Conflict of Interpretations.* Edited by Don Ihde. Evanston, IL: Northwestern University Press, 1974.

————. *Freud and Philosophy: An Essay on Interpretation.* Terry Lectures Series. New Haven: Yale University Press, 1977.

————. *The Symbolism of Evil.* Translated by Emerson Buchanan. Boston: Beacon, 1969.

Rieff, Philip. *Fellow Teachers.* New York: Faber & Faber, 1975.

Rolston, Holmes, III. *Science and Religion: A Critical Survey.* New York: Random House, 1987.

Rorty, Richard. "Untruth and Consequences." *New Republic* (1995) 32–36.

Rue, Loyal. *By the Grace of Guile: The Role of Deception in Natural History and Human Affairs.* New York: Oxford University Press, 1994.

Rupnik, Jacques. "Vaclav Havel." *Civilization* 5 (1998) 44.

Ruse, Michael. *Darwin and Design: Does Evolution Have a Purpose?* Cambridge: Harvard University Press, 2003.

Russell, Bertrand. "A Free Man's Worship." In *The Meaning of Life*, edited by E. D. Klemke and Steven Cahn. Oxford: Oxford University Press, 2008.

Russell, Robert John, et al., eds. *Evolutionary and Molecular Biology: Scientific Perspectives on Divine Action.* Vatican City: Vatican Observatory, 1998.

Sagan, Carl. *Cosmos.* New York: Ballantine, 1985.

Sartre, Jean-Paul. *Existentialism and the Human Emotions.* New York: Citadel, 1983.

———. *Existentialism is a Humanism.* Translated by Carol Macomber. New Haven: Yale University Press, 1970.

Schillebeeckx, Edward. *Christ the Sacrament of Encounter with God.* Translated by Paul Barrett and N.D. Huston. London: Sheed & Ward, 1986.

———. *Church: The Human Story of God.* Translated by John Bowden. New York: Crossroad, 1990.

Schleiermacher, Friedrich. *On Religion: Speeches to Its Cultured Despisers.* New York: Harper, 1958.

Schroeder, Gerald. *Genesis and the Big Bang: The Discovery of Harmony Between Modern Science and the Bible.* New York: Bantam, 1990.

Schumacher, E. F. *A Guide for the Perplexed.* New York: Harper Colophon, 1978.

Skinner, B. F. *Beyond Freedom and Dignity.* Indianapolis: Hackett, 2002.

Smith, Huston. *Beyond the Post-modern Mind: The Place of Meaning in a Global Civilization.* New York: Quest, 2003.

———. *Forgotten Truth: The Primordial Tradition.* New York: Harper & Row, 1976.

Smith, John Maynard. *Did Darwin Get It Right? Essays on Games, Sex, and Evolution.* London: Penguin, 1988.

Smoot, George. *Wrinkles in Time.* New York: William Morrow, 1993.

Taylor, Mark C. *Erring: A Postmodern A/theology.* Chicago: University of Chicago Press, 1987.

Teilhard de Chardin, Pierre. *Christianity and Evolution.* Translated by René Hague. New York: Harcourt Brace, 1969.

———. *The Future of Man.* Translated by Norman Denny. New York: Harper Colophon, 1964.

———. *How I Believe.* Translated by René Hague. New York: Harper & Row, 1969.

———. *The Human Phenomenon.* Translated by Sarah Appleton-Weber. New York: Harper & Row, 1973.

———. *Hymn of the Universe.* Translated by Gerald Vann, OP. New York: Harper Colophon, 1969.

———. "The Mass on the World." In *Teilhard's Mass: Approaches to "The Mass on the World,"* edited by Thomas M. King, SJ. New York: Paulist, 2005.

———. *The Phenomenon of Man.* Translated by Bernard Wall. New York: Harper Torchbooks, 1959.

———. *The Prayer of the Universe.* New York: Harper Perennial, 1958.

———. *Writings in Time of War.* Translated by René Hague. New York: Harper & Row, 1968.

Thiemann, Ronald F. *Revelation and Theology: The Gospel as Narrated Promise*. Eugene, OR: Wipf and Stock, 1985.

Tillich, Paul. *The Courage To Be*. New Haven: Yale University Press, 1963.

———. *Shaking of the Foundations*. New York: Scribner, 1996.

———. *Systematic Theology*. 3 vols. Chicago: University of Chicago Press, 1963.

Toulmin, Stephen E. *An Examination of the Place of Reason in Ethics*. Cambridge: Cambridge University Press, 1950.

Ulanowicz, Robert E. *Ecology: The Ascendent Perspective*. New York: Columbia University Press, 1997.

Waldenfels, Hans. *Offenbarung*. Munich: Max Hueber Verlag, 1968.

Weber, Otto. *The First Three Minutes*. New York: Basic, 1977.

———. *Foundations of Dogmatics: Volume 1*. Grand Rapids: Eerdmans, 1981.

Wells, Jonathan. *Icons of Evolution: Science or Myth? Why Much of What We Teach About Evolution Is Wrong*. Washington, DC: Regnery, 2000.

Wilson, Edward O. *Consilience: The Unity of Knowledge*. New York: Knopf, 1998.

Whitehead, Alfred North. *Adventures of Ideas*. New York: Free Press, 1967.

———. *Modes of Thought*. New York: Free Press, 1968.

———. *Process and Reality*. Edited by David Ray Griffin and Donald W. Sherburne. New York: Free Press, 1978.

———. *Religion in the Making*. London: Macmillan Company, 1926.

———. *Science and the Modern World*. New York: Free Press, 1967.

Weinberg, Steven. *Dreams of a Final Theory: The Scientist's Search for the Ultimate Laws of Nature*. New York: Vintage, 1994.

Wilde, Oscar. *De Profundis*. New York: Philosophical Library, 1950.

Williams, H. A. *True Resurrection*. New York: Harper Colophon, 1972.

Wilson, David Sloan. *Darwin's Cathedral: Evolution, Religion, and the Nature of Society*. Chicago: University of Chicago Press, 2002.

Wyschogrod, Michael. *The Body of Faith*. New York: Harper & Row, 1983.

Young, Louise B. *The Unfinished Universe*. New York: Simon & Schuster, 1986.

Życiński, Józef. *God and Evolution: Fundamental Questions of Christian Evolutionism*. Translated by Kenneth W. Kemp and Zuzanna Maslanka. Washington, DC: Catholic University of America Press, 2006.